Recovered Territory

Recovered Territory

A German-Polish Conflict over Land and Culture, 1919–89

By
Peter Polak-Springer

berghahn
NEW YORK • OXFORD
www.berghahnbooks.com

Published in 2015 by
Berghahn Books
www.berghahnbooks.com

© 2015, 2018 Peter Polak-Springer
First paperback edition published in 2018

All rights reserved. Except for the quotation of short passages
for the purposes of criticism and review, no part of this book
may be reproduced in any form or by any means, electronic or
mechanical, including photocopying, recording, or any information
storage and retrieval system now known or to be invented,
without written permission of the publisher.

Library of Congress Cataloging-in-Publication Data
A C.I.P. cataloging record is available from the Library of Congress

British Library Cataloguing in Publication Data
A catalogue record for this book is available from the British Library

ISBN 978-1-78238-887-6 (hardback)
ISBN 978-1-78533-814-4 (paperback)
ISBN 978-1-78238-888-3 (ebook)

For Halina

Contents

List of Illustrations	VIII
Acknowledgments	X
Note on Place Names, Translations, and Labels	XII
List of Abbreviations	XIV
Maps	XIX
Introduction	1

1.	The Making of a Contested Borderland, 1871–1939	21
2.	A Transnational Tradition of Border Rallies, 1922–34	55
3.	Acculturating an Industrial Borderland, 1926–39	89
4.	Giving "Polish Silesia" a "German" Face, 1939–45	138
5.	Recovering "Polish Silesia," 1945–56	183

Epilogue. From Revisionism to *Ostpolitik* and Beyond	232
Appendix. Rallies at the Voivodeship Government Building (Gmach Urzędu Wojewódzkiego), Katowice/Kattowitz	250
Bibliography	253

Illustrations

Maps

1. Boundaries of Germany, 1922–38, and the situation after 1945 (map by Dariusz Gierczak).   xix
2. Upper Silesia, 1922–38 (map by Dariusz Gierczak).   xx
3. German administrative regions in occupied Central Europe at the end of 1941 (map by Dariusz Gierczak).   xxi

Figures

2.1. Statue of the Insurgent in Chorzów (formerly Królewska Huta/Königshütte), unveiled in 1927.   56
3.1. Voivodeship Government Building (Gmach Urzędu Wojewódzkiego).   96
3.2. Marshal Rydz Śmigły speaking in front of the Voivodeship Government Building at the May Third rally, Katowice, 1936.   99
3.3. The House of Education (Dom Oświatowy), 1928.   101
3.4. The skyscraper, as part of the skyline of Katowice (Kattowitz), completed in 1934.   102
3.5. Postcard of Haus Oberschlesien, Gleiwitz (Gliwice), completed in 1928.   107
3.6. Hitler Youth in front of the Oberschlesische Landesmuseum, Beuthen (Bytom), opened in 1932.   108
3.7. Silesian Museum building, Katowice, completed in 1939.   109
3.8. The Reich Memorial (Reichsehrenmal) and amphitheater, Mount of St. Anne, opened in 1938.   111
3.9. The Borderland Tower in Ratibor (Racibórz), opened in 1938.   112
3.10. Postcard of a wooden church in Knurów.   116
3.11. Baron Reden statue in Königshütte by Theodor Khalide, erected in 1853.   118

3.12.	Parade in Silesian folk costume at the May Third rally in Katowice, 1936.	121
3.13.	Photographs of Adolf Hitler at the Choral Union Festival (Sängerbundfest) in Breslau (Wrocław).	127
4.1.	Heinrich Himmler with Fritz Bracht and other Nazi officials greeted by "*Volksdeutsche* resettlers" (*Umsielder*). Mount of St. Anne (circa 1940–42).	149
4.2.	German postcard of Kattowitz (Katowice), 1940–43.	157
4.3.	Dismantling of the Silesian Museum building, Kattowitz (Katowice), 1942–45.	158
4.4.	Administration Office Building (before 1939) and German Police Headquarters (after 1939) with porcelain bells on the wing of the façade, Kattowitz (Katowice), 1941.	158
4.5.	Nazi Party DAF brochure: Reden Festival, 1941.	168
5.1.	Władysław Gomułka at May Day rally, Katowice, 1946.	198
5.2.	Bishop Stanisław Adamski facing Aleksander Zawadzki, 1946.	199
5.3.	Holy Mass, urns with soil from the battlefields of the military conflict of May–June 1921.	201
5.4.	Folk dance concert at the amphitheater, Mount of St. Anne, 1955.	202
5.5.	Distribution of books at a "Re-Polonization" course.	211
6.1.	Monument to the Insurrectionist Deed.	233
7.1.	May Third rally before the Voivodeship Government Building (Gmach Urzędu Wojewódzkiego), Katowice (Kattowitz).	250
7.2.	Nazi Freedom Day rally, 1 September 1940.	251
7.3.	May Day rally with painting of Bolesław Bierut, 1946.	252

Acknowledgments

I would like to thank the financial supporters that made the research for this book possible. They include the United States Department of Education, the Freie Universität in Berlin, the Social Science Research Council, the Andrew Mellon Foundation, the American Council of Learned Societies, and Qatar University (Start Up Grant). While doing research for this book, I was really fortunate to meet a number of delightful people, who not only helped me find the right sources, but also gave me companionship and encouragement during my extensive stays away from home. In Poland, I am particularly grateful to Sebastian Rosenbaum, Ryszard Kaczmarek, Bernard Linek, Piotr Przybyła, Grzegorz Bębnik, Adam Dziurok, Urszula Biel, Adam Dziuba, Anna Novikov, and Grzegosz Strauchold. In Germany, I would like to thank, in particular, Juliane Haubold-Stolle, Karin Goihl, Simon Donig, Michael Esch, Andrzej Michałczyk, Tobias Weger, Philipp Ther, and Kai Struve. During research in Moscow, I owe great gratitude to the assistance and hospitality of Katja Roshina.

My colleagues, mentors, and friends in the United States and other parts of Europe not only directly helped me with the book, but also in confronting the numerous challenges I faced in my professional life and in general during the time I was working on it. I owe particular gratitude to Belinda Davis for her many years of unrelenting support and guidance on this project and in my career in general, as well as to my dear supporters Paul Hanebrink, Jochen Hellbeck, and Eagle Glassheim, whose critical analyses of this work during its early stages were particularly helpful. I would also like to express my gratitude to a number of esteemed colleagues and dear friends for their stimulating ideas and support, especially William Franz, Andrew Demshuk, Jennifer Miller, Maté Tokič, Mark Keck-Szajbel, Tomasz Kamusella, Winson Chu, Gregor Thum, Jim Bjork, Annika Frieberg, Pieter Judson, Jan Kubik, and T. David Curp. Indeed, only the hard work invested in me by my former teachers made this work possible, and I am in particular grateful to Vivian Gruder, Bonnie Smith, Richard Wolin, Bradley Abrams, Istvan Deak, and Jan T. Gross.

I was able to write this book mainly in Doha only because so many kind and friendly people did so much to help make this place into a new home for me.

Discussions and support from colleagues and students provided fresh perspectives and the new energy and enthusiasm that allowed me to finish this book. I would like to thank, in particular, Mahjoob Zweiri, Steven Wright, Todd Thompson, Edward Moad, Karl Widerquist, Basak Ozoral, and Alaa Laabar.

During the writing process, I owe Amy Hackett a great debt for her truly devoted, careful, and critical reading and editing of various drafts, and her many brilliant suggestions for revisions and improvements. Likewise, I would like to thank Brendan Karch for his careful critical reading of earlier drafts, as well as for the insightful comments and critiques of the anonymous readers. I am also grateful to Dariusz Gierczak for drawing the maps, as well as the Polish National Digital Archives, the State Archives of Katowice, the Silesian Library Special Collections, and the Herder Institute in Marburg for providing access and publication rights to valuable photographs. I thank copyright and licensing librarian Janice T. Pilch for her assistance as well as Teresa Delcorso, a masterful fellowship advisor, for her critical reading of the grant applications that made this book possible. I am particularly grateful to the editors and staff at Berghahn Books for all their hard work in putting this work together. This book is the product of the gracious effort and support of far more people than those I was able to mention. Indeed, no one but I bears any responsibility for its shortcomings.

Words cannot express my gratitude for the patience, love, and support from my family, without which I would have certainly never been able to complete this project. I am referring especially to my parents, Eligius and Iwona Polak, and to Katrin and Halina Polak-Springer, the Boryslawscy, and Springer. I wrote this book to contribute to the ongoing dialogue, reconciliation, and integration among Europeans, and other people across the world, who have been hampered in understanding one another by various borders, from which I hope Halina and her future will prosper.

Doha, 22 April 2014   Peter Polak-Springer

Note on Place Names, Translations, and Labels

All local place names in this volume have German and Polish names. During the era I examine, the choice of language was often a political choice meant to underscore one or another nation's "right" to the area the name identified. In an effort to be impartial, and to acknowledge the multiple identities of localities, in more recent years historians have written place names in the various languages they commonly appeared. This is the approach I take here. During each era, I refer to places by the official name given by the government controlling it at the time, and place the competing name in parentheses the first time I mention the place, for example, Gliwice (Gleiwitz). I refer to countries, regions, and localities commonly translated into English (e.g., the Mount of St. Anne) by their English name.

When using the terms "western" or "eastern" Upper Silesia, it is not my intention to echo the irredentist political equivalents used during the era I examine—the German *Ostoberschlesien*, or Polish *Śląsk Opolski*—but rather to refer to the two sides of the border of 1922, the former belonging to Germany and the latter to Poland. I purposely avoid overusing the terms "German" or "Polish" Upper Silesia, since such descriptors were used for irredentist purposes to mask the region's ethnocultural fluidity. Instead, I use the term the Provinz (Oberschlesien, or O/S), the official name of the German part of the region during the interwar era, interchangeably with "western Upper Silesia," and the Voivodeship (Silesia), the English translation of the Polish official name for "eastern Upper Silesia" (Województwo Śląsk) during this era.

Very often politicized historical foreign terms defy exact and undisputed English-language equivalents. All the translations in this volume are my own, unless pointed out otherwise. Whenever there may be a discrepancy between the foreign term used by contemporaries and my own term, I usually justify my own translation in the notes. For example, I use the term "Germanization" to refer to *Eindeutschung* even though the latter was used by Nazi officials to avoid the Bismarckian term *Germanizierung*, which contradicted their racially based idea of nationality. Another term that I translate with an approximate English equivalent that hardly promotes the emphatic and symbolic idea of the original German concept is "local homeland" for *Heimat*. Indeed, in German this term also promotes connotations of "home," "attachment" to place, and a sense of "belonging." I often use such terms in the German/Polish equivalents in the text after translating them once.

Just as place names had a political charge, so did labels for ethnic/national groups. Very often "Pole" and "German" ("Polishness," "Germandom") had specific connotations based on the ideology of their authors. I therefore also sometimes place these descriptions in quotation marks. When referring to Jews I am mainly referring to the category created by government officials and organizations claiming to represent this group. Indeed, very often the people counted as part of this or other ethnic/national categories, be they Jews, Poles, Germans, or Silesians, had their own multiple identities, which unfortunately were ignored by the categorizing agents.

Abbreviations

AA	Auswärtiges Amt (Foreign Office)
AAN	Archiwum Akt Nowych (New Records Archive), Warsaw
Amb. Ber.	Ambasada Polska w Berlinie (Polish Embassy in Berlin)
APK	Archiwum Państowe w Katowicach (Polish State Archive in Katowice)
APK-Gl.	APK Gliwice Section
APO	Archiwum Państwowe w Opolu (Polish State Archive in Opole)
APWr.	Archiwum Państwowe we Wrocławiu (Polish State Archive in Wrocław)
BArch	Bundesarchiv (Federal Archive)
BDM	Bund Deutscher Mädel
BdO	Bund der Oberschlesier/Związek Górnoślązaków (League of Upper Silesians)
BDO	Bund Deutscher Osten (League of the German East)
BdV	Bund der Vertriebenen (League of the Expelled)
BŚ-ZS	Biblioteka Śląska – Zbiory Specialne (Silesian Library – Special Collections)
ChD	Christian Democratic Party (Korfantists or Chadeci)
DAF	Deutsche Arbeitsfront (German Labor Front)
DNVP	Deutschnationale Volkspartei (German National People's Party)
DVL	Deutsche Volksliste (German Ethnic List)
DZ	*Dziennik Zachodni* (newspaper)
FPZOO	Federacja Polskich Związków Obrony Ojczyzny (Federation of Polish Unions for the Defense of the Fatherland)

Genkons.	Deutsche Generalkonsulat in Kattowitz (German General Consulate in Kattowitz)
GDR	German Democratic Republic (East Germany)
GG	Generalgouvernement (Nazi-occupied parts of Poland)
GGŚl.	Głos Górnego Śląska (newspaper)
GOP	Górnośląski Ośrodek Przemysłowy (Upper Silesian industrial district)
GStA PK	Geheimstaatsarchiv Preußische Kulturbesitz (Secret State Archives, Prussian Cultural Heritage Foundation)
IPN	Instytut Pamięci Narodowej (Institute of National Remembrance)
Kat.	Kattowitz (Katowice)
KdF	Kraft durch Freude (Strength through Joy)
KH	Königshütte (Chorzów, formerly Królewska Huta)
Kon. Byt./Kon. Op./Kon. Br.	Konsulat Generalny Rzeczypospolitej Polskiej w (General Consulate of the Republic of Poland in) Bytomiu/Opolu/Breslau
KOS	Kuratorium Okręgu Szkolnego (School District Administration)
KPD	Kommunistische Partei Deutschlands (German Communist Party)
KPP	Komunistyczna Partja Polski (Polish Communist Party)
Krsl.	Kreisleitung (County Head)
KVP	Katholische Volkspartei (Catholic People's Party)
KW	Komitet Wojewódzki (Voivodeship Committee)
KZ	*Kattowitzer Zeitung* (newspaper)
LdO	Landsmannschaft der Oberschlesier (Upper Silesian Homeland Society)
MO	Ministerstwo Oświaty (Ministry of Education)
MRN	Miejska Rada Narodowa (National Council, Municipal Level)
MSZ	Ministerstwo Spraw Zagranicznych (Polish Foreign Ministry)
MZO	Ministerstwo Ziem Odzyskanych (Ministry of Recovered Territories)
NAC	Narodowe Archiwum Cyfrowe (National Digital Archives)

n.d.	not dated
NOFG	Nord und Ostdeutsche Forschungsgemeinschaft (North and East German Research Society)
n.p.	not paginated
NSLB	Nationalsozialistische Lehrerbund (Nazi Teachers' Union)
NSF	Nationalsozialistische Frauenschaft (Women's League)
ODM	*Ostdeutsche Morgenpost* (newspaper)
OHB	O/S Heimatbund (Upper Silesian Regional Homeland League)
O/S (O.S.)	Oberschlesien (Upper Silesia)/Oberschlesische (Upper Silesian)
OSW	*Oberschlesische Wanderer* (newspaper)
OP	Oberpräsidium/Oberpräsident der Provinz Oberschlesien or (Governorship/Governor of the O/S Province.
OSV	*Oberschlesische Volksstimme* (newspaper)
Pr. MdI.	Preußische Ministerium des Innern (Prussian Ministry of the Interior)
PA-AA	Politisches Archiv des Auswärtigen Amtes (Political Archive of the Foreign Office)
PPR	Polska Partia Robotnicza (Polish Workers' Party, the Polish Communist Party before 1948)
PSL	Polskie Stronnictwo Ludowe (Polish Peasants' League/Party)
PPS	Polska Partia Socialistyczna (Polish Socialist Party)
PZPR	Polska Zjednoczona Partia Robotnicza (Polish United Workers' Party/the Polish Communist Party)
PZ	*Polska Zachodnia* (newspaper)
PZZ	Polski Związek Zachodni (or Polish Western League, same as previously called the ZOKZ)
RAŚ	Ruch Autonomii Śląska (Silesian Autonomy Movement)
RGVA	Rossiskii Gosudarstvennyi Voennyi Arkhiv (Russian State Military Archive)
RKF	Reichskommissar für die Festigung des deutschen Volkstums (Reich Commissioner for the Strengthening of Germandom)
RP	Rzeczpospolita Polska (Republic of Poland)

RPA	Reichspropagandaamt (Reich Propaganda Bureau)
RH	Reichszentrale für Heimatdientst (Central Office for Service to the Heimat)
SD	Sicherheitdienst (of the Nazi RF-SS Security Service)
SPD	Sozialdemokratische Partei Deutschlands (German Social Democratic Party)
SR	Situation Report
StP	Starostwo Powiatowe (Polish County Government)
TRZZ	Towarzystwo Rozwoju Ziem Zachodnich (Society for the Development of the Western Territories)
UB or (UBP)	Urząd Bezpieczeństwa or (Urząd Bezpieczeństwa Publicznego) (State Security Agency of People's Poland)
VB	Volksbund (Deutsche Volksbund für polnische Oberschlesien)
VBW	Volksbildungswerk (National Cultivation Agency)
VDA	Verein für das Deutschtum im Ausland (Association for Germandom Abroad)
Woj. Śl.	Województwo Śląskie (Voivodeship Silesia)
VGB	Voivodeship Government Building (Gmach Urzędu Wojewódzkiego (Voivodeship Government Building))
VVHO	Vereingte Verbände Heimattreue Oberschlesien (or United Organizations of Upper Silesian Homeland Patriots/German Homeland Patriots)
Woj.	Województwo (voivodeship)
WUIP	Wojewódzki Urząd Informacji i Propagandy (Voivodeship Agency of Propaganda and Information)
Wyd.	Wydawnictwo (Press)
Wydz.	Wydział (Department)
ZBOWiD	Związek Bojowników o Wolność i Demokracje (League of Fighters for Freedom and Democracy)
ZIOF	Zentralinstitute für Oberschlesische Landesforschung (Central Institute for Upper Silesian Regional Research)
ZM	Zarząd Miejski (Municipal Government)

ZOG	Związek Obrony Górnego Śląska (Upper Silesian Defense League)
ZOKZ	Związek Obrony Kresów Zachodnich (or Western Territories Defense League, from 1934 on called the Polish Western League or PZZ)
ZPwN	Związek Polaków w Niemczech (Union of Poles in Germany)
ZPŚl.	Związek Powstańców Śląskich (or Silesian Insurgent League)
ZWPŚ.	Związek Weteranów Powstańców Śląskich (or Veterans League of Silesian Insurgents)

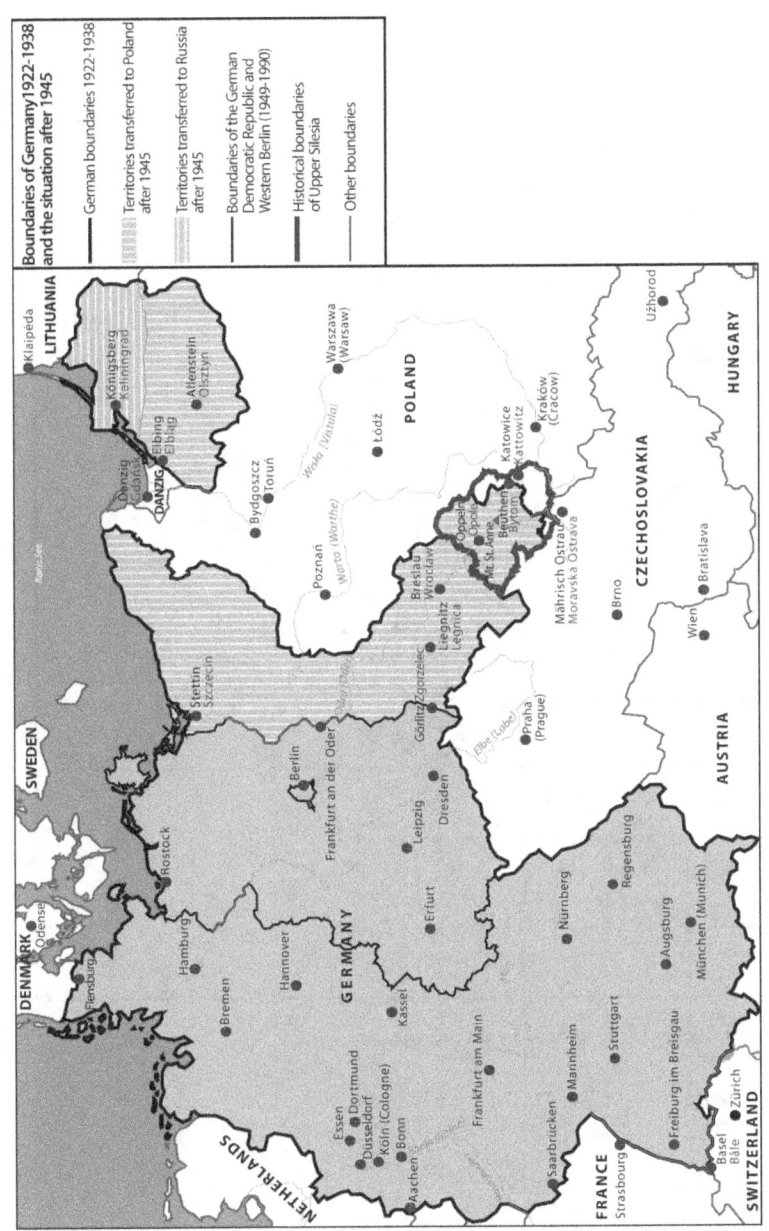

Map 1. Boundaries of Germany, 1922–38, and the situation after 1945 (map by Dariusz Gierczak).

Map 2. Upper Silesia, 1922–38 (map by Dariusz Gierczak).

Map 3. German administrative regions in occupied Central Europe at the end of 1941 (map by Dariusz Gierczak).

Introduction

On 31 August 1939, Nazi SS (*Schutzstaffel*) agents carried out a ploy to disguise Hitler's imminent attack on Poland as a defensive measure. In this legendary subterfuge, armed SS men dressed in Polish military uniforms broke into the German radio station in Gleiwitz (Gliwice), located near the border with Poland in Upper Silesia. (Some historians believe they were actually dressed in civilian clothing.) After holding up the station's personnel, the fake soldiers went on air to announce that the station was in Polish hands. On the next fateful day, as the Wehrmacht attacked Poland, the Nazi Party's newspaper, *Völkische Beobachter*, reported the Gleiwitz incident as an attack on "German soil" by members of the "Polish volunteer corps of Upper Silesian insurgents." Yet the incident went unmentioned as one of "fourteen border incidents" the previous night in Adolf Hitler's war declaration speech before the Reichstag on 1 September 1939. Perhaps "the Führer" chose not to draw attention to an incident whose logistical feasibility should have puzzled anyone familiar with Gleiwitz at the time. Just to reach the radio station, the "Polish invaders" would have had to make their way through a well-patrolled border, not to mention a densely populated city full of German soldiers preparing to invade Poland.[1]

Nonetheless, a Polish attack on German soil seemed at least plausible to residents of the industrial border city. That summer, as for nearly twenty years, Polish paramilitary members organized by a government-sponsored Insurgent League had marched with firearms to the German-Polish border, vowing to use force to "recover" the western (German) part of Upper Silesia for Poland. Long before the Gleiwitz incident, Nazi propaganda had been using such theater, as well as exaggerated stories of Poland's persecuted German minority, to persuade the public of their neighbor's aggressive threat to Germany. Even in Upper Silesia, where locals often questioned the regime's exaggerated anti-Polish rhetoric, observers of the public mood in Gleiwitz in May 1939 noted that "the anti-Polish agitation is beginning to gain influence even among leftist-oriented people," and "that it is quite possible that in the event of a real outbreak of war against Poland Hitler could indeed win over large masses for such a war."[2] Well-versed in the irredentism endemic to this borderland and other eastern territories, Nazi borderland specialists wrapped their propaganda in the publicly familiar discourses and symbols of the long-standing German-Polish conflict over Upper Silesia.

Since Germany's defeat in 1918, followed by territorial losses in the Treaty of Versailles, even proponents of the Weimar Republic and fervent opponents of Nazism and nationalism as well as defenders of international peace, moderation, and diplomacy gave lip service to the notion that, in the words of historian Erich Marcks, "the current borders" were "just impossible."[3] Thus, the republic's defenders commonly agreed with its opponents in calling for the "recovery" of the "German east." Similarly, long before the Nazis seized power, ordinary Germans had become activists on behalf of saving the "bleeding border" from "Polonization."[4] In Upper Silesia and the other "lost" eastern provinces whose cause he had inherited, Hitler found a valuable grievance around which to rally German support for his own imperialist dreams of military expansion.

To win domestic and international sympathy for the invasion of Poland, Hitler's 1 September war declaration speech consciously avoided appeals to such Nazi principles as Germany's need for *Lebensraum* (living space) and the mixture of social Darwinism and racism that justified the right of the stronger. Rather, he invoked a more traditional line of argument that affirmed Germany's right as a nation-state to its eastern borderlands. At the outset, he underscored that these provinces "were and remain German," and that although they "owe their cultural development exclusively to the German people," they "had been annexed by Poland," where "the German minorities living there [have been] ill-treated in the most distressing manner!"[5] These phrases reflected a familiar language of popular irredentism that long before the Third Reich had been endorsed by the Weimar Republic's supporters and opponents alike.

The Gleiwitz incident—a sideshow in Hitler's invasion of Poland—drew its symbolic power from a deeply entrenched irredentist culture that emerged from post–World War I territorial conflicts between Germany and Poland. By "irredentist" and "irredentism" (and interchangeably "revisionist" and "revisionism"), I refer to the politics of contesting and claiming territory in general, whether based on purely historical and geopolitical or ethnic arguments or, more commonly, ones of a mixed sort.[6] Indeed, I make a claim for the inherent similarity of irredentist politics between two nations that long contested control over Upper Silesia, the geographical focus of this book. This holds true despite changes in governments and across different time periods. The area of primary interest is known as the "industrial district," a cluster of densely populated industrial urban centers, one of them being Gleiwitz. This center of coal mining and metallurgy made the larger region one of Central Europe's most industrially valuable areas. Moreover, in 1922, the League of Nations drew the German-Polish border—an object of unrelenting quarrel and contestation—right through this industrial district, making it the most coveted area to each of the two nation-states.

Throughout the interwar era, governments in Germany and Poland struggled against one another to reacculturate landscapes and renationalize inhabitants in the district and larger region. Each side deployed its own cadre of borderland nationalists (activists supported by the government, including state agents, paramilitants, scholars, folklorists, literati, and other specialists of irredentist politics) dedicated to promoting to its locals, its nation, and the international community its own irredentist myth that the borderland "always was and remained" German or Polish. These nationalists waged a cultural contest over this borderland in reaction to, and in imitation of, one another's "cultural propaganda," namely, discourses, propaganda tactics, and nationalization policies. They were spread through traditional written media, the new technologies of radio and film, politically symbolic enclaves such as architecture, urban planning projects, museums, mass rallies, education, and other venues.

This book represents a transnational history of irredentism as a popular culture, and its promotion at the grassroots.[7] It aims not only to give equal attention to both sides of the conflict but also to demonstrate how they interacted with one another in disputes over territories, spaces, and symbols, as well as with the locals they sought to mobilize to actively support their side of the struggle. I utilize this interactive transnational approach to highlight my main argument, namely, that although claiming to be emphatically opposed to one another, both of the conflicting (German and Polish) national camps and their propaganda enterprises were actually but two sides of one political culture, in which the policies and discourses of each were not only strikingly similar, but also inherently interwoven. Interaction, mutual reaction against one another's policies and propaganda, and even mutual influence between both national camps formed the basis of this irredentist culture and the territorial conflict that it sustained. This culture played a central role in Upper Silesia's multiple territorial "recoveries"— successive renationalizations by Germany and Poland following border revisions in 1922, 1939, and 1945. Between 1922 and 1953, the book's primary focus, it evolved over several historical periods and under German and Polish governments of diverse ideological orientations. Since the early 1920s, regional and national governments on each side of the border—liberal and authoritarian alike—profited politically from borderland nationalism. They found it helpful for boosting Upper Silesia's national importance, legitimizing authoritarian rule, and, in the cases of the German National Socialists and Polish Communists, for building "ethnically cleansed" societies.

Between 1939 and 1950, the institutions, discourses, policies, and proponents of this transnational irredentist culture served the acculturation goals of larger forces working to forge ethnic and political homogeneity in the borderlands. Thus, this culture became an essential instrument for social engineering projects that employed violence, expulsion, resettlement, forced assimilation—and in the case of the Nazis, genocide. Upper Silesia was part of the larger politics of constructing utopian societies—in the annexed territories for the Nazis and in the western borderlands for the Communists. Each of these projects occurred under unique circumstances and employed different if also similar means. Whereas the Nazis focused on "re-Germanizing" the eastern parts of Upper Silesia that had belonged to Poland during the interwar era, the Polish Communists worked to "re-Polonize" the formerly German western part.

Yet each treated the vast majority of locals in its new territory as "recovered peoples" who needed to be renationalized, that is, reengineered as its model "new man." For this purpose, each drew heavily on the transnational irredentist culture, and even appropriated and repurposed the "other's" institutions—for example, museums, conservatories, institutes—for its own nationalizing work. By analyzing these commonalities, this book contributes to recent scholarship that breaks down the conceptual border between the imperialist policies of Nazism and communism in East-Central Europe.[8] On a broader scale, it aims to contribute to the history of the contestation and nationalization of borderlands, and more specifically with regards to German-Polish relations, but also to studies of regionalism and a phenomenon more recently described as "national indifference."

Borderland Nationalism

World War I clearly revealed the destructive potential of nationalism and the chauvinism, militarism, and racism—in this case, cultural racism[9]—that accompanied it. At the same time, by hastening the end of four multinational conglomerations—the German, Habsburg, Russian, and Ottoman empires—the war created opportunities for a number of previously unacknowledged nations to assert their own territorial claims. Calls for the "liberation" and "recovery" of "stolen" territories, or for their "return" to their proper national "motherland," resounded beyond Germany's borders. Rogers Brubaker characterized this politics of claiming a "homeland" beyond one's nation-state borders as "external homeland nationalism."[10]

This irredentism was particularly strong in multiethnic Central Europe, where the victorious Allies tried to accommodate Woodrow Wilson's ideal of the congruity of peoples and "their lands" in their task of drawing and redrawing borders. Thus, if a nation has a right to territories inhabited by its own people, then it followed that "an independent Polish state should be erected which should include the territories inhabited by indisputably Polish populations."[11] As a basic tenet for rebuilding the continent's postwar political order, Wilsonian principles thus reinforced the dominance of nationalism in European politics. The conflict between these ideals and demographic realities often led to brutal territorial wars and population exchanges between successor states of the fallen monarchies.[12]

The mass mobilizing potential of territorial conflicts made grassroots irredentism a characteristic feature of interwar diplomacy. By the end of World War I, territorial conflict ceased to be the concern only of diplomats and government elites. Government agents strove to mobilize the broader public around disputed borderlands, made more graphic by irredentist symbols and slogans. Radio and film, still new media technologies, played a pivotal role in providing both informative and entertaining ways to bring irredentist discourses to the masses.[13]

The Hungarian-Romanian conflict over Transylvania offers a case study in irredentist mass politics. Holly Case has recently described how Hungary accompanied its annexation of the northern part of this region in 1940 with a whole "language and science of legitimacy" that identified the new territory as a "liberated" or "reannexed" Hungarian province, thereby promoting a "sense of interrupted continuity being restored." Social scientists, such as ethnographers, racial anthropologists, and geographers, along with natural scientists, such as climatologists and botanists, worked to create a myth of this region's "national belonging." Urban planners, architects, and builders assisted in this enterprise by giving Transylvania's capital, Koloszvar, a Hungarian appearance. State cultural politics aimed to resocialize the masses to accept this national identity by creating symbolic spaces and staging mass rallies that celebrated "liberation" and "reannexation." Thus, Case argued, the territorial conflict "between Hungary and Romania ran much deeper than high diplomacy, saturating domestic politics, social science, cultural institutions, and ideas of statehood."[14]

This popular irredentism was part of a larger innovation in mass politics in twentieth-century Europe, where, as Philipp Ther argued, "nationalism had been transformed from a political ideology into a social reality."[15] This process began in the second half of the nineteenth century with what Rogers Brubaker referred to as "the nationalizing nation-state."[16] Early nation-building policies involved a degree of cultural homogenization, as exemplified by the German chancellor Otto von Bismarck's Kulturkampf, a cultural struggle to cripple the political influence of Catholicism in the newly united Germany. According to Brian Porter, by the fin de siècle, a new nationalism had emerged, which in reaction to the liberal model of an inclusive multicultural nation based on patriotic ideals defined the nation by exclusivist ethnic and linguistic criteria.[17] Exemplified by the Pan-German League and Roman Dmowski's (Polish) National Democracy, the new nationalists worked to standardize the physical and cultural characteristics of the essential (or core) elements of their respective nations, their particular peoples (*Volk* in German, *lud* in Polish), and their territories. (From *Volk* comes the commonly used *völkisch* for these politics.) Their insistence that the state should safeguard the supremacy of its core people, who often inhabited areas of Central Europe that extended beyond the borders of one nation, gained enormous political influence in the midst of postwar revolutions and dislocations.

Wilsonianism strengthened "the spell" of building homogenous nation-states in Central Europe.

In its role as social engineer, the nationalizing nation-state often employed procedures that have come to be known as "ethnic cleansing"—defined by Norman Naimark as "the removal of a people and *all traces of them* from a concrete territory."[18] By promoting "population exchange" between Greece and Turkey, the Treaty of Lausanne (1923) formally made expulsion an internationally endorsed "solution" to the "problem" of diversity within a given nation, particularly in contested border areas. Moreover, mass migrations—in Brubaker's words, the "unmixing" of populations—followed post–World War I border revisions, usually in response to more informal cultural and economic pressures in nationalizing nation-states. Hitler's extreme nationalism and ethnic cleansing policies emerged within this broader context.[19]

Fearing irredentist aggression from an adjoining nation-state, governments of multiethnic borderlands often resorted to "cleansing," "unmixing," and nationalization. Caitlin Murdock's work on the Saxony-Bohemian borderland (separating Germany and Austria-Hungary and, later, Czechoslovakia) demonstrates that postwar state authorities imposed unprecedented control and surveillance over frontier regions. Nation-states categorized the inhabitants of these areas along ethnic-national lines and demanded that they constantly reaffirm their identity with and loyalty to the nation-state. A specific "borderland rhetoric" reinforced these politics by positing the politically constructed "borderland" as an "endangered" and "bleeding" entity that at the same time represented the nation's "fortress."[20] This ideology, which I refer to as borderland nationalism, legitimated an intrusive politics of nationalization and homogenization. For example, restrictions on border crossing threatened the traditional rhythms of local life in regions that prior to their classification as "borderlands" were marked by unimpeded movement and nonnational identities.[21] As Tara Zahra's work has demonstrated, such policies even invaded family life in cases where national activists pressured parents to send children to schools that instructed in "their" language.[22]

The German-Polish Borderlands

Following the post–World War I territorial settlements, the German government increased control over its remaining, but now "endangered," eastern provinces, to which the new nation-states of Poland and Czechoslovakia laid continuing claims. Fervent opposition to territorial losses imposed on Germany united otherwise divided Germans of almost all political orientations, and in turn weakened faith in the new Weimar Republic. The "bleeding border"—a term that depicted territorial loss as an amputation of vital parts of the German nation—became a symbol of national victimization, as did the many displaced individuals, both those who fled their "lost *Heimat*" (local homeland) and those stranded on now Polish territory.[23] Interwar Germany's claims to its *Volksdeutsche*—ethnic Germans who were citizens and inhabitants of other countries—amplified calls for the return of "German cultural soil" (*Deutsche Kulturboden*) on which these groups resided. As Annemarie Sammartino demonstrates, this irredentist discourse presupposed an official conceptualization of citizenship along the specific ethnic and cultural lines of "Germanness"—itself a result of border revision.[24]

Throughout the interwar period, Germany posed the greatest threat to the territorial integrity of the new Polish state. Long before the Nazis assumed power, the Weimar Republic explicitly called for the return of Poland's most vital territories: Danzig and the Polish Corridor, which provided Poland's only access to the sea, and eastern Upper Silesia, its only center of industry. This perceived threat provided a justification for the discriminatory treatment of Germans and the persecution of German minority organizations in Poland.[25] These groups helped fan the flames of Polish irredentism, which aimed not just to defend the republic's existing borderlands, but also to expand them with claims to territories in Germany, Czechoslovakia, and other neighboring states.

The brutality of the Third Reich's acts of territorial aggression has long cast a shadow on the historical memory of the irredentist politics of other nations during the interwar era, particularly on the part of those who became Hitler's main victims. Defending and expanding "endangered" borders was integral to the irredentist political culture common to most countries of Central Europe. The new Polish state—born of six territorial military conflicts against its neighbors and plagued by the resulting grievances—serves as a prime example of how the quarrelling successor states of the former Habsburg Empire contributed to making Central Europe a powder keg for World War II.[26] In the end, the establishment of the German-Polish border by western European statesmen at Versailles was met with protests from political elites within *both* nations. Interest in the "struggle" to protect and expand the borderlands aroused widespread and serious interest among the publics of both Poland and Weimar Germany. Like the *Volksdeutsche* in Poland, so Poles in Germany's borderlands had their own minority organizations, which became the state's tools for irredentist politics.[27] Poland's invasion and annexation of the Czechoslovakian border region of Teschen Silesia (Tešin or Zaolzia) in the wake of Hitler's annexation of the Sudetenland following the Munich Conference in October 1938 marked a culmination of this irredentist fervor. Hungary followed suit that November by taking territory in southern Czechoslovakia, including Carpathian Ruthenia. Clearly, Germany's annexation of the Sudetenland—however great its iconic role as a premonition of the war to come—represented broader discontent over Central Europe's borders.

Responsibility for the war that enveloped Europe clearly rested with the Nazi regime's unilateral determination to build a continental German empire stretching even into Soviet Eurasia, not with this widespread irredentist fervor. Nevertheless, in Munich Hitler was able to exploit the internationally accepted ideal of a nation's "right" to "its" territories in order to sufficiently disguise his imperialist aims to suit the European appeasers.[28] Although this ruse failed in the case of Poland, the Nazis portrayed their invasion as a struggle to "recover" territory and "liberate" its "*Volksdeutsche*."[29] For many ordinary Germans, including some who may not have been Nazis, this notion conferred moral value to at least the initial phase of the Third Reich's military aggression. Persuaded by these ideals—the subject of Elizabeth Harvey's work on women's activism in these regions—they zealously engaged in the work of "Germanizing" the annexed formerly Polish western borderlands, which were also known as the "recovered lands" (*wiedergewonnene Länder*).[30] The German myth of "recovering" lands that "were and remain German" functioned as a more familiar and traditional, culturally as well as regionally based nationalist discourse. Part of a larger narrative of the "German east" that legitimated German hegemony over its wider eastern European "sphere of influence," it applied specifically to the formerly Prussian borderlands of interwar Poland.[31] Working in tandem with a more esoteric Nazi discourse on racial hygiene, this mainstream irredentist language legitimized the "Germanization" of the annexed territories through ethnic cleansing, which included acculturation, expulsion, resettlement, and genocide.

Upon liberating Poland from Nazi German occupation in 1945, the Soviet Union installed a Polish Communist regime to govern the country. Likewise, Poland's borders were redrawn to incorporate Germany's eastern provinces (the so-called Oder-Neisse territories, named for the rivers that formed the new border), such as Pomerania, eastern Brandenburg, and Silesia. Indeed, the expulsion of millions of Germans followed. As Hugo Service argues in his work on postwar Silesia, while Poland's westward territorial shift was formally decided only by the "Big Three" Allied leaders (the United States, Great Britain, and the USSR), it marked the realization of the long-standing dreams of Polish nationalists, particularly followers of Roman Dmowski, the original author of claims to these lands. Working with the Communist regime to ensure the success of their longed-for western border, they helped promote the regime's own "recovered territories" myth to rationalize the annexation. Indeed, in some respects similar to how the German territorial myth had functioned as an alternative to Hitler's racism, the Polish counterpart offered a nationalist ideology as a substitute for a widely detested Marxist-Leninism to legitimate Poland's new political order. Borderland nationalists working with the Communists used this myth to justify the expulsion of Germans, to idealize the "recovery" of "Poles from Germany," and to glorify the engineering of an ethnically homogenous society in these provinces.[32]

German and Polish myths of "recovered territories" functioned as the ideological backbone of two inherently interwoven irredentist cultural-political enterprises, whose development stemmed from the conflict fostered by the shared post-1919 border. Throughout the interwar era in particular, cultural politics were at the center of what I will refer to as a territorial *cold war* (or a state of heated political tension but not actual war) between these nations, waged by propaganda and acculturation policies. During the war and immediate postwar era, these cultural-political enterprises worked to nationally (re)integrate the "other's" borderlands and their populations. By focusing on one of Central Europe's most hotly contested borderlands, Upper Silesia, across a number of decades, this book examines successive episodes of border redrawings during the heyday of war and nationalism in Europe from a (trans)national political as well as a local "everyday life" perspective. It is also meant as a contribution to the more recent shift in scholarly interest—particularly with regard to the 1939–50 era—from the politics of exclusion (e.g., genocide and expulsion) to inclusion (e.g., resettlement, nationalization, acculturation).[33]

The Struggle over Upper Silesia

The economic importance of Upper Silesia's industrial district made the region a particular flash point in German-Polish relations. The resulting conflict was fully as fierce as the more celebrated dispute over the Polish Corridor and its port city of Danzig. The bilateral national struggle over the region grew particularly fierce from the late winter through the summer of 1921. Although propaganda played a key role in this conflict, Upper Silesia was the only region in which the Allies' prescription of a plebiscite to resolve the territorial question was followed by open war, which began with a Polish armed offensive. The so-called third Silesian insurgency of May and June 1921 aimed to take the borderland by force after the Germans had won the majority of votes in the plebiscite. It remained the fiercest armed conflict between Germany and Poland until World War II.

The League of Nations resolved the conflict to Poland's advantage, essentially annulling Germany's plebiscite victory. To the great dismay of both Germans and the region's locals, in 1922 it drew a border right through the industrial district, separating residential districts, coal mines, roads, waterways, and railways. Poland received the bulk of the industrial district, one of Central Europe's centers of coal mining and metallurgy. Just as the Polish Corridor represented the country's sole outlet to the sea, eastern Upper Silesia was its only industrial province. Given that Germany retained several ports and richer industrial areas, its stake in these territories was more a matter of honor than of economic necessity. Indeed, holding onto them was also a means for Germany to maintain its foothold in East-Central Europe. Intensifying Germany's sense of grievance, the Upper Silesian decision came after Poland had been awarded all the other formerly Prussian eastern provinces that the German government had hoped to retain. The league's seemingly arbitrary, antidemocratic, and punitive partition of Upper Silesia fueled the already strong public resentment in Germany against the Treaty of Versailles, the Allied Powers, and Poland, thus helping to undermine the legitimacy of the Weimar Republic, which had signed these agreements. Revision of the Upper Silesian border to their respective advantages remained the official policy of both Poland and Germany throughout the interwar era.[34]

As the site of a bloody armed conflict, Upper Silesia became a particular repository of irredentist symbolism, as well as a breeding ground for militant nationalism in both officially revisionist nations. The transnational irredentist culture that dominated regional politics for the next decades had its origins in the propaganda and armed hostilities of 1921, which forged cadres of German and Polish borderland nationalists devoted to advancing their separate nation-state interests at the regional level. These included Weimar Germany's Upper Silesian Homeland Patriots (Vereinigte Verbände heimattreuer Oberschlesier, or VVHO) and Nazi Germany's *Ostforschung* (eastern research) academic network, as well as the League of the German East (Bund Deutscher Osten), and their Polish counterparts, the Western Territories Defense League (Polish Western League/Polski Związek Zachodni) and Western Borderland Thought (Myśl Zachodnia). While these nationalists did not necessarily represent the political views and identity of Upper Silesian society at large, they functioned as the arm of national politics in the region. Whereas the governments and regimes they served came and went, irredentist activism remained constant across the tumultuous decades between 1921 and 1950, when the conflict raged most fiercely, and for at least twenty years thereafter, when it lingered on, albeit with less intensity. Indeed, it was not until 1990, with the collapse of the Soviet Bloc and the reunification of Germany, that the struggle over Silesia and other borderlands formally ended.

In working against each other, German and Polish borderland nationalists together constructed an irredentist culture that represented regional identities as more homogenous—along ethnic/national lines—than they were in actuality. Each nationalist camp denied Upper Silesia any connection to the "other," and indeed vilified the other group. At best, under the politically dominant and formally nonnationalist regional branch of the German Center Party, irredentist agents in interwar western Upper Silesia recognized local (German-Polish) bilingualism but refused to acknowledge the region's connections to Polish history and heritage.[35] Under Polish authoritarian, Nazi German, and postwar Communist regimes, these nationalists conceptualized diversity only in a negative light, as part of their common depiction of Upper Silesia as an eternal "land of struggle" between Germans and Slavs. Nonetheless, for most of the era before World War I, the locals of Upper Silesia—like their counterparts in other would-be hotbeds of ethnic conflict—lived in relative peace and tolerance. Endorsed by state financial, institutional, and political power, German and Polish irredentist networks collaboratively succeeded in overshadowing this reality, particularly in the eyes of audiences outside these regions. During the wartime (World War II) and postwar eras, the transnational irredentist culture (along with its borderland nationalists, institutions, discourses, and "invented traditions") became the ideological and cultural-political precursors to the Nazi German and Polish Communist use of force, population politics, and social engineering to "recover" the borderlands.

In a number of respects the German-Polish contest over Upper Silesia differed from other borderland conflicts. In crafting this book, I was inspired by Gregor Thum's cultural history of how, after World War II, Poland annexed and renationalized the city of Breslau (Wrocław), former capital of the province of Lower Silesia, which until 1945 belonged to Germany's Prussian eastern territories.[36] The population of Lower Silesia, which adjoined Upper Silesia to the west, was largely German both linguistically and in terms of ethnic/national identity; indeed, it first became a seriously contested borderland only when Poland claimed it after the war. In contrast, Upper Silesia's largely multilingual (German, Polish, Silesian dialects) local population lacked a stable patriotic loyalty to either nation. Known for its economic resources and its long and fierce history of national conflict (since 1919), the region was often deemed "problematic" by state officials due to the locals' "indifference" to the desired national patriotism. In 1945 Polish officials in Lower Silesia were able to make a "clean sweep" between "unwanted" (German) and "desired" (Polish) populations.[37] In Upper Silesia, by contrast, none of the three episodes of border revision (1922, 1939, and 1945) facilitated a clean separation. Under both the Nazis and the Communists, the economic need for critical industrial labor, as well as the ideological conviction that Upper Silesia's inhabitants were really "lost" Germans or Poles whom the nation needed to "recover," kept the majority of the population in place.

The region's political masters turned to cultural politics to create the ethnic population they desired, whether German or Polish. As a newly contested territory after World War I, this industrialized "land of work and no culture" suddenly attracted archeologists, ethnographers, and historians, among other scholars, who set up research institutes and created narratives on the identity of the territory's "unknown" population and landscapes. Architects and urban planners decorated the previously mundane or imperial German landscapes with some of Europe's first skyscrapers and other early modernist buildings, as well as awe-inspiring monumental structures. Polish and German folkloric performers, public events coordinators, and museum workers competed to provide entertainment that also instructed the local population on its designated official identity. International law accommodated this irredentist culture by giving each side a plausible right to claim the borderland as "theirs" and by protecting minority organizations—one of the agents of this politics—against persecution.

World War II changed this situation. Whereas previous governments sought to convince local, national, and international communities that the borderland "is and remains" either German or Polish, in 1939—and again after 1945—the new regimes implemented more forceful policies of acculturation and (re)nationalization. Aided by their own border nationalists, both Nazi and Communist regimes worked to integrate the region's locals as a "recovered people." Each regime surveyed and verified its population's backgrounds, enforced "accepted" speech and ideas, and strongly promoted adult education courses that taught locals how to be "good" Germans or Poles.[38] Terror and coercion were inherent to renationalization under both regimes, although in many respects the mainstream Catholic population suffered more under the Communists than under the Nazis.[39] Without competition from the opposing camp, borderland nationalists appropriated the "other's" cultural institutions, architecture, and national monuments for their own purposes. Ironically, however, each nationalist camp found that their success required them to preach the continuing threat from the "other"; indeed, this was so even after the enemy had been militarily defeated. Thus, irredentist myths forged during the interwar era became a basis for creating a new official regional identity.

Despite all its particularities, Upper Silesia bore strong resemblances to irredentist culture in other German-Polish borderlands. For one, German *Ostforschung* and Polish Western Borderland Thought conceptualized individual regions within the larger traditions, narratives, and symbols common to all these borderlands. Characterized by mass cultural elements such as rallies, museums, folkloric performances, architecture, radio auditions, and films, among other elements, the cultural politics of territorial contestation in Upper Silesia were certainly comparable with those in other German-Polish border areas, such as Lower Silesia and eastern Brandenburg/Wielkopolska, as well as other parts of Europe.[40] Although far more widespread, Upper Silesia's strong regional/local sentiment, ethnic fluidity, and indifference to nationality was also a notable feature of Pomerania and Masuria.[41] Nazis and Polish Communists introduced more or less standard policies to win over "recovered peoples" in all the German-Polish borderlands: the Deutsche Volksliste (German Ethnic List) and its Polish counterparts, "verification" and "rehabilitation," and various acculturation schemes.[42] Not just a study of one economically critical borderland that displayed a uniquely widespread sense of "national indifference" among its locals, this book is also intended as a case study of the processes and politics behind the reannexation and renationalization of European borderlands that made irredentism a popular-cultural and grassroots phenomenon.

Regionalisms and "National Indifference"

This book also contributes to the growing historical literature on the role of regionalism in nationalism. More than a decade ago, Celia Applegate and Alon Confino demonstrated that both these identity categories were inherently modern, thus dispelling the view that regionalism represented a remnant of premodern society that would inevitably yield its place to this more recent successor. Disputing the once dominant assertion that the two concepts had a necessarily incompatible and contentious historical relationship, they argued instead for coexistence, even mutual support and reinforcement.[43] More recent research has built on their work to demonstrate that the late nineteenth century, the heyday of nationalism and nation building, was also an era of flourishing regionalism and local sentiment. Indeed, regional "imagined communities" were constructed with the same media (e.g., museums, films, the press) and customs (e.g., language and folk traditions) as their national counterparts, and the two often shared inherently interconnected and overlapping myths and historical narratives. In Germany, the entrenched concept of *Heimat* (local homeland)—one of the most frequently studied subjects for scholars of regionalism—served as the glue between the individual, locality, province, and nation.[44]

After World War I, European governments continued to nurture local traditions, symbols, and landscapes. The interwar years, according to Eric Storm, marked "the golden age of regional popular culture" in Europe, a trend that Shanny Peer called a "folklore vogue."[45] Governments endorsed regionalism as a way of promoting nationalism. Cultural activists meanwhile highlighted folklore—the nation's "rich cultural heritage"—as a vehicle for emotionally bonding the local individual to the larger nation. In France, regional folklore exhibits received significant attention at the Paris Exposition of 1937. Since the late 1920s German radio promoted *Heimat* traditions to the larger nation as a way of eliciting pride in its treasure of local cultures.[46]

This book serves to shed light on the nature of regionalism in contested borderlands. In these areas, the inherently intertwined nature of nationalism and regionalism is evident in the fact that border conflicts become a part of regional traditions. Indeed, the discourses and symbols of borderland nationalism infiltrate at least the official identity of region and locality. At its center are narratives of political and cultural struggle against the national (or "racial") "other," which reinforce myths of these areas as the nation's zones of crisis and struggle in past and present. Indeed, in some cases, the identities of disparate contested borderlands are tied together by overarching narratives, the most typical example being interwar Germany's discourses that depicted the various eastern regions both inside and outside national boundaries as "bleeding borders" and the "German east." Examples of how nationalism shapes regionalism on the one hand, such provincial narratives are also fundamental to the identity of the entire nation on the other. In this regard, borderlands typically symbolize the nation's "bulwarks" within its current boundary lines against the "other" in its neighboring borderlands. Yet simultaneously these borderlands represent "bridges" to its cultural and political affiliations in these neighboring areas, which form the basis of its territorial claims.[47]

Contested territories are also arenas for multiple official regionalisms, whose narratives and traditions symbolically function to mutually exclude one another, even though they remain inherently entwined and interwoven. In Upper Silesia, regionalisms served as weapons in territorial conflicts. German and Polish Silesianisms each used folklore, rural history, and other aspects of local culture to forge what Andrew Demshuk has called an "imagined regional community" with inseparable ties to the nation.[48] In their effort to portray the region as solely German or Polish, both camps of borderland nationalists invented what I call national regionalisms, which reinterpreted local traditions, whether existing or newly invented, in ways that connected them to traditions in the nation's other provinces but excluded any "foreign" associations. This reflected another characteristic common to contested regions, where nation-state actors—for example, governments and irredentist activists—carefully edited, reshaped, manipulated, and monitored these enclaves of discourses, narratives, and symbols to make sure they buttressed not only the region's *official* national identity, but also the irredentist agenda.

Aside from national regionalisms, unofficial nonnational concepts of local and provincial identity also take part in conflicts. In Alsace, one of the most famous contested borderlands, various groups of Alsatians cultivated different regional identities, which competed both against one another as well as against the one-sided regional identities and traditions promoted by rival French and German nation-state actors.[49] By contrast, Upper Silesia had no political parties explicitly devoted to promoting nationally indifferent regionalism—except for a few short-lived autonomy movements. In part, this reflected the regional intelligentsia's national orientation, the ability of nationally oriented regionalist parties, such as the German Center Party, to accommodate nationally indifferent locals, and also German and Polish government measures to combat "separatism."[50] Nevertheless, nonofficial regional identities expressed themselves in the actions, gestures, and opinions of the Silesian in the street. They are evident to us today largely through the records of national officials, who expressed frustration in dealing with locals' "national ambiguity," "national indecisiveness," or even "asocial behavior." Only after the fall of communism were some locals able to designate themselves as "Silesian" on official censuses—with other options being Pole *and* Silesian, German *and* Silesian, Pole, or German. Some chose to declare no ethnic or national identity. Such census results have led many to call for regional autonomy within Poland.

The phenomenon that historians have called "national indifference" has recently attracted scholarly attention to Upper Silesia. Although easier to characterize than to define, it refers primarily to locals who identify less with a particular nation than with some alternative collective identity, such as region, confession, or social class. Their tendency to "switch sides," or engage in what Winson Chu calls "interethnic accommodation,"[51] particularly following the redrawing of borders, also reveals an attitude ultimately indifferent to nationality, and has led Chad Bryant to refer to them as "amphibians."[52] This attitude has been observed in other regions, such as Catalonia, Alsace, Tyrol, the Sudetenland, other parts of formerly Habsburg-ruled Central Europe, and even metropolitan areas, such as Łódź.[53] Tara Zahra, a prominent scholar who has worked on flexible loyalty, singled out Upper Silesia as "the most famously nationally indifferent region in world history."[54] James Bjork identified the role of influential Catholic clerical leaders in averting Upper Silesia's potential for total breakdown into antagonistic German and Polish factions.[55] Tomasz Kamusella, in a broad synthetic work, attributed Upper Silesians' resistance to nationalization to their being an ethnic group of their own, with a shared historical, religious, cultural, and linguistic consciousness.[56] Similarly, Brendan Karch, in a microstudy of the city and suburbs of Oppeln in western Upper Silesia, concluded that during the interwar era both camps of nationalists failed to turn Silesian locals into stable national categories of either Germans or Poles.[57]

One of my arguments here is that the borderland struggle—contrary to the intent of its protagonists—actually helped to perpetuate "national indifference." Strong regional identities do not necessarily suffer "natural extinction" when provinces are incorporated into a nation-state, nor are they unique to contested border areas. However, it is no coincidence that they have been most visible where such conflicts are intense. Because periodic border changes in Upper Silesia destabilized any existing sense of "national belonging," locals had to rely on alternative identities that seemed stable and reliable. The violence, lawlessness, uprooting, ethnic segregation, and expulsion campaigns that often accompanied shifting frontiers made the political contingency of nationality all the more apparent. As Hugo Service argues in his study of postwar Upper Silesia, the locals reacted to forceful "Polonization" efforts not so much with displays of German national pride as with "local patriotism."[58] Indeed, plebiscites and the agitation to support one nation or the other were less brutal, but they presented national identity as a choice, not an innate characteristic.

German and Polish borderland nationalists were aware of, and perplexed by, the slippery slope of promoting regionalism, even if overlaid with nationalism. Both camps expressed concern that by endorsing Silesian identity and reviving old and promoting new regional traditions, as well as by deploying social sciences and new media technology to lend legitimacy to a unique provincial culture, they might swing the balance too far in the direction of regional consciousness. Ultimately, however, regionalism offered greater appeal to locals than did traditional nationalism.

The first chapter of this book provides a historical background of Upper Silesia from the late nineteenth century to the eve of World War II. Chapters 2 and 3 examine the resulting cultural conflict between the two new border societies, as well as the related internal politics of Germany and Poland, during the interwar era. The final two chapters examine Upper Silesia's successive annexation and renationalization under the Nazis and then the Polish Communists, with a focus on acculturation politics and local reactions to them. A postscript takes the Upper Silesian story from the Cold War years to the present, with attention to the role of Upper Silesian expellees in West Germany's Cold War politics. This book is based on extensive research in primary documents in national and regional state archives in Germany, Poland, and Russia—including police records and accounts by political dissidents—as well as on contemporary publications (books, pamphlets, newspapers), in addition to films.

Notes

1. Jürgen Runzheimer, "Der Überfall auf den Sender Gleiwitz im Jahre 1939," *Vierteljahrshefte für Zeitgeschichte* 10, no. 4 (1962): 408–22.

2. These locals, who were opponents of the Nazis, served as informers for the police on the Polish side of the borderland. Situation report (SR), May 1939, Archiwum Państwowe w Katowice (APK), 38 (Policja Województwa Śląskiego), 176, 21ff.

3. Quoted from Ewa Waszkiewicz, *Doktryna hitlerowska wśród mniejszości niemieckiej w województwie śląskim w latach 1918–1939* (Wrocław, 2001), 44.

4. Annemarie H. Sammartino, *The Impossible Border: Germany and the East, 1914–1922* (Ithaca, NY, 2010); Elizabeth Harvey, *Women and the Nazi East: Agents and Witnesses of Germanization* (New Haven, CT, 2003).

5. "Der Führer spricht," *Ostdeutsche Morgenpost* 241 (2 Sept. 1939): n.p.

6. The concept of "irredentism" I use here comes from Markus Komprobst, *Irredentism in European Politcs: Argumentation, Compromise, and Norms* (Cambridge, 2009), 23–24. While the work of Winson Chu distinguishes "revisionism" (also "supra-revisionism") from "irredentism" (also "ethnic irredentism"), this book uses the terms interchangeably to refer to claims to both parts of Upper Silesia—and the common German-Polish borderlands in general. Even as Chu irons out the nuances that distinguish these terms quite well—essentially, that "revisionism" refers to claims to territory, while "irredentism" concerns peoples/ethnic groups—he also asserts that "in practice, of course, there was considerable room for revisionism and irredentism to overlap and to piggyback on one another." This book aims to demonstrate that the overlap was particularly striking in the struggle over Upper Silesia. Thus, I refrain from strictly categorizing the relevant political actors in this case study according to the one term or the other. See Winson Chu, *The German Minority in Interwar Poland* (New York, 2012), 32, 28ff.

7. The most similar work examines the popularization of German and Polish irredentist politics in the media and through rallies and commemoration events in Upper Silesia, mostly during the interwar and early postwar eras, and from a comparative perspective: see Juliane Haubold-Stolle, *Mythos Oberschlesien: Der Kampf um die Erinnerung in Deutschland und Polen, 1919–1956* (Osnabrück, 2008). Otherwise, similar approaches to irredentist politics in regard to German-Polish borderlands

have focused on geopolitical thought and thinkers: see Michael Burleigh, *Germany Turns Eastwards: A Study of Ostforschung in the Third Reich* (New York, 1988); Eduard Mühle, *Für Volk und deutschen Osten: Der Historiker Hermann Aubin und die deutsche Ostforschung* (Düsseldorf, 2005); Markus Kroska, *Für ein Polen an Oder und Ostsee: Zygmunt Wojciechowski als Historiker und Publizist* (Osnabrück, 2003); Jan M. Piskorski, Jörg Hackmann, and Rudolf Jaworski, eds., *Deutsche Ostforschung und polnische Westforschung im Spannungsfeld von Wissenschaft und Politik* (Osnabrück, 2002). Other works focus on politics and diplomacy: see Perti Ahonen, *After the Expulsion: Western Germany and Eastern Europe, 1945–90* (Oxford, 2003); Debra J. Allen, *The Oder-Neisse Line: The United States, Poland, and Germany in the Cold War* (Westport, CT, 2003); T. David Curp, *A Clean Sweep? The Politics of Ethnic Cleansing in Western Poland, 1945–1960* (Rochester, NY, 2006). Recent works that also examine acculturation politics include Gregor Thum, *Uprooted: How Breslau Became Wrocław during the Century of Expulsions*, trans. Tom Lapert and Allison Brown (Princeton, NJ, 2011); Hugo Service, *Germans to Poles: Communism, Nationalism, and Ethnic Cleansing after the Second World War* (Cambridge, 2013). See also works cited in notes 31 and 40 below.

8. See Timothy Snyder, *Bloodlands: Europe Between Hitler and Stalin* (New York, 2010).

9. By "cultural racism," I refer to what Eric Weitz described as the imposition of "indelible, immutable, and transgenerational" culturally defined characteristics imposed on a societal group, and serving to legitimate its discrimination or persecution. See Eric Weitz, "Racial Politics without the Concept of Race: Reevaluating Soviet Ethnic and National Purges," *Slavic Review* 61, no. 1 (Spring 2002): 7; George M. Friedrickson, *Racism: A Short History* (Princeton, NJ, 2002), 137.

10. Rogers Brubaker, *Nationalism Reframed: Nationhood and the National Question in the New Europe* (Cambridge, 1996), 107–78.

11. Woodrow Wilson, "Fourteen Points," http://www.fordham.edu/halsall/mod/1918wilson.html (accessed 27 April 2015).

12. See Aviel Roshwald, *Ethnic Nationalism and the Fall of Empires: Central Europe, Russia and the Middle East, 1915–1923* (London and New York, 2001), 163–96; Perti Ahonen et al., eds., *People on the Move: Forced Population Movements in Europe in the Second World War and Its Aftermath* (New York, 2008).

13. See Peter Fischer, *Die Deutsche Publizistik als Faktor der deutsch-polnischen Beziehungen, 1919–1939* (Wiesbaden, 1991); Peter Polak-Springer, "Jammin' with Karlik: The German-Polish 'Radio War' and the 'Gleiwitz Provocation,' 1925–1939," *European History Quarterly* 43, no. 2 (Apr. 2013): 279–300.

14. Holly Case, *Between States: The Transylvanian Question and the European Idea During World War II* (Stanford, CA, 2009), 2. See also Miklós Ziegler, *Ideas on Territorial Revision in Hungary, 1920–1945*, trans. Thomas J. DeKornfeld and Helen D. DeKornfeld (New York, 2007).

15. Philipp Ther, "The Spell of the Homogeneous Nation-State: Structural Factors and Agents of Ethnic Cleansing," in *Diasporas and Ethnic Migrants: Germany, Israel, and Post-Soviet Successor States in Comparative Perspective*, ed. Rainer Münz and Rainer Ohliger (London, 2003), 85.

16. Brubaker, *Nationalism Reframed*.

17. See Brian Porter, *When Nationalism Began to Hate: Imagining Modern Politics in Nineteenth-Century Poland* (New York, 2000).

18. Norman Naimark, *Fires of Hatred: Ethnic Cleansing in Twentieth-Century Europe* (Cambridge, MA, 2001), 4, emphasis mine.

19. On the renationalization of borderlands, see Timothy Snyder, *The Reconstruction of Nations: Poland, Ukraine, Lithuania, Belarus, 1569–1999* (New Haven, CT, 2003); Kate Brown, *A Biography of No Place: From Ethnic Borderland to Soviet Heartland* (Cambridge, MA, 2004); Ahonen et al., *People on the Move*; Eagle Glassheim, "Ethnic Cleansing, Communism, and Environmental Devastation in Czechoslovakia's Borderlands, 1945–1989," *Journal of Modern History* 78 (March 2006): 65–92.

20. Caitlin E. Murdock, *Changing Places: Society, Culture, and Territory in the Saxon-Bohemian Borderlands, 1870–1946* (Ann Arbor, MI, 2010), 1–13, chap. 4, esp. 128.

21. Ibid., 1–13, chap. 4.

22. Tara Zahra, *Kidnapped Souls: National Indifference and the Battle for Children in the Bohemian Lands, 1900–1948* (Ithaca, NY, and London, 2008).

23. The term *Heimat* refers not just to the small locality, but to the local area that Germans call home and to which they are usually emphatically attached. Indeed, "local homeland," although an approximate English equivalent, often does not express connotations that underscore personal attachment and a sense of belonging.

24. Sammartino, *The Impossible Border*, 10–13, 102–3.

25. See Richard Blanke, *Orphans of Versailles: The Germans in Western Poland, 1918–1939* (Lexington, KY, 1993).

26. See Alexander Victor Prusin, *The Lands Between: Conflict in the East European Borderlands, 1870–1992* (Oxford, 2010); Snyder, *The Reconstruction of Nations*, chaps. 3 and 7.

27. See Chu, *The German Minority*; Blanke, *Orphans of Versailles*. On the Polish minority of German Upper Silesia, see Brendan Karch, "Nationalism on the Margins: Silesians between Germany and Poland, 1948–1945" (PhD diss., Harvard University, 2010).

28. Mark Mazower, *Hitler's Empire: How the Nazis Ruled Europe* (New York, 2008), 54–56.

29. See Vejas Gabriel Liulevicius, *The German Myth of the East, 1800 to the Present* (New York, 2009), 190–91.

30. See Harvey, *Women and the Nazi East*; Otto H. Spatz, *Wiedergewonnenes deutsches Land* (Munich and Berlin, 1941).

31. The term was also used for Alsace-Lorraine, which had been returned to France after World War I. On the myth of the "German east," see Liulevicius, *The German Myth*; Gregor Thum, ed., *Traumland Osten: Deutsche Bilder vom östlichen Europa im 20. Jahrhundert* (Göttingen, 2006).

32. See Service, *Germans to Poles*, 9, chap. 2; Grzegosz Strauchold, *Myśl Zachodnia i jej realizacja w Polsce Ludowej w latach 1945–1947* (Toruń, 2003).

33. The long-standing scholarly interest in the Nazi policies to exclude Jews, Slavs, and other groups from the *Volksgemeinschaft* has recently shifted to a greater focus on their efforts to include and integrate populations; see, e.g., Catherine Epstein, *Model Nazi: Arthur Greiser and the Occupation of Western Poland* (New York, 2010); Gerhard Wolf, *Ideologie und Herrschaftsrationalität: Nationalsozialistische Germanisierungspolitik in Polen* (Hamburg, 2013). Similarly, the previous strong focus on the expulsion of Germans from Poland's postwar, formerly German borderlands—see, e.g., Sebastian Siebel-Achenbach, *Lower Silesia from Nazi Germany to Communist Poland, 1942–49* (New York, 1994)—has shifted to a stronger interest in resettlement and reassimilation. See, e.g., Thum, *Uprooted*; Service, *Germans to Poles*.

34. On the conflict over Upper Silesia, see Timothy Wilson, *Frontiers of Violence: Conflict and Identity in Ulster and Upper Silesia, 1918–1922* (Oxford, 2010); T. Hunt Tooley, *National Identity and Weimar Germany: Upper Silesia and the Eastern Border, 1918–22* (Lincoln, NE, 1997); James Bjork, *Neither German nor Pole: Catholicism and National Indifference in a Central European Borderland* (Ann Arbor, MI, 2008).

35. Brendan Karch draws a similar conclusion in his analysis of German Center Party *Heimat* propaganda in interwar western (German) Upper Silesia in "Nationalism on the Margins," 34, chap. 5.

36. See Thum, *Uprooted*.

37. See Curp, *A Clean Sweep*.

38. For a comparison of German and Polish citizenship politics in wartime and postwar Upper Silesia, including the bureaucratic categorization of locals as Germans or Poles, see Adam Ehrlich, "Between Germany and Poland: Ethnic Cleansing and the Politicization of Ethnicity in Upper Silesia under National Socialism and Communism" (PhD diss., University of Indiana–Bloomington, 2006).

On language politics, see Matthais Kneip, *Die Deutsche Sprache in Oberschlesien: Untersuchungen zur politischen Rolle der deutschen Sprachen als Minderheitensprache in den Jahren 1921–1998* (Dortmund, 1998).

39. On postwar renationalization, see Tomasz Kamusella, "Ethnic Cleansing in Upper Silesia, 1944–1951," in *Ethnic Cleansing in Twentieth-Century Europe*, ed. T. Hunt Tooley, Béla Várdy, and Agnes Huszár Várdy (New York, 2003), 293–310; Philipp Ther, *Deutsche und polnische Vertriebene: Gesellschaft und Vertriebenenpolitik in der SBZ/DDR und in Polen, 1945–56* (Göttingen, 1998); Piotr Madajczyk, *Przyłączenie Śląska Opolskiego do Polski, 1945–1948* (Warsaw, 1996); Bernard Linek, *Polityka antyniemiecka na Górnym Śląsku w latach 1945–1950* (Opole, 2000); Service, *Germans to Poles*.

40. See Peter Oliver Loew, *Danzig und Seine Vergangenheit: die Geschichtskultur einer Stadt zwischen Deutschland und Polen* (Osnabrück, 2003); Peter Oliver Loew, Christian Pletzing, and Tomas Serrier, "Zwischen Enteignung und Aneignung: Geschichte und Geschichten in den 'Zwischenräumen Mitteleuropas,'" in *Wiedergewonnene Geschichte: Zur Aneignung von Vergangenheit in den Zwischenräumen Mitteleuropas*, ed. Peter Oliver Loew, Christian Pletzing, and Tomas Serrier (Wiesbaden, 2006), 9–15; Mühle, *Für Volk und deutschen Osten*; Robert Traba, *"Wschodniopruskość": Tożsamość regionalna i narodowa w kulturze politycznej Niemiec* (Poznań, 2005); Thum, *Uprooted*; Jan Musekamp, *Zwischen Stettin and Szczecin: Metamorphosen einer Stadt von 1945 bis 2005* (Wiesbaden, 2010); Mateusz J. Hartwich, *Das Schlesische Riesengebirge: Die Polonisierung einer Landschaft nach 1945* (Vienna, 2012).

41. See Richard Blanke, *Polish-Speaking Germans? Language and National Identity Among the Masurians since 1871* (Cologne, 2001).

42. See Michael Esch, *Gesunde Verhältnisse: Deutsche und polnische Bevölkerungspolitik in Ostmitteleuropa, 1939–1950* (Marburg, 1998); Epstein, *Model Nazi*; Wolf, *Ideologie und Herrschaftsrationalität*; Service, *Germans to Poles*.

43. See Celia Applegate, *A Nation of Provincials: The German Idea of Heimat* (Berkeley, CA, 1990); Alon Confino, *The Nation as a Local Metaphor: Württemberg, Imperial Germany, and National Memory, 1871–1918* (Chapel Hill, NC, 1997).

44. See Joost Augusteijn and Eric Storm, eds., *Region and State in Nineteenth-Century Europe: Nation-Building, Regional Identities, and Separatism* (Houndsmill, UK, 2012). For connections between locality and nation in Poland, see Keely Stauter-Halsted, *A Nation in a Village: The Genesis of Peasant National Identity in Austrian Poland, 1848–1914* (Ithaca, NY, 2001); Patricia Dabrowski, "Constructing a Polish Landscape: The Example of the Carpathian Frontier," *Austria History Yearbook* 39 (2008): 45–65.

45. Eric Storm, *The Culture of Regionalism: Art, Architecture, and International Exhibitions in France, Germany, and Spain, 1890–1939* (Manchester, 2011), 11; Shanny Peer, *France on Display: Peasants, Provincials, and Folklore in the 1937 Paris World's Fair* (Albany, NY, 1998), 135–36, 140–46.

46. Adelheid von Saldern, "*Volk* and *Heimat* Culture in Radio Broadcasting during the Period of Transition from Weimar to Nazi German," *The Journal of Modern History* 76 (June 2004): 312–46. See also Samuel Godfellow, "Fascism and Regionalism in Interwar Alsace," *National Identities* 12, no. 2 (June 2010): 133–45.

47. See Jeffrey K. Wilson, "Imagining a Homeland: Constructing *Heimat* in the German East, 1871–1914," *National Identities* 9, no. 4 (Dec. 2007): 331–49; Andreas Kossert, "Masuren als 'Bollwerk': Konstruktion von Grenze und Grenzregion von der wilhelmischen Ostmarkenpolitik zum NS-Grenzland- und Volkstumskampf, 1894–1945," and other essays in *Die Grenze als Raum, Erfahrung und Konstruktion: Deutschland, Frankreich und Polen von 17. bis zum 20. Jahrhundert*, ed. Etienne Francois, Jörg Seifarth, and Bernhard Struck (Frankfurt and New York, 2006); Omer Bartov and Eric D. Weitz, "Coexistence and Violence in German, Habsburg, Russian, and Ottoman Borderlands," in *Shatterzones of Empires: Coexistence and Violence in the German, Habsburg,*

Russian, and Ottoman Borderlands, ed. Omer Bartov and Eric D. Weitz (Bloomington, IN, 2013), 10–22; Gregor Thum, "Megalomania and Angst," in *Shatterzones of Empires: Coexistence and Violence in the German, Habsburg, Russian, and Ottoman Borderlands*, ed. Omer Bartov and Eric D. Weitz (Bloomington, IN, 2013), 42–60.

48. Andrew Demshuk, *The Lost German East: Forced Migration and the Politics of Memory, 1945–1970* (Cambridge, 2012), 78.

49. See Christopher J. Fischer, *Alsace to the Alsatians? Visions and Divisions of Alsatian Regionalism, 1870–1939* (New York, 2010); Samuel Godfellow, "Fascism and Regionalism," 133–45.

50. Ryszard Kaczmarek, Maciej Kucharski, and Adrian Cybula, *Alzacja/Lotaryngia a Górny Śląsk: Dwa Regiony Pogranicza, 1648–2001* (Katowice, 2001), 99–242.

51. Winson Chu, "'Volksgemeinschaften unter sich': German Minorities and Regionalism in Poland, 1918–1939," in *German History from the Margins*, ed. Neil Gregor et al. (Bloomington, IN, 2006), 107.

52. See Chad Bryant, *Prague in Black: Nazi Rule and Czech Nationalism* (Cambridge, 2007).

53. On national indifference in these and other regions, see Phillip Ther and Holm Sundhaussen, eds., *Regionale Bewegungen und Regionalismen in europäischen Zwischenräumen seit der Mitte des 19. Jahrhunderts* (Marburg, 2003); Blanke, *Polish-Speaking Germans?*; Pieter M. Judson, *Guardians of the Nation: Activists on the Language Frontiers of Imperial Austria* (Cambridge, MA, 2006); Jeremy King, *Budweisers into Czechs and Germans: A Local History of Bohemian Politics, 1848–1948*, (Princeton, 2005); Murdock, *Changing Places*; Zahra, *Kidnapped Souls*; Winson Chu, "'Volksgemeinschaften unter sich,'" 104–26.

54. Tara Zahra, "Imagined Non-communities: National Indifference as a Category of Analysis," *Slavic Review* 69, no. 1 (2010): 93–119.

55. Bjork, *Neither German nor Pole*.

56. Tomasz Kamusella, *Silesia and Central European Nationalisms: The Emergence of National and Ethnic Groups in Prussian Silesia and Austrian Silesia, 1848–1918* (West Lafayette, IN, 2007).

57. Karch, "Nationalism on the Margins." See also Andrzej Michałczyk, *Heimat, Kirche und Nation: Deutsche und polnische Nationalisierungsprozesse im geteilten Oberschlesien (1922–1939)* (Cologne, 2010).

58. Service, *Germans to Poles*, 248–49.

CHAPTER 1

THE MAKING OF A CONTESTED BORDERLAND, 1871–1939

During the spring and summer of 1921, governments, patriots, and militiamen in Germany and Poland waged propaganda and military campaigns over the disputed Upper Silesian borderland. The League of Nation's decision to partition the province in Poland's favor tamped down the level of violence, but did not resolve the conflict at its core. The ensuing cold war was fed by a transnational irredentist culture propagated by German and Polish geopolitical academic centers and borderland activist leagues, paramilitary fighters, regional governors and political party leaders, and organizations that represented national minorities who had been left on the "wrong" side of the border after the partition. Despite internal conflicts among these borderland nationalists, they waged a common struggle to standardize and stabilize a collective identity in Upper Silesia, which, unlike other German-Polish border provinces, lacked clear-cut confessional or linguistic borders.

This chapter examines the forces that turned a once peaceful province in eastern Prussia into a tinderbox of interwar Central European irredentist conflict. After an overview of Upper Silesia's history and the nineteenth-century origins of the ideological and political tenets of German-Polish territorial conflict and borderland nationalism, it will examine the social, economic, and political consequences of the redrawn borders into the late interwar years, when these factors played critical roles in creating a climate in which irredentist fervor, authoritarian regimes, and the politics of nationalization flourished. This is the wider context in which the cultural struggle over the region—the focus of the next two chapters—took place.

On the Fringes of the Prussian East

Before it became an iconic borderland, contested by two hostile nation-states, Upper Silesia was an area located both at the nexus of three multinational empires and on the fringes of Slavic linguistic influence. Under Prussian rule since 1740, it formed the southeastern frontier of the united German Empire after 1871. Since the late eighteenth century, Upper Silesia shared borders with czarist Russia to its east and the Habsburg monarchy (Austria-Hungary) to its south. In addition, the region shared an unofficial border with Poznania (the Prussian Posen Province), a part of the postpartition Polish nation-without-a-state.

Both the German and Polish languages exerted strong influences on Upper Silesia throughout its history. High German dominated as the official language of public interaction and was widely used within urban centers, particularly by the educated and migrants from other parts of Germany. Introduced as the language of elementary schooling after the Revolution of 1848, High (literary) Polish flourished until after German unification, when Chancellor Otto von Bismarck replaced it with High German as part of a broader campaign against "foreign" influences. Industrialization and state acculturation both acted as catalysts for the German language's gradual eclipse of Polish. High Polish remained an important language for Catholic religious services and prayer, particularly in the countryside and within the urban centers of the industrial district, which drew workers from surrounding rural areas. Yet despite German's gradual domination, Upper Silesian society remained largely bilingual, insofar as the average person understood, and had at least some command of, both German and Polish. This situation created problems for officials charged with categorizing the nationality of the local population, since language was the usual criterion for such determinations in Central Europe. In practice, the multilingual local inhabitant could usually claim to be whatever she or he chose—German, Polish, or Upper Silesian—and indeed, might have changed that identity to another if doing so became advantageous.

A traditional regional "Silesian" was spoken far more widely than High Polish. Now regarded by some scholars as a dialect (or subdialect) and by others as a separate language, it was earlier often known by the pejorative German term *Wasserpolnisch* (watered-down Polish) to acknowledge its Polish-based grammar and syntax and its use of Polish vocabulary and expressions, but also its admixture of German and regional usages. Polish speakers referred to it as the *gwara Śląska*, or Silesian dialect or way of speaking. Silesian, which was widely spoken in both rural areas and the urban centers of the industrial district, varied over time and by locality. Since the late nineteenth century, High German generally exerted a strong influence on Silesian usage, particularly in urban areas with large German populations. After partition in 1922, the tables were turned to favor High Polish in eastern Upper Silesia. Altogether, the multilingual nature of

Upper Silesian society helped promote its sense of otherness vis-à-vis the largely monolingual (German) neighboring province of Lower Silesia.[1]

The traditional dominance of the Catholic religion in Upper Silesia further strengthened regional consciousness. Within a predominantly Protestant Prussia, 90 percent of Upper Silesia's population was Catholic.[2] The region's heavily religious culture made Upper Silesia a target of Bismarck's Kulturkampf, or "cultural war" against "anti-German" influences, in particular Catholicism and—in the eastern provinces—the Polish language. In Poznania and other heavily Polish parts of the Prussian state, the persecution of the Catholic Church spurred the rise of a modern Polish national movement. Nonetheless, Polish consciousness remained relatively marginal in Upper Silesia. Bismarck's war against the region's socially influential clergy played a more important role in the emergence of Catholicism as a dominant political force.[3] Spurred to defend a faith that was seen as the heart of regional culture against the nationalizing German nation-state, the German Center Party (Deutsche Zentrumspartei), which was known in Upper Silesia as the Catholic People's Party (Katholische Volkspartei), became the main guardian and promoter of Upper Silesian regional identity. The local clergy refused to divide their parishioners into "Poles" and "Germans." Instead, they sought to unite them on the basis of a supraethnic/supranational identity that promoted the primacy of the Upper Silesian *Heimat* (regional homeland), multilingualism (German, Polish, Silesian), and Catholicism. Together, the clergy and the Catholic political movement became the main forces that allowed Upper Silesians to resist the strong nationalizing currents that swept Central Europe in the late nineteenth and early twentieth centuries.[4]

The Upper Silesian industrial district, the region's cluster of industrial cities,[5] has always been foremost a society of workers. In 1921, 60 percent of the roughly 680,000–700,000 residents belonged to the working class, and 54.4 percent of those in the labor force worked in coal mining and metallurgy.[6] The rapid pace of industrialization, here as elsewhere, triggered social dislocations and class conflict, in this case primarily between Catholic and largely multilingual workers and the mainly Protestant and culturally German industrial and landowning elites. While this conflict bolstered the local German Center Party, it also strengthened the appeal of a separate Polish national movement.[7] Upper Silesia's regional political consciousness lasted into the immediate post–World War I period, when workers in Upper Silesia, rather than following the Communist Spartacists, preferred to express their class discontent in what Timothy Wilson has called "the idiom of Polish nationalism."[8] Thus, social conflict, along with political Catholicism and multilingualism, helped to forge strong feelings of Upper Silesian otherness.

The forces that created a distinct regional identity contributed to Upper Silesia's penchant for what has been called both "national indifference" and a "pending nationality" (*schwebendes Volkstum*).[9] The intensity of this indifference, however, fluctuated in accord with events and forces. Manfred Alexander, for example, has shown that before World War II, Upper Silesians displayed a range of collective identities, coinciding with their language use and class status.[10] Thus, the native community differentiated between the "nationally indifferent" and groups that, in addition to strong regional bonds, identified to some extent with a particular nation. As Timothy Wilson put it, "the crux here was that the local population was *not* divided into watertight categories of 'Poles' and 'Germans.' And not only did the categories of 'Germans' and 'Poles' overlap heavily in practice, but each had its own internal gradations."[11] Similarly, Andrzej Michałczyk noted that in Upper Silesia "the terms 'Pole' and 'German' were not used as nouns but rather as adjectives." What mattered, in other words, was the extent to which one behaved as "Polish" or "German," and what kind of "Pole" or "German" one was. Thus, locals might label one another as "an even worse Pole," a "better German," a "die-hard German/Pole"—or even "a paid agent" (a "Pole" or "German" who had been bribed) or a "German/Pole out of fear."[12] These fine distinctions were possible because national identity in the region was an option—one that, more often than not, was imposed by others, rather than a self-identification. Such "internal gradations" underscore the rarity of exclusive and reified "German" or "Polish" identities.

Using linguistic competence as a key marker, Alexander classified Upper Silesians as "Polish/German-oriented," "Polish/German leaning," and "German-assimilated." Although the vast majority of all three groups knew the local dialect (which Alexander calls Schlonsakisch or Silesian), the more Polonophile or Germanophile their members were, the more comfortably and actively they used their respective high national language. Class acted as a related marker that distinguished these groups. Since adoption of the high national language advanced upward mobility, the educated and middle classes tended to be fluent in the standard usages. Urbanites—including workers—also spoke German, particularly before the partition in 1922, and on the German side of the border thereafter.[13]

While nationality remained in a state of flux, the more stable and enduring identities were Upper Silesian, Catholic, and, especially in the industrial district, consciously working class. Throughout the twentieth century, the region had significant elites who identified themselves as German or Polish. Some of these individuals, although outspoken nationalists, still advocated a balance between Germanization or Polonization and the maintenance of regional traditions and identities. In addition to Wojciech Korfanty, the leader of the regional Polish movement, they included Carl Ulitzka, the German Center Party leader in Upper Silesia, and Jerzy Ziętek, the postwar Communist Party leader, who because of his service to the regional cause became the only high-ranking Communist activist in Poland to be memorialized with a statue after 1989 (see epilogue).

These identities endure even into the twenty-first century. Census figures from Upper Silesia that show a significant number of individuals who declare Silesian and German identities have raised eyebrows across Poland. In 2011, for example, 817,000 individuals declared themselves to be of Silesian nationality/ethnicity, with only a little over half (423,000) claiming also to be Polish. At the same time, nearly 113,000 residents claimed to be German, most of these also Polish (over 78,000). The 2002 census results were even "worse"—from a national perspective—as over 224,000 individuals declared no specific nationality whatsoever. This "well-known phenomenon in Upper Silesia"—in Michałczyk's words—which is also prevalent in other regions in Central Europe, points to the limited success of Europe's "becoming national."[14]

The Origins of German-Polish Territorial Strife

The shape of German-Polish territorial conflict during the interwar era can, to a large extent, be traced to the aggressive efforts of the new German Empire to assert its national identity in the Prussian east—namely, those provinces that until their annexation by Prussia between 1792 and 1795 had been part of the Polish-Lithuanian Commonwealth. This campaign, initially launched in the form of Bismarck's Kulturkampf (1871–78), ignited resistance by a nascent Polish national movement that struggled to (re)establish an independent Polish state. Striking at the influence of the Catholic Church in politics, civil affairs, and schooling, as well as the Polish language, the Kulturkampf ultimately backfired, strengthening rather than weakening both clerical influence and the Polish national movement. In particular, Bismarck ipso facto united the German Center Party, the representative of German political Catholicism, with Polish nationalism. As a result, the Polish national movement expanded its influence to new regions and new segments of society in the Prussian east. Although the party's influence remained relatively weak in Upper Silesia, there, more than in other eastern territories, the German Center Party assumed the role of guardian of the Polish national cause.[15]

Bismarck's decision to officially set aside the Kulturkampf in 1878 did not end imperial Germany's anti-Polish campaign. During 1885–86, the German government expelled some 26,000 Polish and Jewish individuals, who were non-German citizens, from the eastern provinces to Galicia and Congress Poland. Simultaneously, after 1886, the Prussian Settlement Commission was working to Germanize the ethnic demography of the countryside of Poznania, the provincial center of German-Polish struggle. Like the expulsions, this effort was in large part a reaction to the socioeconomic consequences of industrialization, which turned the eastern territories into Germany's backwaters and reduced jobs in agriculture. Many Germans from the east fled westward in what was known as the *Ostflucht* or left the countryside for cities (*Landflucht*), emptying rural areas for resettlement by Poles and other Slavs. The Prussian Settlement Commission strove to keep this "Slavic flood"—as nationalists referred to it—at bay by buying up land and settling it with Germans. Between 1886 and 1918, it moved an estimated 154,000 Germans onto farms and homesteads, but nevertheless failed in its larger mission of forestalling a predominantly Polish rural population.[16] Removing Polish as a language of instruction was a related attempt by the Prussian government to make public education an instrument of Germanization.[17]

Years after Bismarck's forced departure from office, Germany embarked on a "softer" anti-Polish strategy under the third German imperial chancellor, the Prince of Hohenlohe. It involved a "politics of lifting up" (*Hebungspolitik*) the standards of welfare, culture, economy, and hygiene in the eastern borderlands. According to Richard Blanke, it also marked a shift "from the land and settlement projects to the cities and small towns."[18] The goal was now to turn cities with a growing Polish middle class into "bulwarks of Germandom." Thus, by 1900 the German state sought to make the city of Posen (Poznań), the urban center of German-Polish conflict, a showcase of *Kultur* (German high culture). The university, the Kaiser Wilhelm Library, and a municipal theater and museum, along with a cleaner and more orderly municipality, served as the main icons of the city's official identity.[19]

The government's moderation of its anti-Polish policy sparked a Pan-German movement committed to carrying on the struggle against the "Slavic flood." According to Elizabeth A. Drummond, these nationalists viewed the eastern borderlands as "Germandom's first line of defense against the advancing Slavic hordes" and their German citizens as the imperial "border patrol."[20] In 1894 nationalists founded the German Eastern Marches Society (Deutscher Ostmarkenverein), devoted to promoting a range of Germanization measures in the borderlands, from halting Slavic immigration to fostering German economic and cultural life.[21] These policies later inspired various societies of borderland nationalists—activists devoted to promoting and defending "Germandom" in the frontier regions—the most renowned being the Nazi-affiliated League of the German East (Bund Deutscher Osten, or BDO).

Hebungspolitik implicitly symbolized the superiority of "German work" (*Deutsche Arbeit*) and "German culture" (*Kultur*) over the equivalent products of "lesser peoples," the Slavs. As described by Vejas Liulevicius, "German work" connoted that "the German character expressed itself in a kind of work which—rather than alienating—was creative and holistic."[22] During this same period, imperial Germany legitimated its colonial ventures in Africa and Asia with myths of racial and cultural superiority. *Kultur* and *Arbeit*—often melded as *Kulturarbeit*—also became important elements of the colonial discourse directed at the Prussian eastern provinces, large areas of which had Polish majorities. Poles were themselves widely considered to be "half-Asiatic."[23] Introduced as part of an official imperial German effort to combat German out-migration and Polish/Slavic in-migration, this discourse remained a staple of German irredentist politics after World War I and into the Third Reich. Likewise, the Germanic rebuilding of Posen (Poznań), the symbolic fruit of *Kulturarbeit*, marked an early use of urban planning as an instrument of territorial appropriation.

Anti-Polish Germanization policies spurred the development of an aggressive and determined grassroots Polish national movement, centered in Poznania (the Posen region) and organized in 1905 as Polish National Democracy (Narodowa Demokracja, commonly known as the Endecja after the Polish pronunciation of the abbreviation ND). This middle class–based movement sought to fortify Polish national solidarity through mass mobilization. Authoritarian, militant, and social Darwinist in its ethos, National Democracy was led by the charismatic biologist, politician, and intellectual Roman Dmowski. A central pillar of its geopolitical ideology was the so-called Piast myth, which viewed the German-Polish borderlands as the cradle of the medieval Piast dynasty, which Polish nationalist historiography appropriated as the nation's founding dynasty. Dmowski thus claimed the more industrialized and "western" Prussian east as the bedrock of the Polish nation. Depicting Germans as the Poles' core enemy, National Democracy asserted that Poles could prevail against their foes by becoming like them, particularly by adopting the German model of modernization. The Endecja thus initiated an epoch of Polish history that Brian Porter has characterized as "when nationalism began to hate." Its nationalism—like that of the Pan-German League, the Prussian Settlement Commission, and the German Eastern Marches Society—was based on language, ethnicity, and racism. National Democrats viewed Germans and Jews as the main enemies of the Polish nation, and after World War I—in imitation of Imperial Germany—called for the expulsion of these groups as part of the "Polonization" of all borderlands as well as of the linguistic Slavs living there. Dmowski's followers made explicit claims to Prussia's eastern provinces: Poznania, Pomerania, Masuria, and Silesia.[24]

In the decade before the war, the Endecja primarily concerned itself with the "nationality struggle" between Poles and Germans, building grassroots social, economic, and cultural organizations to compete with their German counterparts. In order to counter and resist Germanization, the Polish movement worked to replicate its enemy's institutions and tactics. It established cultural and athletic societies, libraries, and reading clubs, such as the gymnast Falcon Society (Sokol), the Society for Popular Education (Towarzystwo Oświaty Ludowej), and the Society for Popular Reading Rooms (Towarzystwo Czytelni Ludowej). These Endecja-inspired grassroots societies identified their mission as spreading national and regional Polish high culture, and thereby "awakening" the masses to Polish patriotism, as well as countering the work of similar German organizations. This culture war began a transnational (German-Polish) political tradition of striving to rally the hearts and minds of the masses for the nation, thus laying the foundation for the territorial struggles that followed World War I.[25]

Prior to the Great War, Upper Silesia remained on the margins of this conflict. There the Polish national movement first gained popularity in response to the Kulturkampf. Its leaders included important laymen, such as literati Jozef Lompa and Karol Miarka, and clerics, such as Antoni Stabik, Jozef Szaffranek, and Bernard Bogedain. In Poznania, where the language issue was predominant, the national movement exceptionally became a political force. In Upper Silesia, where the attacks on religion took precedence, the German Center Party arose to defend both Catholicism and Polish, the main language of prayer. The party attracted men like the teacher and writer Miarka, whose earlier efforts to mobilize the masses in support of a secular Polish national identity had failed. Although they fought for the right to use Polish, which like German and Silesian was central to the multilingual regional heritage, most Upper Silesians had no intention of becoming Poles. In this borderland on the fringes of Russian Poland, the "Polack" remained an unattractive figure associated with poverty and backwardness. By contrast, a powerful German state represented industrial, cultural, and military might. Despite this, the inroads of German nationalism into Upper Silesia were more limited than in the largely Protestant and linguistically German Lower Silesia. In Upper Silesia, both Polish and German nationalisms remained largely foreign forces imported into a province that identified primarily with region, religion, and class.[26]

Stubborn popular rootedness in regional ways ultimately led both German and Polish parties to exploit regionalism as a way to win local support. During the 1890s, the German Center Party, which sought to tie locals to the nation along regional and provincial lines, was the main agent and beneficiary of regionalist zeal. Its strategies for winning local support included defending regional identity and culture, including German-Polish bilingualism, from national cultural standardization, while also emphasizing the region's Prussian identity. Given Prussia's dominance in Germany, this approach elicited national loyalty to Germany among local skeptics of German nationalism. Similarly, Wojciech Korfanty, the charismatic Upper Silesian Polish nationalist who led the region's first viable Polish party, the Polish Circle, enjoyed unprecedented political success in large part because of his appeals to regionalism. According to Tomasz Kamusella, this meant fighting for a place within the Polish nation that allowed Silesians to "continue to live in accordance with their own non-national, manifold identity in the rapidly modernizing world of clashing nation states."[27] Korfanty's strongly regionalist Polish identity made him "too German" for many Poles, but "too Polish" for Germans, particularly during the interwar era. He thus became the embodiment of how chauvinist nationalists from both nations viewed Upper Silesians: neither "theirs" nor "ours." To German nationalists, their linguistic ambiguity made them *Wasserpolen*, while Polish nationalists called them *Odroks* (people of the Oder River) to underscore their in-betweenness.[28]

The sense of belonging and identity among Upper Silesians was, then, more complex than just national patriotism or total apathy toward national consciousness. Prussian/German-Silesian and Polish-Silesian identity both recognized the region's ties to the nation but at the same time signified a feeling of "otherness" from the latter. Multilingualism, bipolar national influence, and strong supranational religious consciousness all gave this borderland its own distinct regional character.

By the late nineteenth century, both German and Polish efforts were underway in Upper Silesia to achieve a version of the process famously described by Eugen Weber as turning "peasants into Frenchmen."[29] After Bismarck's death in 1898, German nationalists erected a twenty-meter-high Bismarck Tower in Slupna (Słupna, currently in Mysłowice) to symbolize the region as a bastion of "Germandom" standing on the fringes of *"polnische Wirtschaft"* (Polish mismanagement).[30] Polish nationalists countered with the Piast myth, which depicted the region as a primordial outpost of Polishness in perpetual struggle against Germanization. Nonetheless, local national indifference and the politics of the German Center Party for the moment dampened any outbreak of ethnic war in Upper Silesia.

World War I, the resulting breakup of empires, and the triumph of the popular determination of peoples unleashed forces that threatened the possibility of national indifference. One tool of the victorious powers, the plebiscite, pressured locals of Upper Silesia to choose either Germany or the newly established Poland. In redrawn Central Europe, this region became one of several playgrounds for the nationalism and social utopianism that characterized this era. The grassroots struggle to nationalize minds was superseded by local, national, and international conflicts over territories, waged now between two nation-states. Most of the policies, ideologies, institutions, and actors in this new struggle emerged from the nineteenth-century German-Polish conflict over the Prussian east.

Plebiscite, War, Partition

The collapse of the Hohenzollern, Habsburg, and Romanov multinational empires, along with disagreements among the Allied Powers on how to map out Central Europe, encouraged the successor states to use military force to create advantageous territorial faits accomplis. Although differing on the extent of westward versus eastward expansion, the chief leaders of the new independent Polish nation-state, Roman Dmowski and Josef Piłsudski, agreed that their nation must use force to win territory from its neighbors. Thus, within the first three postwar years, Poland waged war against the Ukraine, Lithuania, the USSR, Czechoslovakia, and Germany. Mainstream Polish historiography refers to the first four conflicts as "wars," while calling the encounters with Germany grass-roots "uprisings" or "insurgencies," despite central government involvement.

The first of these actions, the Wielkopolska Uprising, erupted in the city of Poznań (Posen) in December 1918, enabling the insurgents to secure the city for Poland.[31] A month later, a seven-day war between Poland and Czechoslovakia broke out over Teschen, Upper Silesia's southeast, which the Czechs had annexed. During this time, the Polish army was also fighting a war against the Ukraine over Galicia and Volhynia. On 21 November, the city of Lviv fell, and the army made its way to Kiev, only to be routed by an advancing Red Army, which pushed it all the way back to Warsaw. The capital's near fall to the Red Army in August 1920, which concluded this most important of Poland's frontier wars, greatly worried middle- and upper-class Europeans fearful of communism's westward advance. Shortly after the Polish-Soviet War, Poland, which coveted the city of Vilnius, also fought against Lithuania.

The Treaty of Riga, signed by Poland and the Soviet Union on 18 March 1921, paused Poland's postwar military engagements by setting the nation's eastern border and granting the new state the regions known to Poles as the *Kresy* (borderlands): eastern Galicia, Volhynia, and western Byelorussia.[32] Militarism and expansion thus became core values of the new Polish Republic's political culture. Needing to protect itself on all sides against now disgruntled enemies—in particular, Germany and the Soviet Union—a mainly agrarian Poland needed resources and facilities for heavy industrial production. Soon after the signing of the treaty with the Soviet Union, an opportunity to address this problem arose in the form of the still unsettled fate of the Upper Silesian region, including its industrial district. Nationalists also asserted historical and ethnic claims to this region.

Through the Treaty of Versailles and subsequent postwar agreements, the Allied Powers had directly stripped Germany of such valuable territories as Alsace-Lorraine in the west and the so-called Polish Corridor to the east. In addition, the Hultschin area at the southern tip of Upper Silesia was ceded to Czechoslovakia without a plebiscite, thus adding more fuel to widespread German resentment against the treaty. Germany's victory in other areas where plebiscites were ordered—including East Prussia (Masuria, Warmia), and Schleswig—averted even greater loss of territory.[33] These successes led to German confidence that the plebiscite mandated for industrially powerful Upper Silesia would also go in Germany's favor.

The plebiscite's announcement provoked vociferous and violent antagonisms. Soon after the armistice, the Polish and German governments each began to build up paramilitary forces led by combat veterans to defend their "rights" to this borderland. In August 1919 these groups were involved in what the Poles called the first Silesian insurgency. Launched by Poland and quickly put down by German forces, this offensive was sparked by the repressive treatment of Polish activists and sympathizers by Prussian authorities, who retained administrative control over the region. To restore order and end this misuse of authority, in February 1920 the Allied Powers placed the region under international governance by a French-dominated Inter-Allied Commission, led by the French general Henri Le Rond. Sporadic German-Polish violence continued, however, and terror by German militants, as well as a broader war of nerves between the two antagonists, helped foment the second Silesian insurgency of mid-August 1920, which lasted for several weeks. British officials in the Inter-Allied Commission blamed the extent of this offensive on the French, which intent on limiting Germany's industrial might, were particularly supportive of Poland's claim to the region.[34]

The plebiscite, which was open to all natives of Upper Silesia, both those who lived in the region and "émigrés" who had left, presented what James Bjork notably refers to as a choice of "either-or": leave their homeland in Germany or cede it to Poland.[35] Scheduled for 20 March 1921, it was preceded by vigorous agitation on the part of both the Polish Plebiscite Commission (led by Korfanty) and its German counterpart (led by the German Center Party's Kurt Urbanek), each supported by its respective national government. Each camp produced and distributed propaganda posters, pamphlets, and newspapers that slurred and ridiculed its opponents with nationalistic and culturally ethnic stereotypes. However, most of the German and Polish propaganda emphasized the cultural, social, and economic benefits of choosing one side over the other.[36] In the end, nearly 60 percent of a heavy vote chose to stay in Germany, with decisive majorities coming from areas with upwardly mobile populations: the main urban centers of the industrial district, Kattowitz (Katowice), Königshütte (Chorzów), and the tricity area (Beuthen/Bytom, Hindenburg/Zabrze, and Gleiwitz/Gliwice). Particularly in the region's eastern districts, the surrounding countryside opted for Poland. Contrary to the once dominant German and Polish nationalist historiographies, recent scholarship argues that the average plebiscite voter was motivated not by deeply rooted patriotism, but rather by the everyday issues confronting the typical Upper Silesian.[37]

The "either-or" choice imposed by the plebiscite nonetheless ended any hope of accommodating the complex nature of collective identity in Upper Silesia, in particular its strong regional sentiment. While the Allies could only allow a vote for Germany or Poland, the national contest over the region that they prompted inadvertently unleashed popular calls for regional autonomy. The region's removal from German control and its placement from 1920 until 1922 under the authority of the Inter-Allied Commission, itself answerable to the League of Nations, enabled the region's natives to envision an independent Upper Silesian state. Supporters cited the precedents of the Allies' creation of the autonomous free city of Danzig and the rise of an Alsatian separatist movement that wanted neither French nor German control.

A short-lived independence movement under the League of Upper Silesians (Bund der Oberschlesier/Związek Górnoślązaków, BdO) became the most fervent champion of either full or partial autonomy within a German state. Led by the Germanophile lawyer Ewald Latacz, this openly pro-German and anti-Polish organization nonetheless opposed nation-state centralism. Scholars sympathetic both to regionalism and this movement have accepted the BdO's claim of 300,000 followers, although no statistical evidence supports this number. It is likely that the league attracted considerable sympathy among Upper Silesians, many of whom shared its expressed values, above all opposition to any attempt to partition the region between Germany or Poland.[38] Although not a factor in the plebiscite vote, the BdO reflected the strength of regional identity and the relative weakness of German and Polish nationalisms. Both national camps tried to make concessions to this sentiment with promises of autonomous legal status for the region.[39]

In the end, a Polish military offensive helped determine Upper Silesia's geopolitical fate. Reacting to the outcome of the plebiscite, Wojciech Korfanty ordered the third Silesian insurgency on the symbolic date of 3 May, Poland's national holiday commemorating the constitution of 1793. With this offensive, the Polish nationalists strove to capture by force what legal means had denied them, although in their view the plebiscite results had been illegitimate on a number of grounds, including German terror and the heavy participation of émigré voters. The Polish government and military clearly instigated this offensive, for example, by mobilizing thousands of troops from outside the region to join the local insurgents. Mainstream Polish opinion, however, viewed it as a popular grassroots uprising that reflected the will and conviction of ordinary Upper Silesians.[40] To Germans, it was a Polish invasion of their country. The German government mobilized volunteer units made up of *Freikorps* and *Selbstschutz* troops to stop the aggression and secure the entire region for Germany. As described by James Bjork, "by the late spring of 1921, an undeclared conventional war was raging across central Upper Silesia."[41] For Poland, this was the last of six borderland clashes that the young republic had engaged in against its neighbors, and the second in seriousness after the Polish-Soviet War. For the new Weimar Republic, it marked the culmination of a series of struggles to retain historically German eastern territories against the hostile guarantors of Europe's post-Versailles geopolitical order. The perception that this conflict was Germany's last chance to resist territorial dismemberment—indeed, to save a territory whose population had clearly proclaimed its will to remain in this nation-state—helps explain the eagerness of tens of thousands of young men to join the *Freikorps* and valiantly fight in defense of their borderland. Indeed, locals from the region made up a large part of voluntary forces on both sides.

Although it lasted only two months, this de facto first modern German-Polish war considerably poisoned relations between the two nations for the rest of the interwar era. In addition to significant battlefield casualties, which may have been as many as 1,760, the postplebiscite conflict led to excesses against both combatants and civilians.[42] Moreover, while the nationalist passions may have been imported from Germany and Poland, the actual violence was committed largely by the locals themselves; thus, natives remembered this conflict as an "Upper Silesian war between brothers." Timothy Wilson argues that such excesses as massacre, rape, torture, and even the desecration of corpses and denial of proper burial can be attributed to the absence of clear-cut ethnonational borders, and thus the impossibility of delineating clear-cut and stable "German" and "Polish" camps. By discouraging defections and enforcing loyalty, violence became an instrument in the futile nationalist cause of drawing sides.[43]

The nationalism that swept Upper Silesia during 1921 in the forms of mass politics, grassroots propaganda, brutal violence, and war continued throughout the interwar years. Nationalists on both sides of the border mythologized the events of this year in narratives of heroic Upper Silesian struggle, sacrifice, and martyrdom for "their fatherland," whether Germany or Poland. On both sides, they published photographs of gruesome killings and mutilations with the intent of stoking enduring vendettas against the other. Indeed, the fighting at the Mount of St. Anne (Sankt Annaberg/Góra świętej Anny), the main regional landmark, served as a powerful propaganda instrument not only throughout the interwar period, but also later for both the Nazis and the Polish Communists, when it served as part of the functional ideologies that legitimated ethnic cleansing in this region.[44]

The passions sparked by the plebiscite and ensuing conflict found a new focus in June 1922, when the League of Nations divided Upper Silesia between Germany and Poland. As drawn by the league, the new border partitioned the industrial district. Although Poland gained only one-third of Upper Silesia, it was the economically most important sector, including 79 percent of the industrial district's coal mines, 60 percent of its blast furnaces, and 75 percent of its steel mills. The new Polish territory also encompassed around 43 percent of the population of Upper Silesia, along with the largest urban centers, Kattowitz and Königshütte, whose residents had clearly opted for Germany, in majorities ranging from 65–75 percent.[45] While neither side was completely satisfied with these new borders, the Germans—the undisputed losers in this settlement—expressed the more unrelenting and explicit outrage.

The Making of Two Border Societies

The partition created two separate provincial polities, western (German) and eastern (Polish) Upper Silesia. The second polity received the name of Voivodeship Silesia (Województwo Śląskie).[46] To distinguish *this* territory from the still German area to the west from which it had been sundered, I will use the term Voivodeship (roughly an English rendering of a Polish province) to refer to this new province. With the exception of the Voivodeship of Warsaw City, the Voivodeship Silesia was Poland's smallest but nevertheless most densely populated and heavily urbanized province. Moreover, it consisted entirely of territory that was "foreign" to most of the nation's history: Silesia had never been part of the Polish-Lithuanian Commonwealth, Poland's forerunner from the medieval and early modern era. Three-quarters of the Voivodeship's territory had belonged to Prussia/Germany, and the remainder (the southern Cieszyn/Teschen area) to Austria-Hungary before World War I.[47]

Recognizing that Upper Silesian regional consciousness could exert a dangerous centrifugal force, Polish nationalists approached this issue with tact. Already during the plebiscite, the pro-Polish forces had tried to rally support by using the Silesian dialect and promising the region extensive autonomy within the Polish nation. In this respect, they were arguably more "Upper Silesian" than the League of Upper Silesians, whose propaganda materials were in German and Polish. Making good on their promises, in 1922 Poland made the Voivodeship a semiautonomous region, the only province with its own legislative body (the Silesian Sejm), its own school system, and its own taxing authority.

To the wider Polish nation, the Voivodeship symbolized industrial power. Its proportion of industrial workers out of its total population was the highest among all of Poland's provinces: 71 percent, compared to an average of less than 40 percent.[48] Ironically, Germans owned the vast majority of this area's productive capacity, with their property rights guaranteed under international law. Germans made up 75 percent of managerial personnel in heavy industry within the first decade of the partition.[49] As late as 1932, close to 60 percent of all technical managers in these industries were German.[50] Capital investment in eastern Upper Silesian heavy industry in 1926 was 40 percent German, 22 percent French and Belgian, 20 percent Anglo-American, and only 16.6 percent Polish.[51] Wealthy German industrialists exercised additional influence by bestowing financial support on German minority organizations, the most important being the Volksbund, headed by the charismatic Otto Ulitz, as well as German political parties and German-language schools and cultural institutions. Polish nationalists saw the control of their industry by the revanchist neighbor as the most potent barrier to the borderland's integration with Poland, making it a prime target of "Polonization" during the 1930s under the nationalist governor Michał Grażyński.

The western segment of Upper Silesia continued its existence as Provinz Oberschlesien (which I will refer to as the Provinz) within Weimar Germany's Prussian State. Until the Nazis dissolved all other political parties in 1933–34, the German Center Party, known locally as the Catholic People's Party (Katholische Volkspartei, or KVP), remained dominant. With a Catholic population of

88.5 percent (compared to 32 percent in the rest of Weimar Germany), Upper Silesia was not only the country's most heavily Catholic region, but also the one where clerics exerted the largest political influence. This situation prompted concern elsewhere in Germany that the borderland would become a "papal state" (*Kirchenstaat*). Promises of regional independence or limited autonomy made during the plebiscite campaign came to naught with the results of a referendum held on 3 September 1922, which went nearly three-to-one for remaining an integral part of the Prussian State.⁵² The political experience of this centuries-old German provincial district, whose legal status and political system remained relatively stable even after the transition from an authoritarian monarchy to a democratic republic, was vastly different from that of its Polish counterpart, whose government struggled to integrate the new territory into a country that was largely foreign to its new province's inhabitants. Nor did the Provinz face the threat of a powerful and wealthy minority that identified with the neighboring nation and even collaborated with it on border revision. While the Polish state funded a Polish minority in western Upper Silesia, organized in the Union of Poles in Germany (Związek Polaków w Niemczech, or ZPwN), its mainly agrarian membership was much smaller and poorer than that of the urban-based Volksbund.

At the time of partition, the western European delegates to the League of Nations anticipated that the partition would disrupt the local economy and cause Upper Silesians general hardship. As a result, the league made the two new provinces subject to fifteen years of regulations under a separate Geneva Convention, signed by Germany and Poland in 1922. A German-Polish Mixed Commission, led by Swiss politician Felix Calonder, monitored each side's compliance with these statutes and addressed grievances and alleged cases of violation throughout this period. Designed to limit control by Berlin and Warsaw—and by the German and Polish regional governments—over their respective part of Upper Silesia, the convention imposed regulations on various aspects of government policies, trade, and communications in an effort to cushion any detrimental effects on local society. In addition to barring both Germany and Poland from forcibly nationalizing the borderland, it safeguarded property rights established prior to partition, regardless of the owner's nationality or ethnicity, thus preventing either government from nationalizing local industry or carrying out land reform. It also guaranteed linguistic and cultural freedom to Upper Silesians, including the right of parents on either side of the border to send their children to a German- or Polish-language school. It also outlawed forced population transfers. The vast majority of formerly German citizens partitioned into the Voivodeship became Polish citizens, but they had the right to participate in German minority organizations. Those who chose to retain German citizenship were allowed to remain where they had lived prior to the partition for a period of fifteen years. These "optants" —as they were officially called—numbered around

28,500 in mid-July 1924; some 4,000 of them remained thirteen years later, when the Geneva Convention expired.[53] The convention also protected the locals' continued freedom of movement from one part of the region to the other by issuing all residents of the former plebiscite district (the area that had been bound by the plebiscite) a type of passport called a "circulation card." This permit helped to maintain cross-regional ties and to keep Upper Silesia a socially, culturally, and economically vibrant and interwoven society. Locals commuted across the border in both directions on a daily basis to work, shop, attend church, and visit friends and relatives, among other reasons.[54]

The freedom of movement guaranteed by the Geneva Convention allowed those unhappy with their postpartition lot to move, resulting in an exchange of populations between western and eastern Upper Silesia. By 1931, some 175,000 individuals had migrated from the Voivodeship, most of whom left the region altogether.[55] At the same time, around 160,000 individuals moved eastward.[56] In the mid-1930s, Grażyński's policy of removing Germans from the managerial ranks of government and industry in the Voivodeship led some 15,000 locals to move to Germany.[57] Rogers Brubaker refers to this and similar actions in the interwar German-Polish borderlands as a process of "unmixing," in which Germans and Poles left ethnically mixed areas for their own respective countries.[58]

In actuality, such migrations should be understood not as statements of ethnic identity, but rather as strategies to find a job, improve the person's material situation, or escape social and economic discrimination. Moreover, the number of migrants moving westward in what Richard Blanke calls the postpartition "great exodus" of ethnic Germans was far smaller in Upper Silesia than in other border regions.[59] For example, about 70 percent of the German minority left East Prussia and Poznania, compared to a quarter or so of comparable Upper Silesians.[60] While national indifference—the regional lack of preference for either Poland or Germany—help explain their relative willingness to stay put, a further reason was the Geneva Convention's guarantees of minority rights and protections. Its expiration in mid-July 1937 led to the gradual erosion of these assurances, which in turn fostered "unmixing," particularly on the eve of World War II.[61]

By 1925, the migration of around 117,000 refugees from Poland had exacerbated a housing shortage in the densely populated urban centers of the German part of the industrial district.[62] In the tricity area of Beuthen, Hindenburg, and Gleiwitz, entire municipal quarters and suburban settlements of makeshift barracks arose, where homeless families, particularly migrants from eastern Upper Silesia, lived for months and sometimes years. The overcrowding fostered typhus epidemics, which were more rampant here than elsewhere in Germany. German revanchists exploited such problems to support their calls for eastern Upper Silesia's "return to the Reich."[63]

The Voivodeship experienced the movement of residents from its rural Cieszyn district, and migration from other regions of Poland, especially Galicia and

Poznania, to its industrial district. These ethnically Polish "newcomers" (*ludność napływowa*), as contemporaries referred to them—and especially to those from without the region—were, to a significant extent, educated professionals. At the Polish government's urging, they moved to the Voivodeship to replace Germans as the region's elites.[64] By the 1930s, the newcomers—who numbered between 40,000 and 50,000—still made up only 5 percent of the population and from 2 to 3 percent of the province's professionally active population.[65]

The arrival of these newcomers soon generated cultural and socioeconomic conflict with the native Upper Silesian majority, who saw them as both a threat to their regional way of life and as competitors for jobs and influence. A myth of the "Polish colonization of Upper Silesia" developed, which fueled regional xenophobia against the newcomers, expressed on each side by derogatory stereotypes of the other. Native Upper Silesians, for example, called High Polish–speaking newcomers *pieroński gorol* (damned mountaineers) and "Polacks." The newcomers responded in kind with *Schwab* and *Germanin* against locals.[66] On the typical mental map of native Upper Silesians, the pre-1914, now obsolete, German-Russian border that separated historic Upper Silesia from the Dąbrowa Basin to the east continued to demarcate the "Silesians" from the *gorole* (Poles). Unlike its role before the war, Catholicism, a religion shared by locals and newcomers, now seemed to do little to overcome ethnic and cultural divisions. This new regional conflict of class and culture created a permanent rift between locals and newcomers, alienating many among the first group from Poland.

Ongoing economic problems in the Voivodeship exacerbated the conflict and further alienated eastern Upper Silesians from Poland. While the economy of the German province recovered from partition relatively quickly, its eastern counterpart suffered repeated downturns. The first major crisis hit in 1925, with the lapse of the Geneva Convention's three-year mandate that Germany import eastern Upper Silesia's coal. In protest against the loss of eastern Upper Silesia and other borderlands to Poland, the German government stopped coal imports and raised tariffs on Polish goods in general, sparking a tariff war between the two countries. This aggressive economic policy only exacerbated the detrimental effects of the largely agrarian Poland's inability to absorb the region's industrial products within the Geneva Convention's inadequately short transition period for adjustment. Coal mines were forced to shut down, giving way to more than a 25 percent increase of the unemployment rate in the Voivodeship.[67] The severity of this crisis was ameliorated by the 1926 general strike in Great Britain, which shut down its mines and prompted the British to import Polish coal.[68] No providential customer appeared in 1933, however, when—at the height of the world economic crisis—industrial output reached its lowest point, unemployment its highest, and mines and factories were shut down en masse.[69] Desperate to survive, locals turned to excavating coal on their own in dangerous domestic mines called *biedaszyby* and sold it on the black market. While the productivity of the coal mining, minerals, and metallurgy industries grew steadily after 1934, they never reached prewar levels.[70]

While the economic difficulties on the German side of the border were at times just as severe as on the eastern side, they had less of a political impact. Hit hard by the German hyperinflation of 1923 and the Great Depression a decade later, western Upper Silesia's economy struggled throughout the interwar era, but performed better than that of its neighbor. Spared the burden of having to integrate into a new, and industrially underdeveloped, nation, the German province was able to recover from the partition and even to surpass its 1913 productivity levels, which the Polish side was never able to do. German state funds played an important role in keeping the provincial economy afloat. During the 1920s, western Upper Silesia received low-interest loans amounting to 46 million reichsmarks from the Prussian State Bank (Preußische Seehandlung).[71] During the Great Depression, it received German Eastern Aid (Osthilfe) of about 330 million reichsmarks, which were invested in public works projects.[72] From the other side of the border, the German province's superior economic situation could be seen as a sign that Germany was taking better care of its borderland than was Poland, whose own government aid efforts seemed ineffective. Indeed, all problems related to industry ultimately played into German hands, thus pressuring the Polish government to intervene in order to prevent not just further downturn, but even the "loss" of the border province.

Eastern Upper Silesia's economic woes shaped its political landscape. During the plebiscite campaign, Poland's proponents had promised Upper Silesians prosperity for their vote, thus setting the stage for the widespread feelings of betrayal that arose during the years of economic downturn. Feeling economically and socially neglected by Warsaw as well as exploited and discriminated against by the recently arrived Polish elites, locals in the Voivodeship turned to voting for German, regionalist, and Polish opposition parties. Three political factions gained new prominence in this environment. The first was the German Block, which represented a coalition of political parties and the Volksbund. The second was the Upper Silesian Defense League (Związek Obrony Górnego Śląska, or ZOG), the only party devoted specifically to the cause of locals against newcomers; it was led by Jan Kustos, a former Endecja follower, who by the mid-1920s had become the main proponent of extenuating Upper Silesian autonomy within the Polish state. The third party was the Voivodeship chapter of the all-Polish Christian Democratic Party (Chadeci, or ChD), led by Wojciech Korfanty, the former champion of the Polish nationalist cause in the region. Each of these factions responded to the discontent of locals and addressed their widespread demands, particularly an eastern Upper Silesia run by and for Upper Silesians and not subject to forceful "Polonization" (forceful integration into Poland and standardization along Polish national lines). However, the disparate interests and polarized ethnic identities represented by these three factions prevented their acting in common.

Each of the three opposition groups endorsed regionalist tenets. The most explicitly regionalist of them, the ZOG, denounced the newcomers, demanded equal stature for the German language, and called for official recognition of a "nationally indifferent" Upper Silesian identity—one that was strongly based on Catholic religiosity, but was neither Polish nor German.[73] Yet most discontented voters preferred to back the other two factions, which were more powerful and mainstream. Backed by the German government and by German-managed industry in the Voivodeship, the German Block politically profited from the economic crises afflicting this area, as well as from conflict between newcomers and locals and the latter's alienation from Poland. In the November 1926 communal government elections in Polish Upper Silesia, the German Block triumphed over mainstream Polish parties, with its candidates winning a plurality of the votes (42 percent) and a majority of the posts (thirty-four of sixty).[74] Despite being subject to persecution and disenfranchisement after the appointment of the radically nationalist governor (*voivode*) Michał Grażyński in September, the German minority's electoral success remained significant into the Great Depression years. It captured over 31 percent of the votes and took second place to the ChD in the 1928 elections to the Polish Sejm (national parliament), and emerged triumphant in elections to the Silesian Sejm (regional parliament) in May 1930.[75] Wojciech Korfanty's ChD became the most potent Polish opposition party after Grażyński, also the head of the Silesian branch of the all-Polish Sanacja (Sanation) movement, became governor. The ChD commonly came in second during elections, often failing to triumph over the Sanacja only by dint of terror, persecution, and chicanery on the part of Grażyński's followers. The Sanacja government's deserved reputation for favoring the newcomers, persecuting Germans and their language, and opposing eastern Upper Silesian interests in favor of hasty nationalization and partial secularization led to growing alienation among locals. Korfanty's official adoption of a plank devoted to Upper Silesian traditions, interests, and regional religiosity won the ChD the support of locals as well as the Diocese of Katowice (Polish Silesian).[76]

Economic crises on both sides of the border empowered another important transnational force, the German and Polish Communist parties: the KPD (Kommunistische Partei Deutschlands) and KPP (Komunistyczna Partja Polski), respectively. Like the ZOG, but from a proletarian class perspective, each rejected partition and played up the notion of a common Upper Silesian regional community. Each party was influential on its own side of the industrial district. However, only the KPD was a legal and legitimate political party that contested electorally with other parties. It enjoyed greater electoral support in western Upper Silesia than its average in Germany overall. During electoral contests to the German Reichstag in 1924 and 1930, which were held in the midst of economic crisis in

Germany, the KPD placed second in the Provinz, but remained far behind the German Center Party, which maintained its number-one spot as long as democracy lasted in Germany.[77] By contrast, the KPP was an illegal and underground organization in the Voivodeship, persecuted by the state and largely limited to assertions that it represented the moral force of workers, particularly during times of economic crisis.[78] The KPD and KPP cooperated with one another until the late 1930s, occasionally staging common cross-border rallies on 1 May, thereby accentuating the region's proletarian and nationally indifferent identity.[79] Their common call for social revolution and their rejection of German and Polish claims to the borderland posed a threat to moderate and radical parties on both sides of the border.

Upper Silesia's partition created a crisis of adjustment to its far-ranging impacts, including economic problems and population movement. This was far more serious on the Polish side, where the government struggled to integrate both an industrial region into a largely agrarian economy and a former Prussian border society into a new nation, even as every shortcoming potentially gave validity to Germany's demand for border revision. Indeed, these tensions, which shaped governments, irredentist actors, and nationalization policies from the late 1920s to the end of the 1930s, are critical to understanding the cultural struggle examined in subsequent chapters.

Irredentism and Its Political Effects

German revanchist propaganda was the main beneficiary of the forces questioning government authority in Warsaw and in the Voivodeship. While economic conditions largely underlay local political support for the German Block, officials in Germany easily interpreted it as a preference for German nationality.[80] German officials and political activists ranging from Social Democrats to liberals and centrists, and on to moderate and radical nationalists, supported the demand for eastern Upper Silesia's "return" to the Reich.[81] The government in Berlin openly called for revision of the eastern border. Thus, after German Foreign Minister Gustav Stresemann signed the Locarno Agreements in 1925, recognizing the permanence of the border with France, his refusal to endorse a comparable agreement for the eastern border made it presumably "provisional." Anyone in Poland who might doubt Germany's expansive intentions should have been set straight by openly revisionist public statements from such high-ranking officials as President Paul von Hindenburg, Reich Minister Gottfried Treviranus, and Stresemann.[82]

In the Provinz, the long dominant German Center Party remained officially committed to its prewar agenda of safeguarding local Upper Silesian culture, above all Catholicism, but also bilingualism and regional sentiment. After the partition it defended the rights and freedoms that the Geneva Convention had guaranteed to Polish minority organizations. Such liberal tolerance earned the Center Party the wrath of local nationalists, including sympathizers of the German National People's Party (DNVP), and of the Nazis, who smeared it as the "Poland party" (*Polenpartei*).[83] However, even the Center Party was an open and unrelenting exponent of border revision, although unlike extreme nationalists, it opposed the use of violence or force to achieve this end.[84] The party also collaborated with revanchist borderland organizations and coordinated commemorations of Plebiscite Day, the main forums for border revisionism. In cooperation with the German national government, the Center Party likewise supported the cause of the German minority in the Voivodeship. In these efforts, the party provided influence and legitimacy for the irredentist and anti-Polish mission of their right-wing enemies.[85]

The irredentism that fueled nationalist and right-wing fervor in Germany had a similar effect in Poland. Open calls for border revision and refusals to sign an "Eastern Locarno" raised public fears of a "German threat" to Poland, thus giving credibility to the Germanophobia that was a core principle of the nationalism of Roman Dmowski and the Endecja. This fear gained even more credibility in a Poland threatened not just by German revanchism, but also by other neighbors with expansionist ambitions. As a nation-state with numerous minorities, Poland was particularly vulnerable to what Rogers Brubaker has called "external homeland nationalism."[86] The Voivodeship's large, well-organized, influential, and wealthy German minority enjoyed financial support from German state organizations, the most important of which were the German Foundation (Deutsche Stiftung) and the Association for Germandom Abroad (Verein für das Deutschtum im Ausland, or VDA). The Volksbund leader and main figurehead of the German minority, Otto Ulitz, had right-wing German national (*Deutschnational*) leanings. Although he officially pledged his loyalty to the Polish state, he mobilized Volksbund activists to work for the irredentist cause. This was the political environment, further inflamed by economic distress, in which the German Block made its electoral successes in November 1926.[87]

Polish democracy collapsed in May of that year as Marshal Józef Piłsudski staged a coup d'état in Warsaw and placed his nationalist and authoritarian Sanacja regime in power, extending into eastern Upper Silesia, where he appointed a follower, Michał Grażyński, as governor, an office he retained until the Nazi invasion. A newcomer from Galicia who had led a battalion during the third Silesian uprising, the new governor established a militant, nationalist, and authoritarian borderland regime that earned him the appellation "the little Piłsudski."[88]

Grażyński used the existence of a "German threat" to the Voivodeship as a pretext to attack political rivals and "ethnic" enemies. Above all, he blamed the German electoral victory in 1926 on his archenemy, Wojciech Korfanty, whom he accused of being "soft" on "Polonizing" the Silesian province, as well as being in the pay of German industrialists. The coup that brought Piłsudski and Grażyński to power marked a major turning point in Upper Silesian history. Although Korfanty had initiated the politics of "Polonizing" the Voivodeship, he generally respected democratic principles, civil rights, as well as domestic and international law. Grażyński, on the other hand, endorsed the authoritarian tactics that characterized Sanacja rule: the instrumentalization of the law for political purposes, arbitrary disenfranchisement, electoral falsification, abrupt dissolutions of parliament, favoritism in local government appointments, and the use of violence and terror to maintain power and influence. He also deployed a number of tactics typical of fascist regimes: the promotion of vicious propaganda against "foreign" groups (in this case, Germans and Jews), a personality cult of the *voivode*, the breach and instrumental use of laws, and the use of illegal and arbitrary terror and violence against internal political and ethnic enemies—real and imagined. Similarly, Grażyński had his own enforcers in the form of paramilitary shock troops, the Insurgent League (Związek Powstańców Śląskich, or ZPŚl), composed of veterans from the Polish Silesian uprisings. Its membership ranks increased from 20,000 in late 1921 to between 30,000 and 40,000 during the 1930s.[89] In a country born of six borderland conflicts, with revanchist neighbors on all sides, the Insurgent League was just one of several such militias, which were organized in a state-supported national network, the Federation of Polish Unions for the Defense of the Fatherland (FPZOO). As a former battalion commander, Grażyński used his positions as member and head of the Insurgent League to accentuate his image both as *voivode* and insurgent, a governor and a combatant in one, which formed the basis of his regional personality cult. Like any fascistoid leader, Grażyński saw politics as a continuation of war—in this case the borderland war (third Silesian insurgency) of 1921—in civilian society. In his mind, this conflict would only end through the full integration of eastern Upper Silesia, and eventually *both* parts of the region, into the Polish state, a task he aimed to accomplish through force and terror, as well as through nationalization ("Polonization") and open irredentism against Germany.[90]

Grażyński's politics incorporated Roman Dmowski's Western Borderland Thought (Myśl Zachodnia), the Endecja geopolitical program, which advocated a permanent struggle for the frontier lands against Germany and the engineering there of a homogenous Polish society. As a political movement in eastern Upper Silesia, Endecja was weak, overshadowed by both the ChD and the Sanacja. Yet as a nationalist group working with Grażyński's government to "Polonize" the "endangered" western territories, its influence was vast. Scholars, teachers, and other activists and professionals committed to "defending" Upper Silesia from "German revisionism" collaborated with Grażyński as part of the Western Territories Defense League (Związek Obrony Kresów Zachodnich, or ZOKZ), an organization founded in 1921 during the plebiscite campaign. After the partition, it became an all-Polish "suprapartisan" group of border nationalists committed to "Polonizing" the western borderlands and to agitating for their continued expansion at Germany's cost.[91]

The ZOKZ attracted borderland nationalists throughout Poland who had fought in the conflicts in Upper Silesia, Poznania (Posen/Poznań region), and Masuria. The Silesian section—led by Teodor Tyc, an activist widely known from the plebiscite campaign—was its largest contingent, accounting for more than half its members in 1924: 16,000 out of a total 24,377. Yet with a Voivodeship membership in 1937 of only slightly over 20,000, the ZOKZ could not claim to be a mass organization. Only a quarter of its members in that year came from the region's working-class majority; its remaining members came largely from the educated elites who had migrated to the eastern province.[92] However, it worked with the largely worker-based Insurgent League, the other major borderland nationalist activist group in the province. The Silesian ZOKZ illustrates how the postpartition cold war between Poland and Germany perpetuated the conflicts of 1919–21, waged largely by the same agents but using different means.

On the German side of the border, veterans from the earlier struggles for Upper Silesia became the main borderland nationalist activists of the conflict that followed. German Center Party notables and leading fighters for the German cause during the German plebiscite struggle, such as party leader Carl Ulitzka and Alfons Proske, governor (*Oberpräsident*) of the Provinz from 1923 to 1929, had played a leading role in the German Homeland Patriots (Vereinigte Verbände heimattreuer Oberschlesier, or VVHO), the main propaganda and activist group for the German plebiscite cause.[93] After the partition, this borderland nationalist organization continued its role as the main agitator for the "return" of all of Upper Silesia to Germany. Attracting leftists, liberals, right-wingers, and paramilitaries, the German Homeland Patriots received official endorsement from the German Center Party, some of whose most prominent politicians helped to coordinate its work, in part as a strategy to prevent the party's takeover by nationalists. Like its Polish counterpart, the ZOKZ, the German Homeland Patriots was a nationwide, officially politically neutral organization that functioned as an interest group for the nationalization and territorial revision of the Upper Silesian borderland.[94] They differed, of course, in their views of how the borderlines should be redrawn. The two groups of borderland nationalists also belonged to larger irredentist traditions and networks. While the ZOKZ adhered to the larger Endecja-led Western Borderland Thought circle, the German Homeland Patriots joined Germany's *Ostforschung* devotees, committed to reclaiming the lost "German east." According to Polish consular reports, by the spring of 1923, the German Homeland Patriots had seven regional chapters (with 1,000 local sections) and represented around 100,000 individuals. The same source reported 60,000 members in Gleiwitz alone, a right-wing stronghold by 1932.[95]

Groups consisting largely of veterans of the 1921 skirmishes existed on both sides of the border. While illegal in Weimar Germany, they received official government sanction and support in Poland. Long before the collapse of democracy in the Provinz, the Voivodeship was governed by a militant and authoritarian regime committed to borderland nationalism. Under Grażyński, violent thugs within the Insurgent League had free reign against the Sanacja's political enemies, in particular those they considered to be local Germans. In order to thwart any repeat of the German Block's November 1926 electoral victory, Grażyński resorted to outright chicanery to disenfranchise the coalition's potential voters and even to prevent its candidates from running. Nonetheless, the local consequences of the international economic crisis produced another German Block victory in elections to the provincial Sejm in May 1930. Attaining around 35 percent of the vote, the German Block won a plurality because the various Polish parties were divided against one another.[96] In reaction, the *voivode* mobilized his shock troops for what was officially called a "week of insurgent offensive." Paramilitary terror and violence, reinforced by Grażyński's customary subterfuge, caused the German Block's support to drop to 21 percent of the provincial vote in the November elections to the national Sejm, from which the Sanacja emerged triumphant.[97] Because of Grażyński's use of paramilitary thugs during the campaign, a blatant violation of the Geneva Convention, the German Block's supporters filed a formal complaint before the League of Nations and the German-Polish Mixed Commission overseeing the Upper Silesian borderland. These complaints joined a long list of grievances filed by the German government against Poland, which multiplied exponentially after Grażyński assumed power.[98]

With the German Block rendered relatively powerless through repression and an improving economy after 1934, Grażyński turned his attention to the province's powerful German industrialists. The Great Depression, by legitimating statist expansion throughout Europe, provided a political rationale for "Polonizing" the ranks of industry in the province—in other words, removing the owners and managers of industry from their positions of authority. Using such tactics as forcing firms to disclose their financial records, which he then used to file charges of financial fraud and tax evasion, Grażyński bullied German industrialists into conceding authority to his followers. He also bought out the stocks of companies in financial straits, then used his influence to remove Germans—real or imagined—from positions as managers and directors, often on trumped-up charges of financial abuse, fraud, malicious intent, or engagement in anti-Polish activities. With the help of the ZOKZ, Grażyński had by 1932 assembled dossiers on dozens of firms, including personal profiles of tens of thousands of their employees. These tactics proved effective. Whereas in 1932, 43 percent of the directors and 58 percent of the managers of these firms were German, only three years later, Poles filled close to 73 percent of these posts.[99] This process, which was precipitated by the expiration of the Geneva Convention, meant that on the eve of war no "German industry" remained in the Voivodeship.[100] "Polonizing" the regional bureaucracy, over which Grażyński had full control from the beginning, proceeded more quickly. As a consequence of these "soft" approaches to ethnic cleansing—that is, the removal of unwanted ethnicities by largely nonviolent means—more than 15,000 former employees and leaders of industry and administration left eastern Upper Silesia and moved to Germany.[101]

Grażyński's internal war against the "German threat" affected not only culturally or politically active Germans, but also groups he viewed as aiding the German irredentist cause, including nationally indifferent Upper Silesians. Most Poles, regardless of their political orientation, saw this population as either German or Polish—not "nationally indifferent" or distinctly Silesian. In 1930, Korfanty, who after Piłsudski's coup had become a leading defender of regional cultural autonomy, referred to the nationally indifferent part of the population as "Polish Alsatians," thus comparing Silesians to Alsatians' split identity among their region, France, and Germany.[102] Grażyński, however, viewed Korfanty and his ilk as instruments of German policy, who stirred up nationally indifferent Silesianism in order to subvert the process of integration with Poland. While the Volksbund formally distanced itself from both Korfanty and the Upper Silesian Defense League (ZOG), it openly supported the political recognition of regional cultural distinction. This was enough for Grażyński to accuse the ZOG of being part of the "German threat" to Polish Upper Silesia.[103] The group withered into political insignificance after the death of Kustos, its charismatic leader, in 1932. Because Korfanty was Grażyński's main threat to political supremacy, in 1927 the Silesian Sanacja brought him up on charges of serving as an instrument of German capital. Imprisoned in 1930 and persecuted after his release, Korfanty fled into exile in Czechoslovakia in 1935. Nonetheless, his party, Chadeci (ChD), remained the most popular faction in the Voivodeship until the Nazi takeover in 1933 undermined the appeal of its opposition to Grażyński's Germanophobia.[104]

"Polonization" also affected the Catholic Church, which had provided the primary support behind the ChD's popularity. In 1928, the church in eastern Upper Silesia, which had been part of the German Diocese of Breslau, was incorporated into the Polish Diocese of Katowice under Bishop Arkadiusz Lisiecki. While he and his successor, Bishop Stanisław Adamski, gave Grażyński moral and symbolic support, they opposed his forced nationalization policy, instead preferring Korfanty's policy of gradual, tolerant, and peaceful integration with Poland. After the Piłsudski coup, clerics and ChD politicians united to preserve Upper Silesia's bilingual culture. Bishop Adamski defied Grażyński's pressure to end or severely limit German-language Masses, which would have encouraged many parishioners to cross to the German side of the border to worship. His and other clergy's refusal to divide their flocks between "Pole" and "German" echoed the Upper Silesian clergy's earlier opposition to Bismarck's Kulturkampf. In Grażyński's eyes, the church's defiance made it, along with the ChD, a defender of Germanic culture and regionalism, thus undermining the Sanacja's internal war against the "German threat." In addition to harassing lower-ranking clerics, Grażyński sought to weaken the church's influence over primary education. The church-state battle continued until early 1939, when the threat of German aggression against Poland led Bishop Adamski to end German-language Masses.[105]

Grażyński also viewed Jews as agents of the "German threat," a myth derived from the pro-German orientation of the region's Jews, which led some 7,700 of the 10,500 Jewish residents of eastern Upper Silesia to move westward after the partition.[106] Many of those who stayed identified with the German minority and the German Block, thus providing the Sanacja a rationale for political anti-Semitism. By 1931, the Jewish population in the Voivodeship nonetheless reached approximately 18,938 (or 1.5 percent of the area's total population), representing not natural growth but rather an influx of Jews from further east who neither felt German nor supported the German minority.[107] Nonetheless, the Grażyński regime continued to depict Jews as German sympathizers until 1936, when he adopted the Polish nationalist policy of encouraging their immigration to Palestine.[108]

In western Upper Silesia, by contrast, Jews, self-identified Poles, and the nationally indifferent enjoyed a significant degree of government-enforced tolerance until the rise of the Nazis. Occasional sporadic attacks on minority groups were carried out by radical paramilitary groups and Nazi bands independent of the government. The German Center Party remained committed to preserving the bilingual regional culture of Upper Silesia and to safeguarding the cultural rights guaranteed to all residents by the Geneva Convention.[109]

While the German Center Party's electoral success gradually declined after late 1929, the faction still managed to win majorities so long as free and unhampered elections continued during the Weimar era. The party's main rivals, the Communists and the German National People's Party, each won only about half the Center Party's total in the Reichstag elections of September 1930. The Nazi Party was a largely insignificant presence in local elections until 1932, when it began to offer more competition to the Center Party than any previous party had. Even so, the Nazis received less support in the Provinz than their average in the rest of Germany. In the July 1932 Reichstag elections, for example, the Nazis received just over 29 percent of the provincial vote, as against their more than 37 percent national average.[110] Their radically nationalist, anti-Catholic, neo-pagan, and Pan-German policies, as well as competition from the Communist Party, contributed to the National Socialists' relatively weak support in western Upper Silesia.

This all changed after 1933, when the new Nazi regime purged all levels of government of Center Party followers. The Nazis also employed force, terror, and deception in an effort to weaken the region's deeply rooted Catholic religiosity.

Ordinary priests and worshippers became targets of Nazi harassment, while Masses, processions, and public religious symbols were subjected to intrusive official regulations.[111] In 1934, the Nazis established the League of the German East (Bund der deutschen Osten, or BDO), comprising a national network of scholars, activists, institutes, and societies devoted to the eastern borderlands, including those from Upper Silesia. The BDO served as the Nazi regime's main agent of borderland nationalism, playing a leading role in waging the ongoing cold war over these territories. As a state-sponsored advocate for the "Germanization" and secularization of the borderlands and their expansion to the detriment of Poland, the BDO became a German counterpart to the Polish ZOKZ (renamed the Polish Western League/Polski Związek Zachodni, or PZZ, in 1934), with its mission to defend the western territories.[112]

The BDO took the lead in implementing the regime's policies of *Eindeutschung* ("Germanization"). Working closely with regional Nazi organizations and the Gestapo, it imposed Nazified "German culture," while forcibly removing all cultural traces of "Polishness," "Jewishness," or other "foreign" identities—often loosely and arbitrarily defined. In its efforts to punish anyone "behaving Polish," the BDO used a range of tactics, from social pressure to terror, harassment, intimidation, and finally the threat of incarceration in a concentration camp. The BDO also pressured locals to speak only "pure" German, since the Nazis viewed the Silesian dialect as equivalent to Polish. It focused most of its efforts on pressuring and compelling locals to not attend Polish-language religious services, but it also discouraged participation in Polish minority organizations, activities, and events. By blacklisting locals who refused to conform to these pressures, the BDO subjected them to social discrimination and economic hardship. Until the Nazi's rise to power, the Union of Poles in Germany (ZPwN) escaped the magnitude of the discrimination to which its German minority counterpart in the Voivodeship was subject under Grażyński. This changed in the Third Reich, and particularly after the expiration of the Geneva Convention in July 1937, when the Polish minority became subject to increasing violence, terror, and harassment. Nevertheless, in order not to give the Poles a pretext to liquidate the Volksbund, the ZPwN's counterpart on their side of the border, the Nazis did not dissolve it until after the attack on Poland.[113]

Local repression against the Polish minority went hand in hand with the Third Reich's use of ethnic cleansing to forge national homogeneity. While in force, the Geneva Convention protected Jewish residents of the German *Provinz* against Nazi terror, including the discriminatory Nuremberg Laws of 1935.[114] After its lapse in 1937, they became the prime target of legalized violence and social marginalization. On the night of 28–29 October 1938—in a prelude to the Reich Pogrom Night (*Kristallnacht*) of 8–9 November—officials forcibly compelled about 6,000 "Polish Jews" to move to the Polish side of the border.[115] Just over a week later, the tricity area experienced the all-German pogrom, which included burning down the synagogue in Beuthen, as well as destruction of Jewish stores and other businesses. The Gestapo and bands of the SS and SA (*Sturmabteilung*) conducted house searches and arrested hundreds of Jews. They included some 600 who were used as slave labor to build the autobahn over the Mount of St. Anne.[116]

As part of the national histories of Germany and Poland, Upper Silesia exemplifies a Prussian eastern province that since the late nineteenth century experienced intensive modernization, in particular nationalization and industrialization. Beyond the economic importance of its industrial district, the region has particular importance as a site where the two national movements developed a mutually intertwined culture of "nationalities struggle" (*Volkstumskampf*). Along with the plebiscite and the violent conflict of 1921, this shared culture laid the foundation for the continuing interwar German-Polish national contest over this region, which to a large extent influenced the tone of relations between the two nations.

Imperial German nationalization policies politicized regional identity in Upper Silesia, initially through the German Center Party's reaction to attacks on its loyalty. A Polish national movement arose later, on the eve of World War I. At the same time, calls arose for regional autonomy and separatism, which after the partition found their most potent voice in the German Center Party, the Polish ChD, and German or Polish minority groups with nationalist and even irredentist tendencies. Nevertheless, this "Silesianism," often viewed as a manifestation of national indifference, remained a significant force, manifesting itself most openly in conflicts between locals and Polish newcomers in the Voivodeship. Nationalist actors struggled to come to terms with the strength of this regionalist sentiment, applying forceful means to do so under Grażyński in the Voivodeship and the Nazis in the Provinz. Indeed, these internal struggles against the "other"—be it Silesians, Jews, or German or Polish minorities—formed the backdrop of the cultural politics that will be analyzed in the next two chapters. The promotion of indigenous national regionalisms to win over locals, a practice endorsed before World War I and during the plebiscite struggle, likewise remained an important aspect of the cultural war that originated in the conflict of 1921.

A regional perspective complicates the widely dominant portrayal of German and Polish history during the interwar era. In Upper Silesia, the Weimar Republic—often regarded as a "failure"—outlasted the collapse of democracy in Poland as well as in other nation-states in East-Central Europe; indeed, it fostered multicultural tolerance in the western part of the province. In contrast, in eastern Upper Silesia an authoritarian, militant, and quasi-Fascist regime under Grażyński promoted persecution and various "soft" forms of ethnic cleansing already seven years before the imposition of Nazi rule across the border. Nor was Germany, which nursed resentment over the "Versailles Dictate," the only irredentist actor in the region. Polish government officials called openly for the "return" of western Upper Silesia to Poland. This interaction and mutual influence of irredentist actors on both sides of the border created the irredentist culture that is the subject of the next chapter.

Notes

1. On the language of the Upper Silesians, see Tomasz Kamusella, "The Szlonzoks and Their Language: Between Germany, Poland and Szlonzokian Nationalism," *EUI Working Papers* 1 (2003): 16–17; Tomasz Kamusella, *Schlonzska mowa: Język, Górny Śląsk i nacjonalizmy* (Zabrze, 2005), 12–34; Bogusław Wyderka, "Język, dialekt czy kreol?," in *Nadciągają Ślązacy: Czy istnieje narodowość śląska?*, ed. Lech M. Nijakowski (Warsaw, 2004), 187–216; Kneip, *Die deutsche Sprache in Oberschlesien*, 32–39; Manfred Alexander, "Oberschlesien im 20. Jahrhundert: Eine mißverstandene Region," *Geschichte und Gesellschaft* 30 (2004): 467–68.

2. See Tomasz Kamusella, "Upper Silesia 1870–1920: Between Region, Religion, Nation and Ethnicity," *East European Quarterly* 37 (January 2005): 446.

3. See Bjork, *Neither German nor Pole*, 25, chap. 1; Kamusella, *Silesia and Central European Nationalisms*, 125, chap. 5.

4. See, in particular, Bjork, *Neither German nor Pole*; Kamusella, *Silesia and Central European Nationalisms*, 179; Michałczyk, *Heimat, Kirche und Nation*.

5. Although not a formal place name, both Germans and Poles used—and continue to use— the term "Upper Silesian industrial district" (*Oberschlesische Industriegebiet/Górnośląski Ośrodek Przemysłowy*) to refer to the cluster of industrial cities, the largest and most notable of which include Kattowitz (Katowice), Königshütte (Chorzów), and the tricity area, Gleiwitz (Gliwice), Beuthen (Bytom), and Hindenburg (Zabrze). "Industrial district" is current usage, the Polish official acronym being GOP.

6. See Franciszek Serafin, ed., *Województwo Śląskie: Zarys Monograficzny* (Katowice, 1996), 90, 92.

7. See Waldemar Grosch, *Deutsche und polnische Propaganda während der Volksabstimmung in Oberschlesien, 1919–1921* (Dortmund, 2002), 19; Eugeniusz Kopec, "Zagadnienie społeczne jendości kresów śląskich z organizmem państwowym II Rzeczypospolitej," in *Ziemie Śląskie w granicach II Rzeczypospolitej: Procesy integracyjne*, ed. Franciszek Serafin (Katowice 1985), 121–22; Eugeniusz Kopec, *"My i Oni" na polskim Śląsku, 1918–1939* (Katowice, 1986), 10–45; Philipp Ther, "Schlesisch, deutsch oder polnisch? Identitätswandel in Oberschlesien, 1921–1956," in *Die Grenzen der Nationen: Identitätwandel in Oberschlesien in der Neuzeit*, ed. Kai Struve and Philipp Ther (Marburg, 2002), 174.

8. Wilson, *Frontiers of Violence*, 61.

9. This translation from Philipp Ther, "German History as Imperial History," in *Imperial Rule*, ed. Alexei Miller and Alfred J. Reiber (Budapest, 2004), 56; see also Bjork, *Neither German nor Pole*, 4.

10. Alexander, "Oberschlesien im 20. Jahrhundert," 478–79.

11. Wilson, *Frontiers*, 200.

12. Michałczyk, *Heimat, Kirche, und Nation*, 269.

13. Alexander, "Oberschlesien im 20. Jahrhundert," 478–79.

14. Michałczyk, *Heimat, Kirche, und Nation*, 3.

15. See Richard Blanke, *Prussian Poland in the German Empire (1871–1900)* (New York, 1981), esp. 17–54. See also Elizabeth A. Drummond, "On the Borders of the Nation: Jews and the German-Polish National Conflict in Poznania, 1886–1914," *Nationality Papers* 29, no. 3 (2001): 459–75; Mark

Tilse, *Transnationalism in the Prussian East: From National Conflict to Synthesis, 1871–1914* (New York, 2011).

16. Kamusella, *Silesia and Central European Nationalisms*, 157–58. See also Scott M. Eddie, "The Prussian Settlement Commission and Its Activities in the Land Market, 1886–1918," in *Germans, Poland, and Colonial Expansion to the East, 1850 through the Present*, ed. Robert L. Nelson (New York, 2009), 39–58.

17. See Kamusella, *Silesia and Central European Nationalisms*, 154–61; Blanke, *Prussian Poland*, 55–92.

18. Blanke, *Prussian Poland*, 200.

19. Ibid., 200.

20. Drummond, "On the Borders of the Nation," 460.

21. Until 1899, the organization's official name was the Society for the Advancement of Germandom in the Eastern Marches (Verein zur Förderung des Deutschtums in den Ostmarken). See Kamusella, *Silesia and Central European Nationalisms*, 148–63; Blanke, *Prussian Poland*, 181.

22. Liulevicius, *The German Myth*, 98–103, 114.

23. Ibid., 98–103.

24. On the Endecja, see Porter, *When Nationalism Began to Hate*; Blanke, *Prussian Poland*, 216–31.

25. Kamusella, *Silesia and Central European Nationalisms*, 155–56, 168–69; Blanke, *Prussian Poland*, 182–238.

26. Kamusella, *Silesia and Central European Nationalisms*, 63–84, 114–99.

27. Ibid., 191.

28. Ibid., 124–26.

29. See Eugen Weber, *Peasants into Frenchmen: The Modernization of Rural France, 1870–1914* (Stanford, CA, 1976).

30. Kamusella, *Silesia and Central European Nationalisms*, 161.

31. Blanke, *Orphans of Versailles*, 15–17.

32. Snyder, *The Reconstruction of Nations*, 137–40; Prusin, *The Lands Between*, 72–84.

33. Tooley, *National Identity and Weimar Germany*, 52.

34. Blanke, *Orphans of Versailles*, 26–28; Tooley, *National Identity and Weimar Germany*.

35. See Bjork, *Neither German nor Pole*, 214–53.

36. See Grosch, *Deutsche und polnische Propaganda*.

37. Bjork, *Neither German nor Pole*, 214ff.; Kamusella, *Silesia and Central European Nationalisms*, 238ff.; Ther, "Schlesisch, deutsch oder polnisch?," 176.

38. Whereas Grosch and Bjork point out the difficulty of precisely determining the number of BdO supporters, Kamusella claims that it was between 150,000 and 300,000. See Bjork, *Neither German nor Pole*, 197–203, 252 (and note 132); Grosch, *Deutsche und polnische Propaganda*, 54–63; Ther, "Schlesisch, deutsch oder polnisch?," 176; Kamusella, *Silesia and Central European Nationalisms*, 256–60, 268–69; Przemysław Hauser, "Von der Provinz zum Freistaat? Der oberschlesische Separatismus im Jahr 1918/1919," in *Regionale Bewegungen und Regionalismen in europäischen Zwischenräumen seit der Mitte des 19. Jahrhunderts*, ed. Philipp Ther and Holm Sundhaussen (Marburg, 2003), 113–26.

39. See Guido Hitze, *Carl Ulitzka (1873–1953) oder Oberschlesien zwischen den Weltkriegen* (Düsseldorf, 2002), 491–559; Grosch, *Deutsche und polnische Propaganda*, 61–63.

40. Kai Struve, "Geschichte und Gedächtnis in Oberschlesien: Die polnischen Aufstände nach dem Ersten Weltkrieg," in *Oberschlesien nach dem Ersten Weltkrieg: Studien zu einem nationalen Konflikt und seiner Erinnerung*, ed. Kai Struve (Marburg, 2003), 14ff.; Bjork, *Neither German nor Pole*, 244–46; Blanke, *Orphans of Versailles*, 29–31.

41. Bjork, *Neither German nor Pole*, 256.

42. Wilson, *Frontiers of Violence*, 200.

43. Ibid., 5, 140–55, 200.

44. On the subject of mythology, see Juliane Haubold, "Mythos Oberschlesien in der Weimarer Republik: Die Mythisierung der oberschlesischen Freikorpskämpfe und der 'Abstimmungszeit' (1919–21) in Deutschland der Zwischenkriegszeit," in *Politische Mythen im 19. und 20. Jahrhundert in Mittel- und Osteuropa*, ed. Heidi Hein-Kirchner and Hans Henning Hahn (Marburg, 2006), 279–99; Haubold-Stolle, *Mythos Oberschlesien*; Grosch, *Deutsche und polnische Propaganda*; Waldemar Grosch, "Deutsche und polnische Propaganda in der Zeit der Aufstände und des Plebiszits," in *Oberschlesien nach dem Ersten Weltkrieg: Studien zu einem nationalen Konflikt und seiner Errinerung*, ed. Kai Struve (Marburg, 2003), 69–88.

45. The 43 percent refers to areas of the region that were subject to the plebiscite (*Abstimmungsgebiet/obszar plebiscytowy*). See Pia Nordblom, "Die Lage der Deutschen in Polnisch-Oberschlesien nach 1922," in *Oberschlesien nach dem Ersten Weltkrieg: Studien zu einem nationalen Konflikt und seiner Errinerung*, ed. Kai Struve (Marburg, 2003), 112.

46. Since this was the only part of the larger Silesian region controlled by the Poles, they did not specify that it was really *eastern* Upper Silesia.

47. Matthais Lempart, "Michał Grażyński: Der schlesische Woiwode, 1926–1939," in *Dzieje Śląska w XX. Wieku w świetle badań młodych historyków z Polski, Czechosłowacji i Niemiec*, ed. Krzysztof Ruchniewicz (Wrocław, 1998), 114.

48. This is according to the Polish census of 1931. Anna Obersztyn and Jerzy Jaros, "Przemysł górnośląski w organiźmie gospodarczym II Rzeczypospolitej: Ekonomiczne Aspekty Integracji," in *Ziemie Śląskie w granicach II Rzeczypospolitej: procesy integracyjne*, ed. Franciszek Serafin (Katowice, 1985), 50.

49. Irena Sroka and Tomasz Fałecki, "Die Deutsche Minderheit in der Wojewodschaft Schlesien," in *Wach auf mein Herz und denke! Zur Geschichte der Beziehungen zwischen Schlesien und Berlin-Brandenburg/Przebudź się, serce moje, i pomyśl"—Przyczynek do historii stosunków między Śląskiem a Berlinem-Brandenburgia*, ed. Klaus Bzdziach, Arno Herzig, and Wieslaw Lesiuk (Berlin, 1995), 249; Barbara Danowska-Prokop and Urszula Zagóra-Jonszta, *Wybrane problemy ekonomiczno-społeczne i polityczne na Górnym Śląsku w latach 1922–1939* (Katowice, 1995), 59.

50. Frank Keitsch, *Das Schicksal der deutschen Volksgruppe in Ostoberschlesien in den Jahren 1922–1939* (Dülmen, 1982), 212.

51. Urszula Zagóra-Jonszta, *Etatyzm w polskiej myśli społeczno-ekonomicznej Górnego Śląska, 1922–1939* (Wrocław, 1996), 17.

52. See Hitze, *Carl Ulitzka*, 491–562; Grosch, *Deutsche und polnische Propaganda*, 61–63.

53. Danowska-Prokop and Zagóra-Jonszta, *Wybrane problemy*, 15–28; Serafin, *Województwo Śląskie*, 86–87.

54. Hitze, *Carl Ulitzka*, 477–84.

55. Serafin, *Województwo Śląskie*, 87. These and other population statistics are estimates, and often subject to dispute.

56. See Krystian Heffner and Wiesław Lesiuk, "Ekonomiczne i Społeczne skutki podziału Górnego Śląska w 1922," in *Podział Śląska w 1922 roku*, ed. Andrzej Brożka and Teresa Kulak (Wrocław, 1996), 148–51.

57. Serafin, *Województwo Śląskie*, 88.

58. Brubaker, *Nationalism Reframed*, 160–69.

59. Blanke, *Orphans of Versailles*, 32ff.

60. James Bjork, "The National State and the Territorial Parish in Interwar Poland," in *Germans and the East*, ed. Charles Ingrao and Franz A. J. Schabo (West Lafayette, IN, 2008), 243.

61. See Nordblom, "Die Lage der Deutschen," 114; Serafin, *Województwo Śląskie*, 86–88; Joachim Bahlcke, *Schlesien und die Schlesier* (Munich, 2000), 142.

62. Hefner and Lesiuk, "Economiczne," 148.

63. *Die Provinz Oberschlesien: Ihre Verluste durch das Versailler Diktat, ihre Notlage, ihre Vorschläge zu deren Behebung ihr natürlicher Reichtum* (Ratibor, 1931), 15.

64. Mieczysław Grzyb, *Narodowościowe-polityczne aspekty przemian stosunków własnościowych i kadrowych w górnośląskim przemyśle w latach 1922–1939* (Katowice, 1978), 240ff.; Maria Wanda Wanatowicz, *Ludność napływowa na Górnym Śląsku w latach 1922–1939* (Katowice, 1982), 120–36.

65. Lech Krzyżanowski, "Kościół Katolicki wobec regionalizmu Śląskiego w okresie miedzywojennym," in *Regionalizm a separatyzm: Historia i współczesność, Śląsk na tle innych obszarów*, ed. Maria Wanda Wanatowicz (Katowice, 1996), 69. For newcomer-related statistics, see Maria Wanda Wanatowicz, "Rola ludności napływowej w procesie integracji Górnego Śląska z resztą ziemi Polskiej," in *Ziemie Śląskie w granicach II Rzeczypospolitej: procesy integracyjne*, ed. Franciszek Serafin (Katowice, 1985), 79.

66. *Schwab* and *Germanin* were pejorative Polish terms for German. See Tomasz Kamusella, "The Upper Silesians' Stereotypical Perceptions of the Poles and the Germans," *East European Quarterly* 33, no. 3 (Fall 1999): 395–410; Wanatowicz, *Ludność napływowa*, 265–301.

67. Danowska-Prokop and Zagóra-Jonszta, *Wybrane problemy*, 71.

68. Obersztyn and Jaros, "Przemysł górnośląski," 45.

69. See Józef Popkiewicz and Ranciszek Ryszka, *Przemysł cieżki Górnego Śląska w gospodarce Polski miedzywojenej, 1922–1939* (Opole, 1959), 294–98.

70. Danowska-Prokop and Zagóra-Jonszta, *Wybrane problemy*, 74.

71. Konrad Fuchs, "Zur Lage der Industrie West- und Ost-Oberschlesiens 1919–1939," in *Górny Śląsk po podziale w 1922 roku: Co Polska, a co Niemcy dały mieszkańcom tej ziemi?*, ed. Zbigniew Kapały, Wiesław Lesiuk, and Maria Wanda Wanatowicz (Bytom, 1997), 39–63.

72. Marek Czapliński et al., eds., *Historia Śląska* (Wrocław, 2002), 371.

73. Piotr Dobrowolski, *Ugrupowania i Kierunki Separystyczne na Górnym Śląsku w Ceszyńskiem w latach 1918–1939* (Warsaw, 1972).

74. Lempart, "Michał Grażyński," 119; Maria Wanda Wanatowicz, *Historia społeczno-polityczna Górnego Śląska i Śląska Cieszyńskiego w latach, 1918–1945* (Katowice, 1994), 79.

75. In the May 1930 Silesian Sejm elections, the German Block won fifteen mandates, while the Sanacja only won ten. Danowska-Prokop and Zagóra-Jonszta, *Wybrane problemy*, 87, 90.

76. See Wanatowicz, *Historia społeczno-polityczna*; Edward Długajczyk, *Sanacja Śląska, 1926–1939: Zarys dziejów politycznych* (Katowice, 1983); Serafin, *Województwo Śląskie*, 131–77.

77. See Jan Drabina, ed., *Historia Gliwic* (Gliwice, 1995), 353; Czapliński et al., eds., *Historia Śląska*, (Wrocław, 2002), 369, 372; Franciszek Hawranek, *Niemiecka Socjaldemokracia w Prowincji Górnośląskiej w latach 1929–1933* (Wrocław, 1971), 226.

78. Wanatowicz, *Historia społeczno-polityczna*, 78.

79. Franciszek Hawranek, ed., *Dzieje Ruchu Robotniczego na Górnym Śląsku* (Opole, 1982), 320.

80. Ther, "Schlesisch, deutsch oder polnisch?," 183.

81. Sammartino, *The Impossible Border*, 3–4.

82. Wantanowicz, *Historia społeczno-polityczna*, 88.

83. Hitze, *Carl Ulitzka*, 1054.

84. Guido Hitze, "Oberschlesien im politischen Denken Carl Ulitzkas," in *Śląsk w myśli politycznej i działalności Polaków i Niemcow w XX wieku*, vol. 2, ed. Danuta Isielewicz and Lech Rubisz (Opole, 2004), 177–87.

85. See Haubold-Stolle, *Mythos Oberschlesien*, esp. introduction and conclusion; Sammartino, *The Impossible Border*, introduction.

86. This refers to the state's use of its minorities across the border for irredentist politics. See Brubaker, *Nationalism Reframed*.

87. Serafin, *Województwo Śląskie*, 178–93.

88. Lempart, *Michał Grażyński*, 120.

89. Initially, the organization was called the League of Former Insurgents (Związek Byłych Powstańców). Tomasz Falęcki has written widely on the league; see "Regionalism Powstańców Śląskich do 1939," in Regionalizm a separatyzm: Historia i współczesność, Śląsk na tle innych obszarów, ed. Maria Wanatowicz (Katowice, 1996), 54; "Powstańcy Śląscy w ruchu kombatanckim w II Rzeczypospolitej," in Powstania Śląskie i plebiscyt w procesie zrastania sie Górnego Śląska z Macierzą: Materiały z sesji naukowej historyków powstań śląskich i plebiscytu, ed. Anrzej Brozek (Bytom, 1993), 170–76; Powstańcy Śląscy, 1921–1939 (Warsaw, 1990).

90. See Falęcki, "Regionalism Powstańców," 46–64. On Grażyński, see Lempart, Michał Grażyński; Długajczyk, Sanacja Śląska; Haubold-Stolle, Mythos Oberschlesien; Serafin, Województwo Śląskie, 148–58; Blanke, Orphans of Versailles, 103–6, 117–20; Wanatowicz, Historia społeczno-polityczna; Wanatowicz, Ludność napływowa.

91. In 1934, the organization adopted its more widely known name of the Polish Western League (Polski Związek Zachodni, or PZZ); see chapter 3. See Serafin, Województwo Śląskie, 136; Lempart, Michał Grażyński, 121; Marian Mroczko, Związek Obrony Kresów Zachodnich 1921–1934: Powstanie i działalność (Gdańsk, 1977), 13–36, and sections on Silesia; Wanatowicz, Historia społeczno-polityczna, 66–142; T. David Curp, "'Roman Dmowski Understood': Ethnic Cleansing as Permanent Revolution," European History Quarterly 3, no. 35 (2005): 405–27.

92. Mroczko, Związek Obrony, 50, 54, 56, 64–67.

93. German Homeland Patriots is my simplified version of a name that would more literally translate as United Organizations of Upper Silesian Homeland (Heimat) Patriots. I use it for the sake of clarity, and particularly to emphasize the contrast with its Polish counterpart.

94. See Grosch, Deutsche und polnische Propaganda, 39–43; Hitze, Carl Ulitzka, 843–47; Haubold-Stolle, Mythos Oberschlesien, 90.

95. Konsulat Generalny Rzeczypospolitej Polskiej w Bytom (Kon. Byt.) to Ministerstwo Spraw Zagranicznych (MSZ), 20 May 1923, AAN, 482, 8, 23; Kon. Byt. to MSZ, 12 Feb. 1932, AAN 482, 8, 107. Prussian State Ministry of the Interior reports noted that in November 1926, the VVHO had only around 300 local groups and 20,000 members: VVHO Zentralstellung, 30 November 1926, Geheimstaatsarchiv Preußischer Kulturbesitz (GStA PK), HA I (Preussische Ministerium des Innerns, or Pr. MdI), rep. 77, tit. 856, "Ost-West," no. 393, 221.

96. Blanke, Orphans of Versailles, 99; Karol Gruenberg, Nazi Front Schlesien: Niemieckie organizacje polityczne w Województwie Śląskim (Katowice, 1963), 16.

97. Gruenberg, Nazi Front Schlesien, 16.

98. On Grażyński's anti-German politics, see Blanke, Orphans of Versailles; Wanatowicz, Historia społeczno-polityczna, 88–92; Serafin, Województwo Śląskie, 178–220; Sroka, "Die Deutsche Minderheit," 254; Stanisław Rogowski, Komisja Mieszana dla Górnego Śląska (1922–1937) (Opole, 1977), 70; Lempart, "Michał Grażyński," 120.

99. These statistics are from Keitsch, Das Schicksal, 212; Serafin, Województwo Śląskie, 265–66.

100. On Grażyński's "Polonization" of industry, see Danowska-Prokop and Zagóra-Jonszta, Wybrane problemy, 78; Serafin, Województwo Śląskie, 255–67; Wanatowicz, Ludność napływowa, 120–36; Bogdan Cimała, "Uwarunkowania funkcjonowania gospodarki Górnego Śląska w organizmie Drugiej Rzeczpospolitej," in Górny Śląsk po podziale w 1922 roku: Co Polska, a co Niemcy dały mieszkańcom tej ziemi?, ed. Zbigniew Kapały, Wiesław Lesiuk, and Maria Wanda Wanatowicz (Bytom, 1997), 70; Grzyb, Narodowościowo-polityczne, 240ff.

101. Serafin, Województwo Śląskie, 88.

102. Maria Wanda Wanatowicz, "Polski, Niemiecki i Śląski: Problemy narodowościowe Górnego Śląska w orkesie międzywojennym," in Wrzesień 1939 na Górnym Śląsku, ed. Grzegosz Bębnik (Katowice and Cracow, 2008), 28.

103. Piotr Dobrowolski, Ugrupowania, 148; Wanatowicz, "Polski, Niemiecki, i Śląski," 29.

104. See Maria Wanda Wanatowicz, "Wojciech Korfanty i Chrześcijańska Demokracja wobec mniejszości niemieckiej w województwie śląskim," in, *Wieki Stare i Nowe*, vol. 2, ed. Maria Wanda Wanatowicz and Idzieg Panica, (Katowice, 2001), 211–26.

105. On Sanacja-church relations, see Lech Krzyżanowski, "Kościół katolicki a władza państwowa," in *Wieki Stare i Nowe*, vol. 2, ed. Maria Wanda Wanatowicz and Idzieg Panica, (Katowice, 2001), 177–85; Jarosław Macala, *Duszpasterstwo a narodowość wiernych: Kościół Katolicki w Diecezji Katowickiej wobec mniejszości niemieckiej 1922–1939*, (Wroclaw: Uniwersytet Wrocławski, 1999), 26–148.

106. Wojciech Jaworski, "Kształtowanie się świadomośći narodowej ludności żydowskiej w województwie Śląskim w okresie międzywojennym," in *Studia Historyczno-Demograficzne*, ed. Jurek Tadeusz (Wrocław, 1996), 99.

107. Wojciech Jaworski, *Ludność żydowska w województwie śląskim w latach 1922–1939* (Katowice, 1997), 33. See also Marcin Wodziński, "Languages of the Jewish Communities in Polish Silesia (1922–1939)," *Jewish History* 16 (2002): 131–60.

108. See Jacek Piotrowski, "The Policies of the Sanacja on the Jewish Minority in Silesia, 1926–1939," *Polin: Studies in Polish Jewry* 14 (2001): 150–55.

109. See Karch, "Nationalism on the Margins," 278ff.; and Brendan Karch, "A Jewish 'Nature Preserve': League of Nations Minority Protections and Nazi Upper Silesia, 1933–1937," *Central European History* 46, no. 1 (March 2013): 124–35. See also Hitze, *Carl Ulitzka*; Michałczyk, *Heimat, Kirche und Nation*.

110. Hawranek, *Niemiecka Socjaldemokracja*, 227–52.

111. See Michałczyk, *Heimat, Kirche und Nation*, 135ff.; Karch, "Nationalism on the Margins," 323ff.

112. See Haubold-Stolle, *Mythos Oberschlesien*, 243ff.; Karol Fiedor, *Bund Deutschen Osten w systemie antypolskiej propagandy* (Warsaw and Wrocław, 1977).

113. On the ZPwN, see Karch, "Nationalism on the Margins," 226–36, chap. 4.

114. See Karch, "A Jewish 'Nature Preserve'," 124–60.

115. Bahlcke, *Schlesien und die Schlesier*, 142.

116. Powiatowa Komenda Policji Tarnowskich Gór (10 Nov. 1938) and Świętochłowic (16 Nov. 1938), APK, 38 (Policja Wojewódzka), 178, 98, 141.

CHAPTER 2

A TRANSNATIONAL TRADITION OF BORDER RALLIES, 1922–34

> "We demonstrated under the slogan of 'we will not give up our native land!' They demonstrated under that of 'Drang nach Osten' [thrust toward the east]. We accented support for our government's accepted international agreements; they called for violating the borders and connecting Polish Silesia to Germany."
>
> —*Polska Zachodnia*, 11 April 1926[1]

> "Germany celebrated the commemoration based on a voluntary rally of the Upper Silesian people. The Poles celebrate the victory of violence and everyone who lived through the insurgencies would agree with the following, which even Polish speakers echo: that it's outright frivolous to commemorate the most appalling days of Upper Silesian history with such pomp."
>
> —*Oberschlesische Volksstimme*, 3 May 1931[2]

In October 1927, President Ignacy Mościcki presided over the ceremony unveiling the Statue of the Insurgent in the border city of Królewska Huta (Königshütte; in 1934 "Polonized" to Chorzów). Although consecrated by Catholic clergy in July, the monument was secular in its aim: to symbolize the central founding myth of Polish Upper Silesia (the Voivodeship). The tall statue of an ordinary local industrial worker represented the men who in May 1921 had voluntarily and spontaneously taken up arms as loyal Poles for their nascent homeland. Identified as a metallurgy worker by his tools and uniform, he flaunts a well-built bare upper torso and brandishes a medieval broadsword. As another layer of symbolism, the worker's head was modeled on the historic "awakener" of Polish consciousness in Upper Silesia, the late nineteenth-century writer and humanist Juliusz Ligoń.

Figure 2.1. Statue of the Insurgent in Chorzów (formerly Królewska Huta/Königshütte), unveiled in 1927. (Biblioteka Śląska—Zbiory Specialne / BŚ-ZS)

The worker stands on a pedestal some ten feet in height, which before partition—as property of the Prussian State—had supported a Germania Monument until its destruction by Polish insurgents during the borderland war (fig. 2.1).

Such acts of symbolic recycling by Polish government officials became so common that they generally attracted little media or government attention in Germany until the Nazi era, when propaganda agents looked for any excuse to fuel anti-Polish vehemence. Nonetheless, government officials on the German side of the border expressed concern over the statue's belligerent pose, its location at the border—indeed, it was "turned looking at Beuthen," the nearby German city—and its apparent endorsement by the Polish president. The local German press sought to discredit the rally by downplaying its size and influence. Provinz officials first found an occasion for a properly high-level response to the message sent by the offensive statue eleven months later during a visit of the German president Paul von Hindenburg to the borderland. Speaking in Oppeln (Opole) in front of Hindenburg on 17 September 1928, the Provinz governor (*Oberpräsident*), Alfons von Proske, a leader of the Catholic People's Party (the Upper Silesian German Center Party), argued that the 40 percent of Upper Silesians who had voted for Poland in the plebiscite had done so out of "erroneousness and confusion," for—as he emphasized—the people of this region, rather than sharing cultural or political bonds with Poland, constituted a bilingual provincial community loyal to Germany.[3]

Dueling presidential visits represented only one important aspect of a much larger border standoff of mass rallies, which were often staged to confront and address the government on the other side of the partition boundary. Held yearly on important anniversaries of the postwar conflict over Upper Silesia, particularly the plebiscite (20 March) and the beginning of the third Silesian insurgency (3 May), these spectacles served as the main forum for conveying the respective irredentist cause to local, national, and international audiences. Beyond stating their claims to the borderland through discourses on the region's "true" identity and the memories of 1921 (plebiscite, third Silesian insurgency, and partition), these rallies sometimes evoked the nationalist chauvinism, terror, and violence that had marked the events of that year. The borderland activist groups and governments that organized these events profited politically from the antagonisms they stoked, thereby functioning to turn the hot war of 1921 into a "cold war"—a war of nerves and standing conflict over Upper Silesia. These rallies served as the bedrock of the transnational irredentist culture that kept this conflict at a simmer, with occasional flare-ups. This chapter explores how these events—and the wider irredentist culture they represented—operated largely unchanged across political contexts that spanned from centrist and liberal governments on both sides of the border to Polish authoritarian rule and the encroachment of radical German nationalism.

The Legacy of 1921

Germany was the big loser in the Allies' revision of its Upper Silesian border, which ceded 65 percent of its industry and two of the region's largest cities to Poland. The German government responded to these losses with official and unrelenting calls for revision. As a nation accused by the international community of being responsible for a devastating war, Germany is often remembered as the leading irredentist force in the interwar period and a threat to European peace. At the grassroots level, a more complicated picture emerges. The end of the plebiscite and armed conflict, along with the official resolution to the border dispute as spelled out by the Geneva Convention of 1922, threatened a cadre of irredentist fighters—both agitators and soldiers—with unemployment and the loss of social status tied to their identity. Faced with this prospect, they strove to maintain their prestige by organizing politically and fanning the flames of discontent over the new border, thereby feeding the atmosphere of German-Polish conflict. Borderland nationalists on both sides remained organized within the main rival organizations of the plebiscite conflict, the United Organizations of Upper Silesian Homeland (Heimat) Patriots (VVHO, hereafter referred to as German Homeland Patriots) and the Western Territories Defense League (ZOKZ; after 1934, Polish Western League, or PZZ). Both organizations gained official endorsements and active support from their respective governments, and both, while disseminating grassroots popular propaganda, also collaborated with academic centers that used multidisciplinary scholarship on the region to legitimate their particular Upper Silesian cause.

In addition, veterans on both sides of the May–June 1921 military conflict over Upper Silesia organized themselves in various paramilitary groups. Even as the Social Democratic–led German government opposed the formation of such groups, various provincial defense (*Landeschütz*) militias organized themselves. By contrast, in the Voivodeship, as in Poland as a whole, paramilitary groups flourished with official government support. Reestablished in 1923 with the endorsement of the prominent Wojciech Korfanty and his liberal Christian Democratic Party (ChD), the Insurgent League (Związek Powstańców) remained at the forefront of politics in eastern Upper Silesia, unlike its German counterparts. As soldiers fighting first for the kaiser and then as insurgents in the third Silesian uprising, many of the league's members had risen up the military ranks and enjoyed a prominence they would have hardly been able to attain during times of peace. Demobilization threatened this hard-won status, particularly for the uprising's leaders, such as Rudolf Kornke, who had to leave the public sphere to survive financially before he again headed the reestablished Insurgent League.[4] Veteran insurgents joined former agitators in the Western Territories Defense League to underscore the continuing "German threat" to Polish Silesia, and in turn gave their counterparts in the German Homeland Patriots reason to mobilize against the "Polish threat." Thus, not long after the violence over Upper Silesia subsided, a cold war over the borderland was under way.

Continuing the Borderland Struggle

Within a year following the partition, activist groups on both sides took advantage of the new border's insecurity and the inertia of violence and terror to invent what became a tradition of border spectacles to demand the return of "lost" or "stolen" territory. In the first such event, held on 25 February 1923, several tens of thousands of former insurgents, some of whom had to cross the border, traveled to Katowice (Kattowitz) for a rally in the city square. The former Prussian administrative center of the Upper Silesian industrial district and now the capital of the Voivodeship, Katowice became the main stage for most subsequent rallies in eastern Upper Silesia. The city's large and architecturally distinguished municipal square (*Stadtring/rynek*), which had served as a frequent rally site on the eve of the 1921 plebiscite, had the further advantage of being only twenty or so miles from the partition line.

The demonstrators of this first demonstration denounced the redrawn border, and demanded Upper Silesia's "reunification" within Poland's borders.[5] Some of them even justified the use of force to achieve this aim. Observers from the

German consulate noted with interest the demonstrators' claim that the new border had "cut the living organism of the Polish peoples in Upper Silesia in two parts, thereby creating a situation, which we insurgents have never recognized and will never recognize."[6] Scholars have often associated this notion of partition as the brutal severing of a naturally unified biological entity with Germany—thus the popular imagery of the "bleeding border." However, Polish nationalists clearly—and from early on—shared this organic image of Upper Silesia.

The 1923 Katowice event began the mutual escalation of mass rallies on opposite sides of the border and previewed much of their rhetoric. Two months after the event, the German Homeland Patriots published a report in a mainstream German Center Party newspaper, the *Oberschlesische Zeitung*, which deliberately overestimated its size as "over 50,000 insurgents." The story further claimed that the rally had adopted "a resolution declaring that an attack would soon take place on German Upper Silesia," since "Polish imperialism is still not satisfied with the [advantageous] conditions created for it by Geneva's shameful verdict [*Genfer Schandspruch*]." Indeed, the authors denounced the whole "Versailles Dictate," as well as its abettors, the Poles and the French, for "invading," "occupying," and "stealing" German land. By citing the French, the authors alluded not just to occupation troops in Upper Silesia in 1920, but also to France's occupation of the Ruhr since January 1923 over unpaid German reparations. The story also aimed to rally locals for the German Homeland Patriots' annual Plebiscite Day, held around 20 March to demand the return of eastern Upper Silesia.[7]

A central theme of such rallies on both sides continued to be the threat from the neighbor across the border. While the Poles accentuated German revisionism, the Germans played on existing fears of a Polish invasion, nourished by memories of the pro-Polish insurgents who had stormed the region less than two years earlier, as well as by the events in the Ruhr. The Insurgent League continued to hold military drills that spring, which included nighttime gunfire near the border, startling locals and stirring "rumors of a Polish putsch."[8] This was more than just street paranoia. In mid-April, the German consulate in Katowice reported to Germany's Foreign Office that "it suspects that the French in the Ruhr will do everything in their power in the next days to detract the military's attention from German Upper Silesia to pave way for a Polish attack."[9] Concerned that the Insurgent League was about to strike Beuthen (Bytom) and Gleiwitz (Gliwice) and continue to move toward the Oder River with the Polish army offering support, the consulate turned to negotiations with the Voivodeship's governor, Antoni Schultis, who gave his assurance of nonaggressive intent. The German officials' anxieties—if not that of many borderland residents—were further reduced by the success of Gleiwitz police informers, who penetrated local insurgent societies and discounted the existence of any active plans for an attack on Germany.[10]

While for the German government the demand for borderland restoration remained a matter for diplomatic negotiation, the German Homeland Patriots took their demand for "return" of "eastern Upper Silesia" to the grassroots. For them, the armed exercises at the border by Polish militants and the French occupation of the Ruhr were evidence of a grand conspiracy among the Allies to dismantle Germany. This mentality fueled nationalist passions when German Homeland Patriots from throughout Germany met in May 1923 for a nationwide assembly, symbolically held in the city of Neisse (Nysa), home of the early nineteenth-century German romantic writer Joseph Freiherr von Eichendorff. Denouncing the "occupation" of both regions, the delegates called for accelerated grassroots mobilization in the Provinz in order to form a united front to defend against "continuing plans for theft on the part of Poles."[11]

Just as tensions reached their height in early May 1923, the conflict entered a new phase as the governments on each side of the border became directly involved in endorsing and even helping to stage irredentist border rallies. Neither the German Center Party nor the Christian Democratic (ChD) government to the east endorsed paramilitary violence, let alone indiscriminate attacks on local citizens. However, the large number of militants, some of whom were in the ranks of the Voivodeship police, made it difficult to control their excesses.[12] Government sponsorship of rallies on both sides was partly motivated by their wish to bring the war of nerves under control. In the end, however, these rallies served to fuel and legitimize the border conflict.[13]

The First Polish "May Third" Rally

The first notable government-endorsed rally in the Voivodeship, held 2–3 May 1923, coincided with a broader national celebration of 3 May. This holiday—formally called the Day of the Third of May or Constitution Day—had dual significance. First, it commemorated the ratification of the 1791 Polish Constitution, and thereby the attempt to found the first independent Polish state. More directly relevant to Polish Upper Silesia, it also marked the beginning, three years later, of Poland's long struggle for national independence in the face of constant threat from its rapacious imperial neighbors. According to Polish national history, the struggle began with the 1794 rebellion under General Tadeusz Kościuszko and continued with the post–World War I Silesian insurgencies. The annual "May Third" festivities in the Voivodeship focused primarily on celebrating and preserving the memory of the more recent insurgencies, and particularly the third, which began on this national holiday in 1921.[14]

At midnight on 2 May, the night before the day on which the third Silesian insurgency had begun, the Insurgent League—the main guest of honor at the following day's festivities—invented a self-indulgently esoteric ceremony for its members, although they welcomed any government or military officials, indeed anyone else who turned up at that hour. In front of the turn-of-the-century Prussian theater on the city square, veteran insurgents assembled in rank-and-file order for a military bivouac. They were fully armed with rifles and canons as though prepared for attack. Instead, they lit a large bonfire—officially the "fire of freedom"—to commemorate the borderland's "liberation from the Prussian/German yoke." While the flames blazed and the troops stood at attention, the Insurgent League's leader read the original orders that had initiated the third Silesian insurgency. Well past midnight, as most residents on both sides of the border peacefully slept, the event reached its grand finale with a loud barrage of rifle and artillery fire, along with—according to German sources—exploding hand grenades. As reported in the German press, the insurgents then marched through the city and into its outskirts, finally returning to the city center—their weapons still blazing—after three o'clock in the morning. They then hung the Insurgent League's flag from the theater and celebrated their "victory" with loud shouts of joy.[15]

Rather than expressing alarm, the German press ridiculed the events as the "storming of Kattowitz" (*Sturm auf Kattowitz*), in which the "combatants only fought against an imagined enemy." In actuality, the sound of continuous gunfire was more than enough to awaken startled residents on the German side of the border. Indeed, at a time of widespread anxiety, the event quickly gave rise to suspicions of an imminent Polish invasion. Moreover, the Volksbund daily, *Kattowitzer Zeitung*, blamed the event for inciting local insurgents to assault German-minority citizens, notably a bomb attack on the home of Baron (Freiherr) von Reizenstein, in Pielgrzymowice (Pilgramsdorf), who was fortunately away from home at the time. The main newspaper in the Provinz echoed these accounts.[16] In succeeding years, the mock "storming of Kattowitz" continued to be all-night events in which insurgents marched from the city center to the border, firing off their weapons and laying wreaths at official monuments to their fallen comrades. This new annual "tradition" continued to set off rumors of impending attacks.[17]

Compared to the celebrations on the eve of 3 May, the official events on the following day were less directly provocative. Held in Katowice's municipal park, they began with an outdoor Mass celebrated by the Catholic apostolic administrator of Polish Silesia, August Hlond, who became primate of Poland a few year later. After the "heroism" of the insurgents had received official clerical blessings, they were praised by their civilian commander, and now liberal (ChD) party leader, Wojciech Korfanty. When the speeches had ended, the park became the site of a folk festival, with popular entertainment for the masses, including sports and music. The organizers intended this nonpolitical aspect of the event to attract the larger part of the population, who otherwise remained indifferent to their irredentist politics. German official sources, which normally emphasized the low attendance at Polish rallies, confirmed that such events did attract large numbers of local citizens, at least until 1925, when the economy worsened as a result of the German-Polish tariff war (see chapter 1). Reflecting indifference to genuine patriotic concern, the locals protested the rising unemployment by boycotting these border rallies, thus spiting the government that they knew counted on their presence.[18]

The Plebiscite Celebration in the Provinz

The state orchestration of the 3 May 1923 events in Katowice inspired German officials to stage their own revanchist festivals. In March 1924—about a week before the third anniversary of the plebiscite—the Provinz governor (*Oberpräsident*) Alfons Proske circulated a confidential memo urging all county heads and mayors under his jurisdiction to counter the Polish May Third celebrations. Local leaders and police chiefs, Proske informed them, were aware that "the political resources of the now independent Polish state" were being used "to undermine the [German] national spirit" in Upper Silesia.[19] As a strategy that aimed to "Polonize" residents on *both* sides of the border, the May Third rallies constituted the "preparatory work for a final separation of that part of the plebiscite area that still remains with us."[20] Although the time was short, Proske ordered all county heads to launch campaigns to mobilize local citizens for a rally on Plebiscite Day. He reminded the officials that their rallies would demonstrate to "that part of the province that was torn away from us, as well as to the whole world, that the entire [Upper Silesian] population remains conscious that, by an overwhelming majority, they had decided to remain with Germany on March 20, 1921, and thus do not really recognize the justice of the decision from Geneva."[21]

Proske's memo demonstrates his intent that the German rallies would differ substantially from the Polish celebrations. Beyond his wish not to antagonize Poland, as a leading figure of the German Center Party, Proske also wanted to avoid stoking nationalist passions in his own province, which would only benefit the antirepublican right. The right-wing nationalists (*völkische*-oriented parties and individuals) that concerned him would find common cause with any openly anti-Polish messages at a partition rally.[22] Moreover, these nationalist groups would not be satisfied merely with the "return" of the borderlands. Rather, they sought to undermine the legitimacy of the German Republic and its official credo of cultural tolerance, as well as the political viability of the parties that supported the republic, in particular the German Center Party.[23]

To dampen nationalist sentiments on both sides of the border, Proske sought to avoid the glorification of military prowess, the flaunting of irredentist organizations such as the German Homeland Patriots, and the blatant government presence that characterized the Polish events. On the contrary, he and his centrist allies shared the vision of a democratic, legal, and peaceful process of border revision. The plebiscite festivities they imagined would be spontaneous, broadly supported mass protests that aimed to lobby for a "return" of eastern Upper Silesia to Germany that was recognized in international law. Social Democrats, centrists, and liberals believed that constant large-scale, popular protests would eventually persuade the Allies of their "mistake" and cause them to correct it. To underline the spontaneity of the expressions of discontent and the coming event's peaceful intentions, Proske urged officials and the press to use the term "commemoration" (*Gedenkfeier*) rather than protest to characterize the rallies. The preferred designation was thus Plebiscite Commemoration (*Abstimmungsgedenkfeier*) or just Plebiscite Celebration (*Abstimmungsfeier*). Nevertheless, Proske clearly had protest in mind: the point of such festivities was, after all, to show the international community that the cession of eastern Upper Silesia to Poland had been an "act of injustice, the revision of which must one day arrive."[24]

From the outset, German Center Party government officials knew the challenges they faced in staging these rallies, not alone because of the looming deadline. Proske's memo to Provinz officials made clear his awareness that "it would naturally be for the best if the public itself would initiate the ... celebration."[25] "Unfortunately," he admitted, "the majority of our population lacks the initiative for a conscious national rising," thus putting "the German cause [*der deutsche Gedanke*] at a disadvantage against the Polish national movement."[26] Proske, therefore, had no choice but to mandate that the Provinz, particularly local administrators and their collaborators in irredentist politics among the German Homeland Patriots, organize the rallies and mobilize the population to attend. He was less concerned about the genuine patriotic conviction of those who showed up than that the events would be massive enough to impress their intended audience. His nightmare was that "if the population itself demonstrates apathy toward Upper Silesia's great fateful day only a short time after the plebiscite, then our endeavor for justice will lack resonance."[27]

Like the Polish May Third spectacles, the German plebiscite commemorations were intended to conjure up momentous events in recent history. Whereas, on the Polish side, the event was the third Silesian uprising, on the other side it was the German victory—albeit unrewarded by the Allies—in the plebiscite. In both cases, the critical event undergirded an intent meant—in Proske's words—to "strengthen the locals' patriotic spirit."[28] On both sides, the organizers also aimed to show the international community that the broad masses continued to demand the incorporation of all Upper Silesia into the nation, as they had shown in the plebiscite. Further, like their Polish counterparts, the plebiscite events aimed to integrate the local population into the nation, in particular the nationally indifferent Upper Silesians, whose identity lay more with the region than with the German nation. In the words of Proske's flyer for the 1924 events, those who attended should let the outside world know how "fired up we are to stand firmly together to guard against all further threats."[29]

Local officials heeded Proske's urgent appeals for popular mobilization. On 21 March 1924, rallies were held in the tricity border area (encompassing the cities of Beuthen, Gleiwitz, and Hindenburg) and also in other locations throughout the Provinz, particularly in larger cities and towns. They typically featured crowds marching behind signposts protesting the partition, and speeches echoing this message made by German Homeland Patriot officials and regional political notables, including Proske himself.[30] The turnout failed to attract much notice in the local or regional press. However, the Polish consul in Beuthen, Edward Szczepański, reported to Warsaw that, unlike the previous year, when the plebiscite anniversary occasioned only small, sporadic, and geographically as well as politically fragmented protests, the 1924 activities were of a completely different nature. Notably, they were marked by "fiery government orchestration," with all participants, regardless of political allegiance, joined in a "united German" protest against the "injustice imposed by the League of Nations in contradiction to the popular will" and also in their desire to again make "Upper Silesia an international question."[31] By mid-1924, the duel of border rallies was fully underway.

The Contest for Crowds and Significance

Whereas the plebiscite was central to the Provinz celebrations, Polish borderland nationalists and government officials initially saw little reason to commemorate a vote in which the pro-Germany position prevailed. This was all the more so since the official Polish interpretation of the plebiscite judged it to have been unfair, indeed illegitimate, on two grounds: first, the violence and terror unleashed by German police agents against Poland's supporters; and second, Germany had allegedly brought back hundreds of thousands of native-born Upper Silesians living elsewhere in Germany to cast their votes. Thus, the May Third festivities became the center of events that lionized the insurgencies.[32] In 1925—in reaction to the German plebiscite celebrations—the Silesian section of the borderlands defense group, the ZOKZ, organized rallies in the days preceding the German events to serve as a preemptive protest against "German revisionism."[33] The increasing size and noise of the German border rallies also drove the Poles to up the ante with their own events in order to attract more international attention. Beginning with the fifth anniversary of the plebiscite (1926), large counterrallies took place on the same day as the German events in an effort to outdo them. In addition, Polish officials continued to stage their own annual May Third spectacles, which reached their peak in size and bombast during the 1930s.

On both sides of the border, some of the rallies—in particular those marking the fifth and tenth anniversaries in 1926 and 1931—attracted large crowds.[34] Recorded attendance at each of the Plebiscite Day and May Third celebrations between 1925 and 1931 ranged between 10,000 and 100,000. In the Voivodeship, borderland nationalists mobilized 10,000–15,000 participants in the areas of Rybnik and Tarnowskie Góry (Tarnowitz) to counter plebiscite celebrations across the border in Gleiwitz and other industrial cities on 20 March 1925.[35] Unfortunately, there are no reliable counts of participants at these events, since—like most statistics related to highly contested issues—each side did its own counting. Polish and German officials both tended to overestimate attendance at their own events, while undercounting the crowds at their rival's rallies. Nonetheless, it seems clear that the turnout among native Upper Silesians was not especially impressive at some of the events. For example, only 3,000 or so local residents took part in the 20 March 1925 festivity in Gleiwitz, a city of 90,000.[36] Such a low turnout would neither justify a new plebiscite vote nor demonstrate the "will" of local citizens for a united German Upper Silesia.

In their efforts to boost crowd size, governments and patriotic societies on both sides of the border used organizing and technology strategies that evolved in the context of the transnational contest. The German Homeland Patriots, for example, took advantage of their secondary role as a refugee aid society. Like most modern conflicts, the Upper Silesian insurgencies led to the mass flight of civilians. According to one scholarly estimate, some 100,000 fled westward by 1924 alone.[37] War, political persecution, and both perceived and real loss of social status fed this flight, which left many homeless, jobless, and in need of aid. While taking thousands of refugees, *Verdrängten* (those "driven out"), under its wing, the German Homeland Patriots also used some of them as tools for their revanchist propaganda. They played a central role at the 1925 plebiscite rally in Gleiwitz, where they walked in rank-and-file order holding protest signs with messages such as "We refugees from the stolen part of Upper Silesia protest against the shredding of our *Heimat*."[38] At the rally's culmination, they stood alongside local government officials, who pointed to them as prime examples of the "borderless suffering" caused by the partition.[39] At other events, the German Homeland Patriots mobilized the refugees to support the argument that, unless their homeland and property was restored, the *Verdrängten* might fall prey to radical politics and "Bolshevization."[40]

Upper Silesians who fled to Poland also became pawns in the cold war over the border. According to one estimate, this group numbered 90,000–100,000 by 1926.[41] Much like the German Homeland Patriots, the Insurgent League provided welfare to refugees, especially to their fellow fighters, who feared German retribution. At the league's events, the refugees (*uchódcy*) often served as personifications of "injustice." For example, at the 24 February 1923 rally in Katowice, insurgents and other refugees from the Provinz highlighted the demand for Poland's "recovery" of lost territory. The establishment of a pro-Sanacja Silesian Refugees League (Związek Uchódcow Śląskich) in 1927, which assumed a central role in Grażyński's May Third festivities and other border rallies, marked a more concerted effort to turn these refugees into tools of irredentist politics.[42]

The symbolic importance of the fifth anniversary of the plebiscite in 1926 prompted German officials to step up their mobilization efforts. In the end, they aimed for a compromise between the Provinz governor Proske's idea of an entirely popular event and a grand official spectacle with an all-German national character.[43] The more popular events took place locally throughout the tricity area on the traditional 20 March, with a more official celebration a week later in Oppeln (Opole), the administrative capital of the Provinz. This delay avoided conflict with a nationwide celebration of the anniversary of the Ruhr's "liberation" from "French occupation." During preparations for the local events, Proske urged local officials to put ordinary citizens at the center of the celebrations. Indeed, he was weary of "anti-Polish" propaganda circuses, like the 1925 plebiscite events, which had led Poland to complain to the German-Polish Mixed Commission. As he had in 1924, Proske wanted a more spontaneous demonstration, which led him to prohibit rank-and-file marches by groups such as the German Homeland Patriots. In addition, the governors of local areas along the border issued warnings to activists about making provocative statements against Poland or the League of Nations: this event should solely commemorate Germany's plebiscite victory. This caution was motivated by fear that provocative gestures would give paramilitary groups across the border an excuse to unleash terror and violence against the German minority, as had happened before after rallies in the Provinz. Nor did the government want to incite nationalist passions against its own Polish minority.[44]

In an effort to maximize popular support, the Provinz government created official German and Polish rally posters carrying Proske's name. Civil servants at all levels were told to attend, and teachers mobilized their pupils. (For those unable to attend, Plebiscite Day became a widely celebrated occasion for classroom morning prayers and discussions of the revisionist cause.[45]) In order to promote an atmosphere of fun and entertainment, choirs and orchestras from local factories and schools performed.[46] Beuthen's mayor noted that "unfortunately, the plebiscite festivity has not taken on the character of a great popular rally," and that without the mobilization of local organizations, "the staging of an effective popular rally in Beuthen is impossible."[47] Such observations contributed to the Provinz government's decision to end its promotion of "spontaneous" celebrations.

On the Polish side, officials took full advantage of organizational mobilization in their efforts to outdo their German rivals in 1926. In the words of a nationalist regional newspaper, the celebration would represent a "second plebiscite, this time, one that has not been falsified by the Germans."[48] The resulting rally was more nationalist, militant, and state-orchestrated than those of their German counterparts. Its main organizers, the government, the Insurgent League and the ZOKZ, called out to Poles, wherever they lived, to come to Katowice to demonstrate against "the German revisionist provocations."[49] To boost participation, the Polish event showcased the kind of closed-ranks marching that Proske had shunned. In addition to paramilitary groups from throughout Poland, there were ranks of Polish Scouts, members of women's organizations, and contingents of teachers, as well as ranks of refugees from Gross Strehlitz (Wielkie Strzelce/Strzelce Opolskie), Oppeln, and Gleiwitz. Finally, the miners, who were a fixture at May Third events, marched in their blue ceremonial uniforms, which had not changed in appearance since Prussian times.[50] Indeed, Polish officials were especially eager to show the world that the workers central to Poland's industrial sector supported the national cause.

Beyond these traditional mobilization strategies, for the 1926 plebiscite rally, the organizers introduced the use of railroad trains to transport patriots to Katowice from throughout Poland. In part to compensate for any lack of enthusiasm among local residents, at least ten special trains with reduced or no fares were organized to entice tourists from Lwów (Lemberg/Lviv), Warsaw, Cracow, Poznań (Posen), and Częstochowa, as well as from the southeastern border with Czechoslovakia. The result of all these efforts was an event of unprecedented size, attended by several tens of thousands of participants. (For those unable to travel to Katowice, borderland societies held smaller events in Cracow and Warsaw.) Special trains were also arranged two months later for a huge May Third rally—as well as for both events in succeeding years. The importation of outsiders from traditionally Polish areas was ironic, given the government's argument that Germany's importation of voters had invalidated the 1921 plebiscite. Not surprisingly, then, Provinz officials were quick to point out the nonregional and orchestrated character of the Polish plebiscite event. As was customary, they also reduced claims in the Polish press of 100,000 participants to 10,000.[51]

The 1926 Oppeln rally marked the next step in the evolution of the transnational tradition of border rallies. Rather than the spontaneous and popular celebrations envisioned by the provincial governor Proske, from now on they would be government-orchestrated, with a focus that was national as well as regional. Accordingly, they would feature national, not just regional, government officials and elites. In his reports on the event to Poland's Foreign Ministry, the Polish consul in Beuthen underlined the significance of the unprecedented presence of German government officials from Berlin: the revisionist gestures once made by local patriotic societies now constituted official national policy.[52] In light of strong Polish memories of Prussia's participation in the eighteenth-century partitions of their motherland, these "German" calls for border revision aroused fears of a fourth partition of Poland.

In response to this provocation, the Polish consul urged Warsaw to give Plebiscite and 3 May rallies in the Voivodeship a similar national character.[53] Whatever the weight of this advice, the 1927 Plebiscite Day festivities in Katowice enjoyed the presence of central government officials, including Finance Minister Edward Kwiatkowski. In addition, more efforts were made to ensure a larger-than-ever attendance. This included providing twenty special railroad trains—double the previous number—to bring enthusiastic Polish citizens (or leisure-seeking day-trippers) to the borderland. In addition to again mobilizing civil servants and activist groups, the government also told factories and coal mines to mobilize their workers to march. Workers fearful of losing their jobs readily followed these orders from their supervisors. Voivodeship officials claimed the presence of a crowd of 150,000 at the Katowice rally. German-minority leaders challenged their count, insisting that attendance barely exceeded 100,000.[54] In either case, the event's size overshadowed those on the German side of the border, which in 1927 were not organized for such large numbers. Indeed, local officials in the Provinz had advised against trying to stage grandiose spectacles every year. Not only would the local public find them routine, but their international resonance could be compromised.[55] In contrast, local Sanacja officials spent 200,000 złotys on their event, a hefty sum that earned them criticism from their political opponents.[56] Moreover, only two months later, similar resources were dedicated to staging an equally grandiose May Third festivity in Katowice and smaller events in other border locations. They were succeeding in their stringent effort to outdo the competitor's spectacles.[57]

Although 1927 was not a particularly significant anniversary year and the Polish economy was still suffering, the history of the region had taken a significant turn over the previous year. Poland's new authoritarian leader, Marshal Joseph Piłsudski, installed the militant nationalist, Michal Grażyński, as governor (*voivode*). That year's plebiscite festival presented Grażyński with an opportunity to show the "weak" German Center Party government on the other side of the border that he had forged a massive "united Polish front." His staged defiance of "German revanchism" was as much a self-serving political instrument for the *voivode* and his Sanacja faction as it was a sincere effort to demonstrate that he would be a better "guardian of the border" than his main rival, Korfanty. The plebiscite event on 20 March 1927 was the last time these two political leaders joined together to stage a grandiose event in "defiance of the German revisionist threat." By May of that year, Grażyński was representing himself not only as the former battalion leader of the third Silesian insurgency, but also as the "chief insurgent" and head of the Insurgent League, indeed as Upper Silesia's (sole) "liberator," a designation that previously had been associated with Korfanty.[58] To further this identity, Grażyński turned the May Third festivity into a self-legitimizing political spectacle. Moreover, in an effort to destroy Korfanty's heroic legend, which was entwined with the memory of Poland's struggle to win the plebiscite campaign in 1921, he also decreed an end to official Plebiscite Day commemorations in the Voivodeship. In their stead, he organized annual rallies on 20 March in official observance of Piłsudski's name day, thereby promoting the all-national cult of the marshal in the border area.[59] Once the border rallies became a tool of the new dictatorship, Korfanty and his followers began to boycott them, thereby undermining the message of a "united national front" they were intended to convey to their western neighbors. German officials and occasionally the press were keen to expose this political division in order to exploit the weaknesses in the Sanacja government's base of support.[60]

Ironically, similar divisions were becoming evident on the German side of the border. In March 1927, an internal dispute erupted over logistics for staging that year's plebiscite celebration, in which the right-wingers within the German Homeland Patriots joined paramilitary organizations such as the *Stahlhelm* and various groups of the *Landeschutz* for their own rally at the Monument to the Fallen in Gleiwitz. This event provided an occasion for Polish officials to make a point of the German failure to create a "united front."[61] Thus, nationalists on both sides of the partition line—German right-wingers and Polish Sanacja—were eager to usurp the border rallies for their own political advantage. The revanchist and nationalist ethos of this transnational irredentist tradition made rallies convenient tools for authoritarian regimes seeking to fuel cross-border conflicts.

Amplifying the Border Contest

The late 1920s saw two developments that, in different ways, transformed the transnational culture of border rallies. First, new media technologies expanded the range for irredentist propaganda in both Germany and Poland. While the 1927 German Plebiscite Day celebration failed to match that year's Polish event in terms of attendance, the Germans far outdid the competition in exploiting the still relatively young technology of motion pictures. *The Land Under the Cross: A Film on Upper Silesia's Most Difficult Times*, a half-hour-long silent documentary, was directed by Ulrich Kayser and produced by Bundesfilm AG Berlin. The Provinz government viewed the film as a vehicle for enlightening Germany and the international community on the burdens imposed on Upper Silesia by war and partition. The film's title aptly reflected the official revisionist message that portrayed the region as a victim of Polish violence and Allied dismemberment. Rather than introducing the film as part of some official spectacle, the government held the grand nationwide premier on Plebiscite Day in 1927 at the Deulingpalast Cinema in Gleiwitz.[62] The thousand attendees invited by the regional government heard an address by the "German plebiscite hero" and county governor (*Landrat*) of Beuthen County (Landkreis Beuthen), Kurt Urbanek, who praised the film and called for "faith in the victorious march of *Kultur* to the German east."[63] Although this stereotype of "culture" as a German possession graciously bestowed on lesser nationalities is usually attributed to German right-wing nationalists, Urbanek belonged to the Center Party. Certainly the film echoed the essential discourse conveyed by the plebiscite celebrations, namely, proclaiming the German character of all of Upper Silesia, denouncing the partition, and publicizing its harmful impact on Upper Silesians, as illustrated by scenes of refugees trekking through the winter snow on foot and carrying their life's belongings.[64]

Two days after its grand premier, the film began its run throughout Germany, beginning with a gala screening in Berlin. Outraged by the film itself and the publicity it was garnering, Polish consular officials lodged protests against its revanchist and "anti-Polish" themes to the German government. Despite their efforts, the film was shown in 180 cinemas, including ten in Berlin alone, and in at least one in all of Germany's largest cities, including several that were located near contested German-Polish borderlands, such as Breslau (Wrocław), Danzig (Gdańsk), and Königsberg (after 1945, Kaliningrad). To further promote the film in the *Provinz*, the government offered reduced admissions in cinemas and arranged showings in public schools.[65]

Upon learning about the production of the German film, in late 1926, the Insurgent League commissioned the making of *Silesia, Poland's Pupil*, to be directed by Konstanty Pawlukiewicz and produced by the "propaganda cinema film agency," Kapefilm.[66] Grażyński, along with various national government officials, were the film's official patrons. Almost twice as long as its German competition, the film shared its purpose: to use a motion picture format to disseminate the kind of slanted message previously limited to speeches and the printed media. The film, which both emphasized the eternal "Polish character" of Upper Silesia and celebrated the insurgents for "returning" part of the region to Poland, included shots of crowds at various May Third rallies in Katowice. The film was not finished in time for the 1927 rally, but it did open in Katowice on 31 May, only a few weeks after the premier of its German rival.[67] Its screenings throughout Poland included a special showing for President Mościcki at the Royal Palace in Warsaw. Two years later, the film was shown to the public at the Polish General Exhibition in Poznań, one of the nation's most important international exhibits devoted to demonstrating its achievements in modernization after a decade of independence. The film's creators concluded that *Silesia, Poland's Pupil* had "attained a record successful propaganda impact."[68] It did not, however, extend its reach beyond Poland, whereas *The Land Under the Cross* was shown in England, France, and Austria. The fact that the German media and government hardly paid the Polish film any attention, while the Polish press poured out article after article denouncing and protesting against the German work, reflects the latter's wider resonance.

Radio was the second transforming technology to enter the escalating cross-border competition in the late 1920s. Germany opened a radio station and tower in Gleiwitz on 15 November 1925, thus boosting the signals of broadcasting stations in Breslau and other cities and even reaching across the border into Poland. In the words of radio official Hans Christian Bredow at the opening ceremony, "with the Gleiwitz broadcasting station our brothers on each side of the border will be given the opportunity to take part in the cultivation of the national [volkstumliche] arts and general high culture."[69] Apart from all-German programs, these stations also—especially around Plebiscite Day—broadcast Silesian regionalist programs, which aimed above all to present a German national spin to the borderland's particularities.[70]

Instead of a regional broadcasting station in the Voivodeship, organizers of the 1926 plebiscite events set up powerful amplifiers in Katowice's central square to transmit speeches and public singing of the nationally renowned Germanophobic anthem, Maria Konopicka's "Rota" (1908), throughout much of the inner city.[71] According to the Sanacja daily Polska Zachodnia, this setup lent the event "American-style grandiosity." Journalists also effectively used photography to capture the "sea of heads" in the city center during the Polish rallies.[72] Spread through the press, these manipulative visual representations of the "magnificence" of these events replaced any effort to come up with a precise count of the crowds. The concentration of the rallies in the central square inside the regional capital, Katowice, which lay near the border, certainly provided them a visual advantage. By contrast, the Germans dispersed their border rallies across the tricity area, resulting in smaller crowds for each. To turn this situation to Poland's advantage, the Polish consulate in Beuthen urged the Voivodeship government to send comparative shots of the 3 May 1925 rally in Katowice and that year's plebiscite celebration in Beuthen to the international press.[73]

The Sanacja government began to remedy its technological disadvantage when, on 4 December 1927, Grażyński ceremonially opened Polish Radio Katowice. Like the Gleiwitz station, it shared a nationalizing purpose, in its case to allow "our dear brothers in western Upper Silesia to hear Polish word and song … and thus on a daily basis feel as if they were in their [Polish] fatherland."[74] Starting in 1928, the station aired all the rallies in Katowice, as well as programs on "regional lore." Analogous to programs in the Provinz, they were based on the cultural work of borderland nationalists, including the ZOKZ and the geopolitical academic tradition of Western Borderland Thought.[75] Thus, by 1927 radio provided the propaganda spectacles that were part and parcel of both German and Polish rallies a greater transborder reach than the rallies themselves could achieve.

Already in the first years after partition, patriotic societies on both sides sponsored the erection (or sometimes repurposing) of statues in the borderlands. These included a Monument to the Unknown Insurgent in Katowice, which consisted of a tall pedestal still standing from the former Monument to the Two Kaisers that the insurgents had detonated. In 1925, German veterans unveiled a Monument to the Fallen *Selbstschutz* Fighters in Beuthen, followed by similar monuments and plaques in Hindenburg and Gleiwitz. These statues provided symbolic sites for small-scale border rallies. As the cross-border rivalry intensified, the statues became more monumental and aggressive. In October 1927, as previously mentioned, the Polish president Mościcki unveiled the Statue of the Insurgent, a ten-foot-tall statue of a worker wielding a broadsword atop the pedestal occupied in Prussian times by a Germania Monument in the border city of Królewska Huta (Königshütte). On the same visit, he also presided over the ceremonial opening of a new stadium, built not only for soccer matches, but also for border rallies. The Germans responded by building a stadium in Beuthen, just across the partition line, which the German chancellor Heinrich Brüning, from the German Center Party, inaugurated during the particularly important Plebiscite Day celebration of 1931.[76]

The Last Great Showdown

The tenth anniversaries of the plebiscite and the third Silesian insurgency fell in March and May 1931, offering officials on both sides of the border opportunities to stage massive propaganda spectacles that utilized all their technological, organizational, and logistical strategies. Thus, the Plebiscite Day and May Third celebrations in 1931 presented both a microcosm and the high-water mark for the transborder culture of revanchist rallies. The times were inauspicious: the unemployment and social discontent spawned by the world economic crisis radicalized politics in Germany and Poland. In the Provinz, the long-dominant German Center Party was losing ground to antirepublican nationalist parties. In the Voivodeship, the Sanacja party faced growing support for German-minority parties, the Polish Christian Democrats (ChD), and a Silesian autonomy movement led by Jan Kustos. Moreover, the radical left was growing stronger and more influential on both sides of the border. Both the German Center Party and the Sanacja governments saw the tenth anniversaries as a chance—at least temporarily—to distract the public from internal problems by rallying support against "the external threat."[77]

The main German Plebiscite Day celebration in 1931 took place on 21 March in the new stadium in Beuthen. Like the event five years earlier, the tenth anniversary celebration was consciously organized as more than a regional event, as evidenced by the presence of the German chancellor Brüning. As a leader of the

German Center Party, he was warmly received by the crowd in this area where the regional section of the party (officially called the Catholic People's Party) had long dominated. Weeks before the event, the government mobilized the media to make this "threatened border region" a center of attention throughout Germany. Taking advantage of the Gleiwitz radio tower, German stations aired programs that presented Upper Silesia as an inherently "German" province whose partition was an injustice.[78] In addition, a flood of newspaper and periodical articles, books, and pamphlets condemned the partition, not only as a tragedy and an injustice, but as the cause of the terrible economic crisis in the region, or perhaps even the precipitating event behind the worldwide depression. Artists and writers in the institute devoted to regionalism and folklore, the Organization for Upper Silesian Regional Studies (Vereinigung für oberschlesische Landeskunde), came together to create songs and poetry that would increase the popular appeal of the official protest. A notable example of these works was the collection of tragic and heroic poetry entitled *A People under the Hammer* (*Volk unter dem Hammer*) by the well-known Silesian *Heimatkundler* Alfons Hayduk.[79]

The Polish minority press in the Provinz carefully monitored the propaganda campaign, expressing particular outrage over the effort to indoctrinate schoolchildren and youth. At a time when many political movements were making efforts to mobilize youth, the German Center Party—facing particular competition from nationalist groups—established its own regional youth group in the early 1930s.[80] To reach its own youth organization as well as young people more generally, the party's press published *The Upper Silesian Friend of Youth* (*O/S Jugendfreund*). As the tenth anniversary approached, this periodical was full of articles, illustrations, and maps that buttressed the official irredentist cause. Thus, articles that covered the now Polish territories bore titles such as "The Symbol of the Torn-Away German Territories" or "The Lost Homeland" (*Heimatland*). Illustrations often featured German relics, such as the Bismarck Tower in Katowice, cited as "proof" that Poland had no rights to eastern Upper Silesia. In addition to the party organ, officials promoted the publication of an array of brochures, pamphlets, and small regional atlases geared toward a grammar and secondary school audience. Moreover, Polish minority observers reported that, in the months preceding the tenth anniversary, teachers taught this revanchist propaganda to their pupils in the classroom.[81] One widely taught song was the "Upper Silesian Oath" ("Oberschlesische Schwur"), which the government made a sort of new regional anthem. While it contained no anti-Polish slurs, this anthem contained lines that asserted "whether on this side [of the border] or the other one," Upper Silesia remained one "homeland" (*Heimatland*) and that no "border post would divide us."[82]

Young people had their own special role in the anniversary events on 21 March 1931. More than 15,000 pupils, along with their teachers, from schools throughout the region attended the Beuthen Stadium ceremonies, where they sang the "Oberschlesische Schwur," thus reinforcing the desired message that "Upper Silesia must be German and will forever remain German."[83] To augment its didactic intent, the celebration included a history lesson on the events of 1919–22, whose central point was that the German nation transcends the actual borders of the nation-state, extending as far as "the German tongue resounds."[84]

The 1931 celebration also exhibited a heavy instrumental use of Catholicism for political purposes in this devoutly religious region. As part of the festivities, Chancellor Brüning, along with Hans Lukaschek, the plebiscite hero and German Center Party politician who in 1929 had succeeded Alfons Proske as Provinz governor, traveled to the most important regional pilgrimage site, the Mount of St. Anne, to celebrate Catholic Mass in honor of fallen *Selbstschutz* fighters.[85] Beyond its religious significance, this site's resonance derived from its role as a famous battlefield during the third Silesian insurgency. Certainly, the symbolism of this event—in addition to the chancellor's presence—did not improve German-Polish relations.[86] The Plebiscite Day event itself began at 12:30 PM with the simultaneous ringing of church bells across the Provinz as a symbol of protest against the border. This action was facilitated by the blessing of Cardinal Adolf Bertram of Breslau (Wrocław). Across the Provinz churches held Masses "for a reunited Upper Silesia."[87] In Beuthen Stadium itself, the day began with the celebration of a Catholic Mass. A large part of the audience consisted of various regional Catholic organizations, including youth, seniors', and women's political activist and cultural groups. Moreover, officials speaking at the event freely used religious language to assert revisionist claims, for example, "Oh God, make us united and free" (*O Herr, Mach uns Einig und Frei*), by which the return of eastern Upper Silesia was understood.[88] Not surprisingly, the Polish press expressed outrage over how "the Germans" had used "the Catholic Church" to promote "hatred against everything Polish."[89]

To a greater degree than any previous border rally in the Provinz, the tenth-anniversary spectacle was a state-centered and military event that represented a radical departure from the German Center Party's original idea of a spontaneous popular event. The official celebration in the Beuthen Stadium included speeches by Brüning and high-ranking German Homeland Patriots members to a crowd of about 40,000. The chancellor, "with great pain," lamented the duplicitous breech of democratic principles on the part of the Allies, who in 1919 had supported self-determination for Upper Silesia, only to reverse their position two years later, despite the majority vote for Germany. Elsewhere in the Provinz, the Social Democratic (Sozialdemokratische Partei Deutschlands, or SPD) interior minister of the Prussian State, Carl Severing, spoke to an audience of 20,000 at Plebiscite Day events in Hindenburg. In Gleiwitz, the nationalist Karl Hoefer, *Selbstschutz* commander and future high-ranking SS officer, addressed a crowd of 30,000.⁹⁰ His central presence added to the event's military character, which likewise included—for the first time at a Plebiscite Day rally—companies of the Reichswehr (the German army) marching inside the Beuthen Stadium and through the streets of the tricity area.⁹¹

The rally also had its popular attractions. Ordinary participants were attracted to the celebration's less blatantly political events, such as performances by local marching bands, choral societies, and gymnastic clubs. Other local groups, including school classes, civil servants, women's societies, workers' associations, and various cultural and political organizations, marched in a festive parade. Marchers from the industrial district's surrounding countryside wore folk costumes, while industrial workers marched in their ceremonial uniforms. In both cases, they aimed to symbolize support for the German cause among locally rooted Upper Silesians.⁹²

Events from the tenth-anniversary celebration in the tricity area were transmitted beyond the region by radio broadcasts and in the form of a newsreel. In addition, local officials in other parts of Germany staged smaller-scale rallies, the most notable of which took place in Munich's city hall a few days after the official Plebiscite Day. It was presided over by the Provinz's new governor, Hans Lukaschek, as well as by Bavarian officials. This rally's agenda extended beyond "Upper Silesia's tragedy," which was presented as only part of "Germany's bleeding border" (die blutende Grenze). This catchphrase, often associated with the German right wing, referred to all the territory Germany lost after World War I and conveyed the resultant "suffering" of these border areas, especially those lost to Poland and Czechoslovakia. Thus, in Munich, the officials in charge of the rally called for the "closing" of these "wounds of the eastern organism" inflicted by the Treaty of Versailles. These losses not only caused Germany's current economic misery, but they also threatened to condemn these territories to a "desolate," "de-Germanized," and "Slavicized" future.⁹³ The Munich event, as well as the official 1931 Plebiscite Day celebration, was organized and supported by politicians who supported the Weimar Republic. Nevertheless, these events ultimately helped to undermine the internationally sanctioned postwar settlement and endorsed aggression against Germany's neighbors.

The tenth-anniversary May Third festival in the Voivodeship presented a similar combination of official speeches and popular entertainment. Orchestrated by the nationalist Sanacja government, the 1931 event shared many features with the one organized in 1923 by the more centrist Korfanty and the ChD. Like that event, it included a "traditional" midnight bivouac of gunfire and battle cries in the city square, which, as usual, awakened and startled residents on the other side of the border. In 1931, however, this spectacle first enjoyed national endorsement through the presence of President Mościcki, as well as the more common vow on the part of officials, in the name of the "Polish" and "Silesian" people, to defend the Voivodeship "to the end" in case of German attack. These leaders further issued an official statement that they would "never forget 600,000 Polish brothers still suffering under German persecution in Śląsk Opolski," the official Polish name for western Upper Silesia, which served to promote the myth of its Polish character. Although the hall in which state officials made these statements was closed to the public, they were later broadcast to both sides of the border by Polish Radio Katowice.[94]

Like its German counterpart, the official May Third ceremony combined government, religion, and the military (as represented by the veteran insurgents). The central event was a public Catholic Mass celebrated by leading clerics in the Diocese of Katowice that attracted between 60,000 and 80,000 spectators. It was held at the newly built site for such mass rallies in the center of Katowice, composed of a monumental Voivodeship Government Building and surrounding parade grounds (see chapter 3). The symbolic building's large front portico formed a stage of sorts with an altar and a giant cross. During the service, most of the crowd stood in the parade grounds in rank-and-file order according to their organizations, which included paramilitary groups, workers' unions, cultural and social organizations, civil servants, schoolchildren, and Polish Scouts. To respond to the Germans' display of the *Verdrängten* (refugees from the partition) at their event, Polish officials mobilized their own refugee organizations. Indeed, German observers noted that this group had a more prominent and better-organized presence at this rally than on earlier occasions.[95] After the Mass and officials' speeches, the rally ended with the usual singing of the Germanophobic "Rota" song and a giant parade of organizations reviewed by President Mościcki.[96]

Efforts were made to obscure any hint of government orchestration of the more popular events. As across the border, they featured amateur orchestras, marching bands, choirs, performances by amateur theater societies, and marchers from various local organizations, as well as groups wearing traditional folk costumes and coal miners in their ceremonial uniforms. A so-designated folk festival further demonstrated the event's "popular character." To encourage broad participation, the festival offered popular contests for children and adults such as sack and egg-and-spoon races, and in the evening, the general public enjoyed music and dancing. Leaving nothing to chance, officials encouraged workers' unions, mines, and factories to boost attendance. Last but not least, the event offered inexpensive food and drink, including alcoholic beverages. The Sanacja press presented all these activities as "proof" that the event manifested "spontaneous popular will." The government nevertheless continued the tradition of arranging for reduced-fare or even free train travel for nonlocals. Although intended to encourage "patriots" to enjoy the day's events, it also gave at least some ordinary Polish citizens a chance to enjoy a Sunday excursion.[97]

The May Third events included some activities that more clearly combined entertainment and propaganda. These included demonstrations of different varieties of masculine prowess by the Polish gymnastic society, Falcon (Sokol) and the Insurgent League. In an event that was more overtly staged to send a message, before the festival five of Poland's champion cyclists set out on a tour of symbolic Polish sites. Beginning at the northern tip of the Polish Corridor (since 1919 Poland's geographic passage through formerly German territory to the Baltic Sea), where they collected bottles of seawater, they traveled southeast, along the way collecting soil from notable "Polish territories," such as Poznań, until they arrived in Katowice. According to official reports, they covered the 825 kilometers (513 miles) in only 36 hours and 11 minutes. As part of the May Third festivities, the bicyclists ceremoniously delivered the seawater and soil samples to Poland's president, thereby representing the Upper Silesian borderland's ties with the rest of Poland and its leaders. In a similar gesture symbolizing the region's "Polish character," officials released thousands of doves that carried the printed message "Greetings from the Silesian Land," which they were to deliver to other parts of Poland. The organizers of this stunt had to make sure that these birds flew in the right direction, rather than across the border into Germany.[98]

Radicalism and the Rallies of 1931

The two border rallies held in 1931 provoked the usual controversies within and between the two Upper Silesian provinces. Most notably, they revealed—indeed, appealed to—the increasingly contentious internal politics on both sides of the border, in particular the growing influence of right-wing nationalism. In the Voivodeship, Grażyński's propaganda war against Wojciech Korfanty's liberal and regionalist Christian Democrats (ChD) thwarted any possibility of reconciliation, while in the Provinz, the antirepublican right rejected the German Center Party government's offer of a "citizen's peace" (*Bürgerfrieden*).[99] Both the German Center Party and the Polish Christian Democrats had themselves nurtured the irredentist culture that radical nationalists (Nazis and the Sanacja) used for their self-legitimation. By supporting their own territorial interests, they now continued to play into the hands of these right-wing forces.

Working across the border with their supporters in the Volksbund, German borderland nationalists in the Provinz exploited the social fractures that underlay regional political rivalries in the Voivodeship. They took particular advantage of the most significant conflict: that between newcomers from other parts of Poland, who became the new elites and promoters of "Polish civilization," and the resentful native locals, who felt marginalized and "colonized" by them (see chapter 1). To a large extent, this fracture was embodied in the Voivodeship's two rival politicians: the former nationalist-turned-regionalist Wojciech Korfanty, who supported the cause of locals, and the newcomer Michał Grażyński, who privileged the entry of the outside elite into government and industrial management posts. The German camp (the German Center Party and the Volksbund) conveniently represented the conflict in nationalist discourse: namely, as one of "German" Upper Silesians against Polish "colonizers." Whereas it had once referred to Korfanty as an illegitimate "dictator of Upper Silesia," it now portrayed his regionalist and liberal attacks on Grażyński as reflecting local opinion in Polish Upper Silesia. Thus, his boycott of the 1931 May Third festival showed that the newcomer Polish elite had "orchestrated" this irredentist event, which found no support among the "real" Upper Silesians, who remained loyal to Prussia and Germany.[100] As evidence of local opinion, a German Center Party publication cited a report from a pro-Korfanty Warsaw newspaper that thirty trains had transported 40,000 "foreign" guests to the rally—many of them higher-class Poles from other parts of the country; after they left, an equivalent number of unemployed Upper Silesian workers would remain and suffer under Sanacja misrule. The same German Center Party publication backed the ChD's attacks on Grażyński for the damage his radical and capricious politics had inflicted on Poland's international reputation, in particular his abuse of the Geneva Convention's minority protections.[101] The publication's intent was less to laud Korfanty and the ChD than to assert the enduring German self-identity of the *Ostoberschlesier* (eastern Upper Silesian—a German revanchist term) and the "bitter disappointments" suffered by Silesians under Polish governance.[102] In using Korfanty's opposition to Grazyński's more radical borderland nationalism as a propaganda tool for their revisionism, the German Center Party effectively discredited the ChD's moderate position in favor of Sanacja extremism.

The Provinz's German Center Party government intensified the emotional weight of the tenth anniversary of the partition by holding its commemorative rally on 25 May 1931 atop the Mount of St. Anne. This most symbolic battleground of the 1921 conflict had long been a favorite gathering place for former insurgents as well as for nationalist militants and radicals more generally. The 1931 event officially inaugurated its long career as a prime irredentist symbol for both Germany and Poland. The proceedings began when German Center Party leaders Carl Ulitzka and Hans Lukaschek, joined by *Selbstschutz* commander Karl Hoefer, unveiled a plaque memorializing the support of "national comrades of all German roots," thanks to which the *Oberschlesische Volk* had "defended itself against its enemy's thieving passions, and thereby saved a large area of German land from a foreign yoke."[103] This one-sided myth of the region's natives uniting with the German nation to protect German land from Polish marauders continued largely unchanged into the late 1930s, when the Nazis appropriated the site for their own political use (see chapter 3). By placing this plaque inside the youth hostel at the Franciscan cloister, an important rest area for pilgrims and other visitors to the mount, the German Center Party turned this age-old regional religious shrine into a nationalist propaganda symbol.

More than just a rejoinder to the Polish nationalists' use of their May Third rally to honor the insurgents, the event at the Mount of St. Anne represented the German Center Party's effort to maintain its grip on the official memory of the heroic years of 1919–22, which was in danger of being stolen by radical nationalists. Most rally participants marched in rank-and-file formations, including troops from both the Reichswehr and the republic's paramilitary organization Reichsbanner Schwarz-Rot-Gold, as well as veteran fighters from 1919–22. Yet this effort to assert government authority and unity crumbled when antirepublican militants joined Nazi SA men in an attempt to disturb the event and attack participants, which escalated from shouting and whistling down speakers to fistfights before the police restored order.[104]

In unison, the Polish press expressed outrage that "the Germans" had staged such a militaristic event at the region's most controversial and hallowed site. Ignoring the conflict exposed between moderates and radicals, Polish irredentists treated the rally as evidence of imminent German aggression and the need for all Poles to unite under a common cause. By thus reinforcing the myth of an "endangered borderland," the German border rallies of 1931 ultimately served Grażyński's radicalism and marginalized Korfanty's opposition. Their aggressive symbolism drove the Sanacja and the ChD to put their mutual antagonisms aside and stand together in "defense" against "German revisionism." The pro-Korfanty *Polonia* referred to the 1931 Plebiscite Day rally as a German "attack on Poles and the Polish state." It also denounced "Polish citizens"—mainly members of the German minority—who wrote letters to newspapers in the Provinz swearing their loyalty to the German revisionist cause. By claiming that there was a "German fifth column" in the Voivodeship, the ChD fueled the Germanophobic political atmosphere that ultimately legitimated the Sanacja regime.[105] In its reviews of the 1931 German rallies in the tricity area, the pro-Korfanty Polish minority paper in Beuthen, *Katolik Codzienny*, observed that "one must note with strong emphasis that the German Catholic Center and even the SPD hardly distinguish themselves from the *clearly nationalist* parties."[106] In similar bipartisan nationalist agreement, Korfanty's monolithic portrayal of "Germans" undermined his opposition to Grażyński.

Voices of Indifference

It is important to note that some political groups in the region did reject the irredentist and militaristic political culture that otherwise transcended Upper Silesia's border. By and large, the contingent of nationally indifferent Upper Silesians kept their opinions on the German-Polish conflict to themselves. The German Communists were foremost among the few outspoken in their rejection of irredentism. Particularly during times of economic crisis, workers used the border rallies to demonstrate their discontent. For example, at the 1925 May Third event in Katowice, they raised banners calling for "work" and "bread."[107] In 1931, the German Communist Party (KPD) staged an alternate Plebiscite Day event, in opposition to what their press organ, the *Rote Fahne*, described as the "Polish-German nationalist hype over Upper Silesia." Workers from both sides were to meet on the border near the tricity area and demonstrate in "proletarian brotherhood" against "German and Polish capitalists." The rally proceeded in defiance of a ban by local German authorities, leading to street clashes between workers and the police.[108] Although the SPD harbored its own nationalist strains, *Vorwärts*, the national party's paper, denounced some of the most flagrantly militaristic and provocative rallies, including the 1931 Mount of St. Anne event.[109]

In the Voivodeship, the regional autonomy movement led by Jan Kustos, the Upper Silesian Defense League (ZOG), also rejected German and Polish nationalisms and the related transnational irredentist culture. Instead, they sought to protect the rights and welfare of native Upper Silesians against discrimination, in particular their social and economic marginalization by newcomers who migrated from other parts of Poland after the partition. The ZOG also promoted greater autonomy for eastern Upper Silesia within the Polish state, most notably recognition and privileges for its "distinct" bilingual and region-oriented culture. Kustos even made occasional overtures regarding an independent Upper Silesian state. Although the ZOG failed to gain strong electoral support, its views found widespread favor among Upper Silesians.[110]

For proponents of regionalism, the plebiscite marked the moment when Upper Silesians had been granted the kind of internationally sanctioned right of self-determination currently denied them. Thus, Kustos—like Korfanty—called for a revival of Plebiscite Day celebrations after Grażyński banned them, in order to deny Germans a monopoly on memorialization of the event. Nonetheless, Kustos held the ChD leader responsible for having initiated the tradition of May Third rallies, whose glorification of the insurgencies drew attention away from the memory of the plebiscite itself. Consequently, Kustos and his party denounced the 1931 May Third rally, using ChD-like rhetoric that charged the Sanacja and upper-class Poles with "celebrating" while ordinary people went hungry or were "forced to commute across the border to work for the 'Germanians' [a Polish nationalist slur for Germans] just to have bread."[111] The ZOG's newspaper, the bilingual (German and Polish) *Upper Silesian Voice*, addressed the legacy of 1919–22 by calling the sacrifices local citizens had made for Poland's cause "a waste," since the "Upper Silesian peoples" had ended up oppressed, marginalized, and exploited by Grażyński and his newcomer followers.[112] Driven primarily by a desire to use regionalist discourse for German revanchism, the Volksbund tended to echo and support ChD and ZOG propaganda, and thereby also gained local sympathy.

The role of revanchist rallies as the ideological bread and butter for German nationalists ended with the Nazi assumption of power in Germany in late January of 1933. Soon thereafter, the right wing of the German Homeland Patriots wrested control over the plebiscite celebrations from the German Center Party and their prorepublican allies.[113] They promptly began planning a Plebiscite Day spectacle of unprecedented militancy, bombast, and chauvinism that would match or exceed anything Grażyński could contrive for the fifteenth anniversary of the third Silesian insurgency. Their plans were cut short when Hitler quashed the tradition of German border rallies—largely for the supremely ironic reason that in late January of 1934, Germany had signed a nonaggression pact with Poland.[114] Subsequent commemorations of the events of 1921 were modest assemblies for party members organized by the Nazi League of the German East (BDO), which had incorporated the German Homeland Patriots and all similar organizations.[115]

Thus, from 1934 on, old-fashioned border rallies were a one-sided Grażyński-dominated show. While these events continued to glorify the insurgencies, the Warsaw government—to honor its pact with Germany—pressured their organizers, the Western Territories Defense League (ZOKZ), the Insurgent League, and the Sanacja government, to tone down Germanophobic actions and rhetoric. That same year, the ZOKZ changed its name to the less provocative Polish Western League (PZZ) and—at the urging of the Polish government—moved its headquarters from the contested border city of Poznań (Posen) to Warsaw. Even under its new identity, the organization continued to oppose the nonaggression pact, which it interpreted as a sign of German weakness, and to uphold its vow to "defend" the borderlands.[116]

So Who Were the More Rabid Nationalists?

The development of a "tradition" of irredentist spectacles was an inherently transnational process, in which Germany and Poland influenced each other's discourse and strategies. Indeed, the particular features of one nation's rally can often be explained as attempts to outdo the other's efforts in grandeur, resonance, and displays of "unity" and military power. Each nation mobilized a vast array of resources, from media and transportation technology to organizational work and infrastructure building, in an effort to win the contest. In the end, neither side could claim a clear-cut victory, nor can we from this distance easily identify one side as "the victim" of revanchist politics and the other as "the aggressor." Rather, in their contentious interactions, the German and Polish rallies collectively defined Upper Silesia as a borderland dividing two mutually antagonistic nation-states. Beyond their symbolic value, the rallies provided platforms from which officials from each side launched complaints to the German-Polish Mixed Commission in Geneva against the aggressive "excesses" of the other's rallies.[117]

Warmongering became a key feature of border rallies, although only the Voivodeship—with its midnight gunfire at the border announcing the "storming of Katowice"—made it integral from the outset. On both sides of the border, such events seemed to foretell impending *hot war*, especially when elaborated upon by public officials. For example, at the Polish Plebiscite Day festivity in 1927, Marshal Piłsudski's representative, General Jan Romer, told foreign journalists: "One should not fool oneself, because this war [between Germany and Poland] will come." According to observations from the Provinz, at the same event, another member of the military personnel, Major Schranowski, enthusiastically offered "three cheers for the war and for our future march to the Oder."[118] Such comments fed episodes of violence against fellow citizens who were identified as "Germans." The Insurgent League, its reputation burnished by its members' prominent role in the irredentist rallies, became Grażyński's primary enforcer of violence and terror. The existence of such groups in turn provided legitimacy for nationalist and militant groups in the Provinz. Indeed, by supplying evidence of Poland's aggressive intent toward Germany, the rallies provided the Nazis an opportunity in 1939 to use a fake "Polish takeover" of the Gleiwitz radio tower to shift blame for launching the war on the Poles.

In both Germany and Poland the rallies served to bring the respective nation closer to a region far removed from the centers of national culture. They also attracted diverse fellow citizens, from ordinary workers to chancellors and presidents, who joined together for ceremonial expressions of common defiance of the "aggressive neighbor." The press, radio, and film conveyed news of the rallies far and wide across both nations, thereby relaying shared borderland myths, for example, Upper Silesia as a "bleeding" and "endangered" border that demanded a "united national front," both to "stand on guard" and defend its half of the region against an aggressive enemy and to work to "recover" territory that remained under "foreign yoke." This borderland rhetoric, which was also invoked for other contested borderlands, became an important pillar of national identity in interwar Germany and Poland. Centrist regional governments on both sides initially adopted a relatively temperate critique of the border issue; however, their calls for the ultimate "return" of lost territory delegitimized the entire postwar settlement and undermined democracy in both nations. Similarly, while liberals vowed to defend democracy, the rallies gave militant nationalists a stage for promoting their opposition to peace and lawfulness using the irredentist rhetoric first advanced by their centrist opponents. This discourse, developed by German and Polish border nationalists to promote their efforts to scuttle any acceptance of the territorial settlement, later became the bread and butter of the Sanacja, Nazi, and postwar Communist regimes.

While the rallies succeeded in fomenting distrust of the alleged national enemy, they failed—on both sides of the border—to cement the bonds between the average Upper Silesian and the particular nation to which he or she had been assigned. Whether out of political or national indifference, or simply weary from protracted border disputes, residents on both sides of the partition seemed incapable of displaying enthusiasm about the rallies. Those who attended were not necessarily moved by patriotic conviction, nor did they always agree with what they heard.[119] Pressure from trade unions, employers, cultural and social organizations, or—in the case of youngsters—schoolteachers often provided motivation. Discounted railroad tickets attracted still others, including some day-tripping tourists, not to mention the lure of games and entertainment, food and drink, and on occasion even offers of cash. In the end, it was the turnout that mattered to the government authorities and borderland nationalists that organized the rallies. By this criterion, the organizers succeeded, in particular for the special fifth and tenth anniversaries of the events of 1921.

The German and Polish governments saw large-scale commemorations of significant events as vehicles for demonstrating a "vast popular will" in Upper Silesia for their respective national causes. Each side used the media to play up the meager turnout at rallies on the other side of the border—or explained impressive numbers by the use of chicanery or pressure from bosses or unions. Beyond the wish to impress their neighbor with a "united national front," they also sought to "awaken" patriotism in a borderland where national identity was relative, contingent, and fluctuating. Each national camp meant to represent the region with one exclusive national identity; collectively, however, their rallies offered a diverse array of Silesian identities that ultimately undermined every nationalizing campaign. Indeed, because these campaigns used regionalist symbols, dialects, and traditions in the interest of promoting German or Polish identity, they also encouraged Silesian consciousness. As I show in the next chapters, neither Germany nor Poland sought to erase this regionalism; to the contrary, they sought to cultivate it—albeit often by making it an instrument of irredentist politics and eventual nationalization. Through such tactics, national actors officially recognized local indifference to nationalism, even encouraging it within the "other" camp for their own political advantage.

Notes

1. Jan Pyrlik, "My i Oni," *Polska Zachodnia* (PZ) 15 (11 Apr. 1926): 1.

2. "In Ostoberschlesien werden die Aufstände gefeiert," *Oberschlesische Volksstimme* (OSV) 204 (3 May 1931), Archiwum Państwowe w Opolu (APO), 1 (Oberpräsidium Oppeln), 181, 57.

3. "Ansprache des Wojewodes an den polnischen Staatspräsidenten in Ostoberschlesien," 2 Oct. 1927, GStA PK, I. HA, rep. 77, tit. 856, no. 637, n.p.; "Z działalności Prezydenta Ignacego Mościckiego w Chorzowie," PZ 231 (3 Oct. 1927): 1–3; Deutsche Generalkonsulat in Kattowitz (Genkons.) to Auswärtigen Amt (AA), 6 Oct. 1927, GStA PK, I. HA, rep. 77, tit. 856, no. 733, 9–12. See also Hitze, *Carl Ulitzka*, 633–38.

4. Falęcki, "Powstańcy Śląscy w ruchu," 167–70.

5. Genkons. to AA, 25 Feb. 1923, GStA PK, I HA, rep. 77, tit. 856, no. 428, 19; Leitendes Grenzkommisariat Oppeln, 6 April 1923, APO, 1, 242, 33; Falęcki, *Powstańcy Ślascy*, 56.
6. Genkons. to AA, 25 Feb. 1923, GStA PK, I HA, rep. 77, tit. 856, no. 428, 19.
7. "Denkt an Oberschlesien," *Oberschlesische Zeitung* 65 (20 March 1923): n.p. Plebiscite Day rallies were sometimes held on days other than the actual anniversary, depending on when the date fell in a particular year.
8. "Nachtübung der Aufständischen," 25 June 1924, GStA PK, I HA, rep. 77, tit. 856, no. 429, n.p. Most likely, they were firing blanks.
9. Genkons. to AA, 17 April 1923, GStA PK, I HA, rep. 77, tit. 856, no. 428, 5. See also "Ordnung!," *Ostdeutsche Morgenpost* (ODM), 17 Apr. 1923, 1; Kon. Byt. to MSZ, 11 Apr. 1923, AAN, 482, 8, 15.
10. Genkons. to AA, 17 April 1923, GStA PK, I HA, rep. 77, tit. 856, no. 428, 5; Staatskommission für Öffentliche Ordnung, "Polnische Bewegung in Oberschlesien," 17 May 1923, GStA PK, I HA, rep. 77, tit. 856, no. 428, 83–84.
11. Kon. Byt. to MSZ, 20 May 1923, AAN, 482, 8, 23.
12. Staatskommission für Öffentliche Ordnung, "Polnische Bewegung in Oberschlesien," 17 May 1923, GStA PK, I HA, rep. 77, tit. 856, no. 428, 84. See also Blanke, *Orphans of Versailles*, 136.
13. See Andrzej Michalczyk, "Celebrating the Nation: The Case of Upper Silesia after the Plebiscite in 1921," in *Four Empires and an Enlargement: States, Societies and Individuals in Central and Eastern Europe*, ed. Claire Jarvis, Daniel Brett, and Irina Marin (London, 2008), 51ff.; Haubold-Stolle, *Mythos Oberschlesien*, 213.
14. See Haubold-Stolle, *Mythos Oberschlesien*, 214.
15. "Der Nationalfeiertag," *Oberschlesische Grenzzeitung* 51, no. 101 (4 May 1923): and "Die polnische Nationalfeiertag in Kattowitz," *Schlesische Zeitung* 206 (4 May 1923) in APO, 1, 180, 2–4.
16. "Bombenatentat auf die Wohnung des Freiherrn von Reizenstein in Pilgramsdorf," *Kattowitzer Zeitung* (KZ) 199 (5 May 1923); Oberpräsident (OP) to Pr. MdI, 8 May 1923, APO, 1, 180, 4, 8.
17. Leitendes Grenzkommisariat to OP, 10 May 1925, APO, 1, 180, 47ff.
18. Ibid.
19. OP to Landräte and Oberbürgermeister, 17 March 1924, APO, 1, 34, 17–18.
20. Ibid.
21. Ibid.
22. These parties and allied groups included the mainstream German National People's Party (DNVP), whose views were promoted by Hans Schadewaldt's *Ostdeutsche Morgenpost* in Beuthen, as well as by the (still relatively marginal) Nazi Party and illegal paramilitary groups such as the *Stahlhelm* and *Freikorps*. Many of these right-wingers were also in the ranks of the VVHO, another reason why the centrists sought to master this organization and its activities, the rallies in particular. See Haubold-Stolle, *Mythos Oberschlesien*, 90–93; Hitze, *Carl Ulitzka*, 843–47.
23. Kon. Byt. to MSZ, 26 Mar. 1924, AAN, 482, 196, 1ff. See also Haubold-Stolle, "Mythos Oberschlesien," 297–99.
24. OP to Landräte und Oberbürgermeister, 17 March 1924, APO, 1, 34, 17–18.
25. Ibid.
26. Ibid.
27. Ibid.
28. Ibid.; Alfons Proske, "Oberschlesier!," 20 Mar. 1924, APO, 1, 34, 9.
29. Proske, "Oberschlesier!"
30. Kon. Byt. to MSZ, 26 Mar. 1924, AAN, 482, 196, 1.
31. Ibid., 7.

32. "Senatmarschall Tramczyński und die Abstimmung in Oberschlesien" [Polish newspaper article translated into German], *Polonia* 81 (22 March 1926), APO, 1, 180, 85–86. See also Michałczyk, "Celebrating the Nation," 55.

33. Several tens of thousands (around 50,000 according to *Polonia*) participated in these events in Katowice and in the border areas, including Rybnik and Tarnowskie Góry. The ChD worked with the patriotic societies to maximize the turnout. See Bogdana Cimała, "Obchody Rocznic Plebiscytowych na Górnym Śląsku w latach 1924–1927," *Kronika Katowic* 6 (1996): 119–31.

34. Andrzej Michałczyk, "Deutsche und polnische Nationalisierungspolitik in Oberschlesien zwischen den Weltkriegen: Ein Vergleich auf Makro- und Mikroebene," in *Die Destruktion des Dialogs: Zur innenpolitischen Instrumentalisierung negativer Fremd- und Feindbilder Polen, Tschechien, Deutschland und die Niederlande im Vergleich, 1900–2005*, ed. Dieter Bingen, Peter Oliver Loew, and Kazimierz Wóycicki (Wiesbaden, 2007), 75.

35. Kon. Byt. to MSZ, 9 Apr. 1925, AAN, 482, 196, 20.

36. The actual numbers were probably larger. Kon. Byt. to MSZ, AAN, 482, 196, 35. According to the Polish consulate, the VVHO had some 60,000 followers in Gleiwitz in early 1932. Kon. Byt. to MSZ, 12 Feb. 1932, AAN, 482, 8, 107. Hitze (*Carl Ulitzka*, 1054) also mentions the city as a VVHO stronghold.

37. See Franciszek Serafin, "Stosunki demograficzne i społeczne," in *Województwo Śląskie*, ed. Franciszek Serafin (Katowice, 1996), 87. The estimate is 217,000 by 1925 according to Heffner and Lesiuk, "Ekonomiczne i Społeczne Skutki," 148.

38. Kon. Byt. to MSZ, 26 Mar. 1925, AAN, 482, 196, 35.

39. Ibid.

40. Kon. Byt. to MSZ, 22 July 1927, AAN, 492, 196, 54; Oberbürgermeister Beuthen to Regierungspräsidenten Oppeln, 28 July 1922, APK, 635 (Akta Miasta Bytomia), 4335, 1. On the political use of refugees during the Weimar and Nazi eras, see Peter Polak-Springer, "'Borderless Misery': The Political Use of Refugees in German Upper Silesia during the Weimar and Nazi Eras," in *Cultural Landscapes: Transatlantische Perspektiven auf Wirkungen und Auswirkungen deutscher Kultur und Geschichte im Östlichen Europa*, ed. Andrew Demshuk and Tobias Weger (Oldenbourg, 2015).

41. See Franciszek Serafin, "Stosunki demograficzne i społeczne," in Województwo Śląskie, ed. *Franciszek Serafin* (Katowice, 1996), 80. The estimate is 60,000 by 1923 and another 100,000 in later years according to Heffner and Lesiuk, "Ekonomiczne i Społeczne Skutki," 148–51.

42. "Walny zjazd delegatów i prezesów Związku Uchódców Śląskich w Katowicach," 27 July 1927, APK, Urząd Wojewódzki Śląski 27/I (Wydział Społeczno-Polityczny), 491, 296 (and others in this file set).

43. OP to Preussische Ministerpräsidenten, 29 December 1925, APO, 1, 34, 166.

44. Regierungspräsidenten Oppeln to various officials, 7 March 1926, APO, 1, 34, 296; Urbanek to OP, 8 March 1926, APO, 1, 34, 301; Bürgermeister Beuthen to OP, 1 Apr. 1926, APO, 1, 34, 363–64.

45. Kon. Byt. to MSZ, 23 Mar. 1926, AAN, 482, 196, 81.

46. "Deutsche vergesst es nie!," OSV 80 (21 Mar. 1926); Kon. Byt. to MSZ, 18 Feb. 1926, AAN, 482, 196, 39.

47. Bürgermeister Beuthen to OP, APO, 1, 34, 363–64.

48. "Hunderttausend Menschen haben in Kattowitz zum Beweis ihrer heissen Anhänglichkeit an Polen manifestiert" [trans. from Polish to German], *Goniec Górnośląski* 77 (22 Mar. 1926), APO, 1, 180, 93.

49. "Na straży potężny głos!," PZ 13 (28 Mar. 1926): 1–6; Leitendes Grenzkommissariat to OP, 24 Mar. 1926, APO, 1, 180, 82.

50. "Kattowitz," *Oberschlesisches Kurier* 83 (19 Mar. 1926), APO, 1, 180, 83; "Hundertausend Menschen haben in Kattowitz zum Beweis ihrer heissen Anhänglichkeit an Polen manifestiert" [trans. from Polish to German], *Goniec Górnośląski* 77 (22 Mar. 1926), APO, 1, 180, 93.

51. "Kattowitz," *Oberschlesisches Kurier* 83 (19 Mar. 1926), APO, 1, 180, 83; Reichszentrale für Heimatdienst (RH), Oberschlesische (O/S) Grenzbericht, Apr. 1926, GStA PK, I HA, rep. 77, tit. 856, no. 592, 153ff.; Polizeipräsident to OP, 27 Mar. 1926, APO, 1, 180, 87.

52. "Uroczystość rządowa w Opolu," *Katolik Codzienny* 72 (30 Mar. 1926): 1; Kon. Byt. to MSZ, 30 Mar. 1926, AAN, 482, 196, 60, 65; "Die Abstimmungsgedenkfeier in Oppeln," *Oberschlesische Zeitung* 88 (29 Mar. 1926).

53. Kon. Byt. to MSZ, 30 Mar. 1926, AAN, 482, 196, 60, 65.

54. "Abstimmungsdemonstrationen in Kattowitz," KZ 66 (22 Mar. 1927), GStA PK, I HA, rep. 77, tit. 856, no. 732, 187; OP to Pr. MdI, 6 Apr. 1927, GStA PK, I HA, rep. 77, tit. 856, no. 732, 208; RH, O/S Grenzbericht, Mar. 1927, GStA, PK, I HA, rep. 77, tit. 856, no. 592, 321ff. See also Michałczyk, "Deutsche und polnische Nationalisierungspolitiken," 75–78.

55. Landrat Gross Strehlitz to OP, 12 Mar. 1925, APO, 1, 34, 58.

56. Wojciech Korfanty, "Po Manifestacji," *Polonia* 80 (22 Mar. 1927): 2.

57. RH, O/S Grenzbericht, May 1927, GStA PK, I HA, rep. 77, tit. 856, no. 592, 358–59; "Der Nationalfeiertag in der Wojewodschaft," OSV 121 (4 May 1927), GStA PK, I HA, rep. 77, tit. 856, no. 732, 233.

58. "Aufzeihnung über der Errinerungen Grazynskis [sic]," n.d., Politisches Archiv des Auswärtigen Amtes (PA-AA), Warschau 47 (P17), n.p. On Grażyński, see chapter 1.

59. "Ein deutscher Gedenktag," *Ostpreussische Zeitung*, 68 (22 Mar. 1927), GStA PK, I HA, rep. 77, tit. 856, no. 732, 188; Genkons. to AA, 21 Mar. 1928, GStA PK, I HA, rep. 77, tit. 856, no. 733, 45; Polizeipräsident Landespolizeistelle Oppeln to OP, 24 Mar. 1931, APO, 1, 181, 9; "Warum veranstalten die Schulbehörden in Polnischoberschlesien keine Abstimmungsfeiern?!" [German trans.], *Polonia* 2317 (19 Mar. 1931), APO, 1, 181, 15.

60. Polizeipräsident to OP, 27 Mar. 1926, APO, 1, 180, 87; Genkons. to AA, 6 Oct. 1927, GStA PK, I HA, rep. 77, tit. 856, no. 733, 9; Genkons. to AA, 7 May 1929, GStA PK, I HA, rep. 77, tit. 856, no. 733, 129, 135, 138.

61. Konsulat Generalny Rzeczypospolitej Polskiej w Opolu (Kon. Op.) to MSZ, 22 Mar. 1927, AAN, 482, 196, 107.

62. See Urszula Biel, "Płonące premiery: Z diejów polsko-niemieckiego pogranicza na Górnym Śląsku," in *Kino niemieckie w dialogu pokoleń i kultur: Studie i szkice*, ed. Andrzej Gwóźdź (Cracow, 2004), 329–31.

63. Kon. Op. to MSZ, 22 Mar. 1927, AAN, 482, 196, 107.

64. Kon. Op. to MSZ, 28 Feb. 1927, AAN, 482, 190, 44; Ulrich Kayser, dir., *Land unterm Kreuz: Ein Film von Oberschlesiens schwierigsten Zeit*, Bundesarchiv Filmarchiv, Sygn. 21553, Eingangsnr. B 56922-1; Haubold-Stolle, *Mythos Oberschlesien*, 110–115. See also Vejas Gabriel Liulevicius, "The Languages of Occupation: Vocabularies of German Rule in Eastern Europe during the World Wars," in *Germans, Poland, and Colonial Expansion to the East*, ed. Robert L. Nelson (New York, 2009), 128.

65. Kon. Byt. to MSZ, 8 Mar. 1927, AAN, 482, 190, 53; Kon. Op. to MSZ, 30 Mar. 1927, AAN, 482, 190, 89; Biel, "Płonące premiery," 321–25.

66. "Śląski Film propagandowy," PZ 45 (24 Oct. 1926); "Prowokacyjny film antypolski został uroczyście wyświetlony w Gliwicach," PZ 65 (21 Mar. 1927): 2.

67. "Pokaz filmu Śląsk Źrenica Polski," PZ 123 (31 May 1927); Biel, "Płonące premiery," 329–30.

68. Kape-Film to Magistrat Pszczyński, 22 Apr. 1929, APK-Pszczyna, 26 (Akta Miasta Pszczyna), 3319, 191. The Polish General Exhibition (Powszechna Wystatwa Krajowa) was held from mid-May to mid-September 1929.

69. RH, O/S Grenzbericht, Nov. 1925, GStA PK, I HA, rep. 77, tit. 856, no. 592, 117.

70. See Polak-Springer, "Jammin' with Karlik," 279–300.

71. For an English translation of the lyrics of Konopicka's "Rota," see Kamusella, *Silesia and Central European Nationalisms*, 171.

72. "Na Straży Śląskiej Potężny Głos," PZ 13 (28 March 1926): 1–3.
73. Kon. Op. to MSZ, 9 Apr. 1925, AAN, 482, 196, 20.
74. RH, O/S Grenzbericht, Dec. 1927–Jan. 1928, GStA PK, I HA, rep. 77, tit. 856, no. 593, Bd. 2, 71.
75. Polak-Springer, "Jammin' with Karlik.'"
76. See Franciszek Hawranek et al., eds., *Encyklopedia Powstań Śląskich* (Opole, 1982), 430–31.
77. "Das 'Schlesische' Volksfest," KZ 102 (4 May 1931), n.p.; Hitze, *Carl Ulitzka*, 1038–54; Serafin, *Województwo Śląskie*, 158–65.
78. Konsulat Generalny Rzeczypospolitej Poslkiej w Breslau (Kon. Br.) to Ambasada Polska w Berlinie (Amb. Ber.), 17 Mar. 1931, AAN, 474 (Ambasada RP, Berlin), 2468, 136.
79. Kon. Byt. to MSZ, 9 Mar. 1931, AAN, 482, 198, 10; Kon. Byt. to MSZ, 26 Mar 1925, AAN, 482, 196, 39–40; see also "In Treue verbunden: O/S Kundgebungen der Bayern," OSV, GStA PK, I HA, rep. 77, tit. 856, no. 390, 125.
80. See Hitze, *Carl Ulitzka*, 1046.
81. *Gesamtüberblick über die polnische Presse* 26 (4 Apr. 1931), GStA PK, no. 390, 99.
82. "Der Zehnjahrestag der Abstimmung in O/S," *Oberschlesien* 6 (1 June 1930), GStA PK, I HA, rep. 77, tit. 856, no. 390, 141.
83. RH, O/S Grenzbericht, Jan.–Mar. 1931, GStA, I HA, rep. 77, tit. 856, no. 593, Bd. 3, 2ff.
84. Ibid., 2ff.
85. "Der O/S Gedenktag," *Germania*, 23 Mar. 1931, GStA PK, I HA, rep. 77, tit. 856, no. 390, 69.
86. See James Bjork and Robert Gerwarth, "The Annaberg as a German-Polish 'Lieu de Memoire,'" *German History* 25, no. 3 (2007): 379–86; Juliane Haubold-Stolle, "Der heilige Berg Oberschlesiens—der Sankt Annaberg als Errinerungsort," in *Schlesische Errinerungsorte: Gedächtnis und Identität einer mitteleuropäischen Region*, ed. Marek Czapliński et al. (Görlitz, 2005), 202–20.
87. Kon. Byt. to MSZ, 9 Mar. 1931, AAN, 482, 198, 10; Kammer dir. Hoffmeister, "Der Zehnjahrestag der Abstimmung," *Oberschlesien* 6 (1 June 1930), GStA PK, I HA, rep. 77, tit. 856, no. 390, 141.
88. *Gesamtüberblick über die polnische Presse*, 15 Apr. 1931, GStA PK, I HA, rep. 77, tit. 856, no. 390, 103;; "Herr, mach uns einig und frei," *Oberschlesische Wanderer* (OSW) 69 (24 Mar. 1931): n.p.
89. *Gesamtüberblick über die polnische Presse*, 15 Apr. 1931, GStA PK, I HA, rep. 77, tit. 856, no. 390, 103.
90. RH, O/S Grenzbericht, Jan.-Mar. 1931, GStA, I HA, rep. 77, tit. 856, no. 593, Bd. 3, 2–3; "Wie O/S der Abstimmung gedenkt: Fahnen mit Trauerflor," OSW 68 (22 Mar. 1931): n.p.
91. "Górny Śląsk jest Polski i chce Polski pozostać," *Katolik Codzienny*, 24 Mar. 1931, Kon. Byt. to MSZ, AAN, 482, 198, 36ff; Haubold-Stolle, *Mythos Oberschlesien*, 129–33.
92. Descriptions of these events in "Wie O/S der Abstimmung gedenkt: Fahnen mit Trauerflor," OSW 68 (22 Mar. 1931): n.p.; "Herr, mach uns einig und frei," OSW 69 (24 Mar. 1931): n.p.; "Grüsse aus dem Reich: Ganz Deutschland gedenkt den Abstimmungstag," OSW 68 (22 Mar. 1931): n.p.; "Innenminister Severing bei der Hindenburger Kundgebung," OSW 70 (25 Mar. 1931): n.p.
93. "In Treue verbunden: OS-Kundgebungen der Bayern," OSV, GStA PK, I HA, rep. 77, tit. 856, no. 390, 109.
94. "Das 'Schlesische' Volksfest," KZ 102 (4 May 1931), n.p.; "Echa wielkiego dnia," PZ 112 (4 May 1931): 2–3; Polizeipräsident to OP, 4 May 1931, APO, 1, 181, 35.
95. Polizeipräsident to OP, 6 May 1931, APO, 1, 181, 62.
96. Ibid., 62; "Echa wielkiego dnia," PZ 112 (4 May 1931): 2–3; "Die grösste Massenveranstaltung seit der Abstimmung: Amtliche Feier des 3. Schlesische Auffstandes," *KZ Beiblatt* (4 May 1931): 1; Polizeipräsident to OP, 6 May 1931, APO, 1, 181, 62.
97. "Śląski Maj 1921–2 Maj 1931," PZ 111 (2 May 1931): 1. For this in earlier years, see "Abstimmungsdemonstrationen in Kattowitz," KZ 66 (22 Mar. 1927), GStA PK, I HA, rep. 77, tit. 856, no. 732, 187.

98. Descriptions of these events are in: "Śląski Maj 1921–2 Maj 1931," PZ 111 (2 May 1931): 1; "Echa wielkiego dnia," PZ 112 (4 May 1931): 3; "Polonia gegen rauschende 3. Mai Feier," KZ 90 (20 Apr. 1931): n.p., "Schlesien und die polnische Aufstandsfeiern," *Oberschlesische Zeitung* 224 (4 May 1931): n.p.; ZOKZ, SR, May 1931, APK, 27/I, 54, 84–85.

99. Kon. Byt. to MSZ, 24 Mar. 1931, AAN, 482, 198, 78. See also Hitze, *Carl Ulitzka*, 1054–57.

100. "Das 'Schlesische' Volksfest," KZ 102 (4 May 1931), n.p.; "Polonia gegen rauschende 3. Mai Feier," KZ 90 (20 Apr. 1931): n.p.

101. "Polnische Kritik an Grażyński," OSV 124 (6 May 1931), APO, 1, 181, 39. This is a German Center Party review of an article published by the anti-Sanacja Polish newspaper *Gazeta Warszawska*.

102. "In Ostoberschlesien wurden die Aufstände gefeiert," OSV 204 (3 May 1931), APO, 1, 181, 57; "Das 'Schlesische' Volksfest," KZ 102 (4 May 1931), n.p.; "Polonial gegen rauschene 3. Mai Feier," KZ 90 (20 Apr. 1931): n.p.

103. OSV 141 (23 May 1931), GStA PK, I HA, rep. 77, tit. 856, no. 390, 124.

104. See "Oberschlesien darf nicht verloren sein!" Der Tag 125 (26 May 1931), "Die Helden mit der Trillerpfeiffe," OSV 144 (27 May 1931), and other press articles in GStA PK, I HA, rep. 77, tit. 856, no. 390, 125–33. See also Haubold-Stolle, *Mythos Oberschlesien*, 120–23; Hitze, *Carl Ulitzka*, 1060–61.

105. *Gesamtüberblick über die polnische Presse*, 1–4 Apr. 1931, GStA PK, I HA, rep. 77, tit. 856, no. 390, 98–100.

106. Emphasis mine. Ibid., 99.

107. Leitendes Grenzkommisariat to OP, 10 May 1925, APO, 1, 180, 47; Michałczyk, "Deutsche und polnische Nationalisierungspolitiken," 75.

108. "Faschistische Oberschlesier feiern zum 10. Jahrestag der O/S Abstimmung," *Die Rote Fahne*, 22 Mar. 1931 (and similar articles from this newspaper), GStA PK, I HA, rep. 77, tit. 856, no. 390, 45, 48, 81.

109. See Haubold-Stolle, *Mythos Oberschlesien*, 150; Hitze, *Carl Ulitzka*, 1057.

110. The claim of 160,000 followers as of 1926 by the ZOG press in *Głos Górnego Śląska* (GGŚl.) is highly exaggerated. ZOG support did, however, grow once the Sanacja regime was in power. During the 1926 communal elections, the ZOG received 2.3 percent of the vote (9,083 votes). See Dobrowolski, *Ugrupowania*, 136, 154ff.

111. "Po 10 letniej uroczystości plebiscytowej w r. 1921 na Górnym Śląsku," GGŚl. 12 (25 Mar. 1931): 1–2.

112. Ibid., 1–2; "Zum 10. Jahrestag der Abstimmung in Oberschlesien," *Der Pränger* (German language section of GGŚl.) 11 (18 Mar. 1931): 1; "Co każdy Polak o Górnym Śląsku powinien wiedzieć," GGŚl. 125 (15 Apr. 1931): 1.

113. Kon. Byt. to MSZ, 26 Mar. 1933, AAN, 482, 30, 11–14.

114. Kon. Byt. to MSZ, 20 Mar. 1934, AAN, 482, 30, 52.

115. Reichsministerium des Innerns Berlin to OP, 19 May 1936, PA-AA, Warschau, 81, n.p.

116. "Überraschende Erklärung in Warschau: Westmarkenverein entpolitisiert!," KZ 266 (19 Nov. 1934), PA-AA, Konsulat Kattowitz, 45, Bd. 2, n.p.; Deutsche Bottschaft Warsaw to AA, 8 Nov. 1934, PA-AA, Konsulat Kattowitz, 45, Bd. 2, n.p.; Gestapo to Deutsche Konsulat in Kattowitz, PA-AA, Konsulat Kattowitz, 45, Bd. 2, n.p.; Genkons. to AA, 3 Feb. 1936, PA-AA, Konsulat Kattowitz, 45, Bd. 2, n.p.

117. Kon. Byt., correspondence with MSZ in March and May 1925, AAN, 482, 196, 14, 15, 19, 33; OP to Pr. MdI, 25 Mar. 1925, APO, 1, 34, 113.

118. RH, O/S Grenzbericht, Mar. 1927, GStA PK, I HA, rep. 77, tit. 856, no. 592, 321; "Abstimmungsdemonstration in Kattowitz," KZ 66 (22 Mar. 1927), GStA PK, I HA, rep. 77, tit. 856, no. 732, 187.

119. Michałczyk, "Deutsche und polnische Nationalisierungspolitiken," 74–76.

CHAPTER 3

ACCULTURATING AN INDUSTRIAL
BORDERLAND, 1926–39

"The competence of the German technician, the entrepreneurialism of the German businessman, the quality performance of the German worker and craftsman, and the tenacity of the German farmer have ... brought to the world new proof of the German's potential for achievement."

—President Paul von Hindenburg, Oppeln, September 1928[1]

"None of Poland's regions presents such a great cult of diligent and sacrificial work as ... Silesia. Here the production promoted by the hands of the Polish worker and the mind of the Polish technician and engineer are constantly strengthening the nation's power status."

—President Ignacy Mościcki, Katowice, May 1929[2]

Upper Silesia's partition between Germany and Poland caused disruptions and created needs for urban planning and building projects on both sides of the border. Indeed, much of the construction completed during the interwar era was part and parcel of wider modernization programs across the two nations. As part of the contest over the borderland, each side played up these development projects as "achievements" that demonstrated its superior stewardship, and thus supported its "right" to all of Upper Silesia. Showcasing modern architecture and the latest technology, cities on both sides of the border served to exemplify the superior "work," "culture," and "civilization" that—as I argue in this chapter—*both* nations claimed vis-à-vis one another. While governors, politicians, and clergy, as well as parading soldiers, paramilitary troops, and workers, played central roles in the rallies and festivals discussed in the previous chapter, architects and urban planners were also among the agents of progress and modernity examined in this chapter.[3]

Paralleling the futuristic displays, the contest over this region also looked backward. By digging up the past and reviving local traditions, partisans for Germany and Poland aimed to demonstrate their respective nation's historical roots and heritage in Upper Silesia. While the smoggy and congested industrial district was hardly a place for such "high cultural" projects before World War I, after the partition national figures rushed to establish new cultural institutions, including museums, research centers, institutes of higher education, theaters, and libraries. Academics, regionalists, and folklorists of both nations—best known by the German term *Heimatkundler* (regionalist or folklorist)—thus joined the ranks of combatants in this territorial cold war.[4] This chapter shows how they worked to restore, recover, and revive, but also to reinvent, standardize, and manipulate Silesian traditions—from dialects to costumes, songs, and dances—in an effort to demonstrate the links between the regional heritage and that of the larger nation.

German history offers numerous instances of the kinds of state-led patterns of development and advancement that were practiced in the eastern borderlands. Often associated with the term *Kulturträger* (Germany/Germans as culture/cultural missionaries), they refer to historical events ranging from Germanic settlement in the Middle Ages to "Germanization" during the Prussian and imperial eras (up to World War I). The historic Polish states are also known for having promoted similar processes in their own eastern regions. This chapter argues that *both* contenders for their common borderlands promoted notions of the superiority of their own national "work" (*Arbeit/praca*) and "culture" (*Kultur/kultura*, sometimes used synonymously with—though other times in contradiction to—"civilization"). In combination as "cultural work" (*Kulturarbeit/praca kulturowa*), the two concepts presented an uneasily coexisting expression of both modernity and tradition.[5] Each nation used the mandate to modernize and fight for its borderland, to acculturate, and to homogenize the cultural landscapes along national lines. Particularly in the case of the Sanacja and Nazi regimes, these lines were also partisan and ideological. Insofar as the deconstruction, symbolic erasure, and removal of the heritage of the national "other" was intrinsic to cultural politics as widely practiced in postpartition Upper Silesia, it marked an early and "soft" form of the politics of ethnic cleansing that would be imposed on the borderlands in full force during 1939–50.

Throwing Down the Gauntlet

Nationalist leaders and public officials used the border rallies that were regular events in Upper Silesia from the late 1920s to early 1930s to stake their claim to "cultural superiority." The concept of Germany as *Kulturträger* developed in the context of its long history as a colonizer of eastern Europe, including significant numbers of Polish-speaking people. This tradition fed a national myth of Germans as the historical engineers of civilization in the formerly Prussian eastern provinces and beyond. Father Carl Ulitzka, the Provinz's Reichstag deputy and German Center Party leader, both reflected this myth and articulated the irredentist implications of the related *Kulturarbeit* (cultural work) trope in exhorting the audience at a Plebiscite Day event in 1930 to

> never forget that the land that lies on both sides is German land! All that this land brought to bloom and prosperity is owed to German work, German diligence, German productivity, German determination, and German *Kultur*. The mines, metallurgy plants, and production centers that greet us today on the other side [of the border] make us aware that Upper Silesia is one. They tell us that the land on which they stand is German, and must also again become German politically.[6]

The Land under the Cross, the German Center Party–endorsed 1927 propaganda film by Ulrich Kayser, attributed everything valuable in Upper Silesia, from its architecture and industry to its folk culture, to "700 years of German *Kultur*."[7] This message carried further resonance because of a more homespun and age-old German prejudice encapsulated in the dismissive term *polnische Wirtschaft* (Polish management), used broadly to degrade the value of *praca* (Polish work or creativity of any kind) and to describe any economic incompetence, or general mess, in Poland. In contrast to their radical nationalist opponents, centrists actually tended to avoid publically using the term in this sense.[8]

During the interwar period, German borderland nationalists, in particular academic *Heimatforscher* (researchers of the region/locality) and *Heimatkundler*, elaborated on the myth of Germans as the "bearers of culture" in the eastern provinces. According to this narrative, since the Middle Ages they had developed these areas from scratch, building urban centers and cultivating the arts and sciences. Their work had created "culturally German ground" (*Deutsche Kulturboden*) or "the German east" (*Der deutsche Osten*), which extended at least as far as the prewar borders of the German Empire. Indeed, during the Nazi era, *Ostforscher* (eastern researchers) also claimed eastern territories far beyond these boundaries. While their irredentist ambitions were limited to recovering provinces lost to neighboring nations after the war, centrists and liberals nevertheless used aspects of this myth of the "German east" to support their interests. Whereas much of the "German east" narrative projected notions of *Kultur* primarily into fertile agricultural lands, the discourses on Upper Silesia, by contrast, used the language of modernization and industrialization.⁹

Liberals and centrists often invoked a regionalist variation of this larger myth that focused on the "needs" of *Ostoberschlesien* (a German revanchist term for the "lost" eastern territory). This discourse stressed that the severing of Upper Silesia seriously harmed *both parts* of the intrinsically connected region. Nonetheless, the damage was worse in the eastern part of the province, which—as an "inherently German land"—could not thrive under Poland, given the lack of historical, cultural, or economic ties. According to the German Center Party daily, the "metallurgy plants and coal mines had been torn away from the body of Upper Silesia and forcefully tied to a nation with which the region shares no bonds."¹⁰ Similarly, speaking at a 1926 Plebiscite Day rally in Oppeln (Opole), regional German Center Party official Kurt Urbanek stated that while "the Geneva border" had caused "economic chaos" in both parts of Upper Silesia, "over there the situation is still much worse than here with us."¹¹ The interwar years brought frequent economic crises to both Germany and Poland, including Germany's runaway inflation, Poland's loss of exports to Germany in 1925, and the Great Depression, all of which caused the closing of plants and high unemployment (see chapter 1). As part of this regionalist discourse, governors and borderland nationalists in the Provinz exploited any economic crisis that hit the industrial district, even if caused by extraregional factors, to buttress their irredentist claims. Aside from blaming the Allies, such arguments often criticized the Poles for treating the industrial district as a colony for exploitation, rather than as a homeland where social welfare, culture, and prosperity should be cultivated.¹²

The regionalist variation on the myth of the "German east" depicted this "ruin" of the "stolen" eastern Upper Silesia not just in economic, but also in social and cultural terms, beginning with the period from the plebiscite to the immediate postpartition period, when both sides—but especially the Voivodeship—had experienced violence, as well as episodic forced migration. Kayser's propaganda film used documentary footage to convey the loss not only of industries, natural resources, and "one million people," but also the "ancient German folk customs." Moreover, its narrative asserted that "over there" there was "hatred of everything that was once German." Stirring images showed Polish law enforcement officials pulling "Germans" from their homes and "unscrupulously expelling [*vertreiben*] women and children from their homeland." A shot of a freight car implied a systematic and organized expulsion, the kind that Germans in Silesia would experience only after World War II. Behind this "stream of fleeing individuals" the film shows the Poles "clos[ing] the door to the homeland" as though the region's inhabitants were "from two separate worlds." The next scene featured nasty Polish border guards harassing local residents, "where just a few years ago German farmers peacefully harvested."¹³

Both the film's one-sided depiction of violence and its representation of the border as a formidable barrier were significantly exaggerated. In actuality, despite incidents of harassment on both sides, area residents had "circulation cards," intraregional passports that allowed them to freely cross the border back and forth. Clearly Kayser intended his portrayal of Germany and Poland as something akin to two different civilizations to illustrate an assertion voiced by regional officials at the previous year's border rally: "if Polish *Oberschlesien* [sic] wants to see economic and cultural prosperity again, this can only happen when it is reunited with Germany."[14]

The Upper Silesia as "German east" myth was further promoted in official representations of current state policies. The demand for *Aufbauarbeit* (an effort to develop, build up, or construct)[15] became a major theme of the 1926 Plebiscite Day celebration as the Provinz government called on German state officials to support and finance efforts to address the socioeconomic and structural impact of partition. They clothed this request in the rhetoric of national pride in the superiority of German *Kultur* and *Arbeit*. Prussia's interior minister, the Social Democrat Carl Severing, picked up the *Aufbauarbeit* theme as a continuation of "the struggle for Upper Silesia":

> I am not speaking about an arms race; I'm speaking of a struggle that we must wage today as good Germans and as good citizens of the world. I am speaking of the struggle that should be fought with the weapons of the spirit. ... It has already been said that our struggle for Upper Silesia is not just for the retention of German territory. We want to strive for a higher culture. We want to be a part of a more sincere humanity. *And in this struggle for Germandom, and for a German Kultur, we will be victorious just as long as every individual ... strives to be better than the eastern neighbor.* In a contest waged in all areas of public life we want to show the whole world that we are serious about struggling for the welfare of the whole German *Volk* here at the border. We want to make sure that not a single foot-length of soil will be lost. That the German *Volk* and German customs will be maintained undisturbed for Germandom.[16]

Severing's statement symbolically threw down the gauntlet—challenging Poland to a contest over national superiority in industry, culture, and even spirit.

President Paul von Hindenburg echoed this theme during his 1928 border visit (see chapter 2), during which he opened a new kindergarten in the border city of Ratibor (Raciborz), observing that the school exemplified the ongoing "mighty new *Aufbauarbeit*" that offered "proof to the world of Germans' potential for productivity and achievement."[17] In statements such as these, Hindenburg, Severing, and other officials articulated the rules of the territorial cold war: displays of stewardship—marked particularly by development and acculturation—were to become a marker that made the nation's "right" to Upper Silesia authentic.

All this propaganda on Upper Silesia as part of a "German east" was duly noted by Polish observers in the Provinz. In Beuthen, the Polish-minority press expressed outrage at Severing's reference to the Provinz as "a fortress of the east, where German culture will converge." It viewed the minister's speech as evidence of Germany's intent to wage "a battle of the spirit" that aimed to show the world that "the German is a better person than his eastern neighbor," thereby tacitly revealing that "up to now the Germans have not been able to show this."[18] Based in the same city, the local Polish consul, Edward Szczepański, likewise expressed his alarm. Reporting to the government in Warsaw, he noted Severing's assertion that economic crises in the Voivodeship reflected Poland's inability "to maintain its own part of the province," thus proving that the "region's natural unity belongs under Germany."[19] He took particular notice of the skillfully crafted regionalist nature of this propaganda, and expressed concern with its potential grassroots appeal:

> The German government's call for a reunification in the near future is supported by a broad array of German administrative and social institutions, which aim to capture the soul and master the mind of the Upper Silesian. ... All of Germany was murderously working to uphold the faith of the Upper Silesian masses in Polish Silesia's speedy return to Germany.[20]

In his report, Szczepański called on his government to engage the German cultural challenge more aggressively. He took issue not so much with Poland's efforts to promote cultural and economic growth in the Voivodeship, as with the government's failure to exploit them for propaganda purposes as "cleverly" as in the German case—particularly at the regional level. He argued that Poland's considerable efforts "to maintain a standard of living in Upper Silesia" had not reached "the mass consciousness" of ordinary locals, "who feel neglected and rejected by Poland." He warned the government that if it did not improve its "cultural propaganda," "it is very easy to imagine a sad outcome" for Poland.[21]

The consul's admonitions were well heeded by Governor (*voivode*) Michał Grażyński. Assuming power two months after the Prussian minister's speech, Grażyński eventually picked up the gauntlet thrown down by Severing, balancing his campaign of terror against the "German fifth column" with a policy of development and acculturation that challenged *Aufbauarbeit* on the other side of the border. On the one hand, this was a nationalization-oriented ("Polonization") cultural program that aimed to introduce both European (i.e., modern and Western) and Polish national styles to the Voivodeship. On the other, this program was also regional in its orientation. Known officially as "regionalism" or "Silesianism" (I refer to it as Polish Silesianism), it sought to symbolically tie Upper Silesia to the Polish nation by inventing, reshaping, and reviving specific regional traditions. In this regard, Grażyński followed a model already established during the era dominated by his liberal rival, Wojciech Korfanty (1922–26).[22]

Urban development and the symbolic beautification of the region's capital, Katowice—in particular, the exploitation of these "achievements" in local and international propaganda—constituted one of the most visible and enduring features of Polish Silesian regionalism.

The Contest to Build National Regional Landscapes

Giving the Voivodeship a "Polish" Face

Provinz officials buttressed their revisionist claims with the argument that the built landscape across the border, inherited from its Prussian days, was inherently "German." Publications issued around the tenth-anniversary Plebiscite Day in 1931 often featured photographs of Prussian-period relics now under Polish control, in particular German monuments that had been recycled as pedestals for "Polish" symbols or renamed, for example, the former Bismarck Tower in Katowice, now the Freedom Tower. This argument echoed the mythology of a deeply rooted Germanic "culture" in the "German east," as against the superficial "Slavic/Polish" layer imposed by regionally foreign elites. Such notions became incorporated in views of *Ostoberschlesien* as Poland's colony.

In an effort to forge a visible and lasting "Polish rootedness" in the region, the new Voivodeship government first set about renaming streets, plazas, and parks, in effect trying to erase German identity. Even before the Sanacja era, tour guides and popular works denigrated the "Prussian era." Kattowitz's makeover as Katowice—the administrative and symbolic capital of Polish Upper Silesia and its industrial district—started in 1923, when the Silesian parliament (Sejm) voted to increase its size by incorporating ten surrounding districts. Whereas the Prussian city had 70,000 residents in 1914, the new Greater Katowice (Wielkie Katowice) overnight became a city of 125,000. Sejm delegates boasted that the population growth signified rapid "progress" under Polish governance, while Polish travel guides saw it as evidence of greater prosperity than in German times.[23] To Volksbund leader Otto Ulitz, however, the expansion was a Polish nationalist move to "forever eradicate the German character of the city."[24]

The real reconstruction of Katowice's landscape began during the Grażyński era as a hallmark of the *voivode*'s program of "regionalism," which combined the creation of a "Polish" identity with Sanacja regime-legitimating symbolism.[25] Throughout the 1930s the Architects Union of Silesia and the Voivodeship government's Bureau for Architecture and Construction created a Polish Silesian landscape that was both pragmatic and politically symbolic. To more easily give Katowice a "Polish face," Grażyński's planners and builders chose its less developed and thus less "Prussianized" southern side as the new center of social

Figure 3.1. Voivodeship Government Building (Gmach Urzędu Wojewódzkiego). Postcard from the 1930s. (BŚ-ZS)

and political life in Polish Upper Silesia, thus hoping to overshadow the old city center, with its town square, municipal theater, and city hall—earlier the center of many an insurgent rally. Grażyński's most ambitious goal was to create a new plaza—a structure that Polish art historians have referred to as the Forum Katowice[26]—that would serve both political and symbolic ends.

The realization of "regionalism" in architecture and building began with the construction of the premier architectural symbol of the Grażyński era: the Voivodeship Government Building (Gmach Urzędu Wojewódzkiego, or VGB). (As discussed in the following chapter, the VGB would serve different functional and symbolic purposes during the Nazi occupation.) Built between 1923 and 1929, this monumental structure had a footprint of 158,000 cubic meters (206,656 cubic yards).[27] In its dual function, the VGB served as the seat of both the legislative (Silesian Sejm) and executive (*voivode*) branches of the regional government and also symbolized the Polish nation-state in this contested borderland (fig. 3.1).

With four bold square extensions jutting from its main body, the VGB resembled an early modern military bastion, thus symbolizing the nationalist myth of Katowice as Poland's frontier fortress city. The thick and undecorated stone walls accented its military character and foreshadowed Nazi and Italian fascist versions of modern architecture. Relieving the severe functionalism, decorative columns and symbolic friezes on each of the façade's extensions paid tribute to neoclassicism. Art historians have identified monumental classical styles, which stemmed from the Cracovian pre-1914 school of architecture, as characteristic of Polish national architecture during the interwar period.

As an embodiment of Grażyński's national regionalism, the VGB added a Silesian touch to its classic Polish architecture. Most notably, each of the friezes displayed both classical symbols of state power (the fasces and laurel leaves) and the letters "RP" (Rzeczpospolita Polska/Republic of Poland), as well as a large golden-crowned white eagle at the center. The symbol of Piłsudski's legionnaires, a smaller and differently configured eagle, appeared repeatedly around the frieze, and exemplified how the Piłsudskiite Grażyński exploited his role in the city's rebuilding to infuse "Polonization" with his own political symbolism. The VGB made a regional reference by placing the coats of arms of cities in the Voivodeship along the outer walls' frieze. At the center of the building's elegant marble-walled interior, stained glass windows that decorated a large cupola featured coats of arms of cities in German Upper Silesia. While tactfully placed inside this official government building, the irredentist message resounded.[28] As the center of the Forum Katowice, the VGB stood adjacent to a broad street that served as a parade ground, as well as to large empty spaces suitable for political mass rallies. The steep staircase and broad portico functioned as a stage for political ceremonies that fully utilized the structure's symbolism to impress a mass audience.

Tourist guides and the annual May Third rallies promoted the VGB to all Poles as an icon of both Grażyński's "Silesianism" and Poland's national civilizing mission in the borderland, carried out through activities officially known as "cultural work." Grażyński's address at the VGB's opening ceremony echoed the theme of Upper Silesians so long isolated from "their [Polish] motherland [that] only a primitive form of Polishness" remained with them. The challenge was to eradicate "superficial" German and "underdeveloped" regional/local identities. In this effort, the VGB served as "the material symbol of Polish culture and power," while the officials working within it performed the "social, cultural, and economic work [that] aimed at deepening ... Polish consciousness among the popular masses" as well as "the confluence of regional and national achievements." Speaking after the governor, Bishop Arkadiusz Lisiecki lent this message the credibility of the Polish Catholic Church. Speaking in the name of the region's natives, he invoked the "great, beautiful, and wonderful, building ... [that] represented the might of their [the Silesians'] bonds with the [Polish] motherland."[29]

As a symbol of Poland's cultural mission in the borderland, the VGB also asserted the nation's "right" to this territory. In this respect, the tenor of the opening ceremony echoed Prussian minister Severing's claim that "work" (the promotion of economic growth, cultural achievement, and public welfare) entitles a nation and its people to a territory. This theme was directly advanced by Henryk Zawadowski, the engineer who led the Department of Public Works. He contrasted "the no-good landowner ... who neglects his land, who does not cultivate and develop it, build on it, and beautify it," with Grażyński, whom he extolled as a "frontier fighter" for the Polish cause, "not just a fellow insurgent," but also a "*builder* of this region." Poland's president, Ignacy Mościcki, provided a broader perspective in citing the VGB as evidence that "here [in the industrial district] the production created by the hands of the Polish worker and the mind of the Polish technologist and engineer are constantly strengthening the nation's status in the world." In his 1927 visit to the Provinz, President Paul von Hindenburg had similarly invoked the "skilled German" technician as the embodiment of his nation's industrial and cultural prowess, implicitly claiming Germany's "right" to the "stolen" territory.[30]

The VGB attracted even more tourists after 1930, when it housed the new Silesian Museum, another pivotal aspect of Grażyński's "regionalism." (Not incidentally, it also countered a German regional museum in Beuthen just across the border.) Demonstrating the broad nonpartisan political support for this program, an eminent Korfanty ally, Senator Konstanty Wolny (ChD), praised plans for the museum at an event marking the tenth anniversary of Poland's birth on 11 November 1928.[31] Headed by the art historian and regional conservationist Dr. Tadeusz Dobrowolski, the Silesian Museum was both a public museum and a research center for the region's history and folk culture. In line with the Sanacja ideology of "Polishness," the museum devoted one section of its permanent exhibit to the plebiscite and third Silesian insurgency, which served as a central pillar of the Grażyński cult.[32]

In 1936, the museum played a central role in the fifteenth-anniversary celebration of the third Silesian insurgency, which attracted over 100,000 visitors to Katowice from all over Poland. Presiding over the celebration—including the opening of a special museum exhibit—was Marshal Edward Rydz-Śmigły, who as commander in chief of Poland's military forces and de facto successor to Piłsudski (d. 12 May 1935) was the most powerful man in Poland (fig. 3.2). The new exhibit was curated by scholars at various academic centers, including the Silesian Institute, the renowned academy devoted to the "Polonization" of the Voivodeship. It thus illustrates the role of the VGB and the Silesian Museum in promoting the larger region's official "Polish identity." Widely promoted by press and radio, the museum and special exhibit were seen by over 40,000 visitors from throughout Poland, school youth and Polish Scouts in particular.[33]

Those visitors included the eminent German *Heimatkundler* Walter Krause, who had been delegated by the Bureau for Upper Silesian Regional Studies (Amt für Oberschlesische Landeskunde) to send a report to the Third Reich's research consortium for *Ostforschung*, the North and East German Research Society (Nord und Ostdeutsche Forschungsgemeinschaft, or NOFG) in Berlin-Dahlem.[34] Although photography was not permitted—which Krause attributed to the fear of "German spies"—he submitted a detailed written account of the extensive exhibit, which displayed a wealth of items, including archival documents,

Figure 3.2. Marshal Rydz Śmigły speaking in front of the Voivodeship Government Building at the May Third rally with Michał Grażyński (right), Katowice, 1936. (Author unknown, APK)

posters, photographs, military uniforms, and weapons. Overall, he described the exhibit as both anti-German and anti-Korfanty. Above all, it promoted the Polish core historical narrative of the *Lud Śląski* (Silesian people), an "ancient Polish people" who had finally prevailed after centuries of conflict against the Germans.[35] It embodied this myth of the *Lud Śląski* with mannequins wearing regional folk costumes, old Polish-language prayer books, and other folkloric artifacts that portrayed Upper Silesians as "ethnically Polish." As discussed later in this chapter, the Silesian Museum was one of a number of vehicles for promoting a nationalized interpretation of folk culture. The museum's archeological exhibit further reinforced the notion of the region's Polish heritage.[36]

The VGB inaugurated a broader development program to create a new built landscape for Polish Upper Silesia, which itself became a symbolic weapon in the territorial cold war. In addition to the construction of urban apartments, it included more than 1,200 suburban settlements for workers erected between 1929 and 1931. New roads connected the industrial district with other regions of Poland, and an airport opened on the outskirts of Katowice. Among other improvements in public transportation, the most politically symbolic achievement may have been the new Magistrale, a rail line from the Voivodeship's industrial heartland to the North Sea ports of the Polish Corridor, which increased opportunities to export the territory's raw materials. The press and other propaganda vehicles represented this development as a symbol of the superiority of

Upper Silesia's ongoing "cultural" and "civilizational" advancement in Poland and its successful integration with the nation.[37]

The regional governments on both sides of the border undertook such projects during the interwar period for reasons that went beyond any nationalizing or irredentist mission. Housing shortages had plagued industrial Upper Silesia since the massive influx of workers from the countryside during the Industrial Revolution. However, like many other social, economic, and infrastructure problems, postwar territorial upheavals exacerbated the existing dearth of adequate housing, in particular by creating waves of refugees. In 1926, some 65,000 of the circa 90,000–100,000 refugees who had migrated from western Upper Silesia were still in the Voivodeship.[38] In addition, the government built housing to accommodate tens of thousands of newcomers from the former Habsburg Silesia (Śląsk Cieszyński/Teschen Silesia) and various provinces of Poland, who became the core of the region's new elites, including bureaucrats, cultural cadres, and factory managers.[39] The new borders also required the reconfiguration of communication lines, including road, water, and rail. In this regard, Poland faced the particular logistical challenge of connecting territory that for centuries had been a Prussian province to the larger part of the new Polish state. From the late 1920s through the following decade, Polish authorities built up the new southern center of Katowice in order to meet the needs of expanding government institutions, including new cultural and academic centers, as well as technical schools.

Cultural activists transformed these largely utilitarian building projects into symbols of nationalization and irredentism, as the government's mandate to develop Katowice provided an opening to introduce a Polish Upper Silesian architecture that integrated urban development with Grażyński's Polish regionalism. The VGB represented this architecture's initial neoclassicism and monumentalism. By 1928, however, the Architects Union of Silesia began promoting western European and North American modernism. By the mid-1930s, southern Katowice boasted a number of avant-garde and functional buildings, devoid of the VGB's decorative impulses and far removed from either the imperial Prussian or the iconic baroque architecture of such centers of Polish culture as Cracow. Some of these new buildings, for example, the Silesian Technical Science Institutes, used thick walls to convey an image of power and fortitude similar to much Third Reich architecture. Other modern buildings flaunted avant-garde functionalist styles, such as the House of Education (Dom Oświatowy), one of Grażyński's new humanities academies, and the Administration Office Building (Gmach Urzędów Niezespolonych), which faced the VGB's main façade (fig. 3.3; see also fig. 4.4).[40] The choice of the industrial district as Poland's first site for architectural modernism signified the borderland's potential as an engine of Poland's progress and modernization.

Some of the new buildings utilized steel skeletons, which by liberating walls and corners from their traditional support functions made innovative designs

Figure 3.3. The House of Education (Dom Oświatowy), 1928. (BŚ-ZS)

structurally possible. Moreover, Grażyński endorsed such structures as a Polish "native style" befitting a region that produced the raw materials for steel.[41] Steel skeletons also first made possible the high-rise buildings that best symbolized international modernist architecture. Katowice was the site for what in 1931 became Poland's tallest structure, a fourteen-story, forty-meter-high (131.2 feet) structure designed mainly for residential use, but with some government offices. Popularly called the "Skyscraper," it quickly became a legend in a nation where such architectural innovations aroused popular wonder (fig. 3.4). Featured in

Figure 3.4. The skyscraper, as part of the skyline of Katowice (Kattowitz), completed in 1934. (BŚ-ZS)

Steel-Skeletal Building, a 1931 newsreel that was screened as a preview to feature shows in cinemas nationwide, the building quickly became a tourist landmark, especially since a small fee let visitors enjoy the view from its terrace.[42] The building also put the head of the Voivodeship government's Bureau for Architecture and Construction Witold Kłębowski, at the center of architectural modernism in Poland. Contrary to Grażyński's regionalist claims, Kłębowski himself characterized the structure as an importation of the "American style" to "Silesia, this most American region of Poland. ... It is no wonder that Silesia, the fatherland of Polish steel, is the first place to build skyscrapers."[43] Whatever its origins, the Katowice skyscraper failed to spark a trend in the region; it remained the Voivodeship's tallest structure, despite the construction of similar lower-rise buildings in Katowice and the neighboring border city of Chorzów (Königshütte). Two years after its construction, the Katowice tower lost its status as Poland's tallest building to the Prudential Building in Warsaw, which was one story higher.[44] Nevertheless, the tower, along with other avant-garde buildings, won Katowice recognition on both sides of the border as an "American city."

One consequence of the partition was the creation in 1928 of a new Diocese of Katowice, necessitated by the fact that the former Upper Silesian diocese was in the city of Breslau (Wrocław) in the German province of Lower Silesia. The "Polonization" of Katowice using sacred structures followed, beginning with the building of a cathedral as the seat for the new archbishop. Following plans by

Zygmunt Gawlik and Franciszek Mączyński, construction of the cathedral began in the early 1930s, but was not completed until the mid-1950s. Rejecting the modernist trend, their plans foresaw a monumental structure following classic ecclesiastical forms, with elongated gothic windows and a cupola. Gawlik explicitly intended the cathedral to underscore Poland's "right" to its "recovered territory."[45]

Those responsible for designing and building many of the new structures did not intend them to serve primarily as irredentist, nationalist, or even regionalist symbols; rather, the government and borderland nationalists represented them as Polish achievements after.[46] In similar ways, these activists used the May Third and Plebiscite Day celebrations to proclaim their nation's technological and organizational prowess. At the May Third event in 1931, high-powered lights made Katowice's architectural "achievements" visible even after dusk.[47] And of course the VGB and its surrounding squares were the focus of the main event, while a parade through the southern section of Katowice also demonstrated Poland's and, more specifically, Grażyński's achievements in the borderland.

The Polish Western Territories Defense League (ZOKZ) picked up on these themes in its November 1931 Silesian Propaganda Month, which aimed to teach all of Poland, including the Upper Silesians, about the region. The message was that investment and hard work had quickly "restored" more of "their own natural, or Polish, character" to the cities and towns of eastern Upper Silesia. Specifically, the new building and development projects served as evidence that Upper Silesians fared better under Poland than they had under German governance. The head of the Silesian Education Department, Dr. Ludwik Ręgorowicz, also cited material aspects of Polish "cultural work" as evidence that under Polish leadership "Katowice was transformed from a provincial city of German times into a large regional metropolis ... striving for one of the first places in the national culture of independent Poland." He further underscored the region's inherent interdependence with the rest of the country, as shown by both 127.8 kilometers (79.4 miles) of new roads and the new Katowice to Warsaw rail line connecting the Voivodeship to other parts of Poland. This new infrastructure meant that Poles would no longer have to rely on a "foreign railway junction" in Beuthen. Such "cultural work" also had "public welfare" benefits, as Ręgorowicz underscored in pointing to new swimming pools in the industrial district's cities, tourist homes in eastern Upper Silesia's Beskidy (Beskiden) Mountains, a favorite recreation and hiking destination, as well as 3,717 new homes, mostly in suburban settlements. He stressed that the cost of all this public construction had reached 84.8 million złotys, an impressive amount that showed Poland's superior commitment to Upper Silesia and its people.[48]

The Bureau for Building and Planning issued a similar statement in *Polska Zachodnia*, the official Sanacja daily, on the tenth anniversary of Poland's independence. Compared with the "small provincial city" with shabby public structures built by the "Prussian/German colonists" after its cession to Poland, the new Katowice "suddenly became the capital of a powerful and autonomous Silesian Voivodeship."[49] The head of the Architects Union of Silesia, Leon Dietz d'Arma, who had designed the city's avant-garde Military Church, made a similar before-and-after comparison in 1935, recalling his visit to Katowice in 1923, from the lack of commercial activity to the residential buildings, "hopeless in their architecture, grey and soot-covered. ... This was one example—needing no further commentary—of the shortcomings and [inferior] standards of prewar German building culture in the borderlands."[50] While Polish opinion setters did not mean to promote a stereotype of "German inferiority" comparable to their neighbor's dismissive *polnische Wirtschaft*, they did mean that by failing to promote any meaningful "cultural work" in eastern Upper Silesia, Germany had forfeited any claim to the borderland.

The political symbolism of the Polish building campaign was viewed with interest from across the border. Thus, Karl Sczodrok ("Germanized" as Schodrok under the Nazis), the head of the Organization for Upper Silesian Regional Studies (Vereinigung für oberschlesische Landeskunde) and the NOFG's main informant on cultural politics in the Voivodeship, in 1936 reported to the Third Reich's *Ostforschung* headquarters in Berlin-Dahlem the near completion of a market hall in Katowice. Although insignificant in itself, he noted, this structure should be seen in the context of larger grouping of "representative buildings," notably the cathedral, the skyscraper, the avant-garde Technical Science Institutes, and the House of Education, as well as seemingly apolitical sporting facilities. He warned that these projects in their totality conveyed a political message: "'proof' that the economic and cultural development of Upper Silesia was first successfully carried out under Poland."[51]

Somewhat more surprising given the Nazis' common reference to *polnische Wirtschaft* and "Polish unculture" (*Unkultur*), in 1938 the *Ostdeutsche Morgenpost* in Beuthen, a right-wing daily in the Weimar era and now a mouthpiece for the Nazi League of the German East (BDO), published an anonymous full-page, illustrated article that opened with the statement: "Whoever has not seen the city of Kattowitz for a number of years could not help but be quite astounded." In particular, it exclaimed about the technologically advanced and impressive buildings, including the "entirely American" skyscraper, and concluded that the postwar "Kattowitz has undergone a mercurial and forward-storming development, and in the realm of municipal building it has leaped over decades."[52] One could characterize this story as a certainly unbiased recognition of Grażyński's success in making Katowice a showplace for Poland's ability to raise the standard of "civilization" on the eastern side of the border.

Building a "Bulwark of Kultur" in the Provinz

The vaunted reputation of German *Kultur* found few reflections in government efforts to promote politicized "cultural work" in the industrial district before the partition. In fact, Upper Silesia (at the time all within Germany) remained part of the "backward" Prussian eastern provinces, suffering from underdevelopment and *Ostflucht* (westward migration; literally, "flight from the east"). Once it became a contested borderland—and in particular, once Grażyński launched his project to make the Voivodeship a cultural showplace—Germans faced up to the challenge with their own building projects, thereby making modernism a transnational regional style. Regional governors were quick to use the border conflict to attract interest and investment in the area's development from other parts of Germany. As was the case in the Voivodeship, planning and building projects were not as specifically Silesian as they were part of larger urban development efforts underway throughout Germany. Nevertheless, they entered irredentist propaganda as the "achievements" of *Arbeit* and *Kultur* and thereby as arguments for border revision.

As in the Voivodeship, many of the projects responded to urgent social problems, such as overcrowding in the tricity (Beuthen/Bytom, Hindenburg/Zabrze, and Gleiwitz/Gliwice) industrial border area, which had to cope with an influx of some 117,000 refugees by 1925.[53] Some of these migrants were initially housed in a number of makeshift arrangements, ranging from barracks to basements and shared apartments. In spring 1926, close to 6,000 families still lacked adequate shelter just in the city of Hindenburg.[54] From early on in response to this problem, the Provinz government launched a building campaign, which, according to one government report, created 4,800 new apartments between 1923 and 1925.[55] This utilitarian project also became a cultural statement with the introduction of modernist forms based on the Neue Bauen (New Building) movement, such as housing settlements in Hindenburg consisting of three-to-four-story buildings with flat roofs, which broke with traditional regional architectural styles and the tradition of small family houses dominant before 1919.[56]

In the Provinz, as across the border, communication lines and infrastructure had to be adjusted to fit the new boundary. The German-Polish tariff war of 1925 made all the more apparent the tricity's weakening former economic ties with the eastern, now Polish and Czechoslovak, parts of Silesia, and rising dependence on the western parts of the greater province and the rest of Germany. With only two rail lines connecting the tricity industrial area with the rest of Germany, planners called for the building of an S-curve for express train service connecting Gleiwitz, Beuthen, and Hindenburg with Oppeln and Breslau. While the realization of this project suffered from financial setbacks, locals had to rely on new bus lines to travel between the cities of the crowded tricity area, which were not entirely connected to one another by rail.[57] Transformed by the new border into an eastern gateway to Germany, the tricity area experienced an unprecedented increase in cross-border train travel. For example, records of ticket sales show that over 4.6 million individuals crossed this border by rail in 1923 alone, 60 percent of them entering Poland and the rest traveling in the other direction. To accommodate this traffic and facilitate customs inspections, the urban planners in Gleiwitz, Karl Schabik, and Beuthen, Albert Stütz, completed new central train stations in 1925 and 1928, respectively, utilizing the latest developments in building technology.[58]

Altogether these projects became subsumed in a Tricity Project (Dreistadtprojekt), which aimed to give the entire industrial area a façade of *Kultur*. Berlin's building planner (Baurat), Henry Gerlach, drafted this master plan along with the urban planners from the tricity in 1926, Stütz, Schabik, and from Hindenburg, Moritz Wolf. The plan foresaw a merger of the separate municipalities of Hindenburg, Gleiwitz, and Beuthen into one metropolis, or "city," as officials referred to it, using the English term. Through central planning and construction, the new "tricity" would become one legal, administrative, and municipal whole. Like the expansion of Katowice, logistical factors provided the primary motivation for this proposal, notably the need for a centrally planned response to the social and logistical problems created by partition, in particular overcrowding. The new border blocked the "natural" path of urban expansion in the tricity area, which before 1922 was eastward, into the surrounding rural provinces.

Eventually, the exercise in urban planning became a symbolic weapon in the cross-border cold war. While it was also part of a nationwide urban planning trend, the idea of a German metropolis was likewise a reaction to the creation of Greater Katowice as the cultural, administrative, and communications center of Polish Upper Silesia. Recognizing the pragmatic origins of the Tricity Project, Polish scholar Barbara Szczypka-Gwiazda notes that the border cities also needed to "demonstrate a greater economic and cultural status so as to radiate the strength of Germandom vis-à-vis the territories that passed to Poland."[59]

Ultimately, a combination of opposition by some officials, economic crises, and inadequate funding largely thwarted the ambitious plan's realization. When the Nazis attained power in 1933, they rejected the project due to its Neue Bauen architectural modernism.[60] Only some of its aspects came to fruition, notably the Haus Oberschlesien in Gleiwitz, built near the city's center by the Breslau architectural firm Gaze and Böttcher between 1923 and 1928. This elegant hotel, assembly hall, and shopping center, café, and restaurant was part of Schabik's urban redevelopment project, which included a train station and an airport, as well as some structures left unbuilt, such as skyscrapers and a new administrative center for the planned metropolis. Due to its enormous size—comparable to the VGB in that regard—Haus Oberschlesien became a symbol of interwar building along the German side of the border (fig. 3.5).[61]

Figure 3.5. Postcard of Haus Oberschlesien, Gleiwitz (Gliwice), completed in 1928. (BŚ-ZS)

As evidence of its advanced cultural work, Germany also built a number of sophisticated educational institutions during the mid- to late 1920s, including a commercial trade school (Gewerbliche Berufschule) in Hindenburg, designed by Dominikus Böhm; the Staatlich Katholisches Friedrich-Wilhelm Gymnasium in Gleiwitz, by Ing Kluge; and Schabik's Eichendorffschule in Gleiwitz. These buildings combined brick construction with a combination of Jugendstil and art deco embellishments.[62] Polish officials responded to this architectural provocation by building their own elaborate elementary schools and gymnasia along the border. According to one report, seven elementary school buildings were being built in August 1936, with twelve more to be completed by year's end and plans drawn up for an additional eleven.[63] In the words of a local school official who represented Grażyński at the grand opening of an elementary school in the border village of Kończyce (Kunzendorf): "the border schools in the Voivodeship Silesia must serve as guardians of Polish *kultura* and national ideals."[64] The German *Heimatkundler* Karl Sczodrok noted that despite the many "school palaces" being built, other Polish provinces with lower literacy rates were being shortchanged.[65] Of course, these other regions lacked the incentive provided by irredentist politics.

The agenda on the tenth anniversary of Plebiscite Day in 1931, presided over by Chancellor Brüning, included praise for the Provinz's record of construction, in particular the Tricity Project. The Moltkeplatz—the central plaza in Beuthen—was completed in 1931. It included a modernist structure

Figure 3.6. Hitler Youth in front of the Oberschlesische Landesmuseum, Beuthen (Bytom), opened in 1932. (NAC)

designed by Albert Stütz, which made extensive use of glass as well as columns that elevated the façade. While a local savings bank occupied the ground floor, the regional museum for Upper Silesia, the Oberschlesische Landesmuseum, was placed in the top three stories (fig. 3.6).[66] Provinz *Oberpräsident* Hans Lukaschek presided over its opening ceremony on 24 October 1932 and Chancellor Franz von Papen, who had replaced Brüning that June, sent a telegram of support. The guest speaker, veteran Freikorps fighter and borderland nationalist Bolko von Richthofen, who at the time was an archeologist at the University of Hamburg and an expert on excavations in Upper Silesia, declared that the new museum should provide "scholarly weapons to defend against claims of the ancient Slavic or ancient Polish character of the Silesian region [made by Polish academics]."[67]

German nationalists, in particular from the German National People's Party (DNVP), had been pressuring scholars to counter Polish efforts to create an academic underpinning for irredentist claims. For example, the right-wing *Ostdeutsche Morgenpost* criticized the local academic community as well as the Provinz government for insufficient investment in the "border-political (*grenzpolitisch*) struggle." Using language that would become a staple of Nazi-era discourse, the nationalists argued that the Polish Silesian Museum more

Figure 3.7. Silesian Museum building, Katowice, completed in 1939. (BŚ-ZS)

effectively realized its "cultural-political" (*kulturpolitisch*) mission of promoting "cultural propaganda" (*Kulturpropaganda*) than did the Landesmuseum. As explanation, they cited Grażyński's greater commitment to nationalization politics than was shown by the Provinz government.[68]

Polish consular officials interpreted the German nationalists' expressions of patriotic dismay as "a hymn of praise for our wonderfully organized propaganda work at the museum in Katowice, of which all these guardians of 'endangered' German *Kultur* are well aware."[69] Nonetheless, the Voivodeship government vowed to outdo the Beuthen museum with a new, separate building for the Polish Silesian Museum—which became the last politically significant and monumental structure of Grażyński's national regionalist architecture program. In 1934, Dietz d'Arma, the head of the Architects Union of Silesia, used the important national periodical *Architecture and Building* to announce the project. He made no secret of the motivation: "I have to admit, in the last years in Śląsk Opolski [western Upper Silesia], the Germans succeeded in building a magnificent regional museum in Beuthen."[70] Designed by the architect Karol Schayer, the enormous new Polish museum (encompassing 80,000 cubic meters, or 104,636 cubic yards) arose near the museum's old home in the VGB. Its cubic shapes, glass walls, and limited decoration conformed to the functional, modernist trend (fig. 3.7). As it happened, the grand opening ceremony—scheduled for 11 November 1939, the twenty-first anniversary of the Polish Republic's founding—was preempted by Germany's invasion on 1 September.[71]

After 1933, the National Socialists put their own stamp on Germany's mission of *Kulturarbeit*. They continued to build housing complexes, extended the autobahn to the industrial district, constructed the Adolf Hitler Canal (after 1945, the Gliwice Canal) to connect Gleiwitz with the Oder River, and built the Eichenkamp (Oak Camp), a rural settlement for members of the SA on the outskirts of Gleiwitz. A new and stronger radio frequency tower erected in that city became the site of the infamous staging of a "Polish invasion" on 31 August 1939, used as a pretext for the German attack on Poland. Nazi propaganda officials viewed this building campaign less as a competition with Poland than as a demonstration of National Socialism's superiority over the governments it replaced.[72]

Polish officials only accused two Nazi projects of "anti-Polish" symbolism, both of which opened in May 1938. The Reich Memorial (Reichsehrenmal) atop the Mount of St. Anne—where centrists seven years earlier had commemorated the military conflict of 1921 (see chapter 2)—consisted of a fortress-like Mausoleum to the Fallen *Selbstschutz*, supported by a 100-foot-high (30 meters) rock. Below the monument and next to the rock was the largest amphitheater in the Third Reich, which officially seated as many as more than 100,000 (fig. 3.8).[73] The Borderland Tower (Grenzlandturm), a forty-meter-high (131 feet) structure, served the functional purpose of a water tower for the area of higher elevation around Ratibor (Ratiborz), the "city of two borders" (Poland and Czechoslovakia). Nonetheless, the tower's decorations assertively projected a message of territorial domination, including the slogan *Deutschland über Alles* in addition to the Nazi eagle and swastika (fig. 3.9). These two structures countered Grażyński's more modest efforts to symbolically mark the German-Polish border with an array of monuments and plaques in honor of the Polish insurgents.[74]

The building of these two sites symbolized the Nazi regime's pivot from its previously more diplomatic tack toward Poland. This accompanied its shift to a far more aggressive politics of homogenization in the Provinz after expiration in mid-July 1937 of the Geneva Convention (see chapter 1). Harassment of the German minority and anyone else the regime regarded as "German" had been long underway across the border in the Voivodeship. In fact, since the 1931 Silesian Propaganda Month, the ZOKZ had represented the "achievements" of Grażyński's "regionalism" in terms of both "gains"—modernist buildings and infrastructure—and "losses"—namely, Germans in industry and government.[75] Such symbolic ethnic cleansing was even more evident in another important aspect of "cultural work"—the struggle to assert the "national belonging" of the region's local heritage.

Figure 3.8. The Reich Memorial (Reichsehrenmal) and amphitheater, Mount of St. Anne, opened in 1938. (Herder Institute, Marburg)

Figure 3.9. The Borderland Tower in Ratibor (Raciborz), opened in 1938. (Author unknown, Private collection of Sebastian Rosenbaum)

The Mental Mapping of a Regional Heritage

For both Germany and Poland, the competitive building campaigns of the 1920s and 1930s represented a political quest to demonstrate the marvels and superiority of their respective "culture" in a contested border area. These progressive urges coexisted with a more backward-looking impulse in each nation to claim deeper historical roots and a richer folk culture in Upper Silesia. As a strategy for demonstrating the innate national identity of the industrial district, governments and activists in Germany and Poland each sought to construct separate versions of Silesianism, a national regional culture that would symbolically entwine the region with the nation. This strategy involved reviving and modifying existing local customs and folk culture, as well as inventing and cultivating others, as part of emphasizing the uniqueness of Upper Silesian regional identity. These tasks fell to dedicated borderland nationalists and folklore specialists, in particular the German *Heimatkundler* and their Polish counterparts under first Korfanty and then Grażyński. The traditions they promoted had a dual function: both symbolizing the region's historical and cultural bonds with the respective nation and marginalizing or erasing those that tied it to the other.

Each individual regional government influenced and shaped what it meant to be a German or Polish Upper Silesian according to its own ideological values. In the Provinz, the German Center Party emphasized the region's Prussian, Catholic, and bilingual identity, while the Poles promoted the idea of a unique semiautonomous Polish Upper Silesia—although the Korfantists emphasized provincial independence and uniqueness to a far greater extent than did the Grażyńskiites, who called for ever greater centralization and standardization within Poland. All three factions sought to appeal to Silesians' sense of "otherness" vis-à-vis the nation on the other side of the border, their strong ties to local culture, and their relative indifference to nationalism. Despite its lip service to the concept, the Sanacja government remained suspicious of regionalism, viewing it as a temporary strategy for "Polonizing" the locals.

After assuming power in 1933, the Nazis introduced a strikingly different concept of regional identity than the other factions, which mapped the borderland as part of a Pan-Silesia/Greater Silesia (*Gesamtschlesien/Großschlesien*) that encompassed German, Czechoslovak (the Sudetenland), and Polish areas of Upper and Lower Silesia. The Nazis' national regionalism aimed to extinguish rather than uphold Upper Silesian regional peculiarity, which the Nazis associated with Catholicism, the German Center Party, Polish/Slavic culture, regional separatism, and ultimately pro-Polish tendencies. Pan-Silesia was the territorial equivalent of *Gleichschaltung* (alignment), the Nazi policy of subsuming all previously independent entities—from the remaining political parties and social welfare groups to cultural institutions—into Nazi agencies and organizations. The Nazis aligned regional cultural institutes, such as the Organization for Upper Silesian Regional

Studies, into the NOFG and created new organizations, such as the Bureau for Upper Silesian Regional Studies (Amt für Oberschlesische Landeskunde, est. 1935), both based in Oppeln and headed by Karl Sczodrok, and in 1938 subordinated them to the Silesian Bureau for Regional Studies (Schlesische Amt für Landeskunde) in Breslau in accordance with the Pan-Silesianist ideal.[76] The latter also served the Nazi regime's goal not merely to "recover" the "stolen" provinces, but to expand much further eastward. In *Ostforschung* discourse, Pan-Silesia was a uniformly German region that represented both a "fortress of *Kultur*" against "Slavdom" and other "lesser peoples and races," but also the Reich's "bridge" to a greater "German east"—a geopolitical term that denoted Germany's historical cultural "right" to lord over the peoples of East-Central Europe.[77]

Understanding the nature and impact of all these competing national regionalisms demands attention to the promotion of history and folklore that reached the masses in multiple forms, including popular publications, museum exhibitions, films and radio programs, staged performances, and even tourism.

Archeology

Before Upper Silesia became a contested borderland there was hardly any motive to dig in the industrial district except for coal, iron ore, and other resources. After the partition, however, both Polish and German archeologists began to search for the ancient roots of their national cultures. Their findings supplied the regional museums that became popular during this period. For example, an entire room in the permanent exhibit of the enlarged German Landesmuseum in Beuthen was devoted to the "Germanic epoch" of Vandal settlement. An exhibit describing the digs supplemented such artifacts as weapons and jewelry, mannequins dressed in the garb of Germanic tribes, and models of their settlements. Although the average spectator might see these artifacts as objects for diversion or intellectual enrichment, curators designed the exhibit to support the message that "for a long period of time *Oberschlesien* was an ancient Germanic settlement ground and at the time possessed a high-standing culture."[78]

In the early 1930s, Tadeusz Dobrowolski began to expand the ancient history section of the regional museum in Katowice. Whereas their German counterparts focused on "Germanic settlements," Polish archeologists searched for relics of Lusatian culture (*kultura Łużycka/Lausitzer Kultur*, 1500 to 400 BC). Although this Bronze Age and early Iron Age culture extended into eastern Germany and beyond, the exhibit presented it as inherently proto-Polish and the region's cultural base. In this vein, one government-endorsed tour guide boasted about the "discoveries" of these digs:

> Germanic traits were limited to the period from the first century to the middle of the fourth A.D. And even then, they did not represent [the ways and traditions] of

the Upper Silesian peoples, but rather only of the dominant classes, which, thanks to their skillful organization and more advanced weapons, controlled a more populous Slavic local population which had been settled here for decades.[79]

This assertion reflected a larger political myth that depicted German culture as a superficial and brutal imposition on a region whose own cultural roots—it alleged—were inherently Slavic and proto-Polish.

German scholars disputed the asserted connection between the ancient Slavs of the region and twentieth-century Poland. At the Landesmuseum's ceremonial opening in 1932, the archeologist Richthofen cited German archeological findings as evidence that "old Germanic *Kultur* [dominated] in Upper Silesian history," a "fact" that Polish museums and scholars "refuse to come to terms with." He also underscored that "the oldest Slavic settlers, and Upper Silesia in its millennia-long cultural development, were only tied to Poland politically for a very short and transitory time span."[80] Particularly during the Nazi era, *Ostforschung* scholars completely dismissed any notion of connection to Poland by identifying "Lusatian culture" as in fact "Illyrian" and thus "Indo-Germanic."[81] Like their Weimar predecessors and Polish competitors, they used the authority of scholarship to reshape and manipulate the region's official history and identity.

Folk Architecture

The "national character" of historical folk art and architecture also generated heated intellectual debate. Dobrowolski and the academic consortium of Western Borderland Thought, the Polish counterpart to *Ostforschung*, aimed to document the cultural roots of an important token of Upper Silesia's rural heritage: wooden architecture, and in particular churches. About two hundred of these structures had survived in the region, including eighty-five in the Provinz and fifty in the Voivodeship (fig. 3.10). Most of these structures—which typically had a tower and an A-shaped roof—were built between the sixteenth and eighteenth centuries, although some were older.[82] While both Polish and German scholars recognized this wooden architecture as an Upper Silesian "autochthonous" (*autochtońskie/bodenständige*) art, each national contingent claimed the style as its own, thus creating more pawns in the game of revanchist politics.[83]

The contest over wooden architecture did not remain within the ivory tower. Polish and German cultural-political actors promoted these and other relics of local heritage to wider publics as part of their cultural propaganda spectacles. In doing so, they were not merely representing these folkloric forms as inherently tied to the nation, but altogether transforming their meaning and altering their symbolic capital by turning them into the essential icons of Silesian identity. A propaganda pamphlet distributed by ZOKZ activists during Silesian Propaganda Month in 1931 pronounced these buildings to be "the highest expression of

Figure 3.10. Postcard of a wooden church in Knurów. (NAC)

Polish folk art in Silesia, which came to fruition in the architecture of the old wooden churches," whose details, "especially the fragile little towers, ... all differ entirely from German wooden building, and instead are analogous to the wooden architecture of Poland."[84] This architectural analysis accords with their assertion that all of Upper Silesia was "Polish to the Oder River." Along the same lines, a government-sponsored tour guide published in 1937 described the churches as "erected by forefathers of Polish descent," indeed, "the same as those in Małopolska [the Cracow region], constituting typical examples of old Polish [*staropolskie*] woodcraft."[85]

The German cultural discourse on these icons of "autochthonous" art changed during the Nazi era. While Weimar-era scholars challenged Polish assertions, they generally had not claimed the structures as purely German in origin, since they were found over a wide area from Scandinavia to western Germany. Moreover, they represented them as treasures of a distinctly Upper Silesian heritage. The Nazis, in contrast, disputed the identity of these structures—indeed, all aspects of local culture—in accordance with the tenets of their own Pan-Silesianism. To popularly promote the latter, in the late 1930s the League of the German East (BDO) began to stage annual festivities called All-Silesian Cultural Weeks (Kulturwoche des Gesamtschlesischen Raumes). Wooden churches were on the agenda at the last such event, held in 1939 in Breslau, the center of *Ostforschung* in Lower Silesia, where they were described as "the single remaining trait of early

Germanic architecture." As for these structures' presence in Scandinavia, if the Vikings knew how to build these churches, "they mastered this technology from the eastern Germans," since "no other *Volk* had as great a mastery of the art of wooden architecture as our Germanic ancestors."[86]

Such national appropriation of folklore did not always remain a matter of renarration and display, sometimes also involving the actual uprooting and displacing of relics from their historical point of origin to sites that possessed higher symbolic propaganda value. In the Voivodeship, the wooden churches symbolized the "Polish" roots of a region long controlled by Prussia. In keeping with Grażyński's "Polonization" campaign, some of the wooden churches were transported from their rural locations to urban industrial areas that lacked these historical buildings. One such sixteenth-century structure in 1936 received a new home in Katowice's South Park, near the site of a demolished Bismarck Tower.[87] The wooden church also presented a politically useful contrast with the cosmopolitan and futuristic architecture of Katowice. A wooden church transplanted to the border city of Chorzów in 1934 exemplifies not just the manipulation of individual relics, but also the intent to reinvent the meaning of entire folkloric landscapes in order to symbolically tie locality to nation. The move was itself part of a larger effort to counter the strong influence of the local German minority. Formerly called Królewska Huta (a translation of Königshütte or Royal Iron Works), the city had been given the more "Polish-sounding" name Chorzów two years earlier. Indeed, the municipal park that was the church's new home—Reden Hill—bore the name of the German noble and industrial entrepreneur from Hanover, Count (Graf) Friedrich Wilhelm von Reden (1752–1815), one of the earliest founders of Upper Silesian industry.[88] In keeping with the park's transformation into a site of Polish Silesianism, it received a new name: Liberation Hill, a tribute to the city's post-1922 "overcoming" of "Prussian captivity."[89]

German cultural officials were concerned that the next step in "Polonization" would be the destruction or removal of the park's statue of Reden by the famous nineteenth-century sculptor Theodor Kalide (fig. 3.11).[90] For the moment, however, Reden's historical legacy and importance as the city's father gave him a supranational aura. Thus, his statue remained standing—unlike a similar one in the neighboring city of Tarnowskie Góry (Tarnowitz), which Polish nationalists had destroyed in 1930.[91] Cultural officials promoted the wooden church transported to Chorzów, like the one in Katowice, and its green surroundings as a tourist site. Initially, official tour guides included mention of the "monument to Reden."[92] With time, however, local nationalists demanded its removal. In July 1939, the municipal authorities capitulated. While recognizing Reden's "great service to creating industry in the area," they acknowledged that he was, regrettably, "also a Germanizer." The removal and destruction of Reden's statue completed the park's nearly two-decades-long "Polonization."[93] The national

Figure 3.11. Reden statue in Königshütte by Theodor Khalide, erected in 1853. (NAC)

appropriation of local heritage was thus not just a process of renarrating its meaning, but of inventing entirely new folkloric traditions to enliven and popularize it. A similar manipulation of folklore took place with songs, dialects, and costumes, to which the chapter turns next.

Folk Songs and Dialects

The Archive for Upper Silesian Folk Songs (Oberschlesische Volksliederarchiv) in Beuthen, launched in 1928 by the Organization for Upper Silesian Regional Studies, represented the nationalization of yet another folkway. A long-standing pet project of ethnographer and folklorist Alfons Perlick, the archive relied on his connections with two collaborating institutions: Beuthen's Landesmuseum and its Pedagogical Academy. To initiate the project, Perlick requested the public's contributions of songs unique to the region. During its first year, this campaign for "folk song preservation" (*Volksliedpflege*) solicited 1,500 Germanic-based/German and 300 Slavic-based/Polish songs from both urban areas and the remote countryside.[94] The archive aimed both to transcribe for the first time this locally rooted oral culture into written form, but also to create a repository of primarily *linguistically German* folk songs, thus establishing "Upper Silesian folk songs" as part of the "German national heritage."[95] Indeed, Perlick was so intent on this goal that the Polish consulate in Beuthen accused him of "translating old Polish folk songs into German."[96] In 1932, he admitted his deception, but advanced the excuse that he only wanted to promote these Slavic- or Polish-based folk songs "in proper form and beauty in our language."[97] Perlick tacitly conceded that Upper Silesia remained a bilingual (or even trilingual) region, particularly the industrial district, with its mix of Polish, Czech, and German, as well as distinctly local terms and expressions.

Following the pattern established for the interpretation of archeology and wooden churches, Perlick's folk song project changed once the Nazis "aligned" the Organization for Upper Silesian Regional Studies with their own institutions and ideology. Whereas German Center Party governments had officially recognized the bilingual nature of regional culture, the Nazi regime made the *Ostforschung* consortium the arbiter of what in its eyes marked a rigid linguistic border between High (literary or standard) Polish and what it called the regional *Mundart* (dialect; literally, "way of speaking"), also referred to as *Oberschlesisch* (Upper Silesian) or *Wasserpolnisch* (watered-down Polish).[98] According to the *Ostforscher*, only High German speakers—and not their Polish counterparts—could understand this essentially "German" dialect.[99] In 1938, Perlick published an illustrated volume of local German-language folk music under the title *Upper Silesian Folk Songs*, which by "Germanizing" the local language sought to erase any memory of Slavic/High Polish influence in the region.[100]

In response to this threat to the region's bilingual heritage, the Polish consul in Beuthen urged Voivodeship cultural officials to collect and publish their own edited volume, "so that the rich treasure chest of Polish folk songs in Upper Silesia does not remain the property of Germandom" (niemczyzna).[101] In fact, such a project had long since begun, led by Father Emil Szramek, a Catholic (Christian Democracy/ChD) regionalist and leading folklorist and a collector of folk songs. Already in 1927, the Polish Academy of the Sciences published Szramek's edited *Folk Songs from Polish Silesia*. In 1935, the Union of Polish Singing Societies published a similar *Silesian Echoes* in order to promote Polish-Silesian folklore across the border.[102] The fact that both volumes drew their selections largely from nineteenth-century collectors of Slavic-based/Polish Upper Silesian folk songs, such as Józef Lompa and Juliusz Roger, and ignored those Germanic-based/German led Perlick to criticize their approach as purposefully preselective.[103]

Grażyński's attempts to remove German words and locutions from the local dialects and standardize folklore found the support of Polish Western Borderland Thought researchers—the counterparts to the *Ostforschung* academic enterprise. Rather than expecting all Silesians to "speak High Polish in disregard of local traditions," the governor's "regionalist" approach—in the words of the leading scholar in this area, Eugeniusz Kopec—aimed "to eliminate the German language from public life and to officially recognize a local linguistic form that, cleansed of German superficialities, was equal to the high national language and a symbol of [Silesia's] membership in the Polish national community."[104]

Grażyński's cultural agents promoted the *gwara Śląska* (literally, "Silesian way of speaking" or "Silesian talk") as the sole true regional dialect, one that also incorporated elements of the Cieszyn (Teschen) dialect area in the southeast of the Voivodeship, which due to its proximity to Czechoslovakia and Galicia had stronger Slavic influences than the more Germanic dialect of the industrial district. In 1928 Grażyński awarded the novelist and poet Gustav Morcinek (1891–1963), a native of formerly Teschen Karviná (transferred to Czechoslovakia in 1921), the new Silesian Prize in Literature, thereby anointing him as the "father of the Polish Silesian literary tradition." Cultural officials endorsed Morcinek's works, including his 1931 masterpiece, *The Cut-Down Sidewalk* (*Wyrąbany Chodnik*), which glorified the "Silesian insurgencies," as models for proper "Silesian talk." Along with the children's textbook *Our Readers*, by the Cieszyn author Żebrok, the Silesian Education Department promoted Morcinek as a vehicle for promoting the new folk language among the new generation.[105] Polish Radio Katowice supported this effort with a weekly comedy show *Fairy Tales and Stories* (*Bery i Bójki*), hosted by Königshütte native Stanisław Ligoń, which popularized the officially endorsed dialect on both sides of the border—to the open consternation of Nazi and BDO officials.[106]

Folk Costumes

As relics of traditional rural culture, folk costumes provided a particularly inviting target for political manipulation. Although a staple of May Third celebrations, these outfits had been worn less and less as industrialization and urbanization undercut all kinds of rural customs (fig. 3.12). As with other forms of folklore, however, the borderland conflicts prompted a reinvigorated, and politically driven, interest in costumes among cultural elites. Some locals in the rural parts of the industrial district still wore traditional costumes (*Volkstracht*) on special occasions, such as weddings and folk holidays—for example, the annual harvest festivals (*Erntedankfest*/*Dożynki*)—as well as on religious holidays. Women's costumes varied greatly by area, in details and colors, but usually included long dresses, aprons, blouses, and various accessories, including headpieces that ranged from floral crowns to veils and head scarves. Men's outfits—typically not as colorful as women's—varied less, but generally included long jackets, vests, breeches, round hats, and boots. The most frequently noted "costume areas" (*Trachtgebiete*) advertised in German and Polish publications included the German villages of Roßberg (Rozbark) outside of Beuthen and Schönwald (Bojków) outside of Gleiwitz, and the Polish areas of Piekary Śląskie (Deutsche Piekar) and Pszczyna (Pleß).[107]

Like other forms of politicized folklore, costumes won the attention of both scholars and the popular media. Much like the wooden churches, their national origins provided a source of contention. Perlick, an expert on the traditional garb

Figure 3.12. Parade in Silesian folk costume at the May Third rally in Katowice, 1936. (Author unknown, APK)

of Roßberg, claimed that it had developed during the seventeenth century under the influence of the German bodice and skirt costume (*Rock-Mieder-Tracht*).[108] Polish ethnographers agreed that the "Rozbark (Roßberg) outfit" was "the most beautiful" of its type in the region, but referred to it as "the typical *Polish* folk costume."[109] The visual nature of these costumes made them ideal subjects for the propaganda film *The Land under the Cross*, which represented traditional rural culture as (German) *Kultur*. Focusing on Schönwald, the film used costumes to illustrate how the rooted *Kultur* of this "ancient German [*Urdeutsche*] village" had withstood the "ruinous" influence of being "surrounded by the Polish border."[110] Voivodeship officials accused the film's director of "representing Polish costumes and customs in Upper Silesia as purely German."[111]

Edward Szczepański, the Polish consul in Beuthen, betrayed some envy of German prowess in cultural politics. Citing both Kayser's film and an ethnography exhibit curated by academics in Beuthen and Oppeln that was traveling throughout Germany, in 1927 he complained to Warsaw that Poland was "behind" the Germans in this area of "cultural work."[112] By the mid-1930s Polish cultural officials had made efforts to "catch up." In 1936, a film featuring religious pilgrimages to Piekary Śląskie—an equivalent site to the German Mount of St. Anne—premiered in Katowice before high-ranking church clerics and Grażyński himself. In one scene, pilgrims in traditional costumes enthusiastically attended a church ceremony to unveil a memorial plaque to Piłsudski. Like *The Land under the Cross* and its rival Polish film, *Silesia, Poland's Pupil* (see chapter 2), this film was shown in cinemas throughout the country, as well as at Polish-minority centers in the Provinz before 1933.[113]

As discussed in the previous chapter, locals in folk costumes regularly appeared at political festivals on both sides of the border, marching in parades and taking part in ceremonies. In the Provinz, for example, costumes played a visible role at the tenth-anniversary Plebiscite Day event in 1931, where Chancellor Heinrich Brüning was the guest of honor. In reviewing the festivities, the Polish-minority paper in Beuthen noted the "German men and women clothed in our folk costume. But they did not wear these costumes as they should have been worn. Everyone could notice that they did not understand how to move freely in the manner intended for these costumes."[114] Thus, while German officials mobilized costume wearers at their rallies in order to underline the voluntary and enthusiastic presence of locals who were visibly rooted to the region and its traditional ways, the Polish minority saw an unnatural spectacle of Germans wearing costumes that truly belonged to "Polish Silesian" natives.

Minority groups on each side of the border made their own political uses of folk culture. Polish minority organizations in the Provinz, for example, used the harvest festival to showcase the "Polish Silesian" character of the local culture. During the Nazi era, however, such events allowed a form of defiance against local NSDAP intimidation tactics to enforce assimilation with a "German" identity. For example, at a harvest festival held in Beuthen in October 1935, somewhere between 800 and 1,000 participants came from local Polish minority societies and students at the city's Polish gymnasium, who were joined by border crossers from the Voivodeship. After celebrating Mass at a church in the folk costume center of Roßberg, participants assembled at the gymnasium and marched in procession through the streets of Beuthen. A number of the marchers, including two men on horseback in the lead, wore the local costumes of Roßberg, which Perlick and his allies had identified as relics of "age-old German *Kultur*." In an even more provocative act, marchers displayed red-and-white (Polish) flags and children held banners that read (in High Polish): "We are the future of the nation" and "We will fight on with the power of righteousness."[115] Local members of the Nazi Farmer's Union (*Bauernschaft*) debunked the authenticity of the harvest festival. According to their observations, not only were the horseback riders not from Roßberg, but "true Roßbergers" had stayed away. Moreover, the women's and girls' costumes "were borrowed from the Ogoreki Costume Institute of Beuthen."[116] Despite the protections of minority groups and their cultures guaranteed in the 1922 Geneva Convention, such open displays of "otherness" might result in more than a derisive report. Having one's name recorded or photograph taken could be followed by various forms of economic reprisal or violence.[117] The belief that folk costumes represented a nation's rootedness in the industrial border area led Poles and Germans to mobilize "their own" to pose and express themselves in costumes, songs, and words.

Folkloric Performance

Folkloric performances of all kinds grew increasingly popular on both sides of the border during the 1930s. In the Voivodeship, the ZOKZ (the PZZ after 1934) formed folk song and dance groups that performed songs, dances, and theater geared to "revive" and promote traditional rural "Polish Silesian" culture. In this context, "revival" often required some alterations. One of the groups came from Dąmbrówka Wielka (GroßDombrowka), a center of folkloric activity, on the outskirts of Piekary Śląskie and Katowice. In tours through Poland, they performed traditional songs whose words had been edited to more closely resemble High Polish, as published in collections such as *Folk Songs from Polish Silesia* and *Silesian Echoes*.[118] The local "traditional" dances in their repertoire were similarly nationalized, notably the "Wedding in Dąmbrówka," which itself resembled *The Silesian Wedding*, a play written in 1934 by radio comic Stanisław Ligoń that used officially approved "Silesian talk" in order to represent the intrinsic ties between local folklore and Polish national culture. This play was performed both in Poland and for Polish minority societies in the Provinz. The German folklorist Karl Sczodrok referred to *The Silesian*

Wedding as "an effective propaganda piece," and noted that it was being performed in schools and the workplace and at Polish minority centers in the Provinz.[119]

In the tricity area after 1933, the BDO led the campaign for cultural nationalization with the aid of Beuthen's Pedagogical Academy and the regional section of Strength through Joy (Kraft durch Freude, or KdF), the NSDAP's organization for workers' tourist and leisure activities. Together, these organizations set up thirty choral groups (Singgemeinschaften) in the industrial district by 1938, including groups in Hindenburg and Beuthen. One group included workers from local mines and metallurgy plants; another had students from the Pedagogical Academy.[120] In touring local villages, such groups fulfilled the mission of teaching peasants about officially accepted traditional customs. The BDO also organized "Picture Evenings" (Bildabende)—visited by some 60,000 locals from Beuthen and its surrounding district throughout 1935—that aimed to teach locals about "correct" folk customs, along with other propaganda, through song and dance as well as film and projected photographs and other activities.[121]

The Polish minority offered its own counteroffensive to Nazi *Kulturarbeit*: a group of students and faculty from the prestigious Polish gymnasium in Beuthen performed traditional dances, songs, and theater in ways that signified their connections with Polish high culture. Although the Geneva Convention and concern that Poland might retaliate against its German minority prevented the Nazis from banning these performances, they made it difficult for the group to rent venues and obtain necessary permits. Copies of the "Polish Upper Silesian" folk song collection *Silesian Echoes* were among suspect materials confiscated by the Gestapo during house searches of Polish minority members in 1936.[122] More commonly, the Nazis held competing events, as they did in September 1936, when the Polish minority organized a folk festival in Randsdorf (Wieszowa) outside Beuthen. To avert participation by "curious locals," the BDO organized a rival festival in the town center "to demonstrate the German character of Randsdorf." The larger Nazi event, which featured a local costumed folk song group, followed by an evening of music and dancing, drew the larger audience.[123]

Both Germany and Poland sought to reach national and international audiences beyond Upper Silesia by disseminating nationalized versions of their respective folk cultures. Polish Silesian folklore groups from the Voivodeship went on tours around the country and even to western Upper Silesia, as well as to London in 1935.[124] At the end of the following June, vocal groups from throughout Poland and abroad attended the national Choral Congress (Sejm Śpiewaczy) in Warsaw. Although not officially a government event, it aimed to represent the Polish national community united in song across national borders. The Nazis did not stand in the way as Polish minority choral groups from the Provinz travelled to Warsaw to participate in the event.[125]

The Nazis' reason for what might have seemed a gesture toward international fellowship was strategic. The following year, German government agents reminded Polish diplomats of this "favor" and requested permission for 4,000 German-minority singers, including a number from the Voivodeship, to attend a similar event in Breslau—the capital of Nazi Germany's Silesian Province (Gau Schlesien)—to be held on 28 July–1 August 1937. The Nazis assured the Polish consulate in that city that the festival would be an act of "cultural exchange to deepen understanding and closeness between the two neighboring states," and "not a political event." The Polish government agreed.[126]

Rather than an "apolitical" act of friendly "cultural exchange," the Choral Union Festival (Sängerbundfest) was the largest and most politicized event in Germany since the 1936 Berlin Olympics. Marking the seventy-fifth anniversary of the founding of the German Choral Union, the event—like its earlier counterpart in Warsaw—aimed to demonstrate the cross-border extent of a particular "national community." The gathering of folkloric choral and dance groups, which traveled to Breslau from homes throughout Europe and beyond, was intended to represent the German *Volksgemeinschaft*. With Adolf Hitler and his top ministers presiding, this event of over 100,000 participants (20,000 from outside Germany) far exceeded the Choral Congress in Warsaw in size and political bombast.[127] As a propaganda spectacle, it conflated two of the central geopolitical concepts that supported Nazi irredentist and expansionary policies. The first was the notion of a Pan-Silesia, which justified Germany's cultural, historical, and ethnic/national claims to the entire Silesian (Lower and Upper) region, including those parts officially belonging to Poland and Czechoslovakia. The second was the Nazi concept of the "German east," which asserted that, above all, the former Prussian provinces, but also territories as far east as Cracow and beyond, were inherently "German." Speaking at Breslau's Centennial Hall (Jahrhunderthalle)—a monumental and architecturally revolutionary structure of reinforced concrete erected in 1913—the vice governor of Gau Schlesien, Fritz Bracht, hailed those gathered as

> follow[ing] the path of every courageous early medieval German frontier settler, who with the song of "let us ride to the East" [*nach Osten wollen wir reiten*] regained ancient German territory for Germandom and emphatically gave this Silesian land its eternal German face. They recovered this ancient German heritage for Germany not with the sword, but through honest and peaceful German work. They never took anything away from anyone, but rather founded our German cities and villages "on plain green grass."[128]

Setting aside any notion of seeking good relations with their eastern neighbors, the Nazis clearly announced their intentions for the "recovery" of the contested borderlands. The principle underlying their claims had been echoed well before 1933, even by centrists and liberals: that a legacy of "work"—in particular *Kulturarbeit*—entitles a nation to territory. In representing the "east" as a land of German *Arbeit* and *Kultur* and in committing to continuing cultivation, Bracht followed in the path of such Weimar-era leaders as Prussian Interior Minister Carl Severing.

Over three days the hundreds of participating choral and dance societies performed at various sites across the city of Breslau. As a reminder that they were here for politics and not entertainment, Fritz Bracht's address to the Upper Silesian singers depicted them as cultural fighters "mobilized for the *Volkstumskampf* [struggle between peoples]."[129] The groups from the Voivodeship included the leading musical figure from its German minority, Andreas Dudek from Katowice, who headed the consortium of German choral societies from all of Poland. Despite the wealth of performances, the singing and dancing paled in comparison to the grand parade of all participants before Hitler and his lieutenants (fig. 3.13). According to the Polish consul in Breslau—who was seated behind the Führer—many performers were tired and irritated after waiting for hours in rank-and-file order, only to march for another two hours.[130] Dressed in folk costumes, the marchers represented the rootedness of the "German *Volk*" in the territories to which the Third Reich had laid claim, and in Hitler's words to the assembled masses, they were "proof" that the *Volksgemeinschaft* consisted of "98 million Germans" who transcended political borders.[131] Beside him stood Propaganda Minister Joseph Goebbels, the mastermind behind this shameless hijacking of folklore enthusiasts, whose speech only further underscored the irredentist, and not merely artistic, purpose of this festival. In Goebbels's words, "one can erect wooden or steel barriers on borders, but all that is German will nevertheless feel an unrelenting bond for eternity."[132]

The mass rally at the tenth-anniversary Plebiscite Day celebration in 1931 had similarly challenged Germany's eastern borders. However, a liberal ethos still lay behind its message. By contrast, the instrumental Nazi discourse of "overcoming politically imposed divisions" aimed only to justify expansionist goals. And whereas the German Center Party's earlier rallies had an essentially regional, Upper Silesian focus, Nazi rallies such as the Breslau parade bespoke an all-national German agenda that saw the "recovery" of the former Prussian provinces as a first step in building a continent-wide Großdeutsches Reich (Greater German Empire).

Irredentist Cultural Politics at the Local Level

While governments and patriotic elites in both Germany and Poland often expressed envy over the other's "cultural work," the picture was often quite dif-

Figure 3.13. Photographs of Adolf Hitler, crowds, and folk costume parade (bottom right) at the Choral Union Festival (Sängerbundfest) in Breslau (Wrocław). Headline: "Unforgettable hours at the Palace Plaza" (*Schlesische Tageszeitung*, 5 August 1937, Biblioteka Uniwersytecka we Wrocławiu, Kolekcja Śląsko-łużycka).

ferent at the local level. In the Voivodeship, the regional autonomy party, the Upper Silesian Defense Union (ZOG), led by Jan Kustos, continued to attack Grażynski's "Polonization" policies and vowed to protect the rights of Upper Silesian locals, whether German, Polish, or nationally indifferent (see chapters 1 and 2). Although the ZOG was never an electoral threat, the Sanacja shut it down in 1934 as a dangerous "separatist movement."[133] Its bilingual newspaper, *The Voice of Upper Silesia* (and its German section, *Der Pränger*), nonetheless provides a valuable resource on regionally oriented and nationally indifferent citizens in the Voivodeship.

The ZOG rejected Grażyński's regionalism as favoring the Polish newcomers and national interests over Upper Silesian natives. Newcomer elites received appointments to head the new research institutes devoted to Polish Silesianism, such as the Silesian Institute, Music Academy, and the Katowice Pedagogical Academy. During the economic crisis of the early 1930s, Kustos criticized the "waste" of taxpayer funds on these "Polonization" institutions as well as on the construction of architecturally avant-garde buildings and "the usurpation of [Upper Silesia's] customs ... and rights."[134] Kustos reserved special disdain for the Cieszyn Poles, on whose dialect Grażyński based his "Silesian talk," for thinking that they were "better Poles" than natives of the formerly Prussian parts of Upper Silesia.[135]

Such "constructive" measures of Polish Silesianism as the building and development projects in Katowice, and in particular the cathedral, enjoyed considerable support from the leaders of the Diocese of Katowice and Wojciech Korfanty's Christian Democratic Party (ChD) and its coalition, which in turn had the support of most of the Voivodeship's locals. However, both church leaders and Korfanty's supporters opposed those aspects of "Polonization" that discriminated against German speakers and even apolitical Germanophiles. Grażyński ran into particular trouble with the church over his insistence that the clergy either halt or limit German-language church services. Stubborn resistance by Bishop Stanisław Adamski made the church a counterforce to nationalization, even though he continued to celebrate Mass at official ceremonies that promoted the cult of the *voivode*.[136]

In the Provinz, Nazi "Germanizing" policies also encountered local discontent and defiance, notably any efforts to impose linguistic homogeneity. To this end, BDO agents sought to stamp out local use of the Silesian dialect, which they slandered as *Wasserpolnisch*—or in other words, a variation of "Slavic/Polish," and thus a threat to the Reich's territorial integrity, particularly in the workplace and in places of worship.[137] This campaign proved particularly hypocritical, since *Ostforscher* within the BDO had also classified the dialect as "German." Proudly referring to it as *Oberschlesisch*—in other words, a folkloric treasure of German Upper Silesian regionalism—they called for an end to the use of the derogatory term *Wasserpolnisch*.[138]

During the German census campaign in the spring of 1939, the BDO used leaflets, local rallies, and radio programs to popularize the assertion that *Oberschlesisch* had just about nothing to do with the literary Polish language. Its propaganda, therefore, called on all dialect speakers—effectively the majority of locals—to identify themselves as "German" for census purposes, and thus demonstrate the region's national homogeneity and the success of Nazi "Germanization" measures.[139]

This instrumental promotion of national regionalism backfired after the census, when officials reverted to their policy of harassing and threatening dialect speakers. (The census project was all the more irrelevant because the results did not come out before the start of war).[140] Locals were quick to use the recent national appropriation of their dialect to defend their right to speak it. Thus, when a Nazi agent tried to intimidate coal miners near Hindenburg for speaking the local dialect among themselves, one of the workers pulled out a BDO census-related propaganda sheet that instructed *Oberschlesisch* speakers to declare "German" as their mother tongue. The agent ultimately gave in and departed to the defiant laughter of the workers. This episode, which was not an isolated incident, demonstrated that locals took advantage of the new official recognition and important status that national regionalism gave to their local heritage in order to not give into, and instead protect themselves against, nationalization.[141]

Nazi attacks on Catholicism as an instrument of Polish irredentism also encountered significant levels of local defiance. As an icon for both Nazis and Catholic pilgrims, the Mount of St. Anne became a particular object of contention in this struggle. For local Catholics, the mountain's "neopagan" Reich Memorial was an affront to the site's religious identity and heritage. Nazi anti-Catholicism in combination with the party's attacks on multilingualism and regional identities provoked defiant displays of increased participation in pilgrimages and other religious festivities in the late 1930s, often leading to confrontations between the two forces.[142] One such face-off occurred on 18 June 1939, when the local NSDAP staged a folk music festival at the Reich Memorial as a ploy to depress participation in a pilgrimage at the nearby cloister that was expected to attract political opponents, most of them supporters of the Catholic German Center Party. In addition to instructing workplace folk song groups to participate in its event, which included a singing and dance contest, the party also banned car, bus, and train travel to the religious site and closed the hostel where pilgrims normally spent the night. Party officials also made clear that anyone involved in the pilgrimage or similar religious activities would be treated as a "Pole," and thus risk job loss and other sanctions. Yet despite all their efforts, the folk song festival attracted an audience of only 5,000, compared to the 80,000 who took part in the Catholic rally of devotion and defiance. While events such as this one surely attested to the devotion of Upper Silesian Catholics, they also attracted other opponents of the regime, including dedicated communists.[143]

Opposition to the Nazi regime's persecution of the Polish minority—especially after July 1937—was not limited to ordinary local residents. In particular, such policies as the forced transport of suspected "Poles" from the borderland to locations further within Germany and the expropriation of farmers' land divided state functionaries who were native to the region from those who came from other parts of Germany. In the words of an account by Nazi opponents, "these measures even raise disappointment within Nazi circles, a part of the population that recognizes these so-called Polish fellow citizens as equal human beings [and thus] rejects these policies."[144] Internal divisions also arose over the party's program to cultivate a Pan-Silesian identity that was markedly German nationalist in tone, instead of the older concept represented by Upper Silesian folklorists such as Karl Sczodrok, whose circle of regional scholars and cultural activists lamented the Nazi's banning of Weimar-era Plebiscite Day events as well as the *Gleichschaltung* of their own work and institutions. Subject to the directives of the BDO and the regional government (*Gauleitung*) in Breslau, they were expected to conform to the Pan-Silesian orthodoxy. Although the *Heimatkundler* formally acquiesced, they warned that the party's refusal to recognize a German identity that was distinctly Upper Silesian risked alienating a local population that would be convinced that the Third Reich viewed their *Heimat* as a "colony" rather than a "true part of Germany."[145]

Thus, many locals of the Upper Silesian borderland, including many native elites devoted to irredentist and nationalization politics, increasingly questioned the degree to which interwar nationalizing projects brought "progress" and "cultural uplift." On both sides of the border, residents saw efforts to change their ways of life in order to integrate them into the nation as inherently foreign and colonial in nature, serving primarily the regimes in charge. Efforts to homogenize and standardize the multilingual culture, pluralist identities, and religiosity of this borderland alienated precisely the native population whose support both Germany and Poland hoped to win for their irredentist and nationalizing policies. To this extent, the policies of both the Nazi and the Grażyński regimes failed. Both the regionally foreign NSDAP elites in Breslau and the Polish newcomers who assumed leading positions in the Voivodeship instilled among local natives a stronger sense of the cultural peculiarity of their own Upper Silesia.

Conclusion

The contest to impose cultural uniformity, including mass rallies to promote that theme, was a prime facet of the German-Polish cold war for control over all of Upper Silesia. In pursuit of their territorial interests, governments and cultural-political agents on both sides sought to create and impose their own national regional traditions that borrowed from the region's heritage but symbolized their ties to one or the other nation. From urban landscape design to museum exhibitions, popular scholarship, and folkloric performances, the cold war over Upper Silesia thus also took the form of a struggle for the identity of regional culture. Yet the revival of regional culture also conveyed to locals the fundamental importance of their home region. In using regionalism as an instrument of irredentist propaganda, neither the German nor the Polish borderland nationalists outdid their rivals in convincing locals that their region was—exclusively—a cultural component of their respective nation. Just as they had made the border rallies integral to this regional cultural war, the two sides collectively emphasized the region's multifaceted character and gave official sanction to an Upper Silesian identity. Indeed, promotion of various manifestations of Silesianism was part of a larger European-wide regionalist and folklore vogue of the 1930s. Yet unlike the cultural celebrations that characterized the national heartlands of Germany or Poland, Silesianism was the object of multipolar (German, Polish, local) struggle, which in turn distorted and complicated the national identity that each camp of borderland nationalists aimed to project.

In addition to their nationalizing intent, German and Polish national regionalisms aimed to convey each nation's "right" to the borderland, based on a discourse that emphasized a modern nation-state's duty to advance "civilization" to marginal areas. While such rhetoric is reminiscent of European overseas imperialism, it was routinely employed from the days of imperial Prussia onward for German efforts to bring *Kultur* and development to Polish territory. In the interwar period, not just German, but also Polish irredentist actors—moderates and radicals—used variations of this discourse, in particular citing their respective modernist architectural landmarks, although these hardly differed stylistically from one side of the border to the other. Moreover, both Germany and Poland accused the "other" of neglecting and exploiting the borderland as a mere colony, while promoting its own buildings and cultural institutions as symbols of its own superior stewardship.

The constructive aspects of inventing national regional cultures went hand in hand with deconstructive measures, particularly under the Sanacja and Nazi regimes. These policies aimed to deny, discredit, and erase the "work" and heritage of the national rival as well as of nonnational regional identities. Initially motivated by nationalist programs to construct culturally uniform border societies, the various cultural cleansing schemes practiced during the interwar era helped to legitimate the more extreme policies that came thereafter, starting with the outbreak of World War II.

Notes

1. RH, O/S Grenzbericht, July–Sept. 1928, GStA PK, I HA, rep. 77, tit. 856, no. 593, Bd. 2, 108ff.
2. "Wielki Dzień Śląska," PZ 123 (6 May 1929): 1–2.

3. Parts of this chapter appeared in Peter Polak-Springer, "Landscapes of Revanchism: Building and the Contestation of Space in an Industrial Polish-German Borderland, 1922–1945," *Central European History* 45 (2012): 485–522.

4. *Heimatkundler* refers to scholars, experts, and cultural activists or enthusiasts that specialize in the history, folklore, and customs of a particular locality/region or *Heimat* (local homeland). It comes from *Heimatkunde* (regional/locality studies).

5. The political use of terms such as *Kultur*, *Deutsche Arbeit*, and *Kulturarbeit* was intensified by the German occupation of eastern Europe during World War I and connote an aura of superiority for German work, ideas, and creative potential. For political purposes, German nationalists deliberately avoided using *Zivilisation* interchangeably with *Kultur* to distinguish themselves from their French rivals, with whom they identified the former. See Liulevicius, "The Languages of Occupation," 127–30. The political undertones of Polish *praca* (work) or *praca kulturowa* (cultural work) were nowhere near as well understood internationally as the German counterpart.

6. RH, O/S Grenzbericht, Jan.–Mar. 1930, GStA PK, I HA, rep. 77, tit. 856, no. 593, Bd. 2, 174ff.

7. Kayser, *Land unterm Kreuz*.

8. See Hubert Orlowski, *"Polnische Wirtschaft": Zum deutschen Polendiskurs der Neuzeit* (Wiesbaden, 1996).

9. See Gregor Thum, "Mythische Landschaften: Das Bild vom 'deutschen Osten' und die Zäsuren des 20. Jahrhunderts," in *Traumland Osten: Deutsche Bilder vom östlichen Europa im 20. Jahrhunder*, ed. Gregor Thum (Göttingen, 2006), 181–211; Liulevicius, *The German Myth*; Piskorski, Hackmann, and Jaworski, *Deutsche Ostforschung*.

10. Quoted by the Polish consulate in Oppeln from OSV 81 (21 March 1924), Kon. Op. to MSZ, 26 Mar. 1924, AAN, 482, 196, 2.

11. "Die Abstimmungs-Gedenkfeier in Oppeln," *Oberschlesische Zeitung* 88 (29 Mar. 1926); "Abstimmungsfeier in Oppeln," OSV 88 (29 Mar. 1926).

12. Kon. Op. to MSZ, 26 Mar. 1925, AAN, 482, 196, 39–40; "Nach fünf Jahren," OSV 52 (20 Mar. 1926).

13. Kayser, *Land unterm Kreuz*.

14. "Nach fünf Jahren," OSV 52 (20 Mar. 1926).

15. In regard to development, building up, or renovation in principle, here *Aufbau* (with *Arbeit* referring to work) likewise conjures up the politically charged meaning of a struggle to build, cultivate, and create in places where this is needed.

16. "Abstimmungsfeier in Oppeln," OSV 88 (29 Mar. 1926), emphasis in original.

17. RH, O/S Grenzbericht, July–Sept. 1928, GStA PK, I HA, rep. 77, tit. 856, no. 593, Bd. 2, 108ff.

18. "Uroczystość rządowa w Opolu," *Katolik Codzienny* 72 (30 Mar. 1926): 1.

19. Kon. Op. to MSZ, 30 Mar. 1926, AAN, 482, 196, 65ff.

20. Ibid.

21. Ibid.

22. See Maria Wanda Wanatowicz, "Między regionalizmem a separatyzmem Śląskim," in *Regionalizm a separatyzm: Historia i współczesność, Śląsk na tle innych obszarów*, ed. Maria Wanda Wanatowicz (Katowice, 1996), 18–24; Barbara Szczypka-Gwiazda, *Nieznane Oblicze Sztuki Polskiej: W kręgu sztuki województwa śląskiego w dobie II Rzeczypospolitej* (Katowice, 1996), 29.

23. A. Mikulski, ed., *Przewodnik Po Ziemi Śląskiej* (Warsaw, 1935), 24.

24. Otto Ulitz, "Groß-Kattowitz," KZ, 23 July 1924, GStA PK, I HA, rep. 77, tit. 856, no. 731, 159. Also quoted in Polak-Springer, *Landscapes of Revanchism*, 492.

25. Szczypka-Gwiazda, *Nieznane Oblicze Sztuki Polskiej*, 27–29.

26. Szczypka-Gwiazda, "Reprezentacyjne założenie placu forum Katowic jako próba stworzenia 'przestrzeni symbolicznej,'" in *Przestrzeń, Architektura, Malarstwo: Wybrane Zagadnienia Sztuki*

Górnoślaska, ed. Ewa Chojecka (Katowice, 1995), 105ff.; Waldemar Odorowski, *Architektura Katowic w latach międzywojennych, 1922–1939* (Katowice, 1994), 31–43.

27. Helena Surowiak, "Gmach Urzędu Wojewódzkiego i Sejmu Śląskiego w Katowicach oraz jego program ideowy," *Roczniki Katowic*, 1983, 162.

28. Odorowski, *Architektura Katowic*, 56–57; Szczypka-Gwiazda, "Reprezentacyjne," 106–7. German officials took notice of the irredentist meaning of this symbolism: Karl Sczodrok to NOFG, 6 May 1936, Bundesarchiv (BArch), 153 (Publikationsstelle Berlin-Dahlem), 1302, n.p.

29. "Wielki Dzień Śląska," PZ 123 (6 May 1929): 1–2. Also quoted in Polak-Springer, "Landscapes of Revanchism," 495.

30. "Wielki Dzień Śląska," 1–2. Also quoted in Polak-Springer, "Landscapes of Revanchism," 495.

31. "Uroczyste posiedzenie Sejmu Śląskiego," PZ 313 (11 Nov. 1928): 3.

32. Haubold-Stolle, *Mythos Oberschlesien*, 228–29.

33. Sczodrok to NOFG, 2, 4 and 6 May 1936, BArch, 153, 1307, n.p.; Sczodrok to NOFG, 12 Aug. 1936, BArch, 153, 1302, n.p.

34. On *Ostforschung*, see Burleigh, *Germany Turns Eastwards*, 11–12, 53; Ingo Haar, "German Ostforschung and Anti-Semitism," in *German Scholars and Ethnic Cleansing, 1920–1945*, ed. Ingo Haar and Michael Fahlbusch (New York, 2005), 7–20.

35. Sczodrok to NOFG, 6 May 1936, BArch, 153, 1307, n.p.

36. Sczodrok to NOFG, 6 May 1936, BArch, 153, 1302, n.p.

37. "Wyniki Akcji Budowlanej Śląskiego Urzędu Wojewódzkiego," PZ 105 (17 April 1936): 5; LudwikRęgorowicz, "Dorobek rządów polskich w Województwie Śląskim, 1922–1930," in *Śląsk: Przeszłość i Teraźniejszość*, ed. Adam Benisz et al. (Katowice, 1931), 21–29. See also Dorota Głazek, "Kolonie Robotnicze w Autonomicznym Województwie Śląskim," in *O sztuce Górnego Śląska i Zagłębia Dąbrowskiego XV–XX w. Sztuka Śląska odkrywana na nowo*, ed. Ewa Chojecka (Katowice, 1989), 109.

38. Heffner and Lesiuk, "Ekonomiczne i Społeczne Skutki," 148; Franciszek Serafin, "Stosunki demograficzne i społeczne," in *Województwo Śląskie*, ed. Franciszek Serafin (Katowice, 1996), 80.

39. Krzyżanowski, "Kościół Katolicki wobec regionalizmu," 69; Wanatowicz, "Rola ludności," 79. See chapter 1.

40. Odorowski, *Architektura Katowic*, 103–17; Szczypka-Gwiazda, *Nieznane Oblicze Sztuki Polskiej*, 7–31.

41. "Budownictwo stalowo-szkieletowe na Śląsku i w reszcie Polski," PZ 118 (10 May 1931): 4; Odorowski, *Architektura Katowic*, 103–17; Szczypka-Gwiazda, *Nieznane Oblicze Sztuki Polskiej*, 7–31; Ewa Chojecka, *Sztuka Górnego Śląska od średniowiecza do końca XX w.* (Katowice, 2004), 325–36.

42. See Waldemar Odorowski, "Wieżowce Katowic i ich treści ideowo-propagandowe," in *O sztuce Gornego Slaska i przyleglych ziem Malopolskich*, ed. Ewa Chojecka and Lech Szaraniec (Katowice, 1993), 268–71.

43. Witold Kłębowski, "Pierwsze Drapacze Slaskie," *Architektura i Budownictwo* 6 (1932): 169. Also quoted in Odorowski, "Wieżowce Katowic," 268.

44. "Budownictwo stalowo-szkieletowe na Śląsku i w reszcie Polski," PZ 118 (10 May 1931): 4; Odorowski, "Wieżowce Katowic," 277.

45. Barbara Szczypka-Gwiazda, "Historia budowy katedry w Katowicach," in *O sztuce Górnego Śląska i Zagłębia Dąbrowskiego XV–XX w. Sztuka Śląska odkrywana na nowo*, ed. Ewa Chojecka (Katowice, 1989), 87.

46. See, e.g., Stanisław Bereżowski, *Turystyczno-Krajoznawczy Przewodnik po województwie Śląskim* (Katowice, 1937), 156ff.; Ludwik Łakomy, *Ilustrowana Monografia Województwa Śląskiego* (Katowice, 1936) 18–19, 39–40.

47. "Śląski Maj 1921–2 Maj 1931," PZ 111 (2 May 1931): 1.

48. Ręgorowicz, "Dorobek rządów polskich," 21–25.
49. "Akcja budowlana Śląskiego Urzędu Wojewódzkiego," PZ Ekstra, 3 June 1928, 2.
50. Leon Dietz d'Arma, "Nowe Gmachy Muzealne: Muzeum Slaskie w Katowicach," Architektura i Budownictwo 2 (1936): 66.
51. Sczodrok to NOFG, 21 July 1936, BArch, 153, 1302, n.p.
52. "Monumentalbauten geben Kattowitz ein neues Gesicht," KZ, 26 June 1938, n.p.
53. Heffner and Lesiuk, "Ekonomiczne i Społeczne Skutki," 148.
54. RH, O/S Grenzbericht, Apr. 1926, GStA PK, I HA, rep. 77, tit. 856, no. 592, 165ff.
55. RH, O/S Grenzbericht, July 1926, GStA PK, I HA, rep. 77, tit. 856, no. 592, 207ff.
56. Joachim Masurczyk, "Wohnungsbau in Oberschlesien," in Die Architektur der Weimarer Republik: Ein Blick auf unbeachtete Bauwerke, ed. Nikolaus Gussone (Ratingen Hösel, 1992), 28, 77.
57. Barbara Szczypka-Gwiazda, Pomiędzy praktyką a utopią: Trójmiasto Bytom-Zabrze-Gliwice jako przykład koncepcji miasta przemysłowego czasów Republiki Weimarskiej (Katowice, 2003), 49; Roland Lesniak, "Verkehrswesen und Bauten des Verkehrs in Oberschlesien," in Die Architektur der Weimarer Republik in Oberschlesien: Ein Blick auf unbeachtete Bauwerke, ed. Nikolaus Gussone (Ratingen Hösel, 1992), 30–31, 38.
58. Lesniak, "Verkehrswesen," 31–32, 37, 39–41.
59. Szczypka-Gwiazda, Pomiędzy praktyką a utopią, 43–44; Barbara Szczypka-Gwiazda, "Trójmiasto Bytom-Zabrze-Gliwice jako przykład nowej koncepcji urbanistycznej," in Sztuka Górnego Śląska na przecięciu dróg europejskich i regionalnych, ed. Ewa Chojecka (Katowice, 1999), 255. See also Stephanie Hoffmann, "Stadtplanung in O/S am Beispiel der Städte Beuthen, Gleiwitz, und Hindenburg," in Die Architektur der Weimarer Republik: Ein Blick auf unbeachtete Bauwerke, ed. Nikolaus Gussone (Ratingen Hösel, 1992), 10–28.
60. Szczypka-Gwiazda, Pomiędzy praktyką a utopią, 150; Szczypka-Gwiazda, "Trójmiasto Bytom-Zabrze-Gliwice," 279.
61. Lesniak, "Verkehrswesen," 32, 39–41; Masurczyk, "Wohnungsbau," 77.
62. Ilka Minneker, "Schulbauten in Oberschlesien," in Die Architektur der Weimarer Republik: Ein Blick auf unbeachtete Bauwerke, ed. Nikolaus Gussone (Ratingen Hösel, 1992), 86–99.
63. Sczodrok to NOFG, 18 August 1936, BArch, 153, 1302, n.p.
64. Sczodrok to NOFG, 15 Dec. 1936, BArch, 153, 1302, n.p.
65. Ibid.
66. "Wie O/S [Oberschlesien] die Abstimmung gedenkt," and "Grüsse aus dem Reich," both in OSW 68 (22 Mar. 1931): n.p.; "Herr, mach uns einig und frei," OSW 69 (24 Mar. 1931): n.p.; "Innenminister Severing bei der Hindenburger Kundgebung," OSW 70 (25 Mar. 1931): n.p.
67. "Oberschlesien ist urdeutsches Land," ODM, 25 Oct. 1932, AAN, 482 (Kon. Op.), 183, 30.
68. "Hilfe für das Beuthener Museum," ODM, 30 Apr. 1932, AAN 482, 183, 17ff.
69. Kon. Op. to MSZ, May 1932, AAN, 482, 183, 17ff.
70. Dietz d'Arma, "Nowe Gmachy Muzealne," 66–68.
71. See Dorota Głazek, "Budynek Muzeum Slaskiego na tle architektury europejskiej lat trzydziestych XX wieku," in Roczniki Katowic, 1980, 113–21; Szczypka-Gwiazda, Nieznane Oblicze Sztuki Polskiej, 30–31.
72. See Kulturarbeit in Oberschlesien: Ein Jahrbuch, 1936, 18–20, 115, 131–36, 143–46; 1937, 125. See also Chojecka, Sztuka Górnego Śląska, 379–80.
73. See Gunnar Brands, "From World War I Cemeteries to the Nazi 'Fortresses of the Dead:' Architecture, Heroic Landscape, and the Quest for National Identity in Germany," in Places of Commemoration: Search for Identity and Landscape Design, ed. Joachim Wolschke-Bulmahn (Washington DC, 2001), 240–42.

74. *Gesamtüberblick über die polnische Presse* 41 (22 Nov. 1935), Deutsche Generalkonsulat Kattowitz to die Deutsche Botschaft Warschau (30 Dec. 1935), and "Ausland: Enthüllung eines Denkmals für den Lehrer Vincent Janas in Ruda" [German trans.], *Illustrowany Kurier Codzienny* 315 (13 Nov. 1935), all in PA-AA, Warschau 81, n.p. See also *Ratibor: Die Stadt an zwei Grenzen: Der Grenzlandturm* (May 1938), 11. The tower's height was also extended by its location on a hill 250 meters above sea level.
75. W.K., "Polacy i Niemcy w Granicach: Województwa Śląskiego," in *Śląsk: Przeszłość i Teraźniejszość*, ed. Adam Benisz et al. (Katowice, 1931), 31–36.
76. Karl Schodrok, "Die Aufgaben des Amtes für Landeskunde," 6 July 1941, BA, 153, 1354, n.p.; Fiedor, *Bund Deutscher Osten*, 267ff.
77. OP, Abschrift betr. "Gegenwärtige Lage der Deutsche Kulturarbeit in West O/S," 23 Apr. 1936, PA-AA, Kattowitz, 63 A (Politik, Bd. 10), 9ff. See also Wojciech Kunicki, " ... *auf dem Weg in dieses Reich": NS-Kulturpolitik und Literatur in Schlesien 1933 bis 1945* (Leipzig, 2006). Parts of the rest of this section appeared previously in Peter Polak-Springer, "Kultura ludowa, rewanżyzm i tworzenie narodowo-regionalnych kultur wysokich na polsko-niemieckim pograniczu w latach 1926–1953," in *Górny Śląsk i Górno-Ślązacy: Wokół problemów regionu i jego mieszkańców w XIX i XX w.*, ed. Sebastian Rosenbaum (Katowice and Gliwice, 2014), 116–43.
78. "Eine neue Oberschlesische Kulturstätte," OSV, 22 Oct. 1932, AAN, 482, 183, 32.
79. Mieczysław Orłowicz, *Ilustrowany Przewodnik po Województwie Śląskim* (Warsaw and Lwów, 1924), 7, 8–12.
80. "Oberschlesien ist urdeutsches Land," ODM, 25 Oct. 1932, AAN, 482, 183, 30.
81. Regierungsassessor Dr. Gerber to Preussische Ministerium des Innern (circa 1935), APK, 117 (Oberpräsidium Kattowitz), 113, 1; Flott, ed., *Heimatland O/S*, 13.
82. O/S Grenzbericht, Dec. 1927–Jan. 1928, GStA PK, I HA, rep. 77, tit. 856, no. 593, Bd. 2, 64ff.
83. See Tadeusz Dobrolowski, *Sztuka Województwa Śląskiego: L'art en Silesie Polonaise* (Katowice, 1933), 84–110; Herbert Dienwiebel, *Oberschlesische Schrotholzkirchen* (Breslau, 1938).
84. Olga Ręgorowiczowa, "Polskość kultury śląskiej," in *Śląsk: Przeszłość i Teraźniejszość*, ed. Adam Benisz et al. (Katowice, 1931), 49.
85. Bereżowski, *Turystyczno-Krajoznawczy*, 78.
86. "Die letzten Holzkirchen in Schlesien," *Schlesische Tageszeitung*, 13 Feb. 1939, AAN, 482, 31, 237ff.
87. Szczypka-Gwiazda, *Pomiędzy praktyką a utopią*, 140–41.
88. Sczodrok to NOFG, Mar. and Apr. 1936, BArch, 153, 1302, n.p.
89. Bereżowski, *Turystyczno-Krajoznawczy*, 182–3.
90. Sczodrok to NOFG, Apr. 1936, BArch, 153, 1302, n.p.
91. O/S Grenzbericht, Oct.–Dec. 1930, GStA PK, I HA, rep. 77, tit. 856, no. 593, Bd. 2, 207–9.
92. Bereżowski, *Turystyczno-Krajoznawczy*, 151; Ludwik Łakomy, *Ilustrowana Monografia Województwa Śląskiego* (Katowice, 1936), 81.
93. Zespoł Stowarzyszeń Polskich w Chorzowie to Karol Grzesik, 30 June 1939, APK, 646 (Akta Miasta Królewskiej Huty), 2712, 3–4; "Königshütte Wahrzeichen von Polen zerstört: Das letzte Denkmal ein Opfer polnischen Haßausbrüche," ODM, 19 July 1939.
94. Kon. Op. to Województwo Śląskie, 12 April 1928, AAN 482, 183, 1; Kon. Op. to MSZ, 13 Mar. 1929, AAN, 482, 183, 6.
95. See Felicitas Drobek, "Alfons Perlick jako badacz folkloru niemieckiego w regionie Bytomskim," in *Z dziejów i dorobku folklorystyki śląskiej (do 1939 roku)*, ed. Jerzy Pośpiech and Teresa Smolińska (Opole, 2002), 91–107.
96. Kon. Op. to MSZ, 13 Mar. 1929, AAN, 482, 183, 6.

97. Alfons Perlick, "Oberschlesische Volkskunde," in *Das Deutschtum in Polnisch-Schlesien: Ein Handbuch über Land und Leute*, ed. Viktor Kauder (Leipzig, 1932), 107.
98. See Tomasz Kamusella, *Schlonska mowa: Język, Górny Śląsk i nacjonalizm* (Zabrze, 2005), 22.
99. Flott, *Heimatland*, 51.
100. *Oberschlesische Volkslieder: Aus den Beständen des Oberschlesischen Volksliedarchivs* (Kassel, 1938).
101. Kon. Op. to Województwo Śląskie, 12 April 1928, AAN, 482, 183, 1.
102. Emil Szramek et al., eds., *Pieśni Ludowe z Polskiego Śląska* (Cracow, 1927); Związek Kół Śpiewawczych na Śląsku, *Echa Śląskie: Pieśni dla ludu polskiego na Śląsku Opolskim* (Katowice, 1935).
103. Perlick, "Oberschlesische Volkskunde," 107.
104. Eugeniusz Kopec, "Z zagadnień integracji językowej śląskich kresów Rzeczypospolitej," in *Z problemów integracji i unifikacji II Reczypospolitej*, ed. Jósef Chlebowczyk (Katowice, 1980), 26.
105. Ibid., 22–28, 37–41. See also Zdzisław Hierowski, *Życie literackie na Śląsku w latach 1922–1939* (Katowice, 1969).
106. See Polak-Springer, "Jammin' with Karlik," 279–300.
107. See Seweryn Udziela, "Lud Polski na Górnym Śląsku," *Ziemia* 13, nos. 15–16 (1928): 242–251; E. Grabowski, *Die Volkstrachten in Oberschlesien* (Breslau, 1935).
108. Perlick, "Oberschlesische Volkskunde," 92.
109. Ręgorowiczowa, "Polskość kultury śląskiej," 48. Emphasis mine.
110. Kayser, *Land unterm Kreuz*.
111. Kon. Byt. to MSZ, 17 June 1927, AAN, 474, 2429, n.p.
112. Ibid.
113. The film's title remains unknown. Sczodrok to NOFG, Jan. 1936, BArch, 153, 1302, n.p.
114. *Katolik* 25 (Apr. 1931), *Gesamtüberblick über die polnische Presse*, GStA PK, I HA, rep. 77, tit. 856, no. 390, 98.
115. Sczodrok to NOFG, 15 Oct. 1935, BArch, 153, 1302, n.p.
116. Ibid.
117. See Wanatowicz, *Historia społeczno-polityczna*, 145–59.
118. Sczodrok to NOFG, 3 Jan. 1936, BArch, 153, 1302, n.p.
119. Sczodrok to NOFG, "Verschiedene Nachrichten," 10 Feb. 1937, BArch, 153, 1302, n.p. On Ligoń and folklore, see Irena Bukowska-Floreńska, "Uwarunkowania społeczne i kulturowe folkloru śląskiego (do 1939 r.)," in *Z dziejów i dorobku folklorystyki śląskiej (do 1939 roku)*, ed. Jerzy Pośpiech and Teresa Smolińska (Opole, 2002), 21.
120. Max Brammer, "Die Chorarbeit in Oberschlesischen Industriebezirk," and Franz Chomale, "Grenzlandarbeit der Hochschule für Lehrerbildung Beuthen i. O.S. [sic]," *Die Musikpflege*, (Jan. 1938) in Archiwum Państwowe we Wrocławiu (APWr.), 171 (wydział samorządowy prowincji śląskiej), 935, 128–9, 132.
121. The NSDAP boasted an average of 500 attendees at each event from the Kreis Beuthen-Tarnowitz. "Kulturelle Tätigkeit der Kreisfilmstelle der NSDAP, Beuthen O/S," first half of 1935, APWr., 171, 905, 117ff.
122. See Kon. Op. reports to Amb. Ber., 1936–1937, AAN, 482, 98, 249–247; Kon. Op. to Amb. Ber., 31 Nov. 1938, AAN 482, 98, 276; "Die Polnische Leienspielbewegung in Oberschlesien," ODM, 26 July 1936; "Feier der polnischen Nationalfeste durch die polnische Minderheit in Deutschland," ODM, 1 March 1936. See also Teresa Smolińska, "Dorobek Polskiej folklorystyki na Górnym Śląsku: Do drugiej wojny światowej," in *Z dziejów i dorobku folklorystyki śląskiej (do 1939 roku)*, ed. Jerzy Pośpiech and Teresa Smolińska (Opole, 2002), 44.
123. Sczodrok to NOFG, 15 Sept. 1936, BArch, 153, 1302, n.p.
124. Sczodrok to NOFG, 3 Sept. 1935, BArch, 153, 1302, n.p.
125. "Dobrze spisali się nasi śpiewacy," *Nowiny Codzienne* 148 (2 July 1936), 1ff; Amb. Ber., 10 June 1937, AAN, 482, 375, 68.

126. Kon. Br. to Amb. Ber., May and June 1937, AAN, 474, 375, 58–67, 68, 72.
127. Kon. Br. to MSZ, 3 Aug. 1937, AAN, 474, 375, 57, 75ff.
128. "Der Führer kommt nach Breslau," *Schlesische Tageszeitung* 206 (29 July 1937), 1, Kon. Br. to MSZ, AAN, 474, 375, 57, 73.
129. Ibid., 73.
130. Kon. Br. to MSZ, 3 Aug. 1937, AAN, 474, 375, 57, 75ff.
131. "Bekenntnistag der Nation," *Schlesische Tageszeitung* 210 (2 Aug. 1937), AAN, 474, 375, 74.
132. Kon. Br. to MSZ, 3 Aug. 1937, AAN, 474, 375, 57, 75ff.
133. Serafin, *Województwo Śląskie*, 140, 162; Dobrowolski, *Ugrupowania*, 136.
134. "Ludności Górnośląskiej ku uwadze," GGŚl. 26 (1 July 1930): 1; "Zakusy Cieszyniaków na Górnym Śląsku," GGŚl. 15 (7–13 Apr. 1926): 1.
135. "Oni to mogą bo to 'swoi': Zalew Górnego Śląska przez Cieszyniaków," GGŚl. 14 (31 Mar.–6 Apr. 1926): 2.
136. See Bjork, *Neither German nor Pole*, 269; Bjork, "The National State," 243–52; Kopec, "Z zagadnień integracji," 31–34; Krzyżanowski, "Kościół katolicki a władza państwowa," 177–85; Krzyżanowski, "Kościół Katowicki wobec regionalizmu," 75–77; Macala, *Duszpasterstwo a narodowość wiernych*, 44–148.
137. See Kneip, *Die deutsche Sprache in Oberschlesien*, 134–42. Ordinary locals usually prayed in the high languages (German or Polish) but spoke in dialect among themselves.
138. F. Flott, "Wie spricht der Oberschlesier," in *Heimatland O/S: Ein Heimatbuch f. die oberschlesische Jugend*, ed. F. Flott (Breslau, 1937), 51–52.
139. SR, June 1939, APK, 38/I, 176, 45. The authors of these documents are clearly opponents of the Nazis, most likely Communists and/or German Center Party sympathizers. They most likely served the Polish police as informants since their situational reports on Gleiwitz are found in the files of the Polish police. See also Polak-Springer, "Jammin' with Karlik," 277–89.
140. See Maria Wanda Wanatowicz, *Od indyferentnej ludności do śląskiej narodowości? Postawy narodowe ludności autochtonicznej Górnego Śląska w latach 1945–2003 w świadomości społecznej* (Katowice, 2004), 48.
141. SR, June 1939, APK, 38/I, 176, 33–35, 57; Polak-Springer, "Jammin' with Karlik," 289.
142. Ibid., 37. See also Bjork and Gerwarth, "The Annaberg," 388–89.
143. SR, May and June 1939, APK, 38/I, 176, 12–14, 36–37; SR, Apr.–June 1939, APO, 1191 (Regierung Oppeln), 1937, 562.
144. SR, May 1939, APK, 38/I, 176, 16.
145. OP, "Gegenwärtige Lage der Deutsche Kulturarbeit in West O/S," 23 Apr. 1936, PA-AA, Kattowitz, 63 A (Politik, Bd. 10), 9ff.

CHAPTER 4

GIVING "POLISH SILESIA" A "GERMAN" FACE, 1939–45

"You [eastern Upper Silesians] have returned home [to Germany] under the conditions of a war that had been imposed on us. No German ... wants war for war's sake. But [he] wants that which is owed to him. No one could prevent that our brothers of the eastern provinces [*Ostmark*] unite themselves with the Reich, and even so could no one impede the Sudeten Germans' return home [*Heimkehr*] again. ... The times when the German *Volk* is betrayed in its holiest of rights are over. ... You return home to Greater Germany and your mother province. There is only one Silesia."

—Joseph Wagner, *Gauleiter* of Gau Schlesien, address before rally commemorating Freedom Day, 15 October 1939

"No one in Germany thought about destroying the Polish state and the Polish peoples. The hatred that stood between the two nations was unilateral. And we have to always remember this track record of Polish hatred against everything German—yes, also for our continued work on this territory we have to, indeed, keep that before our eyes."

—Walter Gottschalk, inspector for the establishment of the BDO in annexed eastern Upper Silesia, speech at the Concert Hall (*Reichshalle*) in Kattowitz, 16 February 1940[2]

The Nazi attack on the Voivodeship Silesia—an ideologically central piece of the Wehrmacht's broader assault on Poland—began shortly before five o'clock in the morning on 1 September 1939. In support of the fundamental myth that all of Upper Silesia "was, is, and remains" a "German land," the Nazi regime mobilized *Freikorps* battalions made up largely of men who had recently fled across the border to Germany, where they received military training and weapons. As "volunteers" sent off to "retake their *Heimat*," they gave the Nazi invasion of eastern Upper Silesia (*Ostoberschlesien* in German irredentist vocabulary) an aura of righteousness.[3] To bolster the appearance of local support for the "liberation," fifth-column groups from the German minority in Polish Upper Silesia assisted the Wehrmacht in seizing industrial plants. Evoking memories of the border war of 1921, the *Freikorps* were met by armed battalions of former insurgents—only this time, a German army was invading.

As the Wehrmacht waged *Blitzkrieg* from the west, Soviet troops helped bring down Poland by invading from the east, as agreed to by the two powers in the Molotov-Ribbentrop Pact. With military victory quickly achieved, the Nazis annexed eastern Upper Silesia, other parts of the former Prussian eastern borderlands, and areas beyond them. These annexed territories—or "recovered lands," as they were also called—were contrasted with parts of Poland the Nazis claimed to be occupying, designated by the French term *Generalgouvernement*. The Nazis extended Upper Silesia's administrative border to include the province's Teschen area (Tesin/Zaolzia/Olsagebiet), which passed from Habsburg to Czechoslovakian control after World War I before being annexed by Poland in October 1938 in a ploy to prevent Hitler, who had claimed the entire Sudetenland (which encompassed this area), from taking it. The Nazis also expanded Upper Silesia beyond its provincial historical boundaries to include the Dąbrowa industrial basin and other areas previously in the provinces of Kielce and Cracow, including the city and county of Oświęcim, which the Germans renamed Auschwitz.[4]

The economic resources of Germany's "new Ruhr," as Nazi officials referred to industrial Upper Silesia, had key economic importance for the war economy. During the war years, this enlarged region provided an increasingly larger percentage of the Reich's coal supply, from about 9 percent in 1939/40 (34 million tons) to 22.8 percent (98.5 million tons) in 1943/44. In 1942, this industrial region began to produce synthetic benzine and oil from coal, a resource that assumed fundamental importance to the Reich's motorized armed forces once Germany's fuel sources in Romania fell under enemy attack. When the Allies began heavy bombardment of the Ruhr, Upper Silesia provided almost 30 percent of Germany's iron ore and more than 28 percent of its steel, in addition to other metals and chemicals. Once this industrial district fell under Soviet military control in January 1945, Albert Speer, one of the Reich's more sober economic planners, informed Hitler that Germany was now severly limited in its capability to produce armaments.[5]

The economic importance of this industrial center certainly influenced the regime's intent to give the formerly Polish parts of Silesia a "German" face, a project that is the focus of this chapter. Yet more than in any other part of the annexed territories, Nazi officials failed to realize their goal of making what they conceptualized as a "clean break" between what constituted "German" and what was "Polish," including the residents. In addition to the lack of defined national or ethnic borders in this region, the need to maintain a sufficiently large and productive labor force contributed to this failure. While such economic considerations failed to constrain the Nazis' ideologically driven effort to expel—and eventually murder—the Jewish population, they kept the regime from removing the vast majority of the "unpatriotic" mainstream Catholics.

To compensate, the regime placed increasing weight on the inclusive and integrative ("Germanization") aspects of its policies of ethnic "cleansing" (*Säuberung*). After 1941, it segregated and classified Upper Silesians into a four-category bureaucratic list (called the Deutsche Volksliste, the German Ethnic List, or DVL) that denoted the degree to which these individuals were "German"—linguistically, culturally, and politically—and thus the extent to which they could be made into full-fledged Germans and thereby "recovered" for the Reich. While implemented throughout the annexed areas, the DVL played a far more important and consequential role in this region, where the vast majority of locals were classified as "the in-between layer" (*Zwischenschicht*) as to Polish and German ethnicity/nationality/"race," and thus designated as having the potential to become "good Germans."

The interwar German-Polish cold war over Upper Silesia handily provided the appropriate discourses, policies, and specialists for "recovering" Polish Upper Silesia for Germany—renationalization politics that long preceded the DVL. This chapter first focuses on the Nazis' use of the "recovered territories" narrative to legitimate the attack on Poland, and thus the start of their imperial schemes. It then moves on to examine the regime's social engineering policies (expulsion, resettlement, assimilation), and how experts among German borderland nationalists—now working in formerly Polish institutes and facilities they appropriated and repurposed—became part of this enterprise. From there, the chapter examines the efforts these experts, and their new collaborators, made to transform cultural landscapes that symbolized a Polish Upper Silesia into a "beautiful Upper Silesian *Heimat*." Rather than actual rebuilding, this process involved appropriation, redecoration, and mass mobilization. The chapter's then looks at similar efforts to shape a new "Upper Silesian person" (*oberschlesische Mensch*), a project that engaged academics and folklorists constructing a suitable regionalist tradition and pedagogues teaching locals to speak "proper German," as well as the police and Gestapo stamping out "Polish behavior." The final sections examine how various national integration efforts not only failed to achieve their goals, but elicited strong local opposition toward the Reich.

From "Recovered Śląsk" to "Recovered Ostoberschlesien"

Long before its troops crossed the Polish border, Germany launched an irredentist propaganda campaign to renew public commemoration of the German defense of Upper Silesia against the Polish insurgency in 1921. While the Nazis had suspended the large-scale rallies that fed revanchist sentiments, activists in the League of the German East (BDO) "Nazified" this conflict by elevating its *Freikorps* and *Selbstschutz* fighters into the Third Reich's pantheon of "old fighters [*Vorkämpfer*] for the National Socialist movement." This campaign also valorized the earlier struggle of a "united German front" against "invading Polish hordes" and their allies, "the Versailles Powers."[6] The Nazi regime used the Mount of St. Anne monument and the Ratibor Borderland Tower with its *Freikorps* and *Selbstchutz* memorial, both opened in May 1938 (see chapter 3), to stage anti-Polish rallies evoking the earlier conflicts. The two architectural landmarks, both popular sites for organized border tourism, regularly offered education for the masses—officially *Volksbildung* (*Volk*/national cultivation)—on Nazi ideology and the Nazified memory of German-Polish struggle.[7]

Recalling earlier violence by "Polish marauders" against Upper Silesians ("Germans" in Nazi discourse), by 1938 the Nazi-controlled press and radio had begun playing up incidents that might be interpreted as persecution on the part of "Poles" and "Poland" against "Germans" in the Voivodeship. They also covered Grażyński's revanchist spectacles, including the Insurgent League's annual march to the Oder as well as the new memorials to the insurgency and the destruction of the Friedrich Wilhelm von Reden statue in Chorzów (Königshütte, see chapter 3). Together, these incidents constituted "evidence" that from 1919 to 1939 "the Poles" had promoted an unceasing "war of destruction [*Vernichtungskrieg*] against everything German."[8] The BDO held propaganda meetings in villages as well as at coal mines and metallurgy plants near the border. Preaching the Nazi version of national regionalism, these events contrasted the "anti-German conspiracy" between "the Poles" and the "Versailles Powers" with Hitler's "honest and ardent commitment" to "peace" with the eastern neighbor.[9]

The locals' generally negative predisposition to the Nazi regime made them natural skeptics of its ideology. For example, underground opponents of the Nazi regime in Gleiwitz reported how locals mocked the BDO as the "League of German Oxen [*Ochsen*]" and questioned its claims regarding Hitler's commitment to peace. However, they claimed that constant agitation asserting "the self-evident need to recover the German territories" lost after the war found "wide agreement."[10]

Rather than openly calling for war against Poland, the BDO echoed Nazism's staunchest opponents, the Catholic German Center Party and their liberal allies, in arguing for peaceful diplomacy as the way to "recover" the "stolen *Ostoberschlesien*." This general political agreement helps explain the acceptance of the group's assertion that in the border conflict with Poland the Nazi regime was simply acting in the best interests of the region and of Germany.[11] In this sense, the irredentist legacy gave the NSDAP an acceptable cover for its otherwise unpopular social Darwinism and imperialism.

The Nazis used incidents of persecution against "Germans" in the Voivodeship to strengthen their case. Although the violence and harassment at the hands of thugs, to which the Polish regional government gave moral support, was often a reaction to the Nazis' persecution of their Polish minority, it fueled local resentment against Grażyński on both sides of the border. The BDO also criticized Polish travel restrictions and harassment by border guards of Polish citizens seeking to enter Germany, which the Nazi propaganda bureau exploited by inviting border crossers to publicly share their "horror stories." In an area with many cross-border families, these stories were often recounted in workplace discussions. In June 1939, Nazi opponents in Gleiwitz admitted that such accounts "make it hard to doubt that in Poland terror is promoted against Germans. And so all this gives substantiation and legitimacy to the Nazi hysteria against Poland."[12]

In this atmosphere, the Nazis promoted the notion that *Ostoberschlesien* needed "the Führer's liberation." The orchestrated takeover of the Gleiwitz radio station by Germans in Polish uniforms on 31 August 1939 provided the initial justification for the attack on Poland as a matter of self-defense. Local headlines on 1 September read "Polish Insurgents Invade German Soil!" To add more substance to this propaganda, on 2 September the Beuthen daily reported that before the German invasion "Polish army" artillery fire on the city of Beuthen had left "two civilians dead and thirty-five injured." This attack allegedly signaled Polish insurgents to stage a night-time invasion of Beuthen (Bytom), Gleiwitz (Gliwice), and Hindenburg (Zabrze), thus clearing a path to the Oder River for regular troops.[13] The Gleiwitz "incident"—which received the most attention—became the first step in a "Polish annexation plan" that uncannily mimicked the Nazis' own diversionary scheme for the Wehrmacht's invasion of Poland.

The propaganda *Blitzkrieg* culminated in Hitler's appearance before the Reichstag only hours after the invasion began. His speech justifying and rationalizing Germany's actions began with a litany of territorial claims against Poland: "Danzig was and remains a German city. ... The Corridor was and is German!" Bolstering these grievances, Hitler invoked the traditional mythology of Germany as *Kulturträger*: "all these areas [eastern provinces] owe their cultural development exclusively to the German people, [and] without them these eastern territories would have been engulfed in the deepest barbarism." Germany's further justification was Poland's own transgressions as an "annexer" of German lands—albeit abetted by the Versailles Powers—and a "brutal abuser of the German minority," beginning with expulsions of Germans after the drawing of postwar borders. In choosing to highlight German claims to Danzig and the

Polish Corridor rather than Upper Silesia, Hitler may have acknowledged the higher international profile of that issue. But the importance of *Ostoberschlesien* to these matters remained clear.[14]

Despite similarities with the mainstream Weimar-era revanchist rhetoric heard at countless Plebiscite Day rallies, the Nazis diverged from its more regional character. In Upper Silesia, in particular, they promoted more inclusive concepts such as Pan-Silesia (*Gesamtschlesien*) or the German east (*der deutsche Osten*), which encompassed territories that had earlier belonged to the Prussian Empire.[15] In September 1939, the Third Reich used these two formulations to legitimize an annexation that extended beyond such long-contested but once Prussian territories as the Voivodeship and Czechoslovakia's Hultschin Province, including the formerly Habsburg Teschen area (Tesin/Olsagebiet/Zaolzia) as well as the formerly Russian Imperial Dąbrowa Basin. Within the Third Reich, this territorial hodgepodge was merged with Lower Silesia and governed by *Gauleiter* (governor) Joseph Wagner from the latter's administrative capital of Breslau, to form a unitary Gau Schlesien (Silesian Province). The new administration mobilized *Ostforschung* academics to create narratives that represented the Dąbrowa Basin, which had never been a part of any Silesian province, much less a Germanic state, as integral to this region.[16]

Territorial "recovery" and "return home" provided a sentimental veneer for both militant empire building and murderous ventures in biological engineering. The term "recovered provinces" (*wiedergewonnene Länder*),[17] initially applied to annexed Polish and Czechoslovak regions, by late 1940 encompassed French Alsace and Lorraine and Belgium's eastern cantons. Further, cultural officials began to promote "homecoming" (*Heimkehr*) to people of "German blood" throughout Europe, particularly those still stranded beyond the borders of the new German Empire. The mission to bring "German blood and soil" "home to the Reich" (*Heim ins Reich*) rallied irredentist-minded idealists to work toward the realization of the regime's ambitious "new European order."[18] Otto Spatz's 1940 popular scholarly publication, *Recovered German Land* (*Wiedergewonnenes Deutsches Land*), proclaimed that "German land and German people in east and west, who were forcefully integrated into foreign states for years have now returned to the Reich, and thanks to the Führer's will are constituents of the Greater German Reich."[19]

German propagandists idealized the annexation of the former Voivodeship and adjacent territories as the rejoining of *Ostoberschlesien* with "its motherland," while obscuring the fact that the Nazi agenda went far beyond "recovering"—alternately, "liberating"—peoples and territories from "Polish tyranny." The regime's General Plan for the East (Generalplan Ost), a comprehensive strategy for taking over East-Central Europe, foresaw cleansing the Reich of "unwanted" groups by the use of expulsion and resettlement, killings, and genocide (in particular against Jews), as well as collateral material expropriation.[20]

A Revival of Border Rallies

Having reclaimed the former irredentist territory, the Nazi regime resumed the interwar tradition of border rallies in Katowice, which once again became Kattowitz. In this new incarnation the rallies avoided any hint of "Upper Silesian particularism." Instead, they became "*Volk* cultivation" (*Volksbildung*) forums to promote the national reassimilation of the inhabitants of a borderland with famously multiple identities.

The Nazis rejected earlier notions of assimilating "foreigners" using the formal term *Germanisierung* (Germanization). Hitler himself viewed such efforts as futile, since they assumed that an individual—for example, a Pole—could somehow switch his or her fundamentally biological ("racial") national identity. The new mission aimed to "win back" for the nation "German blood" that had been "lost" or "stolen" by foreign powers. In an effort to differentiate their policies from earlier assimilation efforts, regional Nazi officials first described their program with the alternative term of *Eindeutschung* (literally, "making German," hereafter refereed to as Germanization). The confusion continued, and in April 1942, *Gauleiter* Fritz Bracht demanded that *Eindeutschung* be replaced with *Rückdeutschung* (retro-Germanization), in order to strengthen the "winning back" aspect of borderland "cultural work." Further exploiting the possibilities of German word formation, officials alternately used the term *Wiedereindeutschung* (making German again, or re-Germanization).[21] *Beseitigung der Polonisierung* (doing away with Polonization) offered a more concrete construction of the same end.[22]

The first Freedom Day (Tag der Freiheit) rally, held on Sunday, 15 October 1939, officially launched the "re-Germanization" program. (Thereafter these events took place on the more fitting 1 September.)[23] In keeping with the aim of shaping a new national identity that represented the former Voivodeship as an intrinsic part of the Third Reich, the 1939 rally invited the region's native "German" population to publicly celebrate "the re-union of *Ostoberschlesien* with the motherland, from which they were never separated in spirit."[24] Joseph Wagner, *Gauleiter* of the new Gau Schlesien and the highest-ranking official speaker, declared that the Third Reich had launched the war to assert its "holiest of rights": union with "our brothers of the eastern provinces [*Ostmark*]." He asserted that by denying Germany its rights, Poland and the Allies had "imposed" a war which the Germans "did not want for war's sake."[25] Evoking Hitler's Reichstag address of 1 September 1939, Wagner thus cited German claims to the formerly Prussian provinces—rather than ideological rhetoric about *Lebensraum*—to justify an imperialist war. In this sense, the Third Reich drew on two decades of broad support for the "recovery" of German lands.

The Gau Schlesien leadership designated the former Voivodeship Government Building (VGB) and Forum Katowice as the site for the first Freedom Day rally.

Although this venue was designed for mass rallies, the choice was an ironic one given its history as a showcase for the concept of "Polish Upper Silesian" identity, which portrayed "Germans" as oppressors and recalled the Prussian era as a time of "captivity" and "slavery." Because of their brief tenure, the new rulers had to improvise cosmetic changes to prepare the VGB and parade grounds for the rally, such as the destruction of Polish statues, the removal of Polish-language signs, the "re-Germanization" of street and place names, and proper NSDAP decorations for the forum area.[26] Attendance at the rally reached 30,000 according to the *Kattowitzer Zeitung*, formerly the provincial daily of the Voivodeship's German-minority organization (the Volksbund) and now the official party newspaper of the industrial district. Aggressive grassroots mobilization by the NSDAP and its organizations contributed to the impressive turnout.[27]

At the same time, many locals showed an eagerness to demonstrate their "loyalty" to the new government, for example, by signing up for Nazi organizations.[28] In Kattowitz and its surrounding county alone, an area with a population of 483,200 in December 1939, 54,629 individuals (roughly 11 percent) had joined the BDO by March 1940.[29] Before 1941, this organization played a key role in determining which local residents were "of German blood" and then in schooling them on becoming "good Germans."[30] Neither party membership nor attendance at rallies necessarily proved either national identity or political conviction. Indeed, party reports often noted that native residents of the industrial district were commonly motivated by social and material interests rather than by genuine commitment in their gestures of "loyalty" to "Germandom."[31] Certainly, the fear of social reprisals and even punitive measures if they did not at least feign political activism also played a role. For insurgents who had survived the combat but did not join Grażyński and other high-ranking government officials in fleeing from the Voivodeship and Poland, BDO membership offered a way to disguise their past activities and adopt a new German image.[32]

In mid-December 1939, the Nazis made the first formal attempt to categorize locals according to nationality by haphazardly carrying out a census (the "fingerprint" census) for the purpose of issuing new identity cards. Only about two-thirds of the local population participated in the census, most from the cities. It offered the least demanding way to declare German nationality, as did 94.97 percent of the Upper Silesian population, while only 4.75 percent claimed the Polish one. Fewer locals declared German as their language (77.81 percent) than their nationality (94.97 percent), while more claimed that Polish was their language (11.9 percent) than their nationality (4.75 percent), and while no one declared Silesian nationality, a number claimed Silesian as their language (10.05 percent).[33] By March 1940 it had become clear that self-identified "Poles" faced loss of jobs and property, and rumors circulated of systematic transfers to the occupied parts of Poland (the *Generalgouvernement*, or GG). Given the consequences of declaring oneself "Polish" and the subjective nature of this decision, a number of initially self-identified "Poles" petitioned local authorities for a change to "German."³⁴ These conversions help explain the regime's skepticism as to the validity of the census results and its interest in devising a less subjective way to determine nationality among Upper Silesians. Until 1941, when the Nazis would introduce a more complex process for accurately separating "Poles" from "Germans," regional authorities estimated that all but a small fraction of "unreliable" residents (10 percent) of the formerly Polish territories were either "reliable" (10 percent) or constituted a "conditionally reliable," "in-between layer" (*Zwischenschicht*, 80 percent), which was to be "entirely recovered" [*gewonnen*] for the Reich following a "probation period." In other words, they could be "reared" to be "good Germans."³⁵

The first Freedom Day rally served this end by touting the popularity of the "liberation" and the regime that delivered it. To emphasize the image of "popular will"—and borrowing from the interwar culture of border rallies—the pageantry included coal miners in uniform marching with contingents in folk costumes. They also harked back to earlier events in celebrating legendary Volksbund leader Otto Ulitz, who himself strode to the podium to thank Hitler for Upper Silesia's "liberation" from "Polish slavery," and was officially dubbed an "old fighter" (*Vorkämpfer*) for "Nazi ideals" "in the struggle for Germandom."³⁶

By attempting to usurp and Nazify the history of the German minority's interwar social and political activism, as they had the heroes of the military conflict of 1921, the NSDAP aimed to insert itself into a new historical narrative of Upper Silesia as a "land of struggle" (*Kampfland*) where the rooted "German" natives had engaged in a protracted "struggle between peoples" (*Volkstumskampf*).³⁷ As a more direct route to the loyalty of Volksbund leaders, the party offered some of them prestigious posts in the regional government. Most notably, Ulitz—a champion of German schooling—became the regional minister of education, even though he had not been a committed Nazi, and indeed had resisted the Nazification of the German minority during the interwar era. Another important personality, Viktor Kauder, former head of the Volksbund's Kulturbund (Cultural Association), was appointed director of the new (German) Silesian Library in Kattowitz.³⁸

Characterizing the era of Polish governance as "the ruin" (*Verdarb*) of *Ostoberschlesien*, *Gauleiter* Wagner's rally speech followed a second theme of the new narrative that justified the war.³⁹ Notions of Polish deficiencies in "German standards" of *Arbeit* and *Kultur* were, of course, a mainstay of Weimar-era revanchist discourse, a trope with even longer roots in German popular culture. Thus, Wagner deployed the old-fashioned insult of "Polish mismanagement" (*polnische Wirtschaft*), implying both incompetence and slovenliness. Along with the revanchist theme of an imminent "Polish anti-German war of destruction," cultural incompatibilities became the second central pillar of Nazi anti-Polish discourse that initially justified the regime's increasingly radical politics of social engineering.[40]

The rhetoric of German-Polish borderland conflict had long linked the promotion of progress and cultural cultivation to a nation's right to territorial appropriation. Thus, Grażyński had tied his promise of borderland improvements to the discrediting of Prussian-era "cultural work" in eastern Upper Silesia. Nazi officials now denigrated the work of their Polish predecessors, albeit in more radical and racist tones. The 1939 Freedom Day rally provided an early opportunity to contrast their predecessors' "degradation" and "disfigurement" of landscape and culture with what, in the words of *Gauleiter* Wagner, would follow now that the NSDAP was in charge: "With time this land will take on a different character in all walks of life than that which was once imposed on it, a character that only exists where there is Germany."[41] Such promises of progress and improvement soon presented authorities with a considerable challenge. Although the regime no longer had to contest the superiority of its "cultural work" against that of an existing Polish state, it still had to live up to public expectations and, in particular, to popular memories of Polish achievements during the interwar era. More problematic in terms of its popular acceptance, Nazi cultural politics provided an ideological overlay for the expulsion of Poles and Jews and the resettlement of Germans from eastern Europe, as well as the "renationalization" (*Umvolkung*) of the native population.[42]

Population Politics and Renationalization, 1939–45

The annexed territories initially provided a site where the Nazi regime had free rein to engineer society according to its ideological premises. Jews, in particular those individuals whom the regime identified as such, became the main victims of Nazi population politics. The deportation of Jews from the former Prussian parts of Upper Silesia (some 2,912 in the former Provinz and 4,486 in the Voivodeship by mid-May 1940) began briefly in October 1939 to the "Nisko reservation" in Lublin, and thereafter to newly established ghettoes in the neighboring Dąbrowa Basin. This area already had a large Jewish population; indeed, the area's main cities, Sosnowitz (Sosnowiec) and Bendsburg (Będzin), had Jewish majorities. By 1943, Jews from both these areas and ninety-three work camps across Upper Silesia were being shipped en masse to perish in the notorious Auschwitz death camp, which was officially located within the administrative borders of what in 1941 became Gau Oberschlesien (Upper Silesia, abbreviated as Gau O/S).[43]

The labor requirements of wartime industrial production forced the regime to defer the full realization of a "clean break" between "Poles" and "Germans" until the ultimately unrealized "final victory" (*Endsieg*). Thus, large-scale expulsions and resettlements focused on the largely agrarian Warthegau (Poznań/Posen and the Wielkopolska region), which became a kind of "model province" (*Mustergau*) for Nazi population politics.[44] Relatively little population movement occurred in most of annexed Upper Silesia. According to official SS statistics for 1943, a total of approximately 80,000 Poles, Jews, and other "foreigners" were expelled since the war's beginning from the entire eastern Upper Silesia and the Dąbrowa Basin—most from the second area—comprising only 3 to 5 percent of the total population. In October 1940 most of the 22,148 Poles in this group were sent to the GG, primarily to clear Saybusch (Żywiec) County, which lay some fifty miles (eighty kilometers) south of Kattowitz, for resettlement by "*Volksdeutsche*" from Galicia, a province extending from eastern Poland to western Ukraine. Another 5,100 were sent to labor camps in the *Altreich* (Germany proper). Beginning in 1943, more than 9,000 individuals were incarcerated in twenty-one *Polenlager* (concentration camps for Poles) throughout the region. These statistics do not account for the extensive forced movement within Upper Silesia, where those classified as Jews and Poles often lost homes and property and suffered transfers to undesirable residential areas.[45]

While economic forces unquestionably were a factor in explaining Nazi population politics in occupied Poland, they played a secondary role to ideology—more specifically, the official project of "recovering German blood and soil" for the Reich. Thus, despite industrial labor shortages, the regime expelled Jews and Poles, and by the end of 1943 transferred most of the 24,585 "*Volksdeutsche* resettlers" (*Umsiedler*) from Galicia and Bukovina to "cleared" agricultural lands in the Dąbrowa Basin and Saybusch (fig. 4.1).[46] This group constituted only a small percentage of the more than one million "resettlers" transferred to other parts of the annexed territories and the GG during the war. They were to be joined by the roughly 80 percent of the local population that, according to regional leaders, were of "German blood" and on their way to become part of the Reich's "recovered people."

The attempt to enumerate all of Upper Silesia's "German" population through the Deutsche Volksliste (DVL) marked a departure from this inclusivity. While already a part of nationalization policy in the Warthegau since late October 1939, SS leader Heinrich Himmler introduced it to the other annexed regions two years later in early March. As Gerhard Wolf's work demonstrates, this policy was met by widespread discontent from *Gau*-level officials, who, in contrast to the more rigidly selective approach favored by Reich-level leaders, wanted an ever more inclusive and pragmatic national integration policy. Particularly in Upper Silesia, officials viewed the locals' uniform integration into the *Herrenvolk* (master race) as the best way of winning their hearts for the Reich's struggle. Instead, the DVL created rifts and discontent among natives by dividing them according to four different categories that represented the quality

Figure 4.1. Heinrich Himmler (center) with Fritz Bracht (next to the left) and other Nazi officials greeted by *"Volksdeutsche* resettlers" (*Umsielder*). Mount of St. Anne, n.d. (circa 1940–42). (Bundesarchiv Berlin)

of the individual's "German" character—essentially, excellent (category 1), good (category 2), the "in-between layer" (*Zwischenschicht*) (category 3), and bad (category 4)—and discriminating against those in the last two groups. Himmler's call to base the segregation on "racial screening" was ignored in practice; instead, regional officials applied the more traditional nationalist idea of "German" based on cultural affiliation and personal history.[47]

From the spring of 1941 to almost the end of the war, authorities screened the backgrounds of over a million people in eastern Upper Silesia. They had a particular interest in their political and cultural behavior during the German-Polish interwar conflict, and especially during 1921, as verified by interviews that officials held with the locals themselves and people who claimed to know them. Ultimately, in the formerly Prussian parts of eastern Upper Silesia, the regime classified 64 percent of the population as "threes" (category 3)—a term used by both officials and the public—which entitled them only to provisional

German citizenship, subject to revocation. In other words, although most Upper Silesians fell short of Nazi standards for "good Germans," they were deemed "Germanizable" (*Eindeutschungsfähig*). Male "threes" of military age were deemed to be "German" enough to be subject (along with "ones" and "twos" but not "fours") to conscription.

This whole categorization process was only feasible because Upper Silesians were willing to cooperate in such an exercise. Bishop Stanisław Adamski, formerly of the Polish Diocese of Katowice, who continued to serve in the region until expelled to the GG at the end of February 1941, had all along encouraged locals to "mask" their Polish/Silesian identity with a German/Germanophile visage in order to escape expulsion and persecution, and to preserve Silesia's "Polishness."[48]

Some 53,000 German newcomers ultimately moved from the *Altreich* to Upper Silesia (20,000 to Kattowitz alone) to assume prestigious bureaucratic, civil service, and industrial functions, and to serve as the region's new economic, political, and cultural elites. They made up 4.77 percent of the region's population by October 1943.[49] These German newcomers replaced the postpartition Polish newcomer elite, most of whom either fled or were ousted from their positions. They now aroused the same kinds of resentment earlier directed at their Polish counterparts. Class conflict—between what regime officials defined as native "*Volksdeutsche*" and migrant *Reichsdeutsche* (Upper Silesian locals and newcomer Germans)—exacerbated existing tensions and grew worse as the war progressed and economic privation increased.

As during the Grażyński years, the air of superiority assumed by newcomers in their relations with the local borderland population fostered resentments. As educated Germans and, more importantly, as "(NSDAP) party comrades" (*Parteigenossen*), they considered themselves inherently superior to the Polish and Slavicized dialect-speaking masses.[50] During the interwar era, the German Center Party, the Polish Catholic Church, and the regional autonomy party, the Upper Silesian Defense League, in Polish Upper Silesia defended the rights of natives against the newcomers, whom they often criticized as "colonists" and "gold diggers" (see chapters 1 and 3). All parties except for the NSDAP were now, of course, strictly prohibited, along with any independent organizations. Even some high-ranking party officials observed that the *Reichsdeutsche* comported themselves as "conquerors," "gold diggers," "careerists," and "opportunists," while treating the annexed territory as their "helot society" and "new America."[51] Locals themselves had their own lexicon of derogatory terms for this group, including "September Germans" (after September 1939) and "western mountaineers" (*Westgorol*), an adaptation of the *gorol* they had earlier used for the Polish outsider elite. They also sardonically made references to such outsiders with the Nazi honorific "P.G.," for *Parteigenosse*, as a subversive allusion to *pierońskie gorole* (damned mountaineers) in the local dialect.[52]

The *Heimatkundler* as Social Engineer

In December 1939, the North and East German Research Society (NOFG) convened in Kattowitz to incorporate eastern Upper Silesia into the regional and national academic and cultural-political *Ostforschung* consortium. The Nazis' policy for ethnic homogenization in the borderlands had long exploited academic research. Consortium members such as the Silesian Union for Heimat Defense (Schlesische Bund für Heimatschutz), the Silesian section of the BDO, the Bureau for Upper Silesian Regional Studies (Amt für Oberschlesische Landeskunde), and the Organization for Upper Silesian Regional Studies (Vereinigung für oberschlesische Landeskunde) now turned their attention to this new terrain. They also welcomed activists from the Kulturbund (the Voivodeship's German-minority cultural/academic union), notably Viktor Kauder and Edgar Boidol, who now openly joined Karl Sczodrok, Franz Pfüntzenreiter, and Alfons Perlick and other *Heimatkundler* from the western part of the borderland, as well as borderland nationalists in Breslau, including Ernst Birke and Hermann Aubin. This expanded organization of 500 to 600 intellectual combatants for Germandom in the borderlands worked under the auspices of the NSDAP and BDO. Subordination to the Third Reich's apparatus for ideology and ethnic cleansing gave greater political importance to borderland nationalists, who were now tasked with implementing the scholarly and acculturation aspects of the regime's ethnic engineering agenda.[53]

As part of the BDO, these activists and scholars were drawn into its efforts not only to physically segregate "Poles" from "Germans," but also to examine Catholic Church parish records—often despite clergy protests—to uncover "Jews" whose ancestors had converted.[54] Over time, the BDO and the entire borderland nationalist culture came under increasing control from the Reich Commissioner for the Strengthening of Germandom (Reichskommissar für die Festigung deutschen Volkstums, or RKF), headed by Heinrich Himmler. Working closely with the SS, the RKF planned and carried out social engineering policies in the annexed and occupied territories.[55] Rather than just focusing on public lectures, approved reading lists, and research, the *Heimatkundler* now also helped develop and implement "*Volk* cultivation" programs aimed at social engineering. For example, the ethnographic work of Alfons Perlick—earlier promoted in lectures at Beuthen's Pedagogical Academy and exhibits at its Landesmuseum—became "the basis for a new [Nazi] education project [*Erziehungsarbeit*] and for a new cultural development [*Kulturaufbau*] for the working class." These terms, along with *Volkstumsarbeit* and "(re)construction" (*[Wieder]Aufbau*) became part of the new lexicon of social engineering–oriented cultural politics.[56]

The Nazis' initial effort to promote an official program of Greater Silesian (Pan-Silesian) identity ended with the creation in January 1941 of a Gau

Oberschlesien (Gau O/S), governed from Kattowitz by *Gauleiter* Fritz Bracht. In terms of geography, this new entity encompassed all the interwar German, Czech, and Polish parts of the former Gau Schlesien, but not its Lower Silesian area. Symbolically, it embodied the revival of German Upper Silesian peculiarity, which the regime had previously tried to marginalize. The official acknowledgment of a *Heimat* tradition was a partial concession to the borderland nationalists, who insisted that "Upper Silesian regionalism" was critical to the intergration of locals into the Reich. However, the Nazis cleansed it of everything they associated with "Polishness" (or the German Center Party), such as Catholic tradition and the Slavophone local dialect.[57]

The difficulty of reengineering society solely through large-scale population transfers provided an opportunity for cultural politics—and thus the *Heimatkundler*—to rise in importance. The primary goal of these cultural agents was to convince the populace and, by 1941, its "re-Germanizable" majority of DVL-identified "threes," that they and their *Heimat* truly belonged to the *Volksgemeinschaft* (national/*Volk* community). To this end, these cultural activists continued the shared interwar German and Polish tradition of inventing a national regional tradition that would extinguish all traces of Grażyński's "regionalism" (the official Polish Silesian identity) as well as the nationally indifferent regional consciousness.

Ensconced in Kattowitz, the new cultural authorities set about creating a traditional identity suitable to the new—but restored—entity. To this end, they repurposed useful artifacts from Grażyński's Polish Silesianism, notably the Silesian Library, the radio station, the Musical Conservatory, and the Silesian Institute. The institute—and its home in the architecturally avant-garde House of Education (see fig. 3.3)—became the Central Institute for Upper Silesian Regional Research (Zentralinstitute für Oberschlesische Landesforschung, or ZIOF). Indeed, the respective missions of these two institutes so closely resembled one another that a regional BDO chief from Breslau tasked with adapting Silesian Institute holdings for its successor observed that: "We Germans have to build up [*aufbauen*] something entirely different. I don't believe it's worthy of us merely to establish a German institute from the inheritance of this Polish propaganda institution."[58] Responsibility for ensuring that the ZIOF fulfilled its mission fell to Dr. Fritz Arlt. A sociologist specializing in racial theory, Arlt was also the regional RKF leader, Himmler's deputy in Upper Silesia, and a chief planner of the Holocaust, in particular the Auschwitz extermination complex.[59]

The Upper Silesian Regional Homeland League (O/S Heimatbund, or OHB), established in 1941 as the academic wing of a larger consortium dedicated to forging a Nazi German regionalism in Upper Silesia, had by 1943 taken over this responsibility from both its parent body and the BDO. Its head, Georg Kate, became the leading figure of cultural politics in Gau O/S.[60] In instrumentalizing traditional German provincialism in the service of nationalization and Nazification, the OHB exemplified a practice that—as the work of Celia Applegate points out—extended throughout Germany.[61] The Upper Silesian group was itself a regional section of the nationwide Deutsche Heimatbund, led by the Nazi ideologist Alfred Rosenberg, one of the main policy makers in the Third Reich's occupied territories. In a pamphlet entitled *What Does the OHB Want?* the *Gauleiter* Fritz Bracht provided a clear answer to this leading question: "To cleanse the *Heimat* of all traits of the degeneration [*Verfall*] that particularly during the epoch of Polish tyranny distorted the face of our land via an alien way of doing things [*artfremde Geschäftenmacherei*]."[62] The transformation of an eastern Upper Silesia that had been "ruined by the Poles" into a "beautiful German *Heimat*" was thus a matter of "cleansing," which would require cultural politics (that is, "Germanization") working hand in hand with more aggressive forms of social engineering.

In the name of national regionalism, the new regime mobilized an array of disciplines and areas of specialization. Writing in the official Gau Oberschlesien daily *Kattowitzer Zeitung*, OHB head Kate noted that "rearing" the local population as "good Germans" presupposed the wholesale "re-Germanization" of the region itself through such tasks as changing the appearance of its landscape, promoting "German" folk traditions, and constructing a new pedagogical tradition of *Heimatkunde*.[63] This agenda, of course, entailed the deconstruction of Grażyński's Polish Silesianism. Historians, museum curators, photographers, writers and poets, landscape developers, language teachers, even puppeteers, and, of course, *Heimatkundler* all had a role in this effort. A new foundation, the O/S Stiftung, financed the dissemination of Upper Silesian culture through such media as schoolbooks, almanacs, pamphlets, the press, radio, film, theater, and public rallies. The OHB's allies in schooling the public in the new *Heimatkunde* included the NSDAP and its organizations, in particular the Nazi Teachers' Union (Nationalsozialistische Lehrerbund, or NSLB), the Labor Union (Deutsche Arbeitsfront, or DAF), the Strength through Joy leisure agency (Kraft durch Freude, KdF), the Women's League (Nationalsozialistische Frauenschaft, NSF), the Hitler Youth (Hitlerjugend), and the BDO.[64]

The ideology behind this effort to "cleanse" and "reconstruct" a "German O/S *Heimat*" presumed enduring ethnic ("racial") struggle in the borderland. Indeed, its usefulness as an instrument for public mobilization required the regime to forestall any notion that simply incorporating eastern Upper Silesia into the Reich would end this conflict. To this end, regime agents contrived the scenario of a new internal war that would supercede earlier German attempts to "recover" the region's eastern territory from the Poles. This new conflict required a "clean break" between "Polishness" and "Germandom," indeed, the excision of any trace of the former. As spelled out in the OHB program, the "re-Germanization" mission required participation from the public, not just the party elite: "In the past the Upper Silesian learned to fight and sacrifice for his *Heimat*, and this deep love for it will now motivate him to mobilize all his strengths for the new shaping of *Oberschlesien* based on German precepts."[65] By this account, 1 September 1939 represented the transition from the era of old-style ethnic conflict to that of mass mobilization for "re-Germanization" based on ethnic cleansing. According to Nazi officials, this new stage of the struggle for Upper Silesia would be long and hard fought. In the words of *Gauleiter* Bracht, "we can hardly make good [*wiedergutmachen*] decades of transgression in only a few years."[66]

Transforming a "Polish" Landscape

The previous transformation of eastern Upper Silesia's landscape, under Grażyński's "regionalist" program, affected primarily the industrial district. Other than replacing artifacts of Prussian rule, it aimed to improve living standards, strengthen the regional (and Polish) economy, and make the Voivodeship an architectural showcase. Much as the Nazis would have preferred a total makeover of their annexed territory, the constraints of war imposed limitations on its "re-Germanization." Aside from some completed reconstruction projects, the new regime's accomplishments in this area mainly involved symbolic relabeling of the existing landscape with an aim to reeducate the public's taste in architecture and topography.

Much as the regime depended on the trope of eternal German-Polish conflict, its cultural officials cultivated a conceptual border once the physical one disappeared, in their case drawing on earlier rhetorical battles over national architectural superiority. The OHB's bureau for "landscape shaping" (*Landschaftsgestaltung*) led the effort to rid Gau O/S of Grażyński's symbolic spaces. Its head, Gerhard Ziegler, had three years of experience in the Reich Office of Regional Planning in Berlin.[67] In Kattowitz, his office employed a strategy that reified distinct Polish and German "approaches" to landscape development that allegedly became visible on crossing from German-governed to Polish-governed territory. As Ziegler explained this phenomenon, whereas in German Upper Silesia one generally sees

> a loving engagement with the landscape, an agreeable exploitation of its resources, a friendly and purposeful embedding of the products of Man, namely houses, villages, cities, communication lines, etc., in mountains and valleys with appropriate trees … , the stream flanked by alders, the forests beautified and cultivated. [In contrast], there [in Polish Upper Silesia] the exploitation and plunder of the landscape, disorderly placement of buildings, no enjoyment of bushes and trees, barren and untamed monocultures of pines and therefore moldy soil, scattered debris, affectionless and neglected villages, bare streets and paths, … flooding on the one hand, and dust and drought, even outright desert on the other. Indeed, the poverty of the

population has much to account for this, but otherwise, this is all a consequence of affectionlessness and thoughtlessness.[68]

By applying the old racist rhetoric of *polnische Wirtschaft* to the landscape, Ziegler contrasted land and human creations consciously designed to reflect harmony with nature, attention to "beauty" and aestheticism, as well as the fruitful use of space and resources with the chaotic and reckless exploitation of territory and resources.[69]

Ziegler's Polish landscape also reflects the Nazis' disdain for what they viewed as the Western and liberal path to modernization and industrialization. This Nazi trope contrasts "civilization" (*Zivilisation*)—characterized by the rootless, "artificial and merely technical achievements of a soulless Western way of life"—with a superior German *Kultur* of "rootedness," "idealism," and "creativity."[70] Although German literati commonly associated "civilization" with French and British ways, Ziegler singled out "Americanism," thereby evoking interwar Katowice's reputation as an "American city," as well as Nazi propaganda that depicted Poland as a tool of Wall Street. Ziegler's description of the American landscape strikingly resembled his portrayal of Polish Upper Silesia: unkempt, barren, dirty, and abused due to exploitative, "affectionless," tasteless, and environmentally harmful practices. In its homeland or in Upper Silesia, "Americanism" was a consequence "of the rash tempo of economic development."[71]

Despite Ziegler's critique of American landscape practices, the Nazi regime's cultural agents tended to find the primary cause for the degradation of Upper Silesia's landscape closer to home. Erwin W. Schramm, a propagandist who in early 1941 became head of the Gau O/S Office for Local Administration (Gauamt für Kommunalpolitik), blamed "liberalism" for urban and even rural degradation in the *Altreich*; yet his greater concern was the far more extensive "disfigurement" (*Verschandelung*) in cities and villages of eastern Upper Silesia under Polish rule. "The integration [*Eingliederung*] of the eastern territories into the Reich peremptorily demands that appearances of the places that had been disfigured during the Polish era quickly again receive a German face."[72] Essentially, Schramm and the other OHB landscape experts labeled as "Polish" whatever contradicted Nazi values.

Befitting the Nazi glorification of the German land as opposed to the decadent city, critics often deployed standard Nazi defamations such as "cosmopolitan," "foreign," "Jewish/American/Polish"—or any combination thereof—for Kattowitz's modernist architecture. In this context, "Jewish" says nothing about the architect's ancestry, but rather reflects the Nazi rejection of avant-garde or modernist forms, which it lumped together—and often banned—as "degenerate art."[73] Perhaps recalling Ziegler's dusty Polish landscape, one OHB activist charged that Kattowitz's "cubic-style" buildings were evidence of the Polish regime's complicity in a "Jewish" conspiracy to create an "eastern stone desert."[74]

Indeed, for another critic, the city's "monuments of Jewish cubist architectural forms ... give the land the flavor of an annex of Jerusalem."[75] Cultural activists also condemned what they viewed as an official Polish ethnic cleansing campaign under Grażyński to destroy German statues, steal Prussian pedestals for Polish memorials, and paint over German-language signs—all part of an imperialist Polish "anti-German war of destruction."[76]

For Minister of Education Otto Ulitz, the region's "German character" was embodied in its Prussian-era "stone buildings, not by the overpriced and overdecorated Polish architectural creations."[77] His comments—like those of other critics—show the regime's willingness to exploit social tensions carried over from the former Voivodeship, such as resentment of the government's investment in expensive high-rise buildings while neglecting worker housing, the preferential treatment of outsiders over natives, and, of course, German resentment against the Voivodeship's "Polonization" campaign.

To their dismay, the OHB had to face the reality that "war is not the time for transforming Germany's architectural profile."[78] It did, however, provide an occasion for the Nazis' first venture in cleansing the Upper Silesian architectural landscape, when, amid the fighting of early September 1939, they burned down Kattowitz's municipal synagogue.[79] By necessity, Grażyński's icons of modernity remained the façade of Gau Oberschlesien's capital. As a Munich newspaper noted, the buildings both "lacked the gigantic presence to be awe-inspiring, but were too large to be overlooked. [They] ... remain as tokens of the curse of Polishness [Polentum], and likewise serve as our scattered memorial to the hard times of foreign rule over the city."[80] Thus, the modernist skyscraper and the Gau House (formerly Grażyński's VGB), along with the Prussian-era municipal theater and train station, continued to represent Gau Oberschlesien on postcards, travel guides, and popular publications (fig. 4.2).[81] To make the best of the situation, the press and travel guides sometimes conveniently failed to mention the once vaunted Polish origins of the newer buildings.[82]

A "German" Face for the Industrial District

Lacking resources for a complete reconstruction of Gau O/S, the regime turned to redecorating with the established symbols of National Socialist might. Thus, the large carving of a Polish eagle and other national symbols were missing from the Gau House façade when the second Freedom Day celebration convened on 1 September 1940—with Propaganda Minister Joseph Goebbels as guest of honor and over 100,000 local residents in attendance. The "R.P.," for Republic of Poland, along its frieze somehow remained, perhaps because—as the seat of Gau Oberschlesien's governor—it could now stand for Regierungs-Präsidium. Symbolically cleansed, the monumental quasi-modernist fortress with classical

Figure 4.2. German postcard of Kattowitz (Katowice): the skyscraper, center and VGB, top right, and Prussian-era buildings (theater, top left, and train station, bottom left), 1940–43. (BŚ-ZS)

motifs might have been built by Mussolini or Hitler; thus, it fit the regime's norms of "healthy architecture." As the central site of "German Upper Silesian" identity, the former VGB was once again suitable for display on guidebook covers as the architectural pride of Upper Silesia.[83]

The "decadent (Polish) architecture" of the Silesian Museum building—a massive avant-garde construction of glass walls and cubic shapes across the street from the Gau House (see fig. 3.7)—made it impossible to repurpose. In any case, since it had not yet opened in September 1939, it had little institutional or popular support. After its holdings were transferred to the former Landesmuseum, now the Grenzland (Borderland) Museum, in Beuthen, the building became for a time an auction house for property confiscated from Jews and Poles who had been expelled, and then was gradually dismantled (fig. 4.3).[84] Its removal, especially given its prominent location, can also be seen as a token payment toward promises by the *Gauleiter* to "re-Germanize" Kattowitz and the larger region.[85]

Above all, this act of aesthetic ethnic cleansing attested to the regime's prowess in *Kulturarbeit*. Other modernist structures were not dismantled but rather modified in some way to carry a stamp of the Reich. The most notable example was the installation in the Administration Office Building of porcelain bells that played Heinrich Gutberlet's "The March of the Germans in Poland," a favorite patriotic song of the German minority during the interwar era, as well as the national anthem of the Third Reich (fig. 4.4).[86]

Figure 4.3. Dismantling of the Silesian Museum building, Kattowitz (Katowice), 1942–45. (BŚ-ZS)

Figure 4.4. Administration Office Building (before 1939) and German Police Headquarters (after 1939) with porcelain bells on the wing of the façade, Kattowitz (Katowice), 1941. (BŚ-ZS)

Although Kattowitz had particular importance as the Gau Oberschlesien capital, the OHB sought to make nearby Königshütte (Chorzów) a second tourist center in the industrial district, with its own appropriate postcard images.[87] The attractions included the new municipal park monument of Reden that replaced the one torn down by local Polish authorities shortly before the invasion, as well as the premodern wooden churches that Polish cultural officials had earlier moved to both modern metropolises. Formerly symbols of the historical rootedness of "age-old Slavic/Polish" culture, they now became "unquestionably important witnesses to German woodworking technique."[88] By the spring of 1941, Kattowitz boasted its first visitors' center, run by the Reich Tourist Association (Fremdenverkehrsverband). Located across from the central train station, it distributed the official postcards along with local maps and tour guides to the interested public, including tourists from outside the region.[89]

Little came of the regime's larger promises to transform the less symbolic landscape. The 20,000 or so apartments in Kattowitz made "habitable" hardly made a dent in the city's housing needs.[90] Throughout the industrial district and the surrounding countryside, Gau Oberschlesien building officials mainly renovated Polish-era housing, public swimming pools, schools, city halls, and the like, none of which ended the chronic housing shortage that had long plagued the area. Also unrealized were ideas for creating new gardens, parks, and recreation areas, or a "greenbelt" surrounding the industrial district, despite its congruence with the Nazi agrarian ideal, which called for protecting the countryside from further urbanization and industrialization.[91] Thus, the "greening" project largely involved planting roadside trees and constructing urban garden plots, including up to 300 plots in Kattowitz.[92] Much of this renovation effort consisted largely of hype in the press. For example, propaganda officials represented Kattowitz's municipal pool, a Grażyński-era construction, as the Nazis' great gift to the local "*Volksdeutsche*," as well as an icon of "German superiority."[93]

Mass Mobilization for Cultural Cleansing

Under the name Operation More Beautiful Silesia (Aktion schönere Schlesien), the Gau Oberschlesien government initiated its most ambitious landscape project in the spring of 1941. A collaboration with the OHB and local administrators, it called for the renovation and "beautification" of buildings, houses, stores, and signage. Its concern was less to create new construction than to remove the traces of Polish "vandalism" on the region's landscape.[94] Indeed, Operation More Beautiful Silesia also aimed to enlist locals in creating the new "German landscape." As a rallying cry, the OHB adopted the slogan, "Cast out the ugly and return home to the beautiful" (*Auskehr des Hässlichen und Heimkehr zum*

Schönen). As head of the Office for Local Aministration for Gau O/S, Erwin Schramm enthusiastically projected the elevating impact of "the new and beautiful *Oberschlesien*" on its residents, who by "beautifying their *Heimat*" would feel more closely connected and "proudly gain fulfillment from common accomplishments."[95]

Local NSDAP cells, administration officials, and OHB block leaders, supported by the press and radio, sponsored public projects to clean up streets, waterways, public parks, signage, monuments, and cemeteries. Owners of private residential and commercial property were exhorted to paint and renovate their property, particularly the façades, as well as to clean up and "green" their surroundings with trees or flower beds.[96] The government gave some homeowners subsidies of up to half of the financial costs of this work.[97] Even renters received notice to clean up common areas and install flower boxes on their balconies, as well as to display appropriate Third Reich paraphernalia, particularly on official holidays. The OHB hoped that such activities would school Upper Silesians in the values of Nazi Germany and connect them emotionally with the effort to "re-Germanize" the border society.[98]

The OHB also organized two exhibits to educate the public on the differences between "Polish" and "German" landscapes. Under the names "Cast Out the Ugly and Return Home to the Beautiful" and "The Beautiful City," they traveled around Gau O/S. In the summer of 1941, the RKF sent its own nationwide traveling exhibit to Kattowitz. "Planning and Development in the East" promoted the new model "German" cities and villages the regime promised to build in the "recovered territories."[99] This bold new society would be based on land—"recovered" German territories—and "blood"—that of the borderland natives and "resettlers" (*Umsiedler*) from eastern Europe. This "constructive" element of Nazi social engineering served to cloud and distract public attention from its darker side, marked by violence, uprooting, expulsion, and genocide.

In the heavily polluted and crowded industrial district, a program to clean up and beautify the environment might have seemed to be desirable public policy. In this case, "beautification" connoted the "cleansing" (*Säuberung*) of all traces of "Polish" and "Jewish" culture, including linguistic, national, and religious symbols. Thus, the regime demanded that ordinary residents remove Polish-language inscriptions from common and public areas such as apartment buildings, workplaces, bars, and restaurants, as well as churches, shrines, and pilgrimage sites. Since larger signs and symbols had long been taken down by 1941, this pronouncement included messages in elevators, on lists of residents, and in basements. Block leaders and other enforcers of party discipline often followed narrow criteria for "Polishness." Failures to abide by their directives could result in fines, harassment, or even arrest.[100]

The few surviving local records for the beautification campaign indicate that citizens resented its intrusions and bullying. For example, business owners had to follow strict rules to ensure that their shop signs used "proper German" written in the "proper way." Such "foreign words" as *Lokale* (pub) and *Restaurant* had to be replaced by the originally German equivalent of *Gaststätte*. In addition, signs had to use official German *Sütterlin*-style (Gothic) letters, rather than the previously standard Roman characters. This regulation imposed particular burdens on the younger generation, who had not learned this German script in Polish schools. As a further annoyance, regulations prescribed specific colors for signs and awnings in order to ensure a "beautiful German" appearance.[101]

By giving Nazi party officials a pretext for meddling in the everyday lives of local residents, the beautification program sparked regular conflicts, notably when they designated Catholic religious symbols in public spaces outside churches as "undesirable kitsch" and ordered their removal. Paintings and statuettes of the Black Madonna of Częstochowa—a revered Polish icon often placed in small public shrines—became a particular target.[102] The cleansing of religious symbols from church interiors sparked conflicts with priests and fueled resentment from congregants. For example, in the late winter of 1940, local party officials in Königshütte demanded that Father Gaida of the Church of St. Hedwig remove the image of a white eagle from the main stained glass window, on the grounds that it represented "the Polish eagle." The priest denied that the image bore any national or political meaning, insisting that it was a symbol from the Gospel of St. John. The image was concealed while party agents pondered the issue before forcing its removal.[103] Such events tainted the beautification effort as just another way for regime officials to harass an institution that the NSDAP deemed to be the vanguard of "Polishness."

Not surprisingly, then, the beautification campaign failed to rally support for the ethnic cleansing and Nazifying of the landscape. Even the regional party paper, the *Kattowitzer Zeitung*, remarked on the public's widespread rejection. Instead of appreciating spotless surroundings like good Germans, they tossed their garbage and food on the city's streets as soon as they had been cleaned. Another story chastised citizens' reluctance to put flowers on their balconies for state holidays. Internal party correspondence reveals awareness of the campaign's ineffectiveness.[104] Undaunted, the regime embarked on a more ambitious "re-Germanization" program.

Conceptualizing the "German" Upper Silesian

Parallel with their efforts to create a "German landscape," academics and Heimatkundler began to conceptualize and shape the implicitly German "Upper Silesian person" (*Oberschlesischer Mensch*). This project required the work of scholars who, soon after September 1939, began investigating the history and ethnography of the industrial district. The leading local archeologist,

Franz Pfüntzenreiter, led several digs in the former Voivodeship, in areas near Deutsche Piekar (Piekary Śląskie) and around the cities of Bendsburg (Będzin) and Sosnowitz (Sosnowiec) in the Dąbrowa Basin.[105] Published in popular scholarly works, travel guides, and the press, their findings of ancient "Germanic settlements" provided "evidence" for the notion that "the blood of the founding German rulers" continued to course through German veins, and thus that "[t]he firm footing of our German Reich on this land is uncontestable."[106]

The OHB used the concept of the "Upper Silesian person" to support its view of the historical, psychological, and ethnographic ideal type of residents native to the former Voivodeship. Thus, it was both a Nazi German counterpart to Grażyński's *Lud Śląski* (Silesian people; see chapter 3), which it sought to supersede, and a nationalist rival to the German Center Party's narrative of an *Oberschlesisches Volk* (Upper Silesian people; see chapter 2). The two otherwise contrasting German narratives shared the notion of "Poles" not only as foreigners in a timelessly "German" region imbued with *Kultur*, but also as intruders, agitators, armed invaders, and postpartition colonizers who "ruined" the region and exploited a native "German" population. The Nazi narrative was, however, far more extreme in its depiction of Upper Silesia as a *Kampfland*, a site of permanent Germanic-Slavic struggle. Its *Oberschlesischer Mensch* was both a victim and a hardened survivor of centuries-long "ethnic and cultural-political struggle" against Poles and Czechs, as well as various greedy "foreign states." The region's historical subjection to "foreign tyranny" (*fremde Willkür*) was a fundamental mark of this tragic narrative.[107]

The *Heimatkundler* also underscored the "victimization" of Upper Silesians at the hands of late nineteenth-century liberalism and "reckless industrialization"—even though they themselves cited industrialization as evidence for "German intelligence and skill." This narrative extended the period of Upper Silesian "suffering" and "struggle" well beyond the less than two decades of "Polish (mis)governance," though it could not compete with the *Lud Śląski* narrative of 600 years under the "Prussian/German yoke."[108]

The *Heimatkundler* also exploited the relatively short duration of "Polish tyranny" by misconstruing the conflict between local natives and high Polish newcomers in the interwar Voivodeship as a struggle between "Germans" and "Poles." Nazi anti-Semitism entered this narrative via the struggle between "Germans" and "eastern Jews" (*Ostjuden*). As explained in a scholarly article by former Kulturbund head Victor Kauder:

> *Ostoberschlesien* marked the wealthiest and most productive "colony" that the new Polish state had received. Galicians, Poseners, and *Ostjuden* inundated "Voivodeship Silesia" and occupied all the leading and lucrative positions to such a degree that even native "insurgents" thought this was too much and had to defend themselves against the regionally foreign element.[109]

As an expert on the Voivodeship's internal affairs, Kauder most likely knew that it had been High Polish–speaking outsiders who had made some veteran Polish insurgents feel like second-class citizens.[110] His purposely twisted testimony helped legitimate the official myth of Nazi Germans "liberating" Upper Silesians from "foreign" Polish colonizers. By creating a conceptual red line between a native population that belonged to the *Volksgemeinschaft* and the Poles and Jews who did not, this master narrative designated these outsiders for cleansing (and in the case of the second group, for murder).

The narrative of the *Oberschlesischer Mensch*, like that of the *Lud Śląski*, recognized only three groups in this borderland: Germans, Poles, and Jews. This stark division designated multilingualism, "national indifference," and regionalism as categories of abnormality caused by local "Germans'" history of domination by "foreigners." An essay in the OHB's 1941 *Heimat Almanac for Kattowitz* attributed the Upper Silesian's characteristic "political ambiguity" to "repeated shifts in state citizenship [*Staatszugehörigkeit*]," which had instilled "indifference regarding who sat at the rudder."[111] And since the official language followed shifting borders, the Upper Silesian clung to his dialect. Ethnographer Alfons Perlick, an expert on the native population of the industrial district, emphasized that "hundreds of years of subservience" (*Untertänigkeit*) had given the regional native an inferiority complex. He believed that education and cultivation—the keys to eradicating this sociopsychological affliction—would lead to the Upper Silesian's "full integration with the Reich."[112]

The construct of the *Oberschlesischer Mensch* thus legitimatized the regime's intent to turn the local into what official discourse called a "flawless German" (*einwandfreier Deutscher*), in other words, a nationally aware National Socialist. Perlick and his colleagues called for all postannexation scholarship to relate to the psychological nuances of the Upper Silesian and his *Heimat*, with the goal of eradicating any "foreign" traces and forging the desired new construct. Under the tutelage of the party and its organizations, the regime's official "education work" (*Erziehungsarbeit*) would help the Upper Silesian make the necessary psychological "clean break" from "Polishness." The *Heimatkundler* and other cultural officials saw this project as the culmination of their acculturation work. Along with creating a "German landscape," public schooling for "re-Germanization" was the second front in this cultural project. The *Kattowitz Zeitung* drew the connection between these two efforts: "Just as our cities and communes today again shine in German cleanliness, so too must we be clean on the inside."[113]

Drawing Linguistic Borders

The decision to eradicate the linguistic artifacts of "Polishness" soon followed the annexation of Upper Silesia. Admonitions from the party and various

Nazi organizations had not stopped many locals from continuing to use the Slavic-based local dialect, officially classified as *Wasserpolnisch* (watered-down Polish), *O/S Mischsprache* (Upper Silesian mishmash), *O/S Haussprache* (Upper Silesian domestic language), or *O/S Mundart/Umgangssprache* (Upper Silesian colloquial speech). Police agents reported that even members of the SS Security Service (*Sicherheitdienst*, or SD), NSDAP trustees, workplace foremen, members of the party and other Nazi organizations, and Wehrmacht soldiers, both on the front and on leave, used the dialect.[114] Young people presented a particular problem, since most had attended only Polish schools and were used to speaking and thinking in that language, whereas German was foreign to them.[115]

Officials from outside the Gau O/S had particular difficulties distinguishing between High (literary) Polish and the various colloquial usages, or even German spoken with a Slavic accent; all were "foreign" and should be eradicated. As explained by *Gauleiter* Bracht, the use of Polish or the local dialect was part of a larger behavioral gestalt "that one is tempted to classify as Polish in spirit," and that Germans found unacceptable. "The German-Polish mish-language [*Mischsprache*], which one is so eager to call *Oberschlesisch*, must disappear from *Oberschlesien*. Upper Silesians have to kick this habit, which is only the result of superficial [influence] and neglect, and proudly embrace the German [language]."[116] Ironically, Nazi propaganda during the interwar era had cited natives' stubborn dialect usage as evidence of their heroic resistance to "forced Polonization" (see chapter 3).[117] But within half a year of the annexation, the Nazis launched an extensive schooling and propaganda campaign to stamp out all variants of the "Polish" language and resocialize the populace into speaking High German. This effort became the crux of the "*Volk* cultivation" program that aimed to forge the "new man" in this borderland.[118]

Underestimating the deep roots of the local dialect in the industrial district, officials new to the region often blamed their use on a "Polish underground." Sanctions faced by individuals accused of speaking "Polish" included public defamation, job loss or employment discrimination (particularly before 1941), denial of rationed goods and other state "benefits," fines, violence, arrest, interrogation and harassment, and expropriation and expulsion to the GG, other parts of Germany, and/or work camps.[119] These were weakly enforced and proved largely ineffective in halting the widespread use of "unacceptable dialects." A number of high-ranking and local authorities understood the futility of this effort. Thus, the mayor of Tarnowitz (Tarnowskie Góry) responded to urgings to penalize or arrest all "Polish speakers" in his municipality by advising that "it will be monstrously difficult to impose legal sanctions against all Polish-speaking persons. As the area's head of police, I just don't have the resources for this. The imprisonment of Polish-speaking persons is completely out of the question since there just wouldn't be enough prisons and detention centers."[120]

Similarly, Walter Springorum, governor of Kattowitz District (Regierungsbezirk Kattowitz)—which incorporated both sides of the formerly partitioned industrial district, in addition to surrounding areas—rejected pressure to make speaking "the Polish language" illegal. District officials had explained that enforcing this prohibition would be just as difficult as efforts in some districts to "impose on Poles the duty of greeting [German officials]." Indeed, trying to implement a language ban "would only make the German Reich look weak."[121] Instead, Springorum recommended *Volkstumsarbeit*, that is, schooling and reacculturation, as the only realistic ways to quash the use of "Polish." He thought he had the support of most cultural and administrative officials, including *Gauleiter* Bracht.[122]

By default, German-language courses became a fundamental pillar of "re-Germanization." The Volk Cultivation Agency (Volksbildungswerk, or VBW), a subsection of the DAF's Strength through Joy (KdF) bureau, had a central role in this effort. In December 1939, the VBW began to offer free or reduced-price language courses to adults. During the first six months, about 47,000 people took these courses throughout the former Voivodeship area. Workers comprised the largest contingent, at approximately 36 percent of participants.[123] Unfortunately, no subsequent attendance records exist, and the courses ended in spring 1943 due to the war. However, internal VBW records indicate that the various schooling programs in its broader *Volksbildung* project attracted over 3.9 million participants from throughout Gau O/S from April 1942 through March 1943.[124] A number of other NSDAP organizations, including the Teachers' Union (NSLB), Women's Union (NSF), Hitlerjugend, Union of German Girls (Bund Deutscher Mädel, BDM), along with local party groups and the BDO, also ran German-language programs for their members. School-age children received language instruction in "reschooling courses" (*Umschulungskurse*) during the school years and summers.[125] In addition, the DAF and KdF organized workplace "Volk cultivation" courses in German, as well as in party-approved history and culture.[126]

Heimatkundler specialists led the effort to develop a pedagogical methodology to "re-Germanize" the borderland populace. Josef Bolick, the head of the regional NSLB and a leading theoretician of linguistic pedagogy, led the OHB's section for "speech training" (*Sprecherziehung*) after mid-1941. His bureau had responsibility for training teachers of both adults and children to inculcate the use of "proper" German, including pronunciation and the formulation of expressions. In keeping with this ethos, Alfons Perlick's treatise on children's pedagogy in the borderland rejected the use of such strategies as grammar drills and vocabulary lessons, which approached German as a "foreign language."[127] Like Bolick, he argued that "speech training" should reconstruct the native's latent mother tongue by mirroring everyday life and experiences. Such a "comprehensive method" (*Ganzheitsmethode*) would not only enforce the speaking of German, it would also remove Slavic words from students' everyday vocabulary and train them to correct what Germans described as the "hammering" Slavic accent typical of borderland locals who spoke German. As Bolick declared during the OHB's inaugural conference, "*Oberschlesien* will never attain a purely German face until the hardness of [locals'] speech disappears."[128] To effect this change, in 1940 he published a teachers' manual that addressed typical borderland speech and pronunciation "errors" and how to "correct" them.[129]

A major conference on the new education program in June 1941 attracted some 800 teachers from throughout Gau O/S. Pedagogues and curriculum planners conveyed the message that, beyond instructing their students on proper German speech, these teachers' responsibilities included the promotion of subservience to the *Volksgemeinschaft*. This agenda encompassed instruction in the Nazi lexicon, which included such terms as "recovered territories" (*Wiedergewonnene Gebiete*) and "the German east" (*Der deutsche Osten*).[130] In addition to curricular reform, Perlick and his colleagues continued their prewar efforts to translate folk songs and sagas from the local dialect into High German. The OHB also looked beyond the classroom to standardize the jargon used by coal miners and metallurgy workers, which involved "cleansing" it of "foreign" terms and substituting proper German equivalents. The party and its various organizations incorporated this work in their mass schooling and resocialization work.[131]

Having acknowledged that Upper Silesians could not be forced to speak proper German, Nazi officials turned to persuasion. By early 1940 local party cells began hanging posters in public places to advertise the benefits of learning and using "good German"—as well as the consequences of speaking anything else. For example, to enforce the message that speaking Polish was "the source of [locals'] inferiority complex," one such placard admonished:

> Whoever speaks Polish is only a half-German!
> Comrade! Do you want to be a confident *Oberschlesier*? Then learn German!
> Comrade! Do you always want to be disadvantaged [*zurückgesetzt werden*]? Then speak Polish!
> Comrade! Do you want to be worse off than, and subordinate to your fellow national [*Volksgenosse*]? Then go on speaking Polish!
> Comrade! Be proud! Speak German and stay away from the Polish-speaking weakling![132]

Similarly, *Gauleiter* Bracht ordered that propaganda addressed to teenagers should emphasize that German was "becoming more and more a world language" and that those who failed to learn it would invite "mockery" by their peers.[133]

The campaign to promote German included local parades of party cell members carrying banners with such slogans as, "Whoever speaks Polish is our enemy!" In addition to hanging up posters in public locations, Nazi ruffians forced workers and business owners to put them up inside their shops, bars, and restaurants, and even to sign a petition that committed them to deny service to clients who spoke

"Polish." They later returned to make sure the posters were still there. These party "storm troopers," as they were widely called, although not officially part of the SA, walked the streets to harass anyone whose language or accent offended them, and even pressured the linguistic deviants to sign up for German-language courses.[134] OHB publications and press articles supported this campaign by labeling dialect words and expressions as "foreign" and "barbaric" and by calling those who used them—that is, the vast majority of Upper Silesians—"dwarfs."[135] As the *Kattowitzer Zeitung* observed, the goal of this effort was to make "a clean break with Polishness."[136]

By May 1940 the BDO had more than 170,000 members.[137] In addition to proselytizing for High German, its cultural officials sought to "re-Germanize" the populace by means of lessons on the "history" and "culture" of their *Heimat* and its "German motherland." As an organ of the NSDAP, the BDO used this work to promote the party and its ideology. Local groups used "cell evenings," "village evenings," and similar assemblies to promote "*Volk* cultivation." Party and BDO block leaders pressured residents of individual residential blocks to attend these events and blacklisted those who ignored their invitations. As with the German lessons, the main targets for ideological schooling were the youth and working-age adults of both sexes who constituted the regime's most valuable human resources. The party's chief goal was to "win back for Germandom" the politically and nationally indifferent majority of Upper Silesians, particularly the "threes," or the over 60 percent of the population that was assigned to that category of the Deutsche Volksliste.[138]

For the first two years after annexation, party officials in the industrial district reported satisfaction with the progress of the "*Volk* cultivation" effort. However, these accounts ignored the reality that protestations of German national consciousness and support for the regime were often feigned in an effort to gain advantage in the competition for jobs, as well as to attain the full rights and benefits of German citizens, not to mention such negative incentives as fear of social alienation or even expulsion to the GG as "Poles."[139]

To reach a broad audience, officials borrowed attractions from the rallies and festivals of the interwar propaganda battle, including films and performances by local and regional choruses and folk song and dance groups. The annual Reden Festival in the municipal park of Königshütte—first organized in July 1940 to mark the unveiling of the restored statue of Reden—closely followed this tried-and-true script, which included peasants in folk costumes, coal miners in their ceremonial uniform, and speeches by high-ranking regional officials on the event's symbolism as a celebration of "overcoming" the "Polish" effort to "destroy everything German" (fig. 4.5). Most of the large crowd (30,000 according to the press) probably came for the later attractions, which included a singing contest for local worker choirs, a miniature amusement park with food and drink, games, and prizes, and the main highlight—a soccer match held at the

Figure 4.5. Nazi Party DAF brochure: Reden Festival, 1941, commemorating the destruction of the statue of Friedrich Wilhelm von Reden by Poles in 1939. (APK)

stadium inaugurated by the Polish president Mościcki in 1927. Press accounts featured photos of jubilant crowds looking on as the metallurgy workers defeated the dynamite factory workers three goals to two as "proof" of the "joyous" era of "freedom" dawning in eastern Upper Silesia.[140]

Like the regime's other "*Volk* cultivation" ventures, its local-level schooling agenda aimed to develop a "new man" who "thinks, feels, and speaks in [High] German" and despises every hint of "Polishness."[141] Reflecting the Nazi conviction that Catholicism was inseparable from Polish identity, *Ostforschung* academics distributed lesson plans to teachers of regional history that portrayed that religion's leading role in the Silesian uprisings of 1921 and, after the partition, the Polish state's efforts to "forcefully Polonize" the local population. (Party functionaries also used the curriculum for their local propaganda events.) Following Nazi propaganda from the Weimar era, this narrative blamed the Catholic German Center Party and its politics of moderation, tolerance, and peace for the "loss of *Ostoberschlesien*."[142]

Like the attack on dialects, the Nazi regime's anti-Catholic campaign sought to eliminate any "trait of Polishness." Initially, the authorities tried to discourage church attendance in the industrial district by limiting Polish-language Masses to very early on Sunday mornings. This effort failed miserably, and indeed led to higher attendance as a symbolic protest against the regime. When in mid-1940 officials banned all Polish-language Masses, services were held in Latin, or worshippers sat in total silence. To counter such resistance, the party staged mass rallies, such as Freedom Day and the Reden Festival, on Sundays and prohibited any competing religious services. Meanwhile, the regime continued its persecution of clerics through house searches, arrests, and deportations to the GG.[143]

In April 1942, *Gauleiter* Bracht, working with ZIOF director Fritz Arlt and others from the OHB consortium, formulated a broad "re-Germanization" (*Rückdeutschung*) curriculum for "recovered peoples" who wished to acquire full and permanent German citizenship. The primary targets for this citizenship education were the "threes" (DVL category 3). The OHB offered similar schooling to "resettlers" from other parts of eastern Europe settled in Gau O/S. This curriculum, which was heavily promoted by public school officials and the party and its organizations, in particular the Volksbildungswerk, offered not just German-language courses and cultural-political schooling, but also homemaking courses and instructions on the "German way" of household hygiene and family rearing. Not surprisingly, it also promoted the official line on national regionalism, including the role of folk songs, tales, and other *Heimatkunde*. Altogether, its lessons aimed to create a psychological boundary between "Germandom" and "Polishness" that forced the individual to make a "clean break" with his or her "foreign" identity.[144]

In 1943 the ZIOF completed its magnum opus, *Regional Studies of the Upper Silesian Industrial District (Landeskunde des oberschlesischen Industriegebietes).*

Edited by Alfons Perlick, this anthology served as both a teacher's reference guide and a textbook for the pedagogical cadres who would implement the "re-Germanization" project. Its heft and the severe paper shortage forced regional authorities to seek Berlin's approval for its publication. They made the argument that publication was in the regime's "eminent political interest," since the work would finally put to rest the "myth of the Polish industrial worker and miner": the iconic *Lud Śląski* developed earlier by Polish regional academics.[145] Through its narratives of the history, folk culture, and literature of the industrial district, the anthology portrayed a region that was both secular and German in character; all nuances that might complicate and distort this homogenized image were relegated to the realm of the marginal, superficial, and undesirable.[146] In this sense, the *Heimatkundler* symbolically constructed the regime's ideal *Oberschlesien*.

The Limits of "Re-Germanization"

Officials soon realized the limits of their efforts to reshape public consciousness in Gau O/S. *Gauleiter* Wagner, for example, noted a rapid decline in enthusiasm for German-language courses: the initial "great excitement" about learning the language "had subsided very quickly," especially among "the older people [who] thought that learning German would be easier. Moreover, we lack a whole array of educational materials, including good textbooks for learning German at home, etc."[147] The lack of teaching material and proficient teachers contributed to a 30–40 percent dropout rate from VBW language courses in 1939–40. Public school officials reported that the largely non-German-speaking school-age youth, the group most critical to "full re-Germanization," picked up German relatively quickly. But as one new teacher in the former Polish border village of Brzeczkowice (Brzezkowitz) pointed out, this was due less to the pedagogical advice of experts such as Bolick than it was to the flexibility and pragmatism of the individual classroom teacher. Thus, rather than unrealistically trying to get his pupils to totally stop using the Slavic-based dialect, as the authorities demanded, one such teacher chose to "improve" their speech by gradually mixing in High German words and phrases.[148]

Unable to rely on the German courses, officials also turned to various other "re-Germanization" schemes. In the early months after annexation, the regime embarked on a program of sending local workers to work in the Altreich, an experiment that would also alleviate local unemployment. According to the few available statistics, over 4,000 individuals were sent from the Tarnowitz area alone in early 1940.[149] Contrary to official expectations, most of those sent off to assimilate with "true German culture" encountered poor treatment and harassment at the hands of their new bosses and colleagues. Their letters to family and friends back home reported that despite their official identification as "Germans," they were reviled as "Polacks" and "Polish pigs." Local officials frequently complained that such letters caused "great dismay among *Volksdeutsche*" circles, thereby undermining hopes of being recognized as citizens equal in status to those from Germany proper—a faith on which assimilationist politics counted.[150] Labor shortages in the industrial district and the rising demand for military conscripts soon ended the program.

The rural service year (*Landjahrdienst*) was another scheme to "re-Germanize" Upper Silesians. This effort sent young volunteers to help reassimilate "resettlers" on their new land plots in the rural easternmost lands of Gau O/S that bordered the GG. The regime hoped that this experience would both place these youth in an "all-German" linguistic setting and excite them about "recovering blood and territory for Germandom." Healthy outdoors work also seemed to be a promising, socially acceptable way to remove young people from the deleterious linguistic and religious influence of their families. However, these largely Polish-dialect-speaking youth tended to socialize with other Polish speakers in their new surroundings. Nor was familial influence so easily averted. For example, parents of young people from the Tarnowitz area sent to the Dąbrowa Basin to help "resettlers" from the Romanian Bukovina region appeared one weekend for a visit, spoke "Polish" with them, and took them to Mass.[151]

The harassment of recalcitrant Polish speakers by regime officials not only brought limited results, but also created new problems for the authorities, especially in the industrial district. Tactics such as dispatching the police or local party "shock troops" to deal with linguistic infractions committed in bars, buses and trams, parks, and other places of public assembly often led to hostile confrontations. The person admonished, as well as friends and even bystanders, sometimes responded with aggressive profanity or even with flying fists. Toward the end of 1942, the county administrator (*Landrat*) for Kattowitz County (Landkreis Kattowitz) reported "more and more incidents in which Germans have been beaten by the Polish-speaking Upper Silesians they had reproached, and none of the many passersby who noticed what was happening came to their aid."[152]

The regional NSDAP also confronted, as the war wore on, what seemed to be an ever increasing wave of religiosity. Attendance at church services and religious processions remained at high levels, while crowds at rallies and other events organized by the party and its organizations declined in size. To signal resistance to restrictions on religious events, worshippers chose the venerated Corpus Christi processions as an occasion to wear yellow and white, the colors of the Vatican—rather than those of the outlawed Polish flag.[153] A party report to *Gauleiter* Bracht noted the particularly distressing sight in May 1941 of some four hundred Wehrmacht soldiers and officers—many from outside Upper Silesia—among crowds taking part in a Mass at Poland's most important site for this ritual at the Shrine of Jasna Góra (Bright Mount) in Tschestochau (Częstochowa), where they prayed before the "Polish national symbol," a portrait of the Black Madonna.[154] At the industrial district's most famous pilgrimage site, Deutsche Piekar (Piekary Śląskie), the large crowd's use of dialect and Polish was so blatant that—in the words of one official—"Germans feel like a minority" and "think they are in the GG."[155] Indeed, in order to escape the ban on Polish-language Masses, some worshippers illegally crossed the "Police Line," the official border separating areas annexed by Germany from occupied Poland, in order to attend the Polish-language services that were allowed for Poles in the GG.[156] Not only did the regime's efforts to secularize the region fail, but Catholic rituals, pilgrimages in particular, provided opportunities for cross-ethnic integration, thus undermining Nazi efforts to create cultural or bureaucratic divisions within the region's population.

Signs of the shortcomings of "re-Germanization" were evident already at the second Freedom Day celebration in Kattowitz on 1 September 1940. At that event, Joseph Goebbels addressed a crowd of over 60,000, mobilized by the regime's organizing apparatus. The propaganda minister focused on the popular sacrifice necessary for building the "Greater German Reich," a mission in which Upper Silesia would play the role of the "Reich's air-raid celler" (*Luftschutzkeller*). In the following days, police agents noted frequent references to Goebbels's speech and the event itself in discussions among locals. In addition to criticizing poor official acknowledgement of the service of Upper Silesia and its people to Germany, local residents made allusions to food shortages by describing the rally as "a celebration without meat in the pot." From an increasingly alienated and war-weary population, Goebbels's sole reference to the region as the Reich's air-raid shelter elicited the observation: "Yeah, it sure won't be long before it [literally] comes to that!" On the eve of the rally, local residents received anonymous flyers by mail urging them to boycott the Freedom Day event.[157] While Nazi officials interpreted these incidents as evidence of an ongoing "Polish conspiracy," they found wide agreement among Upper Silesians—increasingly so over time.

Contrary to the official Nazi mythology of the *Oberschlesischer Mensch*, unrelentingly committed to fighting for "Germandom," many regime officials themselves suspected that Upper Silesians who showed up for patriotic rallies and joined party organizations only did so out of "opportunism" and the possibility of material gain. According to one party report, "among our comrades [*Volksgenosse*] there are those who have been recognized as Germans, even as political leaders, who take advantage of belonging to the German *Volksgemeinschaft* for personal gain, including the attainment of a better position, apartment, etc."[158] Other common charges against natives, especially among Germans new to the region, included fickleness with regard to loyalty, a lack of true patriotism, and indifference to national and political affairs. The propaganda bureau in the Pleß district reported that the 80 percent of the population that constituted the "politically ambiguous elements ... strongly and loudly emphasize their Germandom in pursuit of economic advantages, just as earlier [before the war] they had called themselves Poles for the same reasons."¹⁵⁹ The strong regional or local ethos of the population and its relatively weak psychological ties to the German (or Polish) nation, often interpreted as outright "national indifference," were, of course, important sources of these suspicions.

The Deutsche Volksliste—although intended in part to allay officials' concerns as to the sincerity of Upper Silesians' loyalty to Germany—assumed paramount importance among the many factors that early on alienated locals from the regime. Rather than treating Upper Silesians as the equals of Germans in Bavaria or Brandenburg, the DVL segregated the "re-Germanizable" four-fifths of the Gau O/S population into official categories of "better" or "worse" German nationals. Being categorized as a "three" signified to the majority of the population that the regime regarded them as "inferior" to the rest of German society.¹⁶⁰ The *Landrat* for Kattowitz in 1942 eloquently described the negative consequences of DVL categories for the regime's hope of "winning back German blood":

> He who in September of 1939 thought that bringing peace to this land that had seen centuries of borderland struggle should be the highest principle that the party and state should strive for ... must recognize today ... that despite—and unfortunately as a result of—the three years' worth of effort on the part of various agents of the party and state, such a peace has not yet been attained. Instead, just in the last months a crisis of trust has arisen of the kind that more mature and honest Upper Silesians don't recall ever having existed when Polonization work was undertaken here before the war. ... Nothing has ever stirred up so much rage and prompted so many conflicts that have engulfed nearly every family, as the DVL, even though the latter's proponents had expected to be able to separate Polish from German ethnicity [*Volkstum*] in order to facilitate reconstruction work in all areas of public life.¹⁶¹

Upper Silesian locals whose classification as "threes" denied them permanent German citizenship felt enraged and discriminated against, especially since they were subject to duties and sacrifices of full citizens. According to one estimate, 71,000 "threes" served in the Wehrmacht, 3,100 perished in combat, and 3,200 were injured as of June, 1943. Gau O/S lacked a bureaucratic apparatus large enough to sufficiently deal with the flood of complaints and appeals for upward reclassification from soldiers and civilians.¹⁶²

"Re-Germanization" was thus the prime victim of the discontent that flared with particular intensity throughout the industrial district. From mid-1941 on, party groups in all locales complained about declining participation at their events.¹⁶³ The severity of the crisis even led officials to call it "the *Volksdeutsche* resistance movement."¹⁶⁴ Exacerbated by the war's escalating toll on the region's human and material resources, the Upper Silesian populace increasingly withdrew from public life, turning to what authorities referred to as a psychological state of "waiting out" (*Abwartung*).[165] By mid-1943, the effort to "re-Germanize" the population and to give eastern Upper Silesia a "German" face had all but stalled.

Conclusion

Until the military collapse, the Third Reich remained undeterred in its conviction that it could not only "recover" the previously "stolen province" of Upper Silesia, but that its residents could, with time, be incorporated into the *Volksgemeinschaft*. If the National Socialist era constituted a rupture in German history, the years 1939–45 represented continuity with the shared German-Polish political culture of representing contested borderlands as historical—and eternal—national territories. Well-schooled in irredentist cultural politics, the regime's agents, including local-level *Heimatkundler* and borderland activists from both sides of the once divided region, promoted the myth that this militarily conquered and occupied borderland province was not being colonized, but rather had been "returned" to its age-old "motherland." This discourse of regaining lost "peoples" and "territories" served as an idealistic justification for the Third Reich's occupation of Poland as well as for its genocidal population politics. In making their argument, the Reich's regional agents for cultural politics drew on an interwar tradition of revanchist ideology, popular scholarship, border rallies, and other familiar forms of representational culture.

During the course of the war, the Nazis reversed course on their initial intention to extinguish Upper Silesian regional peculiarity. National regionalism—here, the discourse of a "beautiful Upper Silesian *Heimat*"—provided a lexicon for legitimating the regime's imperialist schemes in this annexed territory. The segregation of the local cultural landscape into National Socialist categories of "German," "Polish," and "Jewish" accompanied ethnic/"racial" selection among locals. The borderland nationalists infused the Weimar-era German Upper Silesianism that underlay their own *Heimat* tradition with Nazi values, and used it as a basis for their effort to reassimilate the "threes" in their regional homeland.

The Nazi regime not only failed to "win back German blood" in Upper Silesia, but its efforts also carried unanticipated and undesired effects. By attempting to coax locals into "being German" with promises of a better tomorrow, with slogans offering opportunities for German speakers and with festivals offering food and entertainment, the Nazis reinforced the contingent and material nature of local ties to the nation. Ultimately, their treatment of Upper Silesian society as a colony that demanded stringent ideologically based reordering and rehaping, amplified by the material shortages caused by Germany's increasingly perilous military situation, condemned the utopian hopes of "recovering *Ostoberschlesien*."

They left behind a legacy of social engineering that the next revanchist regime to govern this homeland put to use for its own agenda.

Notes

1. Hannes Peuckert, "Es gibt nur ein Schlesien!," ODM, 16 Oct. 1939, 2ff.
2. "Losungen unseres Volkstumskampfes: Ganz klare Scheidung vom Polentum," KZ,16 Feb. 1940.
3. Polak-Springer, "'Borderless Misery,'" and Blanke, *Orphans of Versailles*, 229. Aspects of this chapter (esp. parts of pp.144, 147, 154–57, 159–61) appeared in Polak-Springer, "Landscapes of Revanchism," 513–20.
4. Before 1941, the Nazis incorporated *Oberschlesien* within a supra Gau Schlesien, which included formerly Czech and Polish parts of (Lower and Upper) Silesia, but administratively subdivided it into Regierungsbezirk Oppeln (Oppeln District) and Regierungsbezirk Kattowitz (Kattowitz District), which contained the industrial district. After 1941, these two districts were combined into their own separate Gau Oberschlesien.
5. Ryszard Kaczmarek, *Górny Śląsk podczas II wojny światowej: Między utopią niemieckiej wspólnoty narodowej a rzeczywistością okupacji na terenach wcielonych do Trzeciej Rzeszy* (Katowice, 2006), 131–62.
6. Bjork and Gerwarth, "The Annaberg," 373–400.
7. *Volksbildung* was a national project devoted to the continuing cultivation of out-of-school adults that long predated Nazism. It aimed to raise the cultural standards and "improve" the tastes, ideals, and habits of the *Volk*/Germans. (*Bildung* implies education with an additional emphasis on cultivation.) The Third Reich infused its *Volksbildung* programs with Nazi ideology.
8. Hans Schadewaldt's *Ostdeutsche Morgenpost* was full of this propaganda. See "Königshütte: Wahrzeichen von Polen zerstört," 19 July 1939; "Wojewode Grazynski verlangt Schlesien bis zur Oder," 4 May 1939; "Marsch an die Oder, " 22 Aug. 1939; "Aufständische ziehen in den Krieg wie zu einem Tanz," 19 Aug. 1939; "Polnische Vernichtungswille tobt sich aus," 12 July 1939. See also Eugeniusz Cezary Król, *Polska i Polacy w propagandzie narodowego socjalizmu w Niemczech, 1919–1945* (Warszawa 2006).
9. See SR, May 1939, APK, 38 (Policja Województwa Śląskiego), 176, 15.
10. Voivodeship police files contain reports on the mood among wokers in Gleiwitz written by Nazi opponents, most likely former members of the German Center Party and Communists, who served as informants for the Poles describing local propaganda on the eve of the war. SR, May and June 1939, APK, 38, 176, 32, 21ff.
11. Ibid., 32ff., 45–46, 57.
12. Ibid., 32. See also Blanke, *Orphans of Versailles*, 218–32; Polak-Springer, "'Borderless Misery.'"
13. "Polnische Aufständische haben die oberschlesische Grenze überschritten," ODM 240 (1 Sept. 1939): cover; "Polen beschoss die offene Stadt Beuthen," ODM 241 (2 Sept. 1939): cover.
14. "Der Führer spricht," ODM 241 (2 Sept. 1939). See chapter 3 for a discussion of *Kultur/Kulturträger*.
15. See Friedrich Heiß, *Das Schlesienbuch: Ein Zeugnis Ostdeutschen Schicksals* (Berlin, 1938).
16. See Gerhard Sappok et al., eds., *Oberschlesiens Großstädte: Ein Führer und Handbuch für Fremde und Einheimische* (Leipzig, 1943), 94.
17. In addition to this phrase, the areas were also referred to officially as the "annexed territories" (*eingegelierte Gebiete*), the "new east," *new Gauen, Ostland*, and the "German east."
18. See Götz Aly and Susanne Heim, *Architects of Annihilation: Auschwitz and the Logic of Destruction* (Princeton, NJ, 2002), esp. chaps. 73–282; Isabel Heinemann, "'Deutsches Blut': Die

Raseexperten der SS und die Volksdeutschen," in *Die "Volksdeutschen" in Polen, Frankreich, Ungarn und die Tschechoslowakei: Mythos und Realität*, ed. Jerzy Kochanowski and Maike Sach (Osnabrück, 2006); Rainer Schulze, "'Der Führer Ruft!' Zur Rückholung der Volksdeutschen aus dem Osten," in *Die "Volksdeutschen" in Polen, Frankreich, Ungarn und die Tschechoslowakei: Mythos und Realität*, ed. Jerzy Kochanowski and Maike Sach (Osnabrück, 2006).

19. Spatz, *Wiedergewonnenes deutsches Land*, 3.

20. For this discourse, see Peuckert, "Es gibt nur ein Schlesien!," 2ff.; Wolfgang Förster and Friedrich Stumpe, eds., *Schönere Heimat* (Breslau, ca. 1941), 9–18. On the population politics, see Aly and Heim, *Architects of Annihilation*, 253–282; Mazower, *Hitler's Empire*, 205–387ff.

21. Fritz Bracht, Anordnung A 71, *Gau Anordnungsblatt* (17 Apr. 1942), Rossiskii Gosudarstvennyi Voennyi Arkhiv (RGVA), 1232 (Oberpräsident der Provinz O/S, Kattowitz), 35, 112ff. "Im Dienst der Spracheinkeit," *Lokal Anzeiger*, 18 Mar. 1942, APK, 118 (Provinz Oberschlesien), 4735, 2; *Der Angriff* 252 (19 Oct. 1941), BArch, NS 5, VI 19347, 29.

22. SR, Jan. 1940, GStA PK, XVII. HA Rep. 201e, no. Ost 4 Kattowitz 23, n.p. *Eindeutschung* is another term for Germanization, which I will use instead of the more literal translation "to make German," since Germanization signifies the Nazis' actual intent.

23. On a similar event in the Warthegau, see Epstein, *Model Nazi*, 250.

24. "Grossdeutschland nahm uns auf," KZ, 16 October 1939, cover.

25. Peuckert, "Es gibt nur ein Schlesien!," 2ff. Also quoted in Polak-Springer, "Landscapes of Revanchism," 513.

26. Ibid.

27. Ibid.; NSDAP Gau Schlesien to Kreisleitung (Krsl.) Königshütte (KH), 9 Oct. 1939, APK, 149 (Krsl. KH), 23, 28–29.

28. SR, Feb. 1940, APK, 148 (NSDAP Krsl. Kattowitz [Kat.]), 1; Deutsche Arbeitsfront (DAF), SK, Feb. 1940, APK, 149, 119, 68; Polizeipräsident, SK, Feb. 1940, GStA PK, XVII. HA Rep. 201e, no. Ost 4 Kattowitz 7, 19.

29. Ryszard Kaczmarek, "W Granicach III Rzeszy," in *Katowice: Środowisko, dzieje, kultura, język, społeczeństwo*, vol. 1, ed. Antoni Barciak et al. (Katowice, 2012), 364.

30. BDO, Aussenstelle Kattowitz (ca. 1940), APK, 149, 21, 2–4.

31. See Bericht auf den Fragebogen von 15 Dec. 1939, APK, 122 Reichspropagandaamt (RPA), 8, 1ff.; Krsl. Tarnowitz, SR, 5 Jan. 1940, APK, 122, 8, 29; Polizeipräsident, SR, Apr. 1940, GStA PK, XVII. HA Rep. 201e, no. Ost 4 Kattowitz 7, 41–42.

32. NSDAP Treuhänder und Liquidator, 19 Aug. 1940, APK, 119 (Reg. Kat.), 10493, 18. See also Adam Dziurok, *Śląskie Rozrachunki: Władze Komunistyczne a byli członkowie organizacji nazistowskich* (Warsaw, 2000), 36, 38–39.

33. These ID cards used fingerprints rather than photographs as personal identifying markers. See Ehrlich, "Between Germany and Poland," 49–50; Kaczmarek, *Górny Śląsk*, 174.

34. Polizeipräsident, SR, Feb. 1940, GStA PK, XVII. HA Rep. 201e, no. Ost 4 Kattowitz 7, 19; NSDAP Krsl. KH to Ortsgruppen, 4 Apr. 1940, APK, 149, 18, 194.

35. Polizeipräsident, SR, Dec. 1939, GStA PK, XVII. HA Rep. 201e, no. Ost 4 Kattowitz 7, 1ff.

36. Peuckert, "Es gibt nur ein Schlesien!," 2ff.; and "Grossdeutschland nahm uns auf," KZ, 16 October 1939, cover.

37. Peuckert, "Es gibt nur ein Schlesien!," 2ff.

38. Kaczmarek, *Górny Śląsk*, 342, 344.

39. Peuckert, "Es gibt nur ein Schlesien!," 2ff.

40. Ibid. See also Orlowski, *"Polnische Wirtschaft."*

41. Peuckert, "Es gibt nur ein Schlesien!," 2ff. Also quoted in Polak-Springer, "Landscapes of Revanchism," 514.

42. *Umvolkung* is translated as "ethnic conversion" in Aly and Heim, *Architects of Annihilation*, 87.

43. Statistics from Kaczmarek, *Górny Śląsk*, 219–30.
44. See Aly and Heim, *Architects of Annihilation*, 80–81, 102–4ff; Phillip T. Rutherford, *Prelude to the Final Solution: The Nazi Program for Deporting Ethnic Poles, 1939–41* (Lawrence, KS, 2007); Epstein, *Model Nazi*.
45. Kaczmarek, *Górny Śląsk*, 200–2.
46. Ibid., 215.
47. See Wolf, *Ideologie und Herrschaftsrationalität*, esp. 412ff.; Ehrlich, "Between Germany and Poland"; Epstein, *Model Nazi*, chap. 6; Chad Bryant, "Either German or Czech: Fixing Nationality in Bohemia and Moravia, 1939–1946," *Slavic Review* 61, no. 4 (Winter 2002): 683–706; Mazower, *Hitler's Empire*, 179–222.
48. Bishop Adamski believed that this position was shared by the Polish exile government, led by General Władysław Sikorski. While Bishop Adamski had already been deported from Silesia by the time of the DVL's introduction, his previously articulated pragmatic stance on German nationalization policy remained influential. See Andrzej Grajewski, *Wygnanie: Diecezja katowicka w czasach stalinowskich* (Katowice, 2002), 33–37; Jerzy Myszor, *Stosunki Kościół-Państwo Okupacyjne w Diecezji Katowickiej* (Katowice, 1992), 45–52. By December 1941, 800,000 Upper Silesians were included in the DVL. Three-fourths of them were assigned to either category 3 or category 4, while this was only the case for 14 percent of the inhabitants of the Warthegau. See Wolf, *Ideologie und Herrschaftsrationalität*, 412.
49. Kaczmarek, "W Granicach III Rzeszy," 361; Kaczmarek, *Górny Śląsk*, 182.
50. See Hüttenverwaltung Laurahütte, Bericht über die soziale Lage der Gefolgschaft, 27 Feb. 1940, APK, 149, 119, 189ff.; DAF Krsl. KH, SR, May 1940, APK, 149, 119, 257; NSDAP Beuthen-Tarnowitz, SR, Oct. 1941, APK, 142 (NSDAP Gauleitung), 207, 42; Der Bürgermeister der Freien Bergstadt Tarnowitz, SR, Mar. 1940, APK, 1441 (Akta Miasta Tarnowskie Góry), 3092, 12; SS-Sicherheitdienst, "Aufbau der Herman Göring Werke im hiesigen Bereich," 21 May 1940, APK, 140 (SD), 7, 55.
51. Fritz Arlt, "Übersicht über die O/S Bevölkerungsstruktur als erster Beitrag zum Problem des West-Ost Gefällens," APK, 117 (Oberpräsidium Kattowitz), 435, 41ff.
52. Polizeipräsident, SR, Dec. 1939 and Mar. 1940, GStA PK, XVII. HA Rep. 201e, no. Ost 4, Kattowitz 7, 4, 31; Ortsgruppenleiter to NSDAP Krsl. KH, SR, Aug. 1941, APK, 149, 72, 108.
53. "Bericht über die Besprechung der Nord- und Ostdeutsche Forschungsgemeinschaft am 14. Dezember 1939 in Kattowitz," BArch, R 153, 1359. See also Kaczmarek, *Górny Śląsk*, 344; Mühle, *Für Volk und deutschen Osten*, 358–90.
54. RPA in BDO KH to NSDAP Krsl. KH, 19 May 1940, APK, 149, 21, 57.
55. On *Ostforschung* and its agents, see Haar, "German Ostforschung and Anti-Semitism," 8–20; Burleigh, *Germany Turns Eastwards*; Aly and Hein, *Architects of Annihilation*, 74–114; Mühle, *Für Volk und deutschen Osten*, 358–90; Kunicki, "... auf dem Weg in dieses Reich."
56. Alfons Perlick, "Zur Würdigung des oberschlesischen Industriearbeiters," *Heimatkalender Kattowitz*, 1942, 54; Alfons Perlick, "Das oberschlesische Kind und seine raumbedingte volkskundliche Erziehung," *Der Oberschlesier* 24, no. 3 (July–Sept. 1942): 55–58. Here *Kulturaufbau* is a politically charged term that in addition to "cultural development" also connotates the "building up" (creation/construction) of culture where it was allegedly lacking or deficient beforehand. *Volkstumsarbeit* was used by the Nazis to refer to the strengthening and "purification" of Germandom and *Kultur*. See discussion on *Kultur* and *Aufbau* (*Aufbauarbeit*) in chapter 3. See also Liulevicius, "The Languages of Occupation," 127–32.
57. An example of the efforts of Sczodrok and his *Heimatkundler* circle to protect regionalism against the official Pan Silesian regional centrality was their strive to retain the title of the fundamental journal of German Upper Silesianism, *Der Oberschlesier*, which the regime wanted to change in accordinace with the all-Silesian identity. Despite the official regional revival,

Pan-Silesianism still persisted along side of it after 1941, as Oberschlesien symbolically remained a part of Greater Silesia. See Kunicki, "... auf dem Weg in dieses Reich," 114–23, 505–6; Kaczmarek, *Górny Śląsk*, 344.

58. Ernst Birke, 20 Oct. 1939, APK, 117, 416, 4ff. See chapter 3 for the discussion of the term *Aufbau* (vs. *aufbauen*).

59. On Fritz Arlt, see Aly and Heim, *Architects of Annihilation*, 102–14, 132–38; Frank Mecklenburg, "Von Hitlerjugend zum Holocaust: Die Karriere des Fritz Arlt," in *Deutsche, Juden, Völkermord: Der Holocaust als Geschichte und Gegenwart*, edited by Jürgen Matthäus and Klaus-Michael Mallmann (Darmstadt, 2005), 87–102.

60. Hitler liquidated the BDO on 16 Dec. 1942, merging it with the VDA. See BDO Gauverband O/S, Verwaltungsrundschreiben, 21 Dec. 1942, and 23 Mar. 1943, APK-Oddział Gliwice (APK-Gl.), 95 (Kreisverband BDO Hindenburg), 1, 41, 47.

61. See Applegate, *A Nation of Provincials*.

62. "Was will der O/S Heimatbund?," Aug. 1941, APK, 117, 413, 9–11. Also quoted in Polak-Springer, "Landscapes of Revanchism," 515.

63. Georg Kate, "Schönere O/S Heimat," KZ, 17 Oct. 1941.

64. Kaczmarek, *Górny Śląsk*, 352–54.

65. "Was will der O/S Heimatbund?," Aug. 1941, APK, 117, 413, 9–11.

66. Ibid.

67. "Bericht der ersten Tagung des OHB in Gleiwitz," 9 Aug. 1941, APK-Gl., 1, 5746, 10. See also Aly and Heim, *Architects of Annihilation*, 105–14.

68. Gerhard Ziegler, "Landschaftsgestaltung in Oberschlesien," in *Schönere Heimat*, ed. Wolfgang Förster and Friedrich Stumpe (Breslau, 1941), 14.

69. Ibid., 9–10.

70. Liulevicius, *The German Myth*, 131.

71. Ziegler, "Landschaftsgestaltung," 9–10, 43.

72. Erwin W. Schramm, "Die Entschandelung und Verschönerung des Stadt- und Dorfbildes im Rahmen der gemeindlichen Kulturarbeit," *Der Oberschlesier* 23, no. 2 (Sept.–Dec. 1941): 5. Also quoted in Polak-Springer, "Landscapes of Revanchism," 516.

73. For the use of combinations of these three terms, see "Bericht der Oberbürgermeister der Baupolizei," 13 Mar. 1941, APK, 119, 10608, 1–2; "Die Gauhauptstadt auf der Kohle," *Münchener Neuesten Nachrichten* 54 (23 Feb. 1941), BArch, N.S. 5 VI (DAF), 5943, n.p.; Alfred Perret, "Vom guten und vom schlechten Bauen," *Der Oberschlesier* 24, no. 1 (Jan.–Mar. 1942): 4; "Kattowitz im deutschen Aufbau", 10 Dec. 1940, APK, 119, 1175, 71.

74. Heinz Weber, "Als Pan Grazynski [sic!] hier 'fröhlich schuff,'" *Heimatkalender Kattowitz* (1942), 83–85.

75. Alfred Perret, "Vom guten und vom schlechten Baues." Also quoted in Polak-Springer, "Landscapes of Revanchism," 518.

76. See, e.g., "Erst Sockel eines Kaiserdenkmals, dann 'Aufständischen Grab'," KZ, 23 Mar. 1941; "Deutsch unser Raum—Deutsch unser Wort," KZ, 29 Jan. 1940.

77. Otto Ulitz, "1742–1942," in *Heimatkalender Kattowitz* (1942): 95–96. See also Hans Tiessler (Oberbürgermeister of Kattowitz), "Ein Jahr Aufarbeit in der Regierungshauptstadt Kattowitz," *Heimatkalender Kattowitz* (1941), 128.

78. Rundschrift vom Hauptamt für Kommunalpolitik der Reichsleitung der NSDAP, Feb. 1944, BArch, 8086 (Deutsche Heimatbund), 79.

79. "Insurgenten-Überfall in Kattowitz: Schüsse aus der Synagogue auf vorbeifahrendes Militär. Die Judentempel in Brand geschossen," KZ, 6 Sept. 1939.

80. "Die Gauhauptstadt auf der Kohle," *Münchener Neuesten Nachrichten* 54 (23 Feb. 1941), BArch, N.S. 5 VI (DAF), 5943.

81. *Führer durch die Stadt Kattowitz* (Fremdverkehrsverband, 1940), 9–11; Sappok et al., *Oberschlesiens Großstädte*, 126, 198; *Gauhauptstadt Kattowitz, O/S: Die politische, wirtschaftliche und kulturelle Mittelpunkt der neuen Gaues O/S* (unknown publisher, ca. 1941), cover; *Heimatkalender Kattowitz*, 1941, illustrations between pp. 31 and 33; "Kattowitz als Verkehrszentrum," KZ, 20 Feb. 1941.

82. Sappok et al., *Oberschlesiens Großstädte*, 126, 190 (on high-rises in neighboring Königshütte); a sizable illustration of the "skyscraper," without caption, appears with the article "Die Gauhauptstadt auf der Kohle"; pictures of the "skyscraper" (Hochhaus) and Gau House (Gauhaus, the Voivodeship Government Building) appear on the state-endorsed postcard "Kattowitz O/S," from Biblioteka Śląska, Zbiory Specjalne, PA 13.

83. See correspondence from the spring of 1941 between the director of the Staatsarchiv Kattowitz (the prewar Polish Archiwum Akt Dawnych, Katowice) and the Regierungspräsident on the so-called Gauhaus-Gebäude in APK, 137 (Staatsarchiv Kattowitz), 25, 1–20. On the "R.P." issue, see "Die Hauptstadt auf der Kohle."

84. Kreiswirtschaftsberater, Rundschreibung, 26 Jan. 1940, APK, 148, 7, 31; Głazek, "Budynek Muzeum Śląskiego," 115–17.

85. See "Pflege und Verbesserung des Ortbildes im deutschen Osten," BArch, 8086, 79; Peuckert, "Es gibt nur ein Schlesien!"

86. "Kattowitz als Verkehrszentrum," KZ, 20 Feb. 1941; "Symbol des Deutschtums," KZ, 23 Feb. 1941; *Führer durch die Stadt Kattowitz*, 10–11; Sappok et al., *Oberschlesiens Großstädte*, 126.

87. Plakatten "die O/S Landschaft" zu erwerben, NSG 158, 42, 13 Jan. 1942, APK (not filed), Blatt 2. According to this source 1.25 million postcards of eastern Upper Silesia were printed. I am grateful to Prof. Ryszard Kaczmarek for giving me access to the nonfiled documents of the NSG (the Third Reich's news service agency) at the APK.

88. W. Grundmann, "Aufgaben des Denkmalpflegers im befreiten Oberschlesien," in *Schönere Heimat*, ed. Wolfgang Förster and Friedrich Stumpe (Breslau, 1941), 18–19.

89. "Kattowitz als Verkehrszentrum," KZ, 20 Feb. 1941.

90. The Nazi press' statistics are hardly ever 100 percent reliable. See "Schon 26,000 Wohnungen erstellt," KZ, 27 May 1942; "Grossbaustelle Ostoberschlesien," KZ, 22 Mar. 1940. The housing shortage continued to rage, and was only partly alleviated by the expropriation and eviction of "Jews" and "Poles" from their homes and apartments. See reports of Oberbürgermeister Kattowitz from May and Aug.–Oct. 1940 and Sept.–Oct. 1942, GStA PK, XVII. HA Rep. 201e, no. Ost 4, Kattowitz 13, 1-127, esp. 34ff., 46ff., 53ff., 61ff.

91. "Grüne Gürtel für Landschaftsschutzmassen," KZ, 29 Jan. 1940. See also David Blackbourne, "The Conquest of Nature and the Mystique of the Eastern Frontier in Nazi Germany," in *Germans, Poland and Colonial Expansion to the East: 1850 Through the Present*, ed. Robert L. Nelson (New York, 2009), 141–62; Thomas M. Lekan, *Imagining the Nation in Nature: Landscape Preservation and German Identity, 1885–1914* (Cambridge, MA, 2004), 204–51; Epstein, *Model Nazi*, 231–32, 235–37, 240, 254–56, chap. 7.

92. "Über 6000 neue Kleingärten in Kattowitz," KZ 72 (9 Apr. 1940); "4,000 neue Kleingärten in O/S," KZ, 4–6 Apr. 1942.

93. "Badereise rund um Kattowitz," KZ, 28 Apr. 1940.

94. This campaign had an alternate official name: Sonderaktion für die Entschandelung und Verschönerung des Stadt und Dorfbildes. Schramm, "Die Entschandelung," 4–6. See also Epstein, *Model Nazi*, chapter 7.

95. Erwin Schramm, "Gaukommunalamtsleiter: Verschönerung des Stadt- und Dorfbildes," KZ, 21 May 1941.

96. See "Zur Heimatidee gehört Heimatkenntnis," KZ, 2 May 1941; Oberbürgermeister KH to Kreisleiter NSDAP Amt f. Kommunalpolitik, 1 July 1941, APK, 149, 174, 31; Bekanntgabe

B 25 in NSDAP Gau-Anordnungsblatt, 5 May 1941, APK, 118, 4712, 38; "Landreis Kattowitz, Verschönerung des Ortsbildes," KZ, 27 Apr. 1940; *Der Oberschlesier* 2 (1941): 25–26; "Richtlinien für die Pflege und Erhaltung des Dorfbildes," 1941, APK, 646 (Akta Miasta Chorzow), 2715, 8–13.

97. Oberbürgermeister der Stadt Kattowitz, "Pflege und Verbesserung des Straßenbildes," 3 June 1941, APK 119, 3.

98. "Kattowitz muss schöner werden!," KZ, 1 June 1940.

99. OP der Provinz Westfalten to G. Kate, 26 May 1941, APK, 118, 4822, 3, 20; Görg Guntram, "Kattowitz im Jahre 1941," *Heimatkalender Kattowitz*, 1942, 45. See also Esptein, *Model Nazi*, 254–57, chap. 7.

100. "Anordnungen des Gauamtsleiters für Kommunalpolitik, Pg. Schramm: Verschönerung des Stadt- und Dorfbildes—Das Schöne Oberschlesien," *Der Oberschlesier* 23, no. 2 (Dec. 1941): 24–25; "Plege und Verbesserung des Ortsbildes im Deutschen Osten," BArch, 8086, 79; Regierungspräsident Springorum, "Plege und Verbesserung des Strassenbildes," 17 Dec. 1940, APK, 1485 (Gmina Piekary Śląskie), 283, 49; Gemeindeamt, "Entschandelung als Erziehungsaufgabe," KZ, 17 Oct. 1941; Amt für Kommunalpolitik to Oberbürgermeister KH, 9 Sept. 1941, APK, 149, 174, 40; "Deutsche Wort und Deutsche Schrift," KZ, 17 Oct. 1939.

101. "Deutsche Wort und Deutsche Schrift," KZ, 17 Oct. 1939; "Anordnungen des Gauamtsleiters für Kommunalpolitik," *Der Oberschlesier* 23, no. 2 (Dec. 1941): 24–25.

102. "Anordnungen des Gauamtsleiters für Kommunalpolitik," *Der Oberschlesier* 23, no. 2 (Dec. 1941): 24–25.

103. An die NSDAP Krsl. KH, Feb.–Mar. 1940, APK, 149, 21, 27–28.

104. "Entschandelungs als Erziehungsaufgabe," KZ, 17 Oct. 1941; "Ein Aufruf und sein Erfolg," KZ, 25 Feb. 1941; Regierungspräsident Springorum, "Pflege und Verbesserung des Strassenbildes," 17 Dec. 1940, APK, 1485, 283, 49; Amt für Kommunalpolitik to Oberbürgermeister KH, APK, 149, 174, 40; OHB to DAF Abteilung Fremdenverkehr, 12 Apr. 1944, APK, 646, 2715, 16.

105. Sappok et al., *Oberschlesiens Großstädte*, 5. For archeology in the Warthegau, see Epstein, *Model Nazi*, 249.

106. "Zu den vorgeschichtlichen Gräberfunden in Ost-O/S," KZ, 20 Jan. 1940.

107. See Alfons Perlick, "Eigenschaften und Leistungen des Oberschlesischen Menschen," *Mitteilungsblatt des NSLB Gauwaltung O/S* 1 (Jan. 1943): 8, and continued in 2 (Feb. 1943): 3; Alfons Perlick, ed., *Landeskunde des oberschlesischen Industriegebietes* (Breslau, 1943), 169–98; Ulitz, "1742–1942," 90–97; W. Majowski, "Das Werden des Oberschlesischen Menschen," *Heimatkalender Kattowitz* 1941, 131–33; *O/S und Seine Beitrag zum Grossdeutschen Freiheitskampf* (Kattowitz and Breslau, ca. 1941): 6–40; Sappok et al., *Oberschlesiens Großstädte*, 5–95.

108. Sappok et al., *Oberschlesiens Großstädte*, 30, 34; *O/S und Seine Beitrag*, 15; Perlick, *Landeskunde*, 257–68.

109. Erhard Boberski, "Der Gau Oberschlesien," *Deutsche Monatshefte* 10–12 (1941–42): 391.

110. See Tomasz Falęcki, "Regionalizm powstańców śląskich (do 1939 r.)," in *Regionalizm a separatyzm—historia i współczesność, Śląsk na tle innych obszarów*, ed. Maria Wanda Wanatowicz (Katowice, 1996), 46–64.

111. Majowski, "Das Werden," 132.

112. Perlick, "Das oberschlesische Kind," 55–61. See also Perlick, "Eigenschaften"; Perlick, "Zur Würdigung." The Nazis officially embraced the notion that Upper Silesians had an "inferiority complex" and used in their propaganda. See: "Rednerinformation anlässlich der Stossaktion von 18–21. Feb. 1943 in Gau O/S," APK 142, 603, 50ff.

113. "Reinliche Scheidung," KZ, 8 July 1940.

114. Numerous Nazi Party situation reports make this clear. In the factories, see DAF Krsl. KH, SK, May 1940, APK, 149, 119, 247ff.; in churches, see NSDAP Krsl. Kat., SR, Feb. 1940, APK,

148, 1, 26; in the bureaucracy, see Regierungspräsident Springorum to Landräte, Oberbürgermeistern, Polizeipräsidenten, 15 Feb. 1940, APK, 119, 3374, 110; among Wehrmacht soldiers on leave, see NSDAP Krsl. Kat., SR, Apr.–July 1943, APK, 148, 20, 168; see also Dziurok, Śląskie Rozrachunki, 47–60.

115. NSDAP Krsl. KH to Gauleiter, Oct. 1941, APK, 149, 112, 266ff.

116. "Gauleiter Bracht sprach zur Volkstumsfragen," 26 Jan. 1942, NSG 166, 42, APK (not filed); "Schluss mit der polnische Sprachschande," KZ, 30 June 1940.

117. "Deutsch unser Raum—Deutsch unser Wort," KZ, 29 Jan. 1940.

118. DAF Krsl. KH, SK, June 1940, APK, 149, 119, 310ff.

119. Ortsgruppe Süd to NSDAP Krsl. KH, Bericht, 30 July 1941, APK, 149, 72, 38. See also Kneip, Die deutsche Sprache in Oberschlesien, 150–55; Kaczmarek, Górny Śląsk, 242–43.

120. Tarnowitz Bürgermeister to Tarnowitz Landrat, 8 Mar. 1940, APK, 1441, 3092, 1.

121. "Verbot der polnische Sprache in den Ostgebieten" (sometime in 1940), APK, 117, 143, 29–29V. See also Esptein, Model Nazi, 199.

122. "Gauleiter Bracht vor den O/S Erzieher," in Mitteilungsblatt des NSLB Gauwaltung O/S, 2 Feb. 1943, 1–4.

123. DAF to OP, 9 May 1940, APK, 117, 143, 25.

124. DAF, "Übersicht über die von Deutsche Volksbildungswerk," 1 Apr. 1942–Mar. 1943, BArch, NS 5 VI, 6292, 30–35. On the KdF, see Shelley Baranowski, Strength Through Joy: Cconsumerism and Mass Tourism in the Third Reich (Cambridge, 2004).

125. Also referred to as Umschulungslehrgänge. See Oberbürgermeister Kat., SR, 1 Apr. 1940, GStA PK, XVII. HA Rep. 201e, no. Ost 4 Kattowitz 13, 25; SK, March 1940, GStA PK, XVII. HA Rep. 201e, no. Ost 4 Kattowitz 13, 23.

126. DAF Krsl. KH, SR, Feb., May, and June 1940, APK, 149, 119, 68, 247, 259, 310ff.; DAF, SR, Mar. 1941, APK, 149, 118, 73.

127. Perlick, "Das oberschlesische Kind," 58.

128. "Bericht über die erste öffentliche Arbeitstagung des OHB am 9 Aug. 1941 in Gleiwitz," APK-Gl., 1 (Akta Miasta Gliwice), 5746, 8.

129. J. Bolick, Beiträge zur Sprecherziehung im Grenzland (Dortmund and Breslau, 1940).

130. "Schulungslager für Lehrer in Zwardon-Grenzhaus," 22–28 June 1941, APK, 119, 12569, 18–32.

131. Alfons Perlick, "Sitzung des Volksliedauschusses im Rahmen des OHB," 9 Jan. 1942, APK, 118, 5736, 2; "Jahresbericht des OHB," 1 Apr. 1942–31 Mar. 1943, APK-Gl., 1, 5774, 76; Der Oberschlesier 24, no. 1 (Jan./Mar. 1942): 24.

132. NSDAP Krsl. KH to Gauleiter, Nov. 1941, APK, 149, 112, 266ff.; "Anregeln für die Plakatpropaganda," APK, 149, 112, 269.

133. Der OP, 7 May 1940, APK, 119, 2274, 22ff.

134. NSDAP Krsl. KH "Bericht über die Propaganda Woche von 7–11 Febr. 1940," APK, 149, 104, 46–48, 51–56.

135. Richard Maron, "Deutscher, sprich deutsch!," Heimatkalender Kattowitz, 1941, 147ff.

136. "Reinliche Scheidung," KZ, 3 July 1940.

137. Der OP, 7 May 1940, APK, 119, 2274, 22ff.

138. Polizeipräsident, 31 Dec. 1939, GStA PK, XVII. HA Rep. 201e, no. Ost 4 Kattowitz 7, 1ff.

139. Polizei-Oberinspektor, SR, 1–15 Jan. and June 1940, GStA PK, XVII. HA Rep. 201e, no. Ost 4, Kattowitz 7, 19ff., 80ff.

140. "Redens Vermächtnis führt O/S," KZ, 5 July 1940; "O/S Werkvolk ehrt Graf Reden," and "30,000 in Froher Gemeinschaft," Oberschlesiche Kurier, 8 July 1940. On the first Reden Festival, see NSDAP Krsl. KH reports, APK, 149, 105, 1, 2, 29, 104, 227, 250–51. On the second, see NSDAP Krsl. KH, Monatsbericht, 15 Aug. 1941, APK, 149, 72, 77.

141. "Deutsch unser Raum—Deutsch unser Wort," KZ, 29 Jan. 1940.
142. Maria Lowack, "Zum Volkstumskampf in O/S," Aug. 1943, APK, 149, 103, 174–85.
143. Polizei-Oberinspektor, SR, Feb. 1940, GStA PK, XVII. HA Rep. 201e, no. Ost 4 Kattowitz 7, 21–22; Polizeipräsident, 15 Oct. 1940, GStA PK, XVII. HA Rep. 201e, no. Ost 4 Kattowitz 7, 113ff. See also Myszor, *Stosunki Kościół*.
144. Rademacher to Bracht, 16 Feb. 1942, RGVA, 1232, 35, 102; OP, "Vermerk betr. Rückdeutschung," 16 Apr. 1942, RGVA, 1232, 35, 109; Fritz Bracht, Anordnung A 71, *Gau Anordnungsblatt* (17 Apr. 1942), RGVA, 1232, 35, 112ff.
145. Fritz Arlt to Dr. Papritz, 2 Oct. 1943, BArch, 153, 1092.
146. Perlick, *Landeskunde*, 252–99.
147. OP, Vermerk, 27 Mar. 1940, APK, 117, 143, 19.
148. Schulamtsanwärter Beingow, Kreis Kat. (ca. 1942), APK, 119, 12570, 177ff.
149. According to the report, authorities had gathered an additional 1,500 individuals to be sent westward. Landrat Beuthen-Tarnowitz, SK, Jan. 1940, GStA PK, XVII. HA Rep. 201e, no. Ost 4 Kattowitz 23, n.p.
150. Polizeipräsident, SK, Feb. 1940, GStA PK, XVII. HA Rep. 201e, no. Ost 4 Kattowitz 7, 21; Landrat Kat., SK, Apr. 1940 and June 1940, GStA PK, XVII. HA Rep. 201e, no. Ost 4 Kattowitz 18, n.p.
151. Dr. Faust to OP, 16 Oct. 1942, and Landrat Becker, 7 Oct. 1942, APK, 117, 426, 2–3.
152. Landrat Kat., SR, Sept.–Dec. 1942, RGVA, 1232, 26, 61ff.
153. Polizeipräsident, SR, May 1940, GStA PK, XVII. HA Rep. 201e, no. Ost 4 Kattowitz 7, 67–68.
154. NSDAP Krsl. Zawiercie Blachownia to Gauleiter Bracht, 13 May 1941, APK, 142 (NSDAP Gauleitung), 209, 140–41.
155. Sicherheitdienst, Kreis Tarnowitz, 22 Dec. 1942, APK, 140, 10, 30.
156. Polizeipräsident, SR, July 1940, GStA PK, XVII. HA Rep. 201e, no. Ost. 4 Kattowitz 7, 99.
157. Polizeipräsident, SR, 15 Oct. 1940, GStA PK, XVII. HA Rep. 201e, no. Ost. 4 Kattowitz 7, 114.
158. Krsl. KH, 13 March 1941, APK, 149, 106, 295.
159. Bericht betr. den Fragebogen von 15 Dec. 1939, APK, 122, 8, 1.
160. Schlageterschule to Schulrat KH, SR, 8 Nov. 1941, APK, 149, 72, 236.
161. Landrat Kat., SR, Sept.–Dec. 1942, RGVA, 1232, 26, 61ff. Also cited by Wolf in *Ideologie und Herrschaftsrationalität*, 456.
162. The documents confirming this discontent are vast. See, e.g., NSDAP Krsl. Königshütte, SR Nov. 1941, APK, 149, 72, 254; Gauleitung, SR Sept. 1941, APK, 142, 209, 2ff.; NSDAP Krsl. Pleß, 10 Nov. 1941, APK, 142, 209, 14ff.; for complaints by soldiers, see Generalkommandantur, 30 Dec. 1942, RGVA, 1232, 26, 48; for the *Gauleiter*'s reaction to local discontent, see OP to RFSS Himmler, 4 June 1943, RGVA 1232, 35, 274. See also Wolf, *Ideologie und Herrschaftsrationalität*, 460, 479; Ehrlich, "Between Germany and Poland," chap. 1. The Wehrmacht statistic from Ryszard Kaczmarek, *Polacy w Wehrmachcie* (Krakow, 2010), 174.
163. For examples of a decline in participation at events, see Landrat Kat., SR, Sept.–Dec. 1942, RGVA, 1232, 26, 61ff., Ortsgruppe Immelmann—Bismarckhütte, Monatsbericht, 15 Aug. 1941, APK, 149, 72, 77; N.S. Frauenschaft Gauleitung O/S, 17 Apr. 1942, APK, 142, 208, 39–42; RFSS-SD Leitabschnitt Kat., 9 Mar. 1943, APK, 140, 10, 80ff.
164. Landrat Kat., SR, Sept.–Dec. 1942, RGVA, 1232, 26, 63. Also quoted by Wolf in *Ideologie und Herrschaftsrationalität*, 456
165. RFSS-SD, Leitabschnitt Kat., 9 Mar. 1943, APK, 140, 10, 178.

Chapter 5

Recovering "Polish Silesia," 1945–56

"We are not coming as foreign arrivals to colonize the country here, but rather are returning to the land of our ancestors in order to restore to it its true face, but also taking into account the changes that civilization has undergone, including all that which has brought us progress in the last centuries."

—Wacław Barcikowski, director of the Polish Western League[1]

"The following is already an established basic principle: don't waste a single drop of Polish blood. However one will not recover blood immediately in its entirety. It has to regenerate and cleanse itself [as well as] go through the Polish heart and attain a Polish pulse. This is not a task for one year, but rather for one generation. … The Polish nation has won the territorial war, it also has to win the nationality war."

—Edmund Męclewski, leading activist of the Polish Western League[2]

A new Polish nation-state that reunited the eastern and western parts of interwar Upper Silesia emerged at the end of World War II. When hostilities ceased in 1945, Soviet troops had advanced to the east bank of the Elbe. At the Potsdam Conference (7 July–2 August), the leaders of the United Kingdom, the United States, and the Soviet Union confirmed the decision of earlier conferences to redraw Poland's geographic borders and use organized expulsions to align its ethnic and political boundaries. At Stalin's insistence, the Curzon Line became Poland's new eastern border, resulting in the loss of its prewar eastern territories to a Ukraine directly incorporated into the Soviet Union. As compensation, Poland received formerly German lands east of the Oder-Neisse Line, which marked the postwar boundary between Poland and Germany. Officially known to Poles as "recovered territories" (*ziemie odzyskane*), these western borderlands or territories—as I will refer to them—included the provinces of East Prussia, Pomerania, eastern Brandenburg, Lower Silesia, and the western part of Upper Silesia, all of which had for centuries been a part of Germany or Prussia.

Hitler's use of irredentism as an instrument of German aggression made the existence of sizable minorities unacceptable to any of the new East-Central European nations. Thus, Poland was systematically "cleansed"—the term used by the practitioners—of the millions of Germans living in its new territories. Although the postwar conventions gave Poland only temporary administrative rights to the western borderlands, the internationally sanctioned population transfers made the territorial changes irreversible in practice. The intensifying Cold War soon scuttled any possibility of a final settlement. Nonetheless, the possibility of a final agreement, in particular during the early postwar decades, aroused Polish fears of a border revision in Germany's favor, delivering a fatal blow to the new Polish state.

Adding to the sense of insecurity, Hitler's defeat unleashed a new armed conflict—sometimes referred to by historians as a civil war—that until 1949 raged in the country's mainstream provinces, as a guerilla army led by the independent Polish exile government in London fought to defeat a government that most Poles viewed as a tool of Soviet imperialism.[3] There was less armed resistance in the new borderlands, where ordinary Polish newcomers saw themselves as colonizing a "foreign land." The omnipresent insecurity about the permanence of the new Polish state as well as its essential new territories provided a favorable climate for authoritarian government, radical and repressive policies, and dependency on a powerful Soviet Union.

From the final months of the war to the early 1950s, up to fourteen million Germans fled or were expelled from their homelands—most from Poland's Oder-Neisse territories, but some from Czechoslovakia, Hungary, Romania, and Yugoslavia. The vast majority left for West or East Germany. Smaller-scale exchanges between individual countries included the forced transfer of Poles from eastern borderlands ceded to Ukraine to Polish provinces emptied of Germans. Cumulatively, these border revisions and population transfers, most occurring within the first two postwar years, constituted the largest episode of forced population movement in world history.[4] Inevitably, these "cleansings," which extended far beyond expulsion to include resettlement and the reconstruction of societies, cultures, and identities, gave the new Communist governments an internationally sanctioned mandate to socially engineer at least parts of their countries as they saw fit.[5]

The massive project of nationally integrating Poland's new western territories provided status and employment for the activists, scholars, and professionals of the German-Polish borderlands, who had staffed the ranks of the interwar-era Polish Western League (PZZ) and other Western Borderland Thought research institutes. They thus served as Polish counterparts to the *Heimatkundler*, *Heimatforscher*, and *Ostforscher* who under the Nazi regime had constituted the German consortium of geopolitical specialists. Their career-long devotion to "recovering" the lands that had been ruled by the medieval Piast dynasty—the first Polish state according to the national historical master narrative—overcame their otherwise virulent opposition to Soviet communism, which stemmed from their allegiance to Dmowskian nationalist ideology. In 1945, these borderland experts were welcomed as allies by the Communist masters of Poland's new government, which sought to win popular support in a strongly Germanophobic Polish society.[6] These allies shared a common goal of using a powerful state apparatus to engineer a bold new social order via ethnic cleansing, resettlement, and acculturation, and for the first five postwar years, the Communists and the borderland nationalists placed their hopes of rebuilding a bold new Poland in the formerly German annexed territories.

Reversing chapter 4's focus on the Nazis' "recovered east," this chapter examines the role of ethnic cleansing in postwar Poland's "recovered west." It focuses less on the formerly eastern Upper Silesia, which had belonged to Poland before the war, than on the western parts, which were part of Germany until 1945. In this, as elsewhere on the western frontier, the borderland nationalists and their reestablished PZZ worked with the Communists to "de-Germanize" and "re-Polonize"—the terms they used since the interwar era—cultural landscapes and turn those former German citizens whom the government wanted to retain into "good Poles." Thus, in ways similar to the Nazi acculturation project, Poland's cultural politics worked toward a permanent "clean break" between the "German" and "Polish" in the region, a process that presupposed the conceptualization of two separate ethnic-cultural categories.

Also reminiscent of the Nazi period, the postwar Polish project deployed rallies, culturally racist discourses, and an "adult education" program. Postwar socioeconomic and political instability made any significant urban planning project infeasible until the Stalinist years (1950–56), by which point the building of "socialism" had thoroughly replaced the "re-Polonization" agenda of earlier years. After providing a general sociopolitical overview of the early postwar years, this chapter will address the effort to reshape the western borderlands, from its ideological preconceptions to the policies implemented. The last section will examine the role of repressive measures in this program.

From the "Wild West" to a Reengineered Society

The cultural politics of Poland's postwar appropriation of the western borderlands cannot be understood without a grasp of its sociopolitical context, in particular ethnic cleansing as population politics. In Upper Silesia, whose population was largely left in place, this policy primarily meant renationalization rather than outright expulsion. As during the interwar and wartime eras, most of the new elites of postwar Polish society migrated from outside the region. By March 1945, a Soviet-backed government dominated by the Polish Workers' Party (Polska Partia Robotnicza, or PPR, the Polish Communist Party) took over the administration of Poland's new western borderlands, including western Upper Silesia (an area the Poles called *Śląsk Opolski*, or Opole Silesia), which before the war had been the German Provinz Oberschlesien. It appointed Aleksander Zawadzki, a dedicated Communist, as governor (*voivode*) of a newly formed Voivodeship Silesia-Dąbrowa (Województwo Śląsko-Dąbrowskie). Centered administratively once again in Katowice (Kattowitz), this region comprised all the territories of the former Voivodeship Silesia, as well as the Provinz Oberschlesien as of August 1939, in addition to the Dąbrowa Basin.

Much like the Germans before them, the new Polish authorities considered the Upper Silesian locals as "theirs," in this case, inherently "Polish." The same population whom their predecessors knew as *"Volksdeutsche"* or the "Upper Silesian person" (*Oberschlesischer Mensch*), and whom before the war the Poles referred to as the "Silesian people" (*Lud Śląski*), now received the official appellation of "Polish autochthons" (*Polacy Autochtoni*). By underscoring their "rootedness" in the territory, this term meant to convey that both the land and its people "belong to Poland." Fearing that the international community could still revise the border in Germany's favor, PZZ activists used these autochthons as diplomatic capital to defend Poland's "right" to western Upper Silesia and the rest of the western territories. To Communist leaders, this population had additional value as the largely plebian mass whose support they had to win for the new "workers'" and "farmers'" state.[7]

The beginnings were not auspicious for their efforts. The takeover of these areas by the Red Army and then by Soviet government agents in early 1945 was accompanied by pillage, expropriation, violence, and material shortages that continued throughout that year. Red Army soldiers robbed, battered, and occasionally even murdered locals, as part of the wave of vengeful violence unleashed on "Germans" as they pushed west toward Berlin and then took over as occupation forces. In addition to being subject to these acts, women were also targets of rapes commonly committed by soldiers.[8] The heavily industrialized areas of Upper Silesia became a target for state-organized plunder as the Soviets dismantled whole industrial plants and shipped them, along with machinery, coal, and other resources, back to the USSR. This war booty included some 90,000 slave laborers from Upper Silesia, including about 25,000 coal miners, who were sent to labor camps in the Soviet Union, at least half of whom never returned.[9]

Contrary to the official view that Upper Silesians were Poles, the Polish government functionaries and coercive authorities that first cogoverned and then eventually succeeded their Russian predecessors themselves often treated the locals as Germans. A campaign to weed out suspected NSDAP agents led to the incarceration of thousands of locals in forced labor camps for Germans in the industrial district.[10] Uncertain how the Allies might draw the new borders, and taking advantage of the fact that thousands of locals had already fled west from the Red Army, authorities launched an arbitrary and haphazard "wild expulsion" of 150,000–250,000 Upper Silesians (some 220,000 from the western part of the region) toward Germany in the summer months of 1945.[11] Meanwhile, migrants from central Poland as well as expellees from east of the Curzon Line responded to the government's appeals to "Go west!" to find prosperity, and thereby replaced the expelled. By the end of 1945, these "pioneers" numbered almost 160,000 in western Upper Silesia, and 59,444 in its eastern parts.[12] Its ultimate fate still unknown, this open society offered attractions to the impoverished, displaced, and expelled Polish masses. However dismal life might be in the war-torn land, newcomers could hope to claim the locals' property—including land, farms, homes, and personal belongings—on the grounds that their owners were "Germans."[13] In this sense, locals became the prime victims of this resettlement effort, which turned them into objects of pillage, violence, and expulsion.

This initial clash between property-hungry newcomers and a demoralized native population marked a new chapter of social strife between Upper Silesians and outsiders. Indeed, it was likewise a continuation of the locals' history of marginalization by new national authorities and elites, who again took sides and favored "their own"—the settlers. Much like the native-versus-newcomer conflicts during the interwar and wartime eras, this one intensified the natives' alienation from the annexing nation, in this case Poland and "Polishness," while strengthening their regional consciousness.[14] Moreover, as a new oppressive dictatorship entrenched its power in the region, large numbers of Upper Silesians looked toward Germany as their true homeland. This fear and discontent was already evident by October 1946, when the governor noted a "massive withholding" of interest in petitioning for Polish citizenship in western Upper Silesia.[15] This postwar local-versus-newcomer clash of cultures, material and socioeconomic interests, and power was more serious, violent, and long-lasting than that in interwar Polish Upper Silesia or that against the mainland Germans (*Reichsdeutsche*) in Gau Oberschlesien during the war. After all, this population of newcomers was of unprecedentedly large size, numbering 353,000 (over 40 percent of the total population) in the western part of the region and 83,394 (about 5 percent of the total population) in the east.[16] Charges of "Nazi" and "Fascist" now joined old pejorative stereotypes of the natives as "Swabians" (*schwaby*) and "Germanians," while the new invectives for newcomers included *chadziaje* (slanderous local argot for expellees from the east) and "free eaters" (*darmojady*), referring to their alleged "laziness."[17]

Jews were the only newcomer group who in many respects shared the fate of locals. Indeed, most were Holocaust survivors from the east or repatriates who had taken refuge in the USSR during the war. As the work of Jan T. Gross has shown, throughout Poland, Holocaust survivors met with widespread hostility, particularly if they tried to reclaim their former property from its new local owners.[18] The ongoing struggle against the regime, as well as general insecurity, demoralization, and impoverishment in this war-destroyed country fuelled anti-Semitism. The regional Jewish Committees, regime-controlled local organizations set up to govern Jewish affairs, registered 12,887 Jews in January 1946, most settled in Katowice, Upper Silesia's "center of Jewish life."[19] By comparison, at roughly the same time nearly 100,000 Jews lived in neighboring Lower Silesia, the state-endorsed settlement location for about half of Poland's total registered Jews.[20] Despite the lower rate of anti-Semitic violence in the western borderlands compared to less uprooted mainstream Poland, Katowice still experienced the murder of three Jews along with lesser incidences of violence in 1946. Here, as elsewhere in Poland, Jews had a difficult time reclaiming assets that had been taken over by private individuals or by the Polish state, since the law treated all "abandoned" (Jewish) and "formerly German" (left behind by expellees) property equally under the same statute of March 1945. The Jewish Committees encountered this problem in trying to claim the prewar Jewish community's public buildings, which were critical to the resumption of Jewish cultural and religious life. In Katowice, the former communal building containing a ritual bath and prayer rooms now functioned as headquarters for the regime's main regional daily newspaper.[21]

The fate of Poland's Jews was to a large extent interwoven with the project of appropriating the western territories. Indeed, the same official nationalism that promoted the "Polonization" of these territories—and that romanticized an ethnically pure postwar "Poland for the Poles"—also justified the regime's indifference toward the fate of Jews, and indeed its policy of promoting their emigration. In this unwelcoming atmosphere, some 22,400 Jews emigrated from Upper Silesia and the Dąbrowa Basin between early 1946 and mid-1949—particularly after the brutal Kielce pogrom in July 1946. Most left Poland altogether for Palestine/Israel and various countries in the West.[22] Those Jews who still remained in 1949 were pressured to assimilate into an all-Polish secularized society—as many had been doing for years to avoid persecution. Cemeteries and other cultural remnants of Poland's once vibrant Jewish history suffered pillage, neglect, and deterioration.[23]

By 1946, the regional government had initiated an official campaign to "recover" the territory and peoples of western Upper Silesia for Poland. Like the earlier Nazi efforts, it sought a "clear-cut" break between ethnic groups. The operative metaphor was the "separation of the wheat from the chaff, or in other words Poles from Germans."[24] Like the earlier effort under the Nazis that segregated locals according to the Deutsche Volksliste (DVL), this process depended on the screening of personal backgrounds, beginning with one's loyalty during the conflict of 1919–21, and including political/cultural activism during the interwar era, and—most important—one's participation in the public life of the Third Reich, which all contributed to one's official designation as "Pole" or "German." Since Poles and Germans had belonged to different nations before the war, the authorities differentiated between locals in eastern (formerly Polish) and western (formerly German) Upper Silesia. For those in the eastern territory, the core criterion was an individual's classification in the Nazis' DVL. Specifically, "ones" and "twos" were deemed to be Germans, and thus designated for expulsion, while "threes" and "fours" were designated "Poles," who could be "rehabilitated" with full Polish citizenship. In western Upper Silesia, which had never belonged to Poland before 1945, the inhabitants were mainly all German citizens, whose "real Polish identity" had to first be "verified"—the official bureaucratic term for this background screening process—before they could receive their papers. Even then, the authorities had little faith in their loyalty, and thus awarded them only temporary—and revocable—Polish citizenship. In this sense, like the "threes" in Gau Oberschlesien, these former German citizens were officially labeled second-class citizens, thus helping to fuel their resentment toward newcomers and other "full citizens." Indeed, for this and other reasons the "verification" and "rehabilitation" process exacerbated the native-versus-newcomer conflict. For example, some natives whose property was expropriated in 1945 and early 1946 due to their classification as "Germans" were subsequently "verified" or "rehabilitated" as Poles. Reclaiming this property required the newly recognized "Polish" local to evict the newcomer who had taken over the home or land, leading to quarrels, hostilities, and resentment.[25]

Still, amid the enormous demographic upheavals of postwar East-Central Europe, Upper Silesia remained *relatively* stable. As millions of Germans were being expelled from other parts of the western borderlands, only slightly more than 200,000 Upper Silesians were expelled to Germany during the first five postwar years, the majority from the western part of the province.[26] By contrast, 851,454 Upper Silesians who had only recently been German citizens were now legally "verified" as "Poles," while 1.33 million natives of prewar Polish Upper Silesia remained in their homeland.[27] Whereas the overwhelming majority of native residents of the neighboring province of Lower Silesia were expelled to Germany, the opposite was the case in Upper Silesia. The difficulty of segregating "Poles" from "Germans" as well as the labor needs of industry promoted population stability, as they had during the war.[28] As under the Sanacja regime and the Nazis, the task of renationalizing this borderland fell mainly to cultural (and not population) politics, and thus gave old Polish borderland nationalists a new function. The next section examines their uneasy relationship with the Communist regime and the influence of interwar and Nazi borderland politics on their new tasks.

The Communist-Nationalist Alliance

Any of the Sanacja or Endecja nationalists who survived the war and remained in Poland had to have recognized that their country was no longer a sovereign nation. Indeed, it was controlled by the same Stalinist government that in September 1939 had invaded Poland from the east on the heels of the Nazis, with whom it had signed a nonaggression pact, and that had then carried out a campaign of systematic extermination against the Polish intelligentsia. While the Communist-controlled Polish government had some degree of independence in domestic affairs, it remained dependent on the Soviet force that had installed it. As Stalin's semi–puppet regime, it pursued his policies through a combination of indoctrination, co-optation, denunciations, chicanery, coercion, and terror.[29] The PPR cadres confronted not only widespread public opposition; they also had to confront the armed bands supported by the Polish exile government in London.[30]

Rather than openly opposing the regime, many borderland nationalists decided to focus on the most attainable of their long-standing goals under the current circumstances: first, the opportunity to *finally* "recover" those lands that by dint of their history and inherent folk identity "had been and were Polish," and second, to seek retribution against their imagined archenemies, the Germans.[31] The prospects of once and for all settling the German-Polish territorial question as well as exacting vengeance for Nazi crimes offered the one political silver lining for a nation that was otherwise physically and demographically devastated by war, territorially truncated, and politically dominated from without. In this sense, the dreams of the borderland experts of 1945–47 were formed in a sociopolitical environment and context very different from that of their *Ostforscher* counterparts of 1939–41, an era when the Third Reich was at the height of its imperial size and power.

During the first four postwar years, Stalin and the Polish Communists found it expedient to allow borderland nationalist elites to play a role in realizing their long-standing goal to annex and resettle formerly German lands. Already during the war, some of the western territories experts had been planning such a project in the Delegatura, the underground government of occupied Poland that received its directives from the London government in exile. Unlike the Nazis, the PPR cadres needed the support of a nationally rooted intelligentsia—all the more so because the vast majority of Polish elites to survive the war were virulent opponents of communism and Stalin. To win them over, the Communist regime portrayed itself as a defender of the Polish national cause of retaking from Germany the "ancient Piast lands" to the west, and indeed transforming Poland into an unbreachable bulwark against any future German invasion. The western borderlands experts thus followed in the footsteps of Roman Dmowski, who had advocated such accommodation at a time when Poland's lands were partitioned among the German, Austrian, and Russian Empires. Rather than engage in futile resistance against Poland's new hegemon (the PPR and USSR), these elites sought to make the best of an unfortunate situation by taking pragmatic steps toward permanently securing the "recovered territories" for Poland.[32]

During the first two postwar years, leading western borderlands nationalists joined with the new regime to reestablish the PZZ and its various affiliates. This alliance paid off in 1946 with the establishment of the Ministry of Recovered Territories (Ministerstwo Ziem Odzyskanych, or MZO). Although staffed by borderland experts, the MZO was headed by PPR leader Władysław Gomułka, the main proponent of a "Polish national road to communism" that would avoid the rigidity of the Stalinist model. Apart from the PZZ and its activists, the MZO could also rely on the network of irredentist academic institutes, most notably the Western Institute (Instytut Zachodni) in Poznań, the heart of postwar western borderland nationalism, which was directed by Roman Dmowski's right-hand man, the medieval historian Zygmunt Wojciechowski.[33] The PZZ's leadership also included a number of other borderland nationalists, including the organization's head, the prominent scholar and political activist Wacław Barcikowski, and Grażyński's former chief academic supporter, Roman Lutman, who led the revival of the main Upper Silesian institutions of the interwar governor's "regionalism," including the regional section of the PZZ and the Silesian Institute, both of which reopened in the early spring of 1945 in Katowice. Supported by these institutions' renewed commitment to "Polonization," this city once again became the regional cultural-political capital, and—after Poznań—the second most important center for Western Borderland Thought.[34]

The reestablished PZZ not only allowed Communist leaders to secure the collaboration of intellectuals, activists, and professionals; by claiming an alternative identity as head of a broad all-national coalition of "Polish interests," it also diverted attention from the PPR's unpopular servitude to Stalin and the Soviet agenda. To this end, the party elite declared its fealty to "democracy," for example, initially calling the new nation either Democratic Poland or its official name, People's Poland (Polska Ludowa). Although party agitators continued to demand "the end of big landownership and capitalism" as well as "land reform," they did their best to combat rumors about their own Communist convictions or Soviet control. Thus, a grassroots agitator from Pszczyna (Pleß) charged: "Our enemies are spreading propaganda that our government is Communist and that we [Poland] will become the seventeenth Soviet Republic. But this is false, since neither Stalin, nor our government, nor our populace, wants this. Poland is independent and sovereign."[35] Faced with a question from his audience— "What is this 'democracy,' since the people here call it communism?"—a party agitator from Strzelce (Gross Strehlitz) came up with a response he presumably expected to placate any skeptical locals: "The establishment of a democratic society rebuilds destroyed churches and returns land ... to peasants as private property. On the other hand, communism is something that Hitler was introducing, since he was taking down crosses from schools and was turning churches into weapons storage facilities."[36] Indeed, the regime made an effort to win the support of the Catholic Church as well as of the broad public with both its anti-German politics and its support for rebuilding churches destroyed during the war.[37]

In embracing this irredentist project, the PPR thus grounded its legitimacy on long-standing nationalist fantasies of "recovering" "Polish" territories and peoples from Germany. In 1946, the leading activists of the nationwide PZZ published an official pamphlet entitled *Recovered Lands and Recovered People*, which represented the western borderlands as sociologically and economically more advanced than the former Polish eastern provinces lost to Ukraine, as well as more authentically "Polish" by virtue of the resident proletarian "Polish autochthons." It claimed that these ancient "Piast lands" were the cradle where a "bold new Poland" would be nurtured. By contrast, the authors graciously ceded to Ukraine the annexed "foreign" and "backward," mainly agrarian, eastern lands of interwar Poland. Even more than the Communists, who never really meant to recognize the politically insecure new lands as the heartland of People's Poland, the borderland nationalists thought that permanently securing these areas for Poland marked the most urgent and important national mission. To achieve this goal they would rid these areas of all diversity. Like the Communists, the borderland nationalists were committed to a state-planned and engineered society, a one-party political system, and an ideology-based "national" mission marked by ethnic uprooting and homogenizing.[38]

Aside from the absence of a biologically based racism, the notion of "Poland's recovered west" resembled "Germany's recovered east" as imagined by the *Ostforscher* and Nazi BDO activists (see chapter 4). In the minds of borderland nationalists, these western lands would be settled not just by "Poles" from throughout the new state, but also by the worldwide Polish diaspora, thus becoming the incubator for an advanced "new type of Pole." The expulsion of the German population, the destruction of all political factions except "the Polish party" (i.e., the PPR and PZZ), and the eradication of all "foreign ways" would produce the desired ethnically, culturally, and politically homogenous society. By essentially ignoring Jews or other ethnic or religious groups, these nationalists meant to erase them from memory, as well as to wipe out any religious and cultural distinctions. All "minorities" could live together in the new Poland so long as they repressed any unique identity and adapted to the regime's favored models, the "Catholic Pole" or the secularized "new Pole."[39]

The similarities between Nazi and Polish Communist utopian plans for the German-Polish borderlands were not coincidental. The borderland nationalists in both the PZZ and BDO shared the conviction that ethnic and nationally based cultural homogeneity would permanently secure the contested borderland for their respective nations. During the war, western borderlands experts in the Western Bureau of the Delegatura observed the tactics of the occupiers, and they later examined relevant documents left behind by the enemy, in particular those related to the "positive" and "negative" features of Nazi nationalization politics (*Volkstumspolitik*). Edmund Męclewski, a PZZ leader and former Western Bureau agent, took from the Nazis the importance of central planning to the MZO as it guided policies in the new western borderlands. Thus, the new ministry should, "if not take advantage of, then at least consider in its work the strong German experience (nationalization policy, technical organization), so as to prevent errors from being made."⁴⁰ Similarly, an article in the PZZ's Upper Silesian organ, *The Western Guardian* (*Strażnica Zachodnia*), explicitly advocated imitating—but redirecting—the ruthless policies used by the BDO: "We realize that to a large extent the Germans understood many key aspects of the Polish-German showdown. Moreover, to a significant extent they knew how to promote a proper politics."⁴¹ The Nazis' use of genocide and expulsion not only legitimated postwar ethnic cleansing in Poland. By destroying Jewish communities and uprooting society in general, their actions lent an aura of logistical feasibility to activists' long-standing geopolitical dreams of engineering a homogenous western Polish society.⁴²

More than a society of elitist professionals and scholars, the PZZ was a grassroots mass organization that billed itself as "nonpartisan" and "all-Polish." Like the BDO, it sought to exploit seemingly nonpolitical regional concerns to win over the local population of the new territories for the regime. Also like the BDO in the annexed *Ostoberschlesien*, the PZZ in *Śląsk Opolski* saw itself as a mediator between the regime and society. Thus, it used inclusive slogans, such as "Every Pole a Member of the PZZ," and a variety of similar propaganda tools. Such formulations aimed both to confirm Upper Silesians' Polish nationality and encourage their development as "good Poles," that is, activist members of a Communist society.⁴³ Yet whereas the BDO had gained 54,629 members in Katowice and the surrounding countryside alone by March 1940, the PZZ had only 25,000 members in the entire region by the fall of 1947, and only 32,000 in the early winter of 1949.⁴⁴ This lack of enthusiasm suggests that the violence, pillage, and other abuses imposed by authorities and newcomers on locals during the first postwar years alienated them from this new Poland. Although the Upper Silesian PZZ still had more members than any other regional section in the country, the core of its membership—as had been the case during the interwar era—consisted of newcomers.⁴⁵

Veterans of the Insurgent League, the PZZ's old partner from the interwar era, joined in the regional effort to create a new Polish Upper Silesia. Its new incarnation, founded in late April 1945 as the Veterans League of Silesian Insurgents (Związek Weteranów Powstańców Śląskich, or ZWPŚ), welcomed former lower-ranking officials and rank-and-file members. However, the regime excluded the highest leadership ranks of the former Grażyńskiite organization, as it—citing the Piłsudski-Hitler nonaggression pact of 1934—denounced Grażyński and the other Sanacja elite as Nazi German collaborators. Seven members of the new league's twenty-five-member coordinating committee had been notable activists in Grażyński's old organization, and most of its 22,888 members in 1947 had earlier belonged to Christian Democratic (Korfantist) or Sanacja insurgent societies, or had been active in the plebiscite campaign or as Polish minority activists in the interwar Provinz. The regime posthumously rehabilitated Grażyński's rival, Wojciech Korfanty (whose death in August 1939 had spared him from witnessing Poland's fall), thereby allowing his followers to also join the new organization, which was still widely called the Insurgent League, as I will refer to it hereafter. As an incentive to join the pro-regime organization, Governor Zawadzki conferred a number of privileges on Insurgent League members and their families, including nearly guaranteed job security and opportunities for social advancement. Regional Communists appointed loyalist Jerzy Ziętek as head of the organization as well as regional vice governor. As a native of Gleiwitz, and thus a "Polish autochthon," Ziętek was so important to the party cadres that they overlooked his prewar service as a Grażyńskiite local administrator. Indeed, despite his undistinguished role in the third Silesian insurgency, the party constructed a legendary heroic past for him and awarded him the rank of corporal. Another Insurgent League leader was the second vice governor, Arka Bożek, a native of Ratibor (Raciborz) and former Polish minority leader and distinguished activist in interwar Opole (Oppeln). The party hoped to use these men's Upper Silesian backgrounds and their reputations as borderland activists to make inroads into the native population.[46]

Much as the Nazi regime had promoted Volksbund activists and *Selbstschutz* or *Freikorps* veterans as its own ideological "old fighters," the Communist government publicly praised the interwar Polish paramilitants and minority activists as the "avant-garde of Democratic Poland." Their appeal came from their embodiment of the party's early postwar nationalist Communist identity, which combined Germanophobic Polish patriotism with proletarian class and "autochthonic" ethnic identity. During the interwar era, Grażyński had used the Insurgent League not just for propaganda and ceremonial roles, but also as his personal shock troops; its successor's role was limited to the first two activities. The grassroots members of the Insurgent League worked primarily to increase support for a "democratic Poland" and a "homogenous nation-state"—two interrelated projects. In conjunction with the PZZ, they sought to segregate "Poles" from "Germans" and to "rehabilitate" individuals harmed by their Deutsche Volksliste designations. Along with other elites created by the PPR, veteran insurgents served as the regime's prototype of "the new man" (i.e., "new Pole"), best exemplified by a borderlands local of plebeian stock who was a Germanophobic fighter for Poland's territorial cause and in addition supported the Communist regime.

Their primary mission was to make regime-approved "good Poles" out of both displaced newcomers and Upper Silesians who, as formerly German citizens, had been made de facto immigrants by the renationalization of their homeland. As part of the "the battle against provincialism/localism"—the official designation of nonofficial regionalism/regional identity—they pressured both newcomers and natives to forget their old native cultures and identify above all with Poland, and with the new official Upper Silesian "regionalism."[47] Thus, along with the PZZ and a number of other Communist social organizations, the Insurgent League became an important agent of forced assimilation.

The regime also set to work constructing a more useful history of the *Lud Śląski* (Silesian people) and their role in the post–World War I insurgencies. Such a revision was meant to burnish the status of the veteran insurgents and also create a regional historical narrative that valorized the Communist regime and thereby legitimize the current sociopolitical and territorial order—just as earlier versions had legitimated Grażyński's rule. In conformity with PPR ideology, these narratives underlined the plebeian character of the "Polish autochthons" and their eternal struggle against the "German" upper class—from the colonial overlords of the Middle Ages on through the more recent landed estate owners and capitalists. Although the party cadres refused to admit it, this image evoked Grażyński's mythology of the heroic "Silesian" worker, but with a more social revolutionary spin.[48] More importantly, it served the party line that the third Silesian insurgency had worked toward a Poland like the one that the PPR, in alliance with the Soviet Union, had now brought about: a German-free, ethnically Polish nation, founded for and by the proletariat, and that extended to the Oder and Neisse Rivers. This new narrative about the history and meaning of 1921—referred to in Polish as the "insurgent tradition" (*tradycja powstańcza*)—was an inherent part of the official history of the *Lud Śląski*. Indeed, both narratives marked the basic myth of the PPR's new version of national regionalism, which served to connect Upper Silesia with the western borderlands. This regional history—which touted the Polish Workers' Party's national "achievements," ethnic cleansing, and the "recovery" of the borderlands as the historical will of the proletarian "Polish autochthons"—also became an important part of the master narrative of People's Poland. Historians have referred to it as the "western territories myth" (*mit ziem zachodnich*).[49]

Continuity with the interwar period prevailed as well in the political effort to tie the ruling regime to the new nation, a possibility facilitated by the survival from the Grażyński era of a cadre of artists, scholars, and literati devoted to irredentist politics. Upper Silesia's postwar Polish cultural elites received their schooling during the era of Sanacja "regionalism." They included the prize-winning novelist Gustav Morcinek, the historian Franciszek Popiołek, the literati and radio broadcasters Stanisław Ligoń, Zdzisław Hierowski, and Wilhelm Szewczyk, the former head of the interwar Union of Silesian Singing Societies, Jan Fojc, and the leading figure, Roman Lutman, who after the war retained his post as director of a reestablished Silesian Institute. They and other cultural figures worked with such institutions as the Voivodeship Cultural Council (Wojewódzka Rada Kultury), the PPR's propaganda bureau, the reestablished Polish Radio Katowice, and the (Polish) Silesian Museum, which reopened in the building of the former German Upper Silesian regional museum (Landesmuseum/Grenzlandmuseum) in Bytom (Beuthen). These individuals and institutions essentially functioned as agents and organs of the PZZ, the primary coordinator of all political "regionalism" in the western borderlands, and of the Insurgent League, which had its own "cultural section."[50]

The regional elites from the Grażyński era were not necessarily eager to work with the PPR cadres, as demonstrated by conflicts that flared within Polish Radio Katowice over the party's effort to co-opt its star performers to promote the official Marxist-Leninist line. Many of these individuals had gained prominence at the station before the war but were currently active in PZZ and Insurgent League circles. In addition to Hierowski and Szewczyk, they included the station's prewar vice director and now director Edmund Odorkiewicz, as well as Silesian Institute scholar and PZZ notable Eryk Skowron and literary critic Aleksander Baumgarten. All were fired at the PPR's behest in August 1946 for airing such "antidemocratic" features as folk songs from interwar Poland's now lost and officially forgotten eastern territories, as well as "incorrect" accounts of the events of September 1939 and the borderland conflict of 1919–21. In regard to Poland's demise in 1939, impolitic radio broadcasts failed to attribute all the blame to the Germans (indeed, they also recalled the USSR's invasion), while a program on the insurgency—while properly stressing the proletarian backgrounds of its "heroes"—mentioned their connection with the Sanacja (Piłsudski and Grażyński) regime. Moreover, the PPR also accused these individuals of failing to publicly express appropriate interest in Marxist-Leninist ideology.[51]

As creatures of the regime, the Polish Western League and Insurgent League were expected to use nationalism to educate their members on the virtues of "democracy," and thereby to attract people to the new political order. A PZZ membership card was deemed "the best proof of one's Polishness," which itself was synonymous with a sincere "democratic [pro-PPR] worldview."[52] This regime-imposed dutiful servitude to communism bothered a number of members of these nationalist societies. Local cell meeting minutes of the Polish Western League reveal that some members were discomforted by the close ties between the organization and the PPR, in particular the injunction to "spread democracy," rather than to focus on "all-Polish" issues. Complaints also arose that the party's ideology interfered with the policy to expel the Germans, especially since some PZZ functionaries noted that PPR members included some "Germans." In response to this complaint, noted borderland expert Czesław Pilichowski observed that the

PZZ itself had earlier "maintained a proper relationship" to Grażyński's Sanacja government, despite its own ideological allegiance to the opposing Endecja camp of Roman Dmowski; thus, "it would be against our principles to stand in negation when the official politics of Poland is now actually in conformity with our goals."[53] Like PZZ activists, veteran insurgents sometimes used local meetings to voice complaints about the new order, but were similarly told to conform by their leaders. Despite these leaders' efforts to toe the party line, insurgent groups were constantly under the watch of PPR agents, suspected as "reactionaries" because of their indifference to communism and their critical stance toward the regime and its politics.[54]

The Communists distrusted national regionalist traditions as much as they did the nationalists who cultivated them. The Katowice circle of nationalists came under particular suspicion because of its association with the official "autonomous" legal status granted to the Voivodeship in interwar Poland—an autonomy at odds with Communist centralism. Thus, the provision establishing the Voivodeship Silesia-Dąbrowa (Województwo Śląsko-Dąbrowskie) in March 1945 explicitly revoked "Silesian autonomy," which was at odds with the policy of a strictly centralized new Poland.[55] Nonetheless, the Communists recognized the pragmatic value of, and thus tolerated, the PZZ's development of a region-centered rhetoric for the western territories that extolled these "Piast lands." As explained by a leading PZZ activist, Eugeniusz Paukszta, the officially endorsed version of regionalism permitted its cultivation "to the extent that it does not interfere with the aim of developing a homogenous Polish society on the basis of common psychological features."[56] This formulation was not altogether new insofar as it resembled the regionalisms cultivated by prior governments, in some respects even by the German Center Party. All utilized a discourse that to some extent symbolically homogenized the local culture by erasing all associations with the rejected other, variously Germany or Poland. Both Nazi and Communist regionalisms were more radical than those of earlier governments in that they consciously served to legitimate the ethnically cleansed societies they sought to engineer. The next sections examine the public promotion of aspects of this regionalism in the context of regional, national, and international politics.

The Postwar Tradition of Border Rallies

Of all the national governments covered in this book, none placed a more symbolic value on Upper Silesia than did the Polish communists in the immediate postwar era. The borderland's identity as both a long-standing site of German-Polish contention and an important industrial power with a strong working class allowed the PPR to represent itself as a "Polish movement" while still upholding its core Marxist-Leninist principles. Moreover, because the industrial district

Figure 5.1. Władysław Gomułka (first from left) watching coal miners parading in ceremonial uniform at May Day rally, Katowice, 1946. (Author unknown, APK)

had suffered relatively little damage during the war compared to other parts of Poland, the sites that had figured so importantly in prewar ceremonies and political symbolism emerged largely unscathed.

The Forum Katowice (see chapters 3 and 4) became the launch site for a series of revanchist rallies during 1946, as part of a nationwide campaign to gain support for the regime and its policies before the so-called People's Referendum in late June and the Sejm elections in mid-February 1947. Propaganda and terror were the regime's key weapons against widespread public opposition, which included both an armed underground resistance and competition from a prewar party supported by most Poles, Stanisław Mikołajczyk's Polish Peasants' Party (Polskie Stronnictwo Ludowe, or PSL). To avert an election that the PPR knew it would surely lose, the referendum asked for popular consent to three questions: (1) approval of the Senate's elimination; (2) the promotion of land reform; and (3) the annexation of the western borderlands. Because only the last issue had support across the political spectrum, the party played it up.[57] The Katowice rally took place on 3 May 1946, which designated both the national Polish and regional Polish-Silesian holiday, just following the communist-favorite May Day rally two days earlier. (fig. 5.1). The second rally occurred on 19 May atop the symbolic Mount of St. Anne, and the third on 15 September in Opole. High-ranking Communist leaders and their borderland nationalist supporters presided over all three events, which together attracted between 100,000 and 200,000 spectators from throughout Poland.

Harking back to earlier traditions—ironically, given the Communists' dim views of religion—each revanchist rally began with a Mass celebrated by some of the region's highest-ranking clerics. Although this comity would wane, clerics and the

Figure 5.2. Bishop Stanisław Adamski (first from left) facing Aleksander Zawadzki, 1946. (Author unknown, APK)

party-state apparatus cooperated during the first two postwar years, especially on the territorial project. The PZZ, whose ranks included clerics, served as an important intermediary between the Communists and the clergy by underscoring the fundamental role that the church would have to play in "re-Polonizing" the western borderlands, encompassing ethnic cleansing. The highest-ranking diocesan leaders, such as Stanisław Adamski, bishop of the Diocese of Katowice, had earlier given spiritual endorsement to Grażyński. Now, out of patriotic conviction—albeit unintentionally—they endorsed the PPR, as did Boresław Kominek, the Catholic apostolic administrator for Opole and a native Upper Silesian (fig. 5.2).[58]

At the PZZ's behest, the church also largely condoned the regime's ethnic cleansing policies. For example, its Upper Silesian organ, *The Sunday Guest* (*Gość Niedzielny*), rallied the populace to vote yes on the third question of the People's Referendum; indeed, by calling it "the plebiscite of the nation," it evoked the events of 1921.[59] The paper—which according to the government propaganda bureau was the region's most widely read newspaper—also exhorted the populace to remove all traces of "Germandom" from their homes and surroundings, as well as to change their German-sounding names to Polish-sounding ones.[60] Similarly, the church generally followed the authorities' demands that it "de-Germanize" religious services, church buildings, and chapels—that is, remove all linguistic and iconic traces of "Germandom." This compliance stemmed largely from pressure by the regime and its nationalist allies, as well as out of fear that if the borderlands were not "de-Germanized," Poland would lose these territories and thus eventually cease to exist as an independent nation.[61]

Ultimately, this church-state cooperation had limits, in particular due to the two institutions' fundamentally conflicting interests in promoting "re-Polonization." Whereas the regime saw it as an instrument for resocializing the region in accord with its fundamentally secular and materialist ideology and policies, the church sought to ensure that religiosity remained a fundamental aspect of postwar Polish consciousness. That is, clerics responded to ethnic cleansing less out of Germanophobia than in order to prevent the Communists from using social engineering to cripple religious life. In this respect, they followed their interwar stance of offering symbolic support to Grażyński's "Polonization" campaign, while also opposing his efforts to prohibit German-language religious services and secularize the schools, as well as by defending local priests attacked for their "German sympathies." In the same way, Adamski and Kominek sought to prevent the state from using "de-Germanization" to persecute uncooperative priests, disrupt religious practices, and weaken the Catholic base of the regional culture. Clerical opposition to the regime's campaign to remove religion and its symbols from schools, as well as the party's exploitation of religiosity to promote "re-Polonization," played major roles in ending church-state cooperation by mid-1947.[62]

Even before this break, clerics sometimes fell short of the regime's hopes, as was the case with Kominek, guest of honor at the 15 September Opole rally. Styled as a harvest festival (*dożynki*), the event was designed to popularize this "Polish autochthonic" tradition, thus uniting Upper Silesians with their "Polish brothers," including newcomers and visitors from other parts of Poland. As a native Silesian, Kominek was expected to model a "good Pole" who thus cooperated with the new authorities. His homily, however, reminded the crowd of 150,000 that "[w]e are carrying the fruits of our harvest as Poles, but at the same time as people with a deep [religious] faith. And this is what unites us in this soil, and what should unite us, no matter where we come from, into one harmonious society. [This unity will enable us] to settle and root ourselves here so deeply that nothing will ever manage to tear us away from here."[63] The party press chose to ignore this message in its reports on the harvest festival, while *The Sunday Guest*, in publishing Kominek's homily, emphasized the role of "faith," not just "the soil," in "uniting the old and the new people of Opolian Silesia."[64] The party press nevertheless did report that Bolesław Bierut, the hard-line Stalinist delegated by the USSR to help take control of Poland, sat alongside Władysław Gomułka, deputy prime minister of the provisional government, and other regime leaders at the harvest festival. Although an atheist, Bierut even shouted out a "so help me God!" after vowing to "defend Polish Silesia to the last drop of blood."[65]

The party also exploited the national regional symbolism of iconic sites, most notably the Mount of St. Anne, whose importance arose during the post–World War I insurgencies. As part of a harvest festival in 1945, regime agents destroyed the Nazis' fortress-like mausoleum. According to a German-speaking eyewitness, who to her dismay described the event in a letter to a friend in Berlin, after the structure was detonated, the sarcophagi inside the structure were torn apart and donated as raw materials to local industry, while the powdered remains of the fallen *Selbstschutz* fighters were dumped in a hole at a local cemetery.[66] The 19 May rally at the same site in 1946, which commemorated the twenty-fifth anniversary of the third insurgency, provided an opportunity for the Polish nation—and the Communist regime—to officially appropriate the sacred site by creating a final resting place for Polish national heroes. To this end, state officials filled twenty-three urns with soil from both the battlefields of 1919–21 and from the recent Warsaw Uprising. After the urns' display at the Forum Katowice, a military unit of motorcyclists brought them to their future resting site for a ceremonious transfer to regime authorities—a pilgrimage that recalled the bicyclists who had brought soil from the Polish Corridor to Katowice for the 1931 May Third rally (see chapter 2). These urns thus became objects of religious and political veneration before their contents became a permanent part of the Mount of St. Anne landscape (fig. 5.3).[67] In a second symbol of appropriation, a stone plaque was placed at the former site of the Nazi mausoleum, marking the foundation stone of a future monument to the insurgents—which was only completed in 1955. The plaque stated that Bolesław Bierut had laid this stone "in the name of the Poles."

Figure 5.3. Holy Mass, urns with soil from the battlefields of the military conflict of May–June 1921 (right), and Polish Scouts kneeling (left). Mount of St. Anne rally, 19 May 1946. (Author unknown, APK)

Uniting all these rituals was the official remythologizing of the Mount of St. Anne from a site of German victory over Poles to one of Polish victory over Germans. They also demonstrated the regime's intent to create for itself the leading role in an irredentist and Germanophile narrative likely to unite the Polish nation. Indeed, into the early 1970s, the Mount of St. Anne served as a center of national memory and public political ceremony. Every five to ten years, at commemorations of both the insurgencies and the Nazi attack on Poland, it attracted up to 100,000 participants from across Poland, as the most important symbol of Poland's "centuries-long struggle" to "recover" not just western Upper Silesia but the entire borderlands from Germany (fig. 5.4).[68]

Figure 5.4. Folk dance concert at the amphitheater, Mount of St. Anne, 1955. (Author unknown, BŚ-ZS)

The harvest festival in Opole exemplified the Polish state's exploitation of regional folklore for nationalist, irredentist, and pro-regime aims. As a peasant ("proletarian") folk festival that also displayed the joy of postwar Poland's "recovered peoples" (the "autochthons") at being "reunited with their motherland," the festival also bolstered the party's "national Communist" image. Following a well-established pattern, groups in regional folk costumes from across the nation personified this unity, except those that conjured up any reminders of the now lost eastern areas of Poland. This festival also included some 3,000 song-and-dance performances and orchestras. The organizers intended that such events would mobilize ordinary individuals, particularly those from the politically and nationally indifferent countryside.[69] To support such "re-Polonization" activities, hundreds of community and cultural centers (świetlice, domy kultury) were established to teach and encourage locals to sew and wear folk costumes and to perform songs and dances.[70] The harvest festival culminated in a kayak race on the Oder that symbolized the new western border. Even the Catholic *Sunday Guest* got the intended message: "The Silesian harvest festival will manifest to the world our feelings [of love] for the recovered territories, our efforts and achievements, and our eternal yearning and effort to unite ourselves with the ancient Piast territories near the Oder and the Neisse."[71] In this sense, the folk costumes carried the same intended symbolism in 1946 that they had in earlier border rallies, including the Nazis' Choral Union Festival (Sängerbundfest) of 1937 in Breslau (see chapter 3): the consent of the "rooted" population to the respective project of territorial appropriation—whether accomplished or aspirational—as well as to the responsible political authorities.

Like the earlier Upper Silesian border rallies, the 1946 events were carefully planned, orchestrated, and publicized in order to maximize the size of their audiences and impact. To this end, the regime's propaganda bureau mobilized photographers and journalists as well as radio and film crews to bring these events to the rest of the nation. State officials even set up radio amplifiers in public assembly sites throughout the country. Because the intended audience for these rallies extended well beyond Poland's borders, government officials invited delegates of the Allied governments, notably Great Britain, France, and the United States, as well as Red Army officers and other Soviet agents—who, given their role as "government advisors," hardly needed an invitation. To facilitate a maximum turnout, the government quickly renovated and built up communication lines. For the Mount of St. Anne rally, 5,000 quadratic meters of nearby forest were leveled in order to lay new railroad tracks so spectators could better reach the site. The PPR exploited this effort for its propaganda value, boasting that "the building of a railway juncture (800 meters of railway) was carried out in record tempo of just two weeks."[72]

The PPR used the rallies to gain popularity as well as to conceptualize its own political agenda and Marxist ideology on the basis of the nationalist territorial project. At the Mount of St. Anne event, party leader Władysław Gomułka called on Poles to rally around the regime "to wipe from the Silesian lands all traces of Germandom [*niemczyzna*] and remove [all] Germans" and to integrate the "centuries-old Polish local inhabitants" and newcomer settlers into one society.[73] Addressing veterans in the Insurgent League in Katowice's city center at the May Third rally, Jerzy Ziętek, the regime's iconic "recovered person" ("Polish autochthon"), stressed the connections between ethnic cleansing and building the Communist regime's new order: "I call on you insurgents ... to engage in intensive work to strengthen and improve Polish democracy [and] in a grassroots war against Germandom."[74] In accordance with the new official "insurgency tradition," which combined nationalist and Marxist-Leninist motifs, Ziętek asserted that the insurgents had fought not just to liberate the region from foreign rule, but also for its social liberation from "German" industrialists and landowners. He therefore declared that "on the third of May [1921] the nation began its struggle for democracy in Poland," an effort that ended only in 1945, when "state authority was taken out of the hands of capital and big landowners and transferred to those of the nation, [and now] all of Silesia and the Piast lands have been liberated from Prussian yoke."[75]

Despite the large crowds and extensive publicity, the three rallies in 1946 did not achieve the PPR's ultimate aim of winning nationwide majority support for the government and its policies. In fact, Kominek's homily about the role of Catholicism in "re-Polonization" was only one instance when a rally inadvertently revealed the party's unpopularity. During the May Third festivities, all over the industrial district and as far as Cracow protests could be heard from among the spectators calling for freedom from Soviet control and a government led by the Polish Peasants' Party leader Stanisław Mikołajczyk. In response, the party cadres dispatched state security agents to silence the dissent. In the most extreme expression of opposition, unknown individuals blew up one of the railroad tracks built to bring spectators to the Mount of St. Anne rally.[76] The party certainly failed to win over the hearts and minds of Poles for the People's Referendum and Sejm election, the goal toward which it had campaigned at all three rallies, and was thus forced to use pressure, terror, and chicanery in order to emerge triumphant. Particularly in the case of Referendum, the regime responded with blatant and crude manipulation of the results. If the rallies failed to mobilize genuine popular support for the PPR as a governing party, they did increase support for its program of territorial appropriation, or at least allowed the party to capitalize on preexisting support. On 30 June 1946, over 11.8 million Poles (90 percent of eligible voters) took part in the referendum. The actual results (prior to falsification) revealed that the majority of voters rejected all of the regime's policies except for the third, which won the support of over 68 percent of voters nationwide for annexation of the western borderlands from Germany.

Indeed, irredentism was the only policy that conferred legitimacy on the regime as a "Polish party."[77]

"Germandom" as a Political Discourse

In identifying modern "racialist nationalism" as a "necessary" condition for ethnic cleansing, historian Norman Naimark cites the tradition of Dmowski's nationalism in discussing postwar Upper Silesia.[78] Even the Nazis augmented their otherwise biologically "racial" politics of ethnic cleansing and genocide with such cultural references as *polnische Wirtschaft* and the "Polish anti-German war of destruction." The derogatory term *niemczyzna* (Germandom) deployed by Gomułka at the Mount of St. Anne rally, which had been used by borderland nationalists before the war, became the primary culturally racist Germanophobic concept after 1945. It collectively demonized all individuals of German heritage as well as all cultural traits, relics, and behaviors associated with them, designating anyone or anything so labeled—without exception—as an object to be removed from Polish society.[79]

As early as June 1945, the PZZ identified its major goal as "to construct and maintain the hatred of the Polish nation toward *niemczyzna*, organize an anti-German predisposition, and on the basis of this hatred of everything that is German, unite people of diverse worldviews within the ranks of the PZZ."[80] Borderland nationalists moved in this direction by forging a linear historical narrative that timelessly demeaned everything German so as to demonstrate "[t]o the entire world that the deeds of Germans, more precisely, Prussian-German extermination, is one millennia old, and Hitlerism is only the culminating point and the most sincere expression of the Prussian-German worldview and a politics of aggression and never-ending struggles for conquest."[81] This notion of incorrigible Germans put the Nazi invasion of Poland into a larger historical context that could be exploited in the campaign against the eternally demonic *niemczyzna*. For the same reason, the PZZ underplayed the differences between Hitler and other German leaders, before or after. No matter that the "Führer" was dead, that many of his closest cronies had been hanged after international trials, and that Germany had been divided into four occupation zones; the PZZ still detected "the resurgence of German imperialism."[82] Polish Workers' Party cadres endorsed this notion, since they too relied on a permanent state of emergency to justify extraordinary measures against internal threats to "national unity."

The year 1945, like 1922 and 1939, brought a new chapter in the Polish struggle as it played out on the international stage. Winston Churchill posed the new challenge in his "Iron Curtain" speech of early March 1946, which cited the expulsion of ethnically German citizens as part of what he condemned as the lawlessness and chicanery of the "Russian-controlled Polish government." Both the PPR and the PZZ responded to these charges by depicting the Allies as tools of a still Nazified Germany. In early September 1946, US Secretary of State Robert Byrnes, in a speech in Stuttgart that foresaw Germany's eventual rehabilitation and the long-term commitment of American troops in Europe, expanded on critical remarks against the Soviet Union to underscore the still provisional nature of Poland's western border. Aided by their nationalist allies, the PPR exploited the Allied leaders' remarks in order to legitimate the Soviet Union's increasing break with its wartime allies and to attack the London Poles for undermining Poland's territorial rights to its "Piast lands" and thus condoning German anti-Polish aggression.[83] Only the "alliance" with the USSR—as part of the "Slavic front"—guaranteed the permanence of the Oder-Neisse Line as "the border of peace for Poland and the world."[84]

Byrnes's recent Stuttgart speech provided a useful foil for the harvest festival rally in Opole, with its theme of a "united nation standing on guard at the Oder." It also allowed such regime leaders as Gomułka, Bierut, and Michał Rola-Żymierski, Poland's head of military forces and Stalin's former NKVD agent, to present themselves as benevolent protectors of embattled Polish lands. They tapped into the interwar tradition of ritualized tropes that portrayed the border as a bulwark of security against a malevolent enemy—a concept that now provided geopolitical legitimation of the incipient Cold War European order. Thus, at Opole Gomułka proclaimed that together "the united Slavic nations of more than 250 million people ... stand behind our border at the Oder and Neisse." Within this Soviet Bloc based on "pan-Slavic friendship," Poland stood as "the front line of Slavdom in the west."[85]

Anti-Germanism provided the foundation for the regime's self-legitimizing warnings against "(West) German revanchism." Ironically, the incorporation of the German Democratic Republic and other non-Slavic nations into the Soviet Bloc contradicted the party's use of the Dmowskian Slav-versus-Teuton worldview. Nonetheless, the alleged external threat from "Germandom," represented by the Federal Republic of Germany (and its "Western supporters"), continued to justify the "removal" of the internal "German threat." As Edmund Męclewski emphasized in the PZZ's 1946 official pamphlet on the western territories, "the Polish nation has won the territorial war; it also must win the nationality war."[86] In a parallel to the Nazi Upper Silesian Regional Homeland League's earlier "*re*-Germanization" campaigns, Polish officials represented their "*de*-Germanization" efforts as "the completion of the task that was begun in 1919."[87] As with the Nazi case, this "mission" was not just about filtering out the "unwanted," but rather the construction of a new society.

The Avant-garde "New Pole"

PPR cadres de facto turned the Allied-sanctioned license to expel "Germans" from western Upper Silesia and other parts of the western borderlands into a right to reengineer local cultures. In particular, this mandate provided nationalist cover for their goal of creating a "new man" on the Soviet model. Following the Mount of St. Anne rally, Gomułka rushed to Wrocław (Breslau), the symbolic capital of the "recovered territories," to declare that "one cannot seriously speak of merging the recovered territories with the motherland if we don't merge our culture, our national spirit, with the historical period that gave us back these territories."[88] Through such purposely nonpartisan language, the party sought to achieve its ultimate aim of weaving a self-serving moral fabric for Polish society.

During the first postwar years, the party cadres benefited from the PZZ's cultural engineering fantasies. For example, an article in the Katowice-based *Odra*—a regional forum for Western Borderland Thought—described the "recovered territories" as "the theater of a great national experiment, aspiring to rebuild, and where necessary transform, the national psyche."[89] PZZ experts asserted that the cultural mix of displaced individuals in Poland's new west, including both the borderland population of "recovered peoples" and newcomers, would create "a school of national life and citizenship" to produce a "new type of Pole"—"new on the basis of morals, on the basis of consciousness of rights and duties, tasks and [social] role."[90] The PZZ wanted the new state to "fuse" all parties and organizations into one ethnically and politically homogenous society.[91] These specialists justified this with the need for a permanent "bulwark" against external and internal threats. The PZZ made this clear as early as mid-May 1945, when announcing as its primary goal "the thorough cleansing and de-Germanization of the western territories": "On these territories we will create a type of border Pole who will be sensitive to the threatening temptations of the now battered and destroyed Teutonic Knight [German], and will be ready to wage war against him, in case he ever tries to take revenge against his pogrom."[92] In this vicious cycle, the gnawing fear of German revenge for territorial annexation and expulsion justified the very actions that might provoke that revenge.

The PZZ saw the "Polish autochthon" as the core element of their re-nationalization project. Thus, Edmund Męclewski stressed that "re-Polonization" meant "restoring Polishness" to the borderland population. Moreover, native locals constituted "great political capital" in that they legitimated Poland's claim to the formerly German lands.[93] The PZZ director Wacław Barcikowski used a radio address during a May Third rally in Gliwice (Gleiwitz) in 1946 to emphasize that the region's locals "have to be placed under the special care of the state," which he explained elsewhere meant "political, cultural, and educational care, including ... the destruction of remnants of centuries-old German slavery and the influence of Nazism in their worldview."[94] Thus, just as "Germans" and "remnants of Germandom" required *physical* removal, the *minds* of borderland natives also needed ethnic cleansing. Promoted as a pedagogical program, this cleansing project shared Męclewski's aim to "manufacture a new and modern type of Pole."[95]

In order to bring the culture of borderland peoples (including Upper Silesians, Masurians, and Pomeranians) to the same level as the rest of Poland, the western territories experts effectively primitivized these populations. For example, the Slavic words and expressions in their heavily Germanized dialects revealed a "primitive" but "pure form of Polishness."[96] As during the interwar era, they regarded any deviation from Polish national consciousness, including regional/local-based identity (or "national indifference")—and even worse, cultural identification with Germany—as an artifact of centuries of Prussian/German victimization. Silesian Institute ethnographer Joseph Ligęza referred to "national apathy" as one of the "psychological effects" of "centuries of isolation" from Poland. Similar to *Heimatkundler* Alfons Perlick during the war, Ligęza dismissed regional consciousness as a defense mechanism by Upper Silesians against "Germanization." He argued that the Silesians' "inferiority complex," as reflected in a lack of social ambition, resulted from their experience under foreign rule, when social advancement required locals to conform to German nationalization policies. Moreover, as committed "Poles," they resisted these demands by developing regionalism as a false consciousness that, according to Ligęza, must now be eradicated.[97] Similarly, leading Upper Silesian scholar and activist Zygmunt Izdebski declared that "in Silesia the centuries-long German occupation made it impossible for the conquered populace to develop a rightful and uniform [Polish] national consciousness."[98]

This officially approved scholarly rhetoric provided the foundation for plans to turn borderland natives into full-fledged Poles—a process Ligęza described as their "return to normalcy."[99] Yet the ambitions of the western territories intelligentsia went beyond the construction of Polish-speaking and patriotic Poles. Męclewski, for example, intended his pedagogical "re-Polonization" to create not just "a new and modern type of Pole," but a "Pole-Democrat" (reflecting the PPR's equation of "Democrat" with "Communist").[100] Silesian Institute director Lutman similarly argued that the recovered territories, now freed from the burden of Poland's aristocratic (*szlachta*) and Sanacja pasts, would become the breeding ground of a "democratic Poland—a Poland of the working people, who alone constitute the power and strength of the nation."[101] Continuing this theme in the introductory article of the premier issue of *Odra*, he defined the "new democracy" as a proletarian society and culture marked by social justice. By contrast, "nineteenth-century democracy" had faltered due to economic inequality.[102] From the beginning, the PPR exerted significant ideological influence on the pedagogical acculturation program, which aimed to indoctrinate locals under the seemingly neutral guise of "re-Polonization."

Creating the "New Pole"

In late 1945, the PZZ, along with the state's Ministry of Education (Ministerstwo Oświaty), whose separate "recovered territories" section collaborated with the Silesian Institute, introduced "re-Polonization courses" (*kursy repolonizacyjne*). Their most urgent purpose was to strengthen the Polish language and encourage its use among the "verified" former German citizens of western Upper Silesia who used German or even the local dialect. Rather than stopping at language instruction, Communists and nationalists wanted these courses to include lessons on history, culture, and citizenship in "the new Poland." Indeed, they saw these courses as a vehicle for shaping their ideal "new man" of the western territories—or in the words of the Ministry of Education, "a new type of Pole ... [one] positively predisposed to today's Polish reality."[103] Advertised with the slogan, "Get to Know Poland, Its History and Culture," the courses formed an important part of a nationwide postwar "adult education/cultivation" (*oświata dorosłych*) program that was the Polish counterpart to the German "*Volk* cultivation" (*Volksbildung*). This project ran parallel to, and occasionally overlapped with, a campaign to promote literacy among the one-third of the country's population who were illiterate.[104]

"Re-Polonization courses" were aimed primarily at out-of-school adults, although the public school curriculum served similar content. There was no explicit measure or policy to compel locals to join and complete these courses.[105] Nevertheless, authorities applied all sorts of pressures to drive them to do so. Knowing Polish—and speaking it without the use of Germanisms—became particularly important for work, school, and everyday life. Already in 1945, the regional government prohibited the public *and* private use of German, threatening stiff punishments for infractions, ranging from monetary fines to internment in forced labor camps and various other social sanctions, which were intensified in the summer of 1947. Occasionally, individuals were reported to the public prosecutor—either by police officials or hostile neighbors—merely for sprinkling a few Germanisms into the local dialect or High Polish.[106] Indeed, improving one's Polish increased prospects of bettering one's socioeconomic situation. For example, the Ministry of Education tended to refuse to officially recognize and accredit locals' German school certificates and diplomas for legal use in Poland until they demonstrated completion of a "re-Polonization course." Apart from language, there is scattered evidence of local officials occasionally applying fines or other forms of harassment against individuals who failed to sign up for the courses, skipped lessons, or dropped out.¹⁰⁷ Such pressures may have helped the Ministry of Education attain its reported registration number of 93,000 for the "re-Polonization courses" in the first four postwar years.¹⁰⁸

This new pedagogical program accepted the long-standing nationalist premise that Upper Silesia's heterogeneous culture was an unnatural product of German cultural hegemony; hence, all "German" cultural and behavioral expressions—including language and mentality—were a "veneer" (*naloty*) covering an essentially Polish core culture. Like all other aspects of *niemczyzna*, they should be isolated and removed. More grandly, the pedagogical program aimed to "sever the civilizational bonds that connect the Silesian element with the foreign [German] society."¹⁰⁹ In other words, like the Nazi "re-Germanization" pedagogy, the Polish curriculum sought to create a psychological break with all cultural traits—including regionalism—associated with the other.

Pedagogues and curriculum planners considered teaching the Polish language to be the most basic means to achieve their aim, given the reality that fluency in High Polish was relatively uncommon among inhabitants of western Upper Silesia, who, after all, had until recently lived in a German society. Most residents who did not speak High German used the local dialect that contained strong elements of German. The Nazi regime's harsh campaign to discourage use of the Polish language or Slavic-based dialect had degraded natives' command of these tongues—particularly among the younger generation. Indeed, it had promoted more widespread use of German and increased German influence on local dialects.¹¹⁰ Linguistic pedagogy specialists nonetheless rejected any essential link between native language and national identity and instead accepted the borderland nationalist conviction that most native Upper Silesians were "ethnically Polish" regardless of their language. The native who spoke no Polish or whose dialect contained only "disfigured" Polish was the product of "centuries of German hegemony" that must be "undone" and corrected. But these pedagogues sought to do more than teach grammatical High Polish: much like Nazi linguist Josef Bolick's wartime efforts, they aimed to reconstruct the locals' native tongue. Thus, the "re-Polonization" language program developed by Stefani Mazurek, a pedagogy expert in the Silesian Institute and in the Ministry of Education's "recovered territories" section, and Maks Hasiński, the head of the regional school district, emphasized pronunciation and called for intensive drills to rid natives of the German accents with which they pronounced Polish words. Teachers in this program were trained in the physiology of phonetics, and their own speech was expected to be a pristine "proper" and "musical" Polish that would set an example for their students (fig. 5.5).¹¹¹ Realizing the difficulty of teaching native-level Polish fluency to German and dialect speakers, the pedagogues soon came to focus primarily on removing German words and sounds from natives' everyday language. In the words of a coordinator in the regional school district: "Dialect [*gwara*] features give local color to the literary

Figure 5.5. Distribution of books at a "Re-Polonization" course. (Author unknown, APK)

tongue while disturbing nobody. One can speak of an error in pronunciation only when the latter denotes German influence."[112]

The postwar campaign to cleanse German from Upper Silesians' everyday speech can be viewed in the context of a continuing effort to construct one standard and High Polish–based "Upper Silesian dialect." Notably, Grażyński had earlier endorsed the search for an "Upper Silesian talk" (*gwara Śląska*) as a core aspect of his "regionalism," which aimed to strengthen linguistically diverse eastern Upper Silesia's ties to the rest of Poland. So, too, the Silesian Institute continued to play a leading role in the effort to standardize local regional dialects, a project that lasted into the last decade of the Communist period.[113] Although this continuity exemplifies the "re-Polonization" curriculum's reliance on Grażyński's national regionalists, the postwar efforts also responded to more immediate concerns, such as rallying locals to identify with *all* the western borderlands, not just Upper Silesia, the role of language education in ethnic cleansing, and above all, bolstering support for the Communist regime.

These new elements of postwar national regionalism infused political and ideological as well as cultural and linguistic concerns. In line with its ambitious mandate to create a "new Pole," "re-Polonization" courses included lessons on history and politics, as well as on regional (the western borderlands) and national culture. By contrast, the Nazi *Volksbildung* program largely separated language lessons from political schooling. Nonetheless, both nationalizing regimes aimed to draw a clear-cut line between "Polishness" and "Germandom" as a prerequisite to teaching hatred of everything associated with the national "other." The Polish curriculum developers sought "above all to point out the essential differences between Polish and German cultures" in order to cultivate an "emotional bond" for the former and abhorrence of the latter.[114] Thus, the history curriculum meant to dispel any notion that Upper Silesia or any other part of the western territories shared an affinity with Germany and German culture. The literary and historical narratives in course readers portrayed Germans as outsiders transplanted to these lands, while "Poles"—the native population from the earliest times—were the region's rightful inhabitants. The basic theme of these narratives became the "centuries-old Polish struggle against the Germanic flood" into "Polish territories." Thus, the Ministry of Education wanted history lessons to point out

> all the injustices [and] injuries that Germans imposed on the populace of the lands along the Oder River, the Baltic Sea, and in Prussia, the territory in which the autochthonous population is the direct descendant of the victims, [which] is bound to awaken in the participants a loathing of the German past in the name of the basic human rights and all-human ideals that have been trampled upon in the course of the 1,000-year period ... [that ends with the fall of] Hitler.[115]

In these course readers this millennia-long struggle against Germans in the borderlands ended with their redemptive liberation by a heroic Soviet army that graciously transferred the "recovered territories" to the Polish people and guaranteed against any reversal.[116] History lessons thus became tools in an attempt to reconstruct a useful collective identity. For the PZZ, the "new Pole" who displayed indefatigable patriotism, loyalty to the current regime, and abhorrence of "everything German" would himself serve as the desired "guardian of the western border."[117]

Beyond its nationalist geopolitical discourse, the new curriculum praised the Communist regime's redistribution of land and property to the proletarian masses, a policy supported by the populist ranks of the PZZ. More generally, the courses promoted the role of Communist ideology in building "a real democracy." For example, the standard reader defined the role of "democracy" as bringing culture to the masses and promoting "social justice" through "a struggle against capitalism"; only by achieving this "democracy" would "a new, better man be raised." There was no mention of an individual's freedom to choose his or her preferred political path.[118] By disseminating PPR principles while avoiding any explicit use of the unpopular "C word" (communism), the regime instrumentalized the popular national mission of "restoring Polishness" to the "recovered peoples" of western Upper Silesia. Rather than schooling them in a more politically neutral High Polish culture, the regime used its ethnic cleansing mandate to engineer a Communist "new man."

In the classroom, these lessons often diverged from the vision of their pedagogical planners. In many instances, students themselves determined what they wanted to learn and what did not interest them. For example, supervisors in the ministry remarked that participants pragmatically favored language instruction over the political and cultural curricula. Faced with loss of a job or other disadvantages if they did not speak Polish, they sought language instruction but paid little attention to the efforts to shape them into "new Poles." According to one report, "very often students learn the Polish language but run away from history lessons, which is likewise proof of [German] propaganda and [their] attitude against the People's Poland."[119]

The instructors, most of whom were newcomers to the western borderlands, also influenced the final shape of what was taught and how. In some cases, they ignored the curriculum planners' intentions, if only to avoid alienating their students. One such instructor, by day an elementary school teacher from Gliwice, rejected the Germanophobia that offended locals, who shared strong heritage and family ties with Germany. In her words:

> With regard to German Hitlerism and the fate of the Polish nation under German occupation, one had to talk about these affairs tactfully and make it appropriately clear that the whole nation is not responsible for the atrocities. These are sensitive matters due to the fact that even though the listeners have Polish citizenship, their closest relatives, with whom they share blood ties, including parents and siblings, live in Germany. And so denunciation of the German nation is hurtful to them and can create conflicts between lecturer and listener and can awaken an outright aversion to Poles.[120]

In deferring to her students' sensibilities, this instructor thwarted the PZZ's intent that the courses "cleanse" the locals' minds of "everything German." Indeed, by using time constraints as an excuse for skipping entirely the lesson entitled, "Will the Germans Rise Again, and What Should Be Our Attitude toward Them?" she deprived the regime of a number of "guardians of the western border."[121]

The same teacher approached her language lessons with equivalent pragmatism and flexibility. Rather than using pronunciation drills in order to reconstruct her students' native tongues, she focused on removing Germanisms from whatever variety of Polish they knew in order to protect them from harassment for "speaking German." In this regard, she resembled the earlier German schoolteacher in Gau O/S who deemed Nazi efforts to teach locals to speak High German unrealistic. One imagines that other "re-Polonization" instructors might have envied the interest shown by the Gliwice teacher's students in her lessons on the Polish heritage of Upper Silesia, on "Pan-Slavic unity," and even on "the history of democratic Poland." She recognized, however, that their interest in these lessons came from pragmatic reasons, not because they felt themselves to be Poles.[122]

As late as 1947, when the earlier cooperation between the Catholic Church and the state had become seriously frayed prior to a permanent rupture, planners and most teachers promoted Catholicism as integral to the "re-Polonization" curriculum, even as they taught Communist ideology and sang "The Internationale."[123] According to one Silesian school district official, "industriousness and religiosity" were core features of local society that would provide the material for "the rise of a new type of Pole."[124] Yet even the inclusion of religion in the "re-Polonization" curriculum failed to attract the number of students the Ministry of Education had hoped for. The 93,000 individuals who signed up constituted less than an eighth of the "verified" population of western Upper Silesia, and less than half of the ministry's target of 200,000. Still worse, only 71,576 of those who began finished either the basic or advanced level of these courses—the majority having quit after the first level.[125] In addition to the ministry, other agents of pedagogical "re-Polonization," including various sociopolitical activist groups, such as youth and women's organizations, workplaces (notably coal mines and metallurgy plants), and community centers in urban and rural areas, also engaged in the teaching of language, history, and politics.

Both the PZZ and the Ministry of Education—as coordinator of the school system—pursued the important task of capturing the hearts and minds of the younger generation. In the summer of 1946, they jointly established youth camps across the region that attracted over 40,000 participants in June and twice that number in August, 20,000 of whom belonged to the Polish Scouting Association (Związek Harcerstwa Polskiego, or ZHP).[126] The camps aimed to foster the "melding" into a "homogenously Polish" society of various groups—newcomers, former German citizens, and locals, but also residents of the Dąbrowa Basin, all of whom now lived in the Voivodeship Silesia-Dąbrowa. The campaign sought to "awaken" Polish national consciousness in natives of western Upper Silesia, in particular its most politically aloof segment, the rural population. To this end, the PZZ mobilized Polish Scouts to set up eighteen camps in this area, including nine in Gliwice County and nearby areas along the interwar German-Polish border; the other half were located deep within the part of the region that had belonged to Germany before the war. To fulfill their mission to "recover" "autochthons," the scouts invited local residents (adults and children) to campfire sing-alongs, storytelling, and other informative, entertaining, and integrative activities. In addition to efforts to persuade local youth to join them, the scouts worked to "de-Germanize" their surroundings by such activities as removing German signs and inscriptions from public places and "correcting" locals who used Germanisms in their speech.[127]

Locals' reactions to the scouts were lukewarm at best. Most scout leaders reported that residents were hesitant to join their events or to allow their children to do so. Indeed, along the former German-Polish border, many mothers refused to allow sons and daughters to join the scout camps, fearing that the uniformed youths had come to ship them to the USSR—just as in 1945 Soviet troops had sent their husbands away. Other locals noticed the similarities between the Polish Scouts and the Hitler Youth, who had earlier been dispatched to win over *"Volksdeutsche"* for the Third Reich. In light of a still insecure border settlement, they also remembered the social consequences imposed by the Nazis on those who had participated in Polish politics during the interwar era. Furthermore, for a society with omnipresent shortages, the scouts fostered resentment as additional mouths to feed, especially given the locals' experience of confiscations by Soviets, Polish officials, and newcomers. The scouts managed to make headway only with such actions as distributing food and bringing in a local priest to hold an outdoor prayer service. According to a PZZ report that cited a scout supervisor: "The religiosity of the youth and the participation of a priest in the camp activities made the best impression on the religious autochthonic population and positively predisposed them to the scouts. Their comparison of the irreligious Hitler Youth camps with those of our scouts must have worked to the latter's benefit."[128] The PZZ expressed its satisfaction that this use of religion had "awakened the [Polish] consciousness of the autochthons."[129]

Border rallies, Germanophobic agitation, and "re-Polonization" courses all ultimately failed to achieve the regime's primary goal: attracting popular support for either the PPR's interests in the referendum or its "coalition" in the Sejm election. The region's newcomers and natives alike voted for the oppositional Polish Peasants' Party (PSL) led by Stanisław Mikołajczyk. Regime cadres might have found the parliamentary vote less shocking than the majorities in several parts of the region that cast a "no" vote on the referendum's third question concerning the border. Yet the brutal treatment recently endured by locals at the hands of the Soviets and newcomers, as well as the Polish state's suppression of their native language, make it hardly surprising that most of the areas that rejected the cession of the western borderlands to Poland were in the western (formerly German) parts of Upper Silesia. They included the counties of Gliwice (34 percent yes, 65.4 percent no) and Bytom (46 percent yes, 53.5 percent no) and the cities of Bytom (47.8 percent yes, 52.2 percent no) and Strzelce (35.8 percent yes, 64 percent no). Those locals who had formerly been Polish citizens experienced more benign treatment by both Soviets and PPR officials, not least because of their familiarity with Polish language and culture. Most likely this was a factor in the positive vote on question three in all urban and rural areas of the industrial district that had belonged to Poland before the war, with one surprising exception: no votes from the rural county of Rybnik (62.5 percent) nearly approached those from the outskirts of Opole (63.4 percent), one of Upper Silesia's most western areas.[130] The referendum results reflected poorly on the regime's nationalization efforts. In reaction to this slap in the face, once the Sejm elections were over—and manipulated in favor of the Communists—both the party and its borderland nationalists turned away from persuasion and toward a stepped-up campaign of terror, surveillance, and punishment.

Mass Mobilization for Cultural Cleansing

The expulsion process sanctioned by the Potsdam Conference had largely ended by September 1947, when Governor Zawadzki intensified internal ethnic cleansing under the slogan "Struggle against the Resurgence of Germandom" (*walka przeciw nawrotu niemczyzny*; hereafter referred to as the Struggle Campaign).[131] Rather than confront their failure to create a socially harmonious and politically active Upper Silesia, government authorities and borderland nationalists indulged in conspiracy theories involving "German propaganda" and "crypto-Germans." This new campaign alleged that a hidden "German element" within Poland was collaborating with the western Allies to maintain "German influence" and "Germanize" local citizens, with an ultimate goal of border revision.[132] Three key aspects of this multifarious campaign are of particular concern here: its connections to the "re-Polonization" effort; its operations at the grassroots level; and its role in facilitating the onset of Stalinism.

Formalized in mid-August 1947, the Struggle Campaign reorganized and reinvigorated ethnic cleansing policies that had been carried out since 1945. Regime officials believed that during the first two postwar years many aspects of cultural "de-Germanization," in particular, had received inadequate attention in the face of such pressing matters as expulsion and resettlement, combating the armed Polish underground, and ensuring victory in the referendum and Sejm elections. In the view of authorities, "German" remained widely spoken, artifacts of "Germandom" still "defaced" private and public places, and individuals "behaving German" continued to express critical views of Poland.[133] To prepare for a final showdown against *niemczyzna*, the authorities levied new and stronger punishments for such behavior and in 1947 even opened a concentration camp in Gliwice for "crypto-Germans" and "traitors." The campaign mobilized local administrators in special Civic Inspection Committees (Obywatelski Komitet Kontroli) to screen the backgrounds of suspected individuals and search private quarters—often more than once—in the effort to track down Poland's "fifth column" and all traces of *niemczyzna*. These committees welcomed "good Poles," in particular veteran insurgents and plebiscite activists, as well as members of the PZZ, PPR, and their various sociopolitical organizations and activist groups. They also worked with the local organs of coercion and repression, the police and the state security agency, the UB (Urząd Bezpieczeństwa Publicznego, whose formal acronym was UBP).[134]

This campaign resembled the Nazis' efforts to ban the use of Polish in wartime eastern Upper Silesia as well as Operation More Beautiful Silesia, both aiming to remove traces of "Polish culture" from public view. Like the wartime equivalents, the postwar campaign promoted grassroots mobilization for ethnic cleansing as part of the larger effort to raise the "new man" (previously the [German] "Upper Silesian person," and now the "new Pole"). Official directives described the campaign's primary function as "[i]ncluding the Silesian population in the operation to cleanse the terrain of truly German elements and of real traitors. This common engagement in social collaboration is an outstanding social-pedagogical means for shaping a national consciousness that does not know a middle ground between Polishness and Germandom."[135] Grassroots mobilization for "de-Germanization," including engagement in acts of violence against persons and property, was thus supposed to teach Upper Silesians to become full-fledged Poles and ardent activists in regime politics.

While spelled out officially in 1947, grassroots mobilization for cleansing and acculturation had in fact long been ongoing. Since the summer of 1945, officials had been calling on locals and newcomers to "de-Germanize" their everyday surroundings, which meant removing from public view any German-language posting or sign. Local officials made cultural cleansing an activity for school youths; for example, in July 1945, pupils in Bytom County searched private houses for German-language books and periodicals, or anything with German writing, for collection and destruction.[136] By making the cultural cleansing process a more integral part of the Struggle Campaign, the regime sought to ensure that all "traces of *niemczyzna*"—even the tiniest and most trivial home items that had previously gone unnoticed—were cleaned out. This would also give the regime a chance to rally more grassroots support. In Gliwice, for example, the campaign assigned residential building managers and supervisors to instruct tenants and residents on how to properly "de-Germanize" their homes and apartments by painstakingly performing such chores as scraping the "German" fine print from underneath dishes and ash trays and erasing "German" signatures from works of art. While the regime underscored that diligent participation in the campaign was "the duty of all Poles," it failed to mobilize locals in practice.[137]

Administrators tended to dismiss the problems and shortcomings of the Struggle Campaign in their jurisdictions, most likely to avoid being held responsible. Exceptions included reports by the governors of Gliwice and Strzelce Counties, which indicate the unpopularity of home searches, tampering with personal belongings, and requisitioning and destruction of German literature. As one Civic Inspection Committee agent reflected on his assessment of a private home: "[D]uring [our] visit the people demonstrate fear and lack of will. [And] even though it is passive, their resistance nevertheless significantly slows down [our] work."[138] Locals prepared for such an inspection by hiding books and other potentially suspect belongings. Thus, some agents reported better luck in finding "traces of Germandom" in an unannounced *second* search after the inhabitants had let down their guard.[139] One Strzelce governor's report indicated a lack of engagement among Polish newcomer residents, which he found even more troubling than the—more anticipated—passive resistance of native locals. He noted that newcomers shared the locals' complaints about the Polish government's "alliance with the USSR" and "democracy," thus adding fuel to the overall hostility toward state officials.[140] Such accounts are exceptions to the usual reports, which underlined tensions between local Upper Silesians and migrant or expellee newcomers.

The Strzelce reports reveal house searches as a frequent cause of open conflict between locals and commissioners. For example, a commissioner's report on a return search of a house in the locality of Leśnica, conducted to ensure that problems identified on a prior visit had been remediated, noted:

> [The resident] did not allow me to look at anything, telling me that we have to put an end to this, having some mayor or administrator walk around and search your apartment. [He said] I'm a free citizen, have finally awaited the coming of free democratic Poland, and want to feel free inside my own home. ... Only the public prosecutor can allow an official to inspect my home."[141]

This reaction indicates that even the period of Nazi governance had not accustomed locals to such intrusions. Indeed, one inspector recounted the objections of an individual who was ordered to remove the "German" signatures on his paintings: "[D]uring German times I had paintings with Polish inscriptions and the Germans did not bother me, but you (that is, Poles) are making a whole needless comedy about it."[142] A similar comment was reported after an inspection in the locality of Zawadzkie: "[T]he Germans did all this too, but did not make us get rid of our Polish-language prayer books."[143] Such reports demonstrated both understandable discontent over the regime's confiscation of beloved personal items, but also reactions to these events based on a collective experience of dealing with two separate social engineering states, and thus comparing "the Poles" with "the Germans."

In the nationally fluid Upper Silesian borderland, it often proved difficult to identify the real-life targets of "de-Germanization." Just as the Nazis had labeled as "Polish" any speech with Slavic vocabulary, pronunciation, or expressions, so Polish officials often viewed Germanisms in local dialects as evidence of *niemczyzna*.[144] In Bytom, PZZ agents harassed Yiddish-speaking Polish Jews, demanding that they "once and for all stop using this German jargon and German language."[145] As of 1 January 1948, the regime had levied fines for the "harmful use of the German language" against 1,447 individuals throughout Voivodeship Silesia-Dąbrowa (primarily in western Upper Silesia).[146] In the city of Gliwice, 296 individuals had been punished by this date, and by the end of 1948, they had been joined by at least another 900 deemed guilty of language infractions.[147]

Although the regime threatened penalties as high as 30,000 złotys (some $819 today), the actual fines were usually between 300 and 3,000 złotys (between some $8.19 and $81.90). More serious "anti-Polish" offenses were punished with incarceration at the concentration camp in Gliwice, which served both as a correctional institution and a temporary holding site for those designated for eventual expulsion. From its opening in 1947 to the end of 1948, just before its closing, the camp held some 5,000 individuals. Of the nearly 3,000 incarcerated in 1947, 2,200 had their temporary citizenship revoked and were expelled to Germany.[148]

By 1948–49, local administrators reported the public disappearance of "German" as well as of visible symbols of *niemczyzna*. These included German names and statements inscribed on tombstones, which had to be erased, even if they belonged to the prewar German Jewish community. The campaign to expunge Germandom was met with complacency and sullen compliance with the prescribed behavior. According to reports, threats and harassment from officials for using German motivated hundreds of people to sign up for "re-Polonization" classes.[149] The governor of Gliwice County reported that those seeking instruction included individuals who had been in hiding since the war ended. Since reports indicated dissatisfaction regarding the success of these courses, one might assume a high level of passive compliance. In this sense, the participants did what the majority of their fellow students had done all along—improved their Polish-language skills in order to pass as "good Poles" and thus avoid harassment and persecution. To avoid political indoctrination, some individuals resorted to private language instruction. By September 1948, the Gliwice County governor reported that, finally, most individuals in his jurisdiction spoke Polish. As an experienced administrator familiar with the population, he nonetheless recognized that the increased local "interest" in learning Polish had one drawback, namely, "those who had learned Polish in the last three years now have a good way to disguise themselves"—in other words, to hide their true identity and convictions.[150]

The price of these limited "successes" was far more dramatic. Much like Nazi efforts against "Polish" during the war, the cultural cleansing efforts of the nationalist-Communist alliance both during and before the Struggle Campaign almost completely failed to homogenize Upper Silesia. The vast majority of "German" speakers went unpunished, while the language and dialect, as well as the material remnants of the age-old bilingual local heritage, remained a permanent part of the cultural landscape. Indeed, as Hugo Service points out, rather than the regime's intended integration of locals into Polish society, the effort resulted in quite the opposite: their further alienation both from the regime and their newcomer neighbors, as well as their turn to a haven in "local solidarity" and "local cultural distinctiveness."[151]

At the End of the "National Road to Communism"

The Struggle Campaign did ultimately benefit the PPR. Having stolen the Sejm elections, the party worked to further develop and entrench Poland's Communist rule, an effort enhanced by the campaign's use of terror, violence, surveillance, and intrusions into private lives. With its façade of nonpartisan support for a national cause, the search for "crypto-Germans" aided the development of a police and surveillance state that intruded into the private sphere and sought to "cleanse" public institutions of "undesirable" individuals. By 1948, local-level officials were combining searches of homes and businesses for "elements of Germandom" with a nationwide "war on speculation" to ferret out sales of hoarded goods as part of a campaign against private enterprise. Similarly, its leaders "cleansed" the PPR's ranks of a host of undesirables, not just "crypto-Germans" but also "class enemies," "drunkards," individuals "insubordinate to party discipline," the "socially immoral," and those who "abused party membership for personal gain and careerism."[152] In addition to legitimating these efforts, the party's internationally sanctioned mandate to "de-Germanize" contributed to a Stalinist atmosphere that used state terror and capricious punishment against an ever more insecure society.

By 1947 the regime had begun to use the German conspiracy myth to end its expedient "friendship" with the Polish Catholic Church, a relationship that the PZZ in particular viewed as an indispensible tool for integrating once German lands into the nation. Thus, in August 1946, Ziętek along with some 300,000 of the faithful led by Bishop Adamski joined in a pilgrimage to Piekary Śląskie (Deutsche Piekar)—the largest such event of the postwar period.[153] That same year the Strzelce County PZZ organized a pilgrimage for 1,200 locals to Częstochwa, central Poland's main devotional site, an experience that it claimed had both "recovered countless Polish hearts" for the nation and "deepened their trust in Poland's government."[154] A year later, however, the party cadres and Catholic clerics were volubly at odds over the state's efforts to diminish religion's influence over young Poles through such efforts as the secularization of schools and the inclusion of schoolchildren in the Communist Union of Polish Youth (Związek Młodzierzy Polskiej). The PPR also launched a propaganda campaign against Adamski for having encouraged locals to comply with Nazi nationalization politics and sign up for the Deutsche Volksliste during the war. Indeed, whereas earlier it had praised his wartime actions as a heroic effort to protect Silesians from expulsion and thus keep the region "Polish," now it labeled them as treasonous "Germanization." In similar respects, the regime accused lower-level Upper Silesian clerics of German sympathies in an effort to fill clerical posts with its politically compliant newcomer "patriotic priests."[155] In these ways, in Upper Silesia (as throughout the western borderlands), the *de*constructive aspects of territorial appropriation acted as a catalyst for establishing the Stalinist order.

Reconstructive measures benefited the regime as well. "Re-Polonization" courses continued into 1949, although they were increasingly fused with the Struggle against Illiteracy, a pet pedagogical campaign of the now reformed and unabashedly Communist Polish United Workers' Party (Polska Zjednoczona Partia Robotnicza, or PZPR). While Upper Silesia's residents had been almost entirely literate before the war, this changed due to postwar immigration from central and formerly eastern Poland.[156] In 1949 the government mobilized the region's major political activist groups, as well as labor, youth, and teachers' organizations, to identify all "illiterates" living in the region so they could be registered for literacy courses. Because many officials used *Polish*-language literacy as their criterion, 45,000 literate Upper Silesians were identified as "illiterates" for their insufficient command of Polish.[157] Outsider agents involved in this tally used their authority as a weapon in the still heated conflict between newcomers and locals. As a result, some individuals were placed on the "illiterate" register out of spite. In places where separate "re-Polonization" courses were not available, such misplaced individuals had to sit in special literacy courses along with their actually illiterate neighbors.[158] The fusion of "re-Polonization" and literacy courses made sense to government officials, whose primary concern was the dissemination of Communist propaganda. Because "political illiteracy" was the real concern, course textbooks purveyed party-line ideology.[159] The treatment of non-Polish-speaking Upper Silesians as de facto "illiterates" became official in 1952, when "re-Polonization" and anti-illiteracy courses were merged as "reading courses" (*kursy czytelnicze*).[160] By this point, the regime had officially abandoned the project of transforming the borderland native into a "new Pole"—and a catalyst for the regime's "national road" to power—in favor of a regionally neutral and class-based *Homo sovieticus*.

The official abandonment of nationalism, national regionalism, and the "recovered territories" project by 1950 marked a core aspect of Poland's Stalinist turn. In its final phase, the chief agents of the territorial appropriation project themselves fell victim to the dictatorial state apparatus that they had worked to construct and legitimate. The period 1948–50 saw Gomułka's ouster from the government, the liquidation of all borderland nationalist institutions along with the PZZ, and the ostracizing from public life of important borderland nationalists who had supported the party. A regime that was now on a strictly nation-centric and regionally blind path to (Soviet) "socialism" severely restricted public discussion of the cultural politics of "recovering" contested territories.[161] In the most symbolic act of this effort to erase decades of German-Polish revanchism, in 1953 Katowice—the historical hotbed of irredentist national regionalism—was officially renamed Stalinogród. To underscore the meaning of this renaming, the party compelled Gustav Morcinek, the Grażyńskiite national regionalist novelist and a figurehead of the interwar cold war over Upper Silesia, to announce the name change. The city's landscape was increasingly filled with ponderous examples of "socialist realist" architecture—one of the largest erected within the former Forum Katowice on the spot where Grażyński's Silesian Museum had briefly stood. Henceforth—and until it became Katowice again in 1956—Stalinogród officially symbolized the heartland of proletarian and Communist Poland.[162]

Those responsible for this official makeover of Upper Silesia's identity intended to efface not only its heritage of national regionalism but also its more essential localism. The regime's efforts to forcefully and equally assimilate all groups encountered massive discontent from all elements, both newcomers and locals, including the few remaining Jews. In the end, the utopian "nationalist Communist" project to create a harmonious and homogenous society failed. Conflicts between newcomers and locals, as well as broader discontent over the political and socioeconomic order, continued to plague the industrial district and the less industrial western areas for many decades.[163] Widespread uncertainty regarding the permanence of the Oder-Neisse Line presented another obstacle to the official dream of rooting (and rerooting) all of the region's social groups, which in turn restrained their willingness to invest their labor and resources in the region's socioeconomic development. State officials coined a formal name for this problem: the "psychosis of temporariness" (*psychoza tymczasowości*), a term similar to what the Nazis had called "waiting out."[164] The de facto division of Germany and then the establishment in 1949 of an independent Federal Republic of Germany that rejected the legitimacy of the Oder-Neisse Line exacerbated the sense of living in an indeterminate state. As the Cold War heated up, newcomers and Upper Silesians began to prepare for a World War III and a possible return to their lost homelands. The second group imagined this as their reincorporation into Germany.[165] Although both groups were dissatisfied with their material and political circumstances, locals at least held out some hope of a border revision. Among their ethnically Polish neighbors, however, this prospect engendered fears of falling victim to an ethnic cleansing campaign orchestrated by a future German government.

Upper Silesian locals, the region's largest social group and also the primary target of postwar reassimilation policies, were left largely alienated from their new nation. When in 1952 the government circulated a questionnaire asking for Upper Silesians' nationality and citizenship, it was dismayed by the results, which confirmed the failure of the regime's national integration policies: namely, 67,000 locals—the vast majority from the former areas of the Provinz—declared German nationality, and thousands more represented themselves as German citizens, as stateless, or refused to fill out these mandatory surveys altogether. A wave of terror against these nonconformists followed, marked by intimidation, arrests, and prison sentences, compelling thousands to "correct" themselves by declaring Polish nationality or citizenship. But the government's use of coercion did not solve its problem. Over 17,000 individuals failed to collect their state identity cards, which were issued to former German citizens in a further attempt to turn them into Poles. Some shunned the cards out of fear that if the Germans retook Upper Silesia, they would suffer the consequences of openly embracing Polish nationality, just as many locals had under the Nazis.[166] The epilogue to this book will explore how, over the next decades, locals' nonconformity with government policy, and a will to emigrate to (mainly West) Germany, would underscore Poland's failure to "recover" this population.

Conclusion

After World War II, collaboration with Poland's Communist Party–controlled regime allowed Dmowskian nationalists and former Grażyńskiites to realize a central goal: the appropriation of western Upper Silesia. Ethnic cleansing in the new Polish state utilized narratives, discourses, and media developed during the interwar German-Polish cold war. Revanchist border rallies, the culturally racist demonization of *niemczyzna*, as well as fantasies of "recovery" and "liberation" of territory and peoples in order to create an ethnically homogenous territorial bulwark against Germany all characterized the symbolic politics that supported an ambitious social engineering campaign. Its aim was to conceptualize and separate the "German" from the "Polish," as well as to collectively denigrate the former group as a prelude to its removal—both physically and from the *minds* of western Upper Silesia's natives.

This campaign's "constructive" program of "adult education" worked in tandem with a repressive campaign to clear the landscape of *niemczyzna* and "crypto-Germans." It was legitimated by a civilizing discourse developed during the interwar era, but that also echoed the wartime ideology of Nazi social engineering. At its core, this discourse depicted Upper Silesians as historical "victims" and their regional and Germanophile identities as marks of "false consciousness," the term Marxist-Leninists also applied to anti-Communist sentiment among workers. In Upper Silesia, it legitimated a political program to "cleanse" local landscapes and consciousness of all traces of unwanted identities—Germandom, Jewishness, and regionalism or localism alike. In the end, this utopian social engineering project resulted in widespread social conflict, discontent, alienation, and eventually mass flight from Poland and its Communist regime.

This revanchist project nonetheless strengthened the PPR. At border rallies that harked back to the interwar period, party leaders flanked by high-ranking clerics and established intellectual elites represented themselves as a "national Polish movement." Although cooperation with the Catholic Church was precarious and conditional, its connections with popular irredentism helped legitimate the regime. The "re-Polonization" campaign also brought an influx of patriotic activists and professionals into Upper Silesia. Although most were anti-Communist, they provided the PPR with support from a badly needed intellectual elite. The mandate to remake Upper Silesia through force and ideology fortified the regime's role as social engineer and gave it the pretext for creating an intrusive police state and an apparatus for ideological mass indoctrination. Despite the failure to create a bold new society, the nationalist activists in concert with the "re-Polonization" campaign helped establish a nationalist basis for Poland's postwar political order.

Notes

1. Wacław Barcikowski, "Słowo Wstępne," in *Odzyskane Ziemie—Odzyskani Ludzie: Z współczesnych zagadnień Ziem Odzyskanych*, ed. Wacław Barcikowski et al. (Poznań, 1946), 7.

2. Edmund Męclewski, "Ziemie Odzyskane i Odzyskani Ludzie," in *Odzyskane Ziemie—Odzyskani Ludzie: Z współczesnych zagadnień Ziem Odzyskanych*, ed. Wacław Barcikowski et al. (Poznań, 1946), 82.

3. See Anita Prażmowska, *Civil War in Poland, 1942–1948* (New York, 2004).

4. Ahonen, *After the Expulsion*, 20–21ff.

5. On Poland's territorial shift and the establishment of communism, see Curp, *A Clean Sweep?*; Thum, *Uprooted*.

6. See Curp, *A Clean Sweep?*, 5–6ff.

7. See Edmund Męclewski, "Repolonizaja: Programem politycznym i realizacyjnym," in *Odzyskane Ziemie—Odzyskani Ludzie: Z współczesnych zagadnień Ziem Odzyskanych*, ed. Wacław Barcikowski et al. (Poznań, 1946); Bernard Linek, "Mit Ziem Odzyskanych w powojennej Polsce na przykładzie Górnego Śląska (wybrane aspekty)," in *Nationalismus und nationale Identität in Ostmitteleuropa im 19. und 20. Jhd.*, ed. Bernard Linek and Kai Struve (Opole, 2000), 241–44; Grzegosz Strauchold, *Autochtoni Polscy, Niemieccy, czy ... Od Nacjonalizmu do Komunizmu (1945–9)* (Toruń, 2001), 95–146.

8. The classic study on this topic is Norman Naimark, *The Russians in Germany: A History of the Soviet Zone of Occupation, 1945–1949* (Cambridge, MA, 1995). For Upper Silesia, see Service, *Germans to Poles*, chap. 3.

9. The statistic is from Kazimierz Miroszewski, "Armia Czerwona na terenie województwa śląskodąbrowskiego," and Andrzej Topol "Przemysł ciężki w województwie śląsko-dąbrowskim," in Andrzej Topol, ed., *Rok 1945 w Województwie Śląsko-Dąbrowskim* (Katowice, 2004), 24, see also 10–31, 170–71; Gregor Thum, *Die Fremde Stadt, Breslau 1945* (Berlin, 2003), 171–210.

10. As of 1 August 1945, the largest camps were in Świętochłowice (3,233 inmates), Mysłowice (4,902 inmates), and Jaworzno (2,179 inmates). See Adam Dziurok, "Problemy narodowościowe w województwie śląskim i sposoby ich rozwiązania," in *Województwo Śląskie, 1945–50: Zarys dziejów politycznych*, ed. Adam Dziurok and Ryszard Kaczmarek (Katowice, 2007), 578–81.

11. Bernard Linek, "Weryfikacja narodowościowa i akcja osadnicza na Śląsku Opolskim," in *Województwo Śląskie, 1945–50: Zarys dziejów politycznych*, ed. Adam Dziurok and Ryszard Kaczmarek (Katowice, 2007), 612. According to Service, *Germans to Poles*, 195: 120,000 fled or were expelled from western Upper Silesia.

12. Ibid., 620; Dziurok, "Problemy," 596.

13. See Bernard Linek, "'De-Germanization' and 'Repolonization' in Upper Silesia, 1945–50," in *Redrawing Nations: Ethnic Cleansing in East-Central Europe, 1945–1948*, ed. Philipp Ther and Ana Siljak (New York, 2001), 126–28.

14. See Ther, *Deutsche und polnische Vertriebene*, esp. chap. 3.
15. In this case, petitioning for "weryfikacja." Wojewoda, SR, October 1945, APK, 185/1 (UWŚl.-Og.), 49, 157ff.
16. The first statistic is from the end of 1948 and the second from July 1949. See Linek, "Weryfikacja," 620; Dżiurok, "Problemy," 598–99. Some dispute exists over these statistics; e.g., Elżbieta Kaszuba claims that there were 500,000 newcomers in western Upper Silesia in 1948 (45.7 percent of the total population). See Czapliński et al., *Historia Śląska*, 463.
17. Starostwo Powiatowe (StP) Tarnowskich Gór, SR, April 1946, APK, 1430 (StP Tarnowskie Góry), 5, 10ff.; Ther, *Deutsche und polnische Vertriebene*, chap. 3.
18. See Jan T. Gross, *Fear: Anti-Semitism in Poland after Auschwitz—an Essay in Historical Interpretation* (New York, 2006), 33–35.
19. Adam Dziurok and Ryszard Kaczmarek, eds., *Województwo Śląskie, 1945–50: Zarys dziejów politycznych* (Katowice, 2007), 521.
20. Bożena Szaynok, "Jews in Lower Silesia, 1945–1950," in *Jews in Silesia*, ed. Marcin Wodziński et al. (Cracow, 2001), 219.
21. See Wojciech Jaworski, "Jewish Religious Communities in Upper Silesia, 1945–1970," in *Jews in Silesia*, ed. Marcin Wodziński et al. (Cracow, 2001), 247–66.
22. In mid-1949, there were 6,446 Jews in Upper Silesia, most in Katowice (1,597) and Bytom (1,144). See Dziurok and Kaczmarek, *Województwo Śląskie*, 521–22.
23. Jaworski, "Jewish Religious Communities," 247–66; Gross, *Fear*, 47. For connections between the fate of Germans and Jews in postwar Poland, see Curp, *A Clean Sweep?*, 87.
24. Eugeniusz Paukszta, "O właściwą structure społeczną," *Strażnica Zachodnia* 3 (Mar. 1946): 79.
25. On ethnic segregation in Upper Silesia, see Naimark, *Fires of Hatred*, 130–31; Kamusella, "Ethnic Cleansing," 300; Linek, "'De-Germanization' and 'Repolonization' in Upper Silesia"; Ehrlich, "Between Germany and Poland"; Esch, *Gesunde Verhältnisse*; Service, *Germans to Poles*, esp. chap. 7.
26. The total number of expellees from eastern Upper Silesia was 54,841 between 1945 and 1950. Those expelled to Germany from the western part totaled 160,000 by January 1947. See Dziurok, "Problemy," 573; Linek, "Weryfikacja," 628.
27. Kamusella, "Ethnic Cleansing," 618. The second statistic (from Dziurok, "Problemy," 598) refers to the population as of 1 July 1949.
28. See Naimark, *Fires of Hatred*, 131ff; Michał Lis, *Ludność Rodzima na Śląsku Opolskim Po II Wojnie Światowej (1945–1993)* (Opole, 1993), 31. On Lower Silesia, see Sebastian Siebel-Achenbach, *Lower Silesia from Nazi Germany to Communist Poland* (Hampshire: Macmillan Press, 1994).
29. See Andrzej Paczkowski, *The Spring Will Be Ours: Poland and the Poles from Occupation to Freedom* (University Park, PA, 2005), 158–60.
30. The armed opposition was much less active in Upper Silesia than in other parts of Poland, particularly since they found less support among the "nationally indifferent" populace. See Prażmowska, *Civil War in Poland*; Adam Dziuba, "Organizacje podziemnej konspiracji," in *Województwo Śląskie, 1945–50: Zarys dziejów politycznych*, ed. Adam Dziurok and Ryszard Kaczmarek (Katowice, 2007), 363–64.
31. See Curp, *A Clean Sweep?*, 40–48.
32. On this Endecja-Communist collaboration, see ibid.; Strauchold, *Myśl Zachodnia*.
33. See Kroska, *Für ein Polen an Oder und Ostsee*.
34. See Mirosław Fazan, "Wkład katowickiego środowiska naukowego i literackiego w kulturalną integrację Ziem Zachodnich," *Rocznik Katowicki* 13 (1987): 100ff.; Strauchold, *Myśl Zachodnia*, 123–25.
35. StP Pszczyna, Protokoł z odprawy, 11 Jan. 1947, APK-Pszczyna, 140 (StP Pszczyna), 42.
36. Referent UBP (UB) Strzelce, do szefa urzędu UB Strzelce, 10 Dec. 1946, Instytut Pamięci Narodowej oddział we wrocławiu (IPN Wr.), 07/3/1, 54.

37. See Thum, *Die Fremde Stadt*, 434–61.

38. See Męclewski, "Repolonizacja"; Edward Serwański, "Polska na starym dziejowym szlaku" and "O społeczeństwo polskie na ziemiach odzyskanych," both in *Odzyskane Ziemie—Odzyskani Ludzie: Z współczesnych zagadnień Ziem Odzyskanych*, ed. Wacław Barcikowski et al. (Poznań, 1946), 9, 20–32, 98–103. See also Curp, *A Clean Sweep?*

39. See Męclewski, "Repolonizacja"; Edward Serwański, "Polska na starym dziejowym szlaku" and "O społeczeństwo polskie na ziemiach odzyskanych," in *Odzyskane Ziemie—Odzyskani Ludzie: Z współczesnych zagadnień Ziem Odzyskanych*, ed. Wacław Barcikowski et al. (Poznań, 1946), 9, 20–32, 98–103.

40. Męclewski, "Repolonizacja," 14; Edmund Męclewski, "'Volkstumskampf': Szkic analizy polityki niemieckiej na ziemiach wcielonych do Rzeszy w latach 1939–45," *Strażnica Zachodnia* 4 (Apr. 1946): 147–48.

41. R. Ł. (most likely Roman Łyczywek), "Praca na zachodzie," *Sprawy Zachodnie* 2 (15 July 1945): 5–8. Referring to one of the BDO's statements from 1939 on how to "re-Germanize" the Third Reich's annexed eastern borderlands, he advocated that the PZZ should merely replace the word "Pole" with that of "German."

42. See Curp, *A Clean Sweep?*, 25–34; Michael Esch, "'Ethnische Säuberungen' zwischen Deutschland und Polen 1939 bis 1950: Überlegungen zu ihrer Genese und Einordnung," in *Definitionsmacht, Utopie, Vergeltung: "Ethnische Säuberungen" im östlichen Europa des 20. Jahrhunderts*, ed. Micheal G. Esch, Ulf Brunnbauer, and Holm Sundhaussen (Berlin, 2006), 107–24.

43. "Posiedzenie Komitetu org. PZZ na Woj. Śląskim," 22 Feb. 1945, APK, 271 (PZZ Okręg Śląski), 2, 3ff.

44. Norbert Kołomejczyk, "Polski Związek Zachodni (okręg śląski) w latach 1945–1950," *Studia i Materiały z Dziejów Śląska* 6 (1964): 351.

45. Close to 200 Upper Silesians signed up for the Bytomian circle of the PZZ, according to APK, 659 (PZZ-Bytom), 7 (Deklaracje członków kóła), n.d. (ca. 1946), n.p. See also Philipp Ther, "Schlesisch, deutsch oder polnisch? Identitätenwandel in Oberschlesien, 1921–1956," in *Die Grenzen der Nationen: Identitätenwandel in Oberschlesien in der Neuzeit*, ed. Kai Struve and Philipp Ther (Marburg, 2002), 196.

46. See Jerzy Ziętek, *Powstańczy Szlak: Rozważania Powstańcze* (Katowice, 1946); Linek, *Polityka antyniemiecka*, 85–87; Jan Walczak, *Jerzy Ziętek: Biografia Ślązaka (1901–1985)* (Katowice, 2002), 156–58.

47. Ziętek, *Powstańczy Szlak*, 23–40; "Statut ZWPŚ.," APK, 273 (ZWPŚ), 1, 10. See also Haubold-Stolle, *Mythos Oberschlesien*, 314–15, 341.

48. See Ziętek, *Powstańczy Szlak*, 5, 12–22, 33–40.

49. See Linek, "Mit Ziem Odzyskanych," 234–52; Haubold-Stolle, *Mythos Oberschlesien*, 314–15, 340–53.

50. Fazan, "Wkład katowickiego," 100 ff.; Maciej Fic, *Wilhelm Szewczyk: Śląski polityk i działacz społeczny (1916–1991)* (Katowice, 2007), 51–117.

51. Vice-Dyrektor Rozgłośni Polskiego Radia (PR) Katowice to Wojewódzki Komitet Polskiej Partii Robotniczej (KW PPR), 27 Oct. 1945, APK, 1718 (KW PPR Kat.), 243, 85ff.; Dyrektor PR, 25 Oct. 1945, APK, 1718, 243, 102–9; KW PPR, "Postanowienie," 27 Aug. 1946, APK, 1718, 243, 113–15. See also Fic, *Wilhelm Szewczyk*, 51–84.

52. "Uwagi na temat wstępnych prac organizacyjnych PZZ," n.d. (ca. June 1945), APK, 185/4 (UWŚl. Społ-Pol), 22, 76; "Statut ZWPŚ," APK, 273, 1, 10.

53. Protokoł PZZ, 25 Aug. 1946, APK, 185/4, 35, 15–16ff.

54. "Zadania PPR-PZZ-towe," 8 June 1946, APK, 1718, 250, 30.

55. See Linek, *Polityka antyniemiecka*, 58–63.

56. Paukszta, "O właściwą strukture społeczną," 82.

57. See T. David Curp, "The Politics of Ethnic Cleansing: The PPR, the PZZ, and Wielkopolska's Nationalist Revolution, 1944–46," *Nationalities Papers* 29 (2001): 575–603.
58. See Walczak, *Jerzy Ziętek*, 149, 158–59, 172–73, 190; Wanatowicz, *Od indyferentnej ludności*, 36–39.
59. "Plebiscyt Narodu Polskiego," *Gość Niedzielny* 15 (14 Apr. 1946): 120.
60. Wojewódzki Urząd Informacji i Propagandy (WUIP) to Ministerstwo Informacji i Propagandy, n.d. (before 1947), APK, 187 (WUIP), 1, 7.
61. "Usuwanie śladów okupacji hitlerowskiej," *Gość Niedzielny* 13 (31 Mar. 1946): 101. See also Grajewski, *Wygnanie*, 26–27.
62. See Wanatowicz, *Od indyferentnej ludności*, 38–39; Linek, *Polityka antyniemiecka*, 110–36; Service, *Germans to Poles*, 285–88.
63. Quoted from "Ziemia i wiara złączy stary i nowy lud opolski: Przemówienie Arcypasterza Opolskiego na dożynkach 15-go września br.," *Gość Niedzielny* 39 (29 Sept. 1946): 3. Between 150,000 and 200,000 attended the event, according to internal government records and the press. See Wojewoda, SR, Sept. 1946, APK, 185/4, 50, 163ff.; Witold Dobrowolski, "Płon Ziemi Śląskiej," *Ogniwa* (29 Sept. 1946): 1–2.
64. "Ziemia i wiara złączy stary i nowy lud opolski: Przemówienie Arcypasterza Opolskiego na dożynkach 15-go września br.," *Gość Niedzielny* 39 (29 Sept. 1946): 3.
65. "Idea Powstańcza Zrealizowana," *Głos Ludu* 137 (19 May 1946): 1ff.; Dobrowolski, "Płon Ziemi Śląskiej," 1–2.
66. Zarząd Gminy Góry św. Anny, 11 July 1946, APO, 179 (StP Strzelce Op.), 82, 21.
67. "Urny z ziemią mogił powstańczych symbole bohaterstwa ludu śląskiego," *Dziennik Zachodni* (DZ), 19 May 1946, 4.
68. See Bjork and Gerwarth, "The Annaberg," 389–400; Haubold-Stolle, *Mythos Oberschlesien*, 340–53.
69. Dobrowolski, "Płon Ziemi Śląskiej," 1–2; "Dożynki Śląskie w Opolu," *Gość Niedzielny* 36 (8 Sept. 1946): 303.
70. See Wojewoda, SR, Apr. 1946, APK, 185/1, 50, 63ff.
71. "Dożynki Śląskie w Opolu," *Gość Niedzielny* 36 (8 Sept. 1946): 303.
72. "Wielkie uroczystości na Górze św. Anny w 25. lecia rocznicy 3-go powstania Śląskiego," *Głos Ludu* 137 (19 May 1946): 1ff.
73. "Wielki dzień Śląska: Góra św. Anny symbol czynu powstańczego," *Dziennik Zachodni* 137 (20 May 1946): 1–2.
74. "W rocznicę czynu powstańczego," DZ 121 (4 May 1946): 1.
75. This statement was made during another part of the festivity, the unveiling of the restored Tadeusz Kościuszko statue of in the nearby Kościuszko Park. "W rocznicy Konstytucji Majowej i III. Powstania Śląskiego," DZ 121 (4 May 1946): 1.
76. Jerzy Ziętek, SR, May 1946, APK, 185/1, 50, 86; Walczak, *Jerzy Ziętek*, 193.
77. The actual results based on internal government documents are published in Andrzej Paczkowski, *Referendum z 30 Czerwca 1946 r.: Przebieg i wyniki* (Warsaw, 1993), 97. See also Service, *Germans to Poles*, 240.
78. Naimark, *Fires of Hatred*, 7, 134–36.
79. Other commonly used derogatory terms were "Germanian," "Teuton"/"Teutonic Knight" (*teutoń/krzyżak*), and another term for "Germandom" (*niemieckość*). Indeed, *niemczyzna* could be used to refer to the German language only, but in this case it collectively depicted everything German, and therefore can be translated as "Germandom."
80. "Trzy zasadnicze linie wytyczne PZZ," n.d. (ca. June 1945), APK, 1718, 250, 10.
81. Edward Serwański, "Założenia i zadania polskiej akcji dokumentacyjnej," *Strażnica Zachodnia* 1–2 (Jan.–Feb. 1946): 14.

82. "Zadania PPR-PZZ-towe," 8 June 1946, APK, 1718, 250, 30.
83. See Allen, *The Oder-Neisse Line*, 47–57; Curp, *A Clean Sweep?*, 73–75.
84. "Inaguracja Tygodnia Ziem Odyzkanych," DZ, 4 May 1946, 2.
85. Dobrowolski, "Płon Ziemi Śląskiej," 1–2. On the "Pan-Slavic Myth," see Tadeusz Marczak, "Mit Słowiański jako tworzywo koncepcji politycznych w latach 1944–7," in *Polskie Mity polityczne XIX i XX w.*, ed. Zofia Zmyk (Wrocław, 1994), 215–26.
86. Męclewski, "Ziemie Odzyskane," 82.
87. Jerzy Ziętek, "Powstańcy walczą przeciw dzielnicowości," ca. 9 Sept. 1945, APK, 273, 38, 1. For the Nazi case, see chapter 4.
88. Władysław Gomułka, "Musimy odnowić kulturę polską," *Głos Ludu* 158 (20 May 1946): 3. Parts of this section appeared previously in Peter Polak-Springer, "The Upper Silesian 'Dream': Re-Assimilating the Native Population, 1945–50," in *Deutschsein als Grenzerfahrung: Minderheitenpolitik in Europa zwischen 1914 und 1950*, ed. Dietrich Beyrau et al. (Essen, 2009), 247–51.
89. Kazimierz Herz, "Duch Kresowości Zachodnej," *Odra* (23 Feb. 1947): 1. See previous chapters for a discussion of Western Borderland Thought.
90. Quoted from Eugeniusz Paukszta, "Nowa Polska—nowe granice—nowi ludzie," *Polska Zachodnia*, 19 Aug. 1945, 1. See also Serwański, "O społeczeństwo," 97, 101.
91. Quoted from Zygmunt Izdebski, "Przyszłość społeczna Śląska Opolskiego," *Odra* 3, no. 1 (11 Jan. 1948). See also Serwański, "O społeczeństwo," 95.
92. "Trzeba Odniemczyć Ziemie Zachodnie, o nowy typ kresowego Polaka," *Polska Zachodnia*, 20 May 1945, 3.
93. Męclewski, "Repolonizacja," 15.
94. "Inauguracja TZO: Wielka manifestacja polskości w Gliwicach," DZ, 4 May 1946, 2.
95. Męclewski, "Repolonizacja," 19.
96. Eugeniusz Paukszta, "Kultura polska a ziemie zachodnie," 25 Mar. 1947, Archiwum Państwowe w Poznaniu (APP), 883 (PZZ), 725, 46–47.
97. Jósef Ligęza, "Na Co Czeka Opolszczyzna," *Odra* 1, no. 4 (Sept. 1945): 3.
98. Izdebski, "Przyszłość," 1.
99. Ligęza, "Na Co Czeka Opolszczyzna," 3.
100. Męclewski, "Repolonizacja," 18.
101. Roman Lutman, "'Cele i zadania PZZ,'" *Sprawy Zachodnie* 5–6 (Oct.–Nov. 1945): 6.
102. Roman Lutman, "Nowa Rzeczywistość," *Odra* 1 (20 July 1945): 1.
103. "Praca na kursach repolonizacyjnych," 4 Nov. 1947, APK, 186 (Kuratorium Okręgu Szkolnego Śląskiego, KOS), 450, 159.
104. Parts of this section appeared previously in Polak-Springer, "The Upper Silesian 'Dream,'" 251–60. Polish "adult education/cultivation," like its *Volksbildung* counterpart, aimed to shape a more enlightened *Lud/Volk*, and likewise functioned as an instrument of ideological mass indoctrination.
105. See Service, *Germans to Poles*, 234ff.
106. See Bernard Linek, *"Odniemczanie" województwa śląskiego w latach 1945–1950: W świetle materiałów wojewódzkich* (Opole, 1997), 26, 97; Wanatowicz, *Od indyferentnej ludności*, 32–33; Service, *Germans to Poles*, 241.
107. Sprawozdanie inspektoratu szkolnego [ca. 1948], APO, 224 (Wojewódzka Rada Narodowa), 4378, 3; Kuratorium Okręgu Szkolnego (KOS) to Ministerstwo Oświaty (MO), 25 May 1950, APK, 186, 450, 9; Linek, *"Odniemczanie,"* 99.
108. KOS to MO, 25 May 1950, APK, 186, 450, 9.
109. "Materiały programowe do nauki na kursach repolonizacyjnych," n.d. (ca. 1950), APK, 186, 450, 61. See also Izdebski, "Przyszłość," 1.
110. See Kamusella, *Schlonzska mowa*, 20–21, 24; Kamusella, "The Szlonzoks and Their Language: Between Germany, Poland and Szlonzokian Nationalism," *EUI Working Papers* 1 (2003): 16–17; Wyderka, "Język, dialekt czy kreol?," 199; Kneip, *Die deutsche Sprache in Oberschlesien*, 155, 160.

111. Papers of Stefani Mazurek, Archiwum Biblioteki Instytutu Śląskiego (BIŚ), A543, 1ff., 18ff.; Stefani Mazurek, "Uwagi w sprawie położeniu polskiej młodzierzy rodzimej na Śląsku Opolskim," 19 Nov. 1946, APK, 186, 450, 33–37; Toraska Zofia, "Słownictwo na kurs języka Polskiego," APK, 186, 450, 95.

112. "Nauka Języka Polskiego—Wymowa," APK, 186, 450, 71A (and other documents in this file).

113. "Protokoł z zebrania Klubu Pisarzy Powstańców," 30 Apr. 1946, APK, 273, 30, 13.

114. Papers of Stefani Mazurek, BIŚ, A543, 10.

115. "Nauka Języka Polskiego," APK, 186, 450, 80A. See also *Nie Rzucim Ziemi: Czytanka do Użytku na Kursach Dla Dorosłych na Ziemiach Odzyskanych* (Warsaw, 1946), 7–66.

116. *Nie Rzucim Ziemi*, 123–46, 223–24; *Ku lepszej przyszłości: czytanki polskie dla starszej młodzierzy szkół powszechnych i kursów dla dorosłych* (Warsaw, 1945), 195–273.

117. "Trzeba Odniemczyć Ziemie Zachodnie, o nowy typ kresowego Polaka," *Polska Zachodnia*, 20 May 1945, 3.

118. *Nie Rzucim Ziemi*, 4, 177–78.

119. KOS to MO, APK, 186, 450, 9ff.

120. Praca na kursie repolonizacyjnym, n.d. (ca. Nov. 1947), APK, 186, 450, 148ff.

121. Ibid., 148ff.

122. Ibid., 148–51. Hugo Service's analysis of a teacher's reports from Opole District demonstrate similar flexibility and pragmatism in light of planners' unrealistic goals. See Service, *Germans to Poles*, 238.

123. Praca na kursie repolonizacyjnym, n.d. (ca. Nov. 1947), APK, 186, 450, 148ff.; SR, KOS, 19–21 Oct. 1948, AAN, 283 (MO), 3397, 27ff.

124. KOS Gliwice, "praca na kursach repolonizacyjnych," APK, 186, 450, 159ff.

125. KOS to MO, APK, 186, 450, 9ff. See also Service, *Germans to Poles*, 247.

126. Zawadzki, SR, July 1946, APK, 185/1, 50, 113ff. According to Walczak, *Jerzy Ziętek*, 187–88, the total number of child participants was over 80,000. See also Strauchold, *Polska ludność rodzima ziem zachodnich i północnych: opinie nie tylko publiczne, 1944–8*, (Olsztyn, 1995), 100–11, 126–46.

127. PZZ reports from Sept. 1946, APK, 271 (PZZ), 6 (Akcja obozowa org. młodzierzowych), 5–13.

128. PZZ Gliwice to PZZ Katowice, 19 Sept. 1946, APK, 271, 6, 11.

129. Ibid., 10–11.

130. These were the actual results before they were manipulated by regime officials. Paczkowski, *Referendum*, 97, 105; Service, *Germans to Poles*, 239–40.

131. Variations of the operation's name included "The Struggle against *Niemczyzna*" and "The Struggle against the Surfacing of *Niemczyzna*," which was the code name that the Insurgent League used. See "materiał dla prelengentów," n.d. (ca. Sept. 1947), 273, 31, 11. Hugo Service notes that while the campaign was Zawadzki's initiative, it was also officially ordered in June 1947 by the MZO for the entirety of the western territories. See Service, *Germans to Poles*, 270, 277.

132. Bernard Linek, "Walka z Nawrotem Niemczyzny," in *Województwo Śląskie, 1945–50: Zarys dziejów politycznych*, ed. Adam Dziurok and Ryszard Kaczmarek (Katowice, 2007), 631–36.

133. Zawadzki, circular, 19 Aug. 1947, 185/4, 551, 1ff.

134. Linek, "Walka z Nawrotem Niemczyzny," 631–36; Adam Dziurok, "Odniemczanie i Repolonizacja," in *Województwo Śląskie, 1945–50: Zarys dziejów politycznych*, ed. Adam Dziurok and Ryszard Kaczmarek (Katowice, 2007), 587–91. The English translation "Civic Inspection Committees" is from Service, *Germans to Poles*, 271.

135. "Materiał dla prelegentów," n.d. (ca. Sept. 1947), 273, 31, 11ff.

136. StP Bytom, "Dotyczące spolonizowania Śląska Opolskiego," 5 July 1945, APK, 686, 264, 7.

137. "Materiał dla prelegentów," n.d. (ca. Sept. 1947), 273, 31, 14–15; Prezydent Miasta Gliwic, SR, Feb. 1948, APK-Gl., 160 (ZM Gliwice), 33, 9. Hugo Service likewise argues that the campaign failed to achieve local support. See Service, *Germans to Poles*, chaps. 9–10.

138. Protokoł w sprawie komisyjnego usuwana śladów niemczyzny, Leśnica, 13 May 1948, APO, 179 (StP Stzelce), 115, 39ff.

139. Protokoł w sprawie, 10 Dec. 1947, APO, 179 (StP Stzelce), 115, 13, and other documents in this file set, and in APO, 179 (StP Stzelce), 114, esp. 31, 83.

140. Wojt Gminy Gogolin II to StP Strzelce, 30 Oct. 1947, APK, 179, 114, 19.

141. Protokoł w sprawie komisyjnego usuwana śladów niemczyzny, Leśnica, 13 May 1948, APO, 179 (StP Stzelce), 115, 39.

142. Gmina Kielcza Zędowice to Gmina Kielczy, 22 Nov. 1947, APO 179, 114, 30.

143. Komisja Obywatelska do walki z niemczyzną, Protokoł w sprawie, 9 Dec. 1947, APO 179, 114, 83.

144. See, e.g., Używanie języka Niemieckiego wśród pracowników Huty Pokój, 3 Nov. 1947, APK, 220 (StP Katowice), 135, 9.

145. Prezes Koła PZZ Bytom-Zachód to PZZ Bytom, 28 Apr. 1946, APK, 659, 3, 201. In January 1946, there were around 4,040 Jews in Bytom. See Dziurok and Kaczmarek, *Województwo Śląskie*, 521.

146. "Dane Statystyczne z akji," 1 Jan. 1948, APK, 185/4, 552, 1.

147. See the documents in APK-Gl., 160 (ZM/MRN Gliwice), 32 (esp. 46), 33.

148. Diurok, "Odniemczanie," 587–88. See also Linek, "Weryfikacja," 633–35; Service, *Germans to Poles*, 241. For currency value, see M. Kłusek "Zasady przeliczania nakładów finansowych poniesionych w latach 1945-2010 przez Muzeum Pałacu w Wilanowie i jego poprzednika prawnego," *Annales* 17:2 (May 2014): 4.

149. See ZM Gliwice, SR, Feb.-Apr. 1947, APK-Gl., 160, 32, 21, 30, 35, 36, 41; ZM Ujazd to StP Strzelce, 9 Dec. 1947, APO, 179, 114, 82. See also Linek, "Weryfikacja," 636.

150. Quoted from ZM Gliwice, SR, Sept. 1948, APK-Gl., 160, 33, 52ff. See also ZM Gliwice, SR, Apr. and May 1948, APK-Gl., 160, 33, 19ff, 24ff.

151. Service, *Germans to Poles*, 238, 279.

152. ZM Gliwice, SR, Sept. and Oct. 1948, APK-Gl., 160, 33, 50ff.

153. Internal goverment reports give this number, while Walczak claims it was 200,000–300,000. Powiat Tarnowskie Góry, SR, July-Aug. 1946, APK, 1430 (StP Tarnowskie Góry), 5, 64ff. See also Walczak, *Jerzy Ziętek*, 197.

154. StP Strzelce, SR, Sept.-Oct. 1946, APO, 179, 12, 223ff.

155. See Grajewski, *Wygnanie*, 45–67; Piotr Madajczyk, "System władzy na Górnym Śląsku w latach 1945–1956," in *Stalinizm i rok 1956 na Górnym Śląsku*, ed. Adam Dziurok, Bernard Linek, and Krzysztof Tarka (Katowice, 2007), 51; Adam Dziurok, "Władze komunistyczne wobec Kościoła katolickiego w diecezji katowickiej," in *Stalinizm i rok 1956 na Górnym Śląsku*, ed. Adam Dziurok, Bernard Linek, and Krzysztof Tarka (Katowice, 2007), 125–38.

156. "Uwagi o realizacji likwidacji analfabetyzmu, 1949," APO, 224, 4374, 56; Strauchold, *Polska Ludność*, 107. Roughly a third of Poland's population was illiterate just after the war. Parts of this and the following paragraph have previously appeared in Polak-Springer, "The Upper Silesian 'Dream,'" 258–9.

157. KOS to MO, APK, 186, 450, 9ff.

158. "Uwagi o realizacji likwidacji analfabetyzmu, 1949," APO, 224, 4374, 56ff. Natives working on the census also did the same to newcomers.

159. "Osiągnięcia Oświaty Dorosłych" (ca. early April 1949), APK, 186, 411, 1. See also the textbooks used for these courses, e.g., Joanna Landy-Brzezińska et al., *Na Trasie: Pierwsze Czytanki dla Dorosłych* (Warsaw, 1949).

160. Szymon Kędryna, "Rozwój oświaty dorosłych w województwie katowickim, 1945–1963," in *Studia i Materiały z Dziejów Śląskich* (Wrocław and Warsaw, 1964), 436.

161. See Curp, *A Clean Sweep?*, 80–106; Strauchold, *Myśl Zachodnia*, 327–72.

162. See Grzegosz Bębnik, "'Stalinizacja' jako zawłaszczenie sfery symbolicznej (na przykładzie Katowic, 1945–1956)," in *Stalinizm i rok 1956 na Górnym Śląsku*, ed. Adam Dziurok, Bernard Linek, and Krzysztof Tarka (Katowice, 2007), 237–58.

163. See Ther, *Deutsche und polnische Vertriebene*; Eugeniusz Kłocek, *"Swoi" i "obcy" na Górnym Śląsku od 1945 roku: Środowisko miejskie* (Wrocław, 1994).

164. Zawadzki, SR, May 1948, AAN, 199 (Ministerstwo Administracji Publicznej), 117, 11ff.

165. ZM Gliwice, SR, 30 Sept. 1948, APK, 160, 33, 51.

166. Piotr Madajczyk, *Niemcy Polscy, 1944–1989* (Warsaw, 2001), 157, 168.

Epilogue

From Revisionism to Ostpolitik and Beyond

Stalinism in Upper Silesia

While the unambiguously German-conscious population of Lower Silesia, like that of other former Prussian eastern provinces, was "swept clean" out of Poland by 1947, the emigration of Upper Silesians was selective and drawn out over decades. Indeed, most locals remained in their regional homeland as "Poles" through the repressive Stalinist years. As a result, they did not share the typical Lower Silesian expellee's bitterness about being forced to leave the *Heimat*; in fact, many thousands of Upper Silesians wished for a way out of People's Poland. In corresponding with friends and relatives in West and East Germany, or in person if they emigrated at the beginning or after the end of Stalinism, their horror stories conveyed an experience of the "lost *Heimat*" that diverged from that of other expellees. Their experience was closer to those from borderlands with Slavic groups who did not identify themselves as Poles, such as Pomerania (Kaszubs) and Masuria (Masurians), than to those from areas with a clear-cut German-Polish ethnic division, such as Lower Silesia. The complex nature of the Upper Silesian expellees' experience is a topic that still awaits in-depth research.[1] Without pretending to present a complete picture, this epilogue aims to provide an overview of the continuity of the "struggle over Upper Silesia" from Stalinism until the turn of the new century. While it persisted over these four decades, the German-Polish irredentist culture carried less transnational weight than it had in previous decades, and with time—and particularly in regard to Upper Silesia—it rapidly faded from the forefront of each country's politics.

The Stalinist era (1950–56) in Upper Silesia—as elsewhere—was marked by terror and rigid centralization. It was not long before some of the suppressed elements of irredentist cultural politics were partially restored. By 1953, Communist

Party officials were complaining about the increasing alienation of "autochthons" (Upper Silesians) from the system—perhaps most ominously, "the rise of a strong separatism" in the industrial tricity area of Bytom (Beuthen), Zabrze (Hindenburg), and Gliwice (Gleiwitz). Although a numerical minority in these and other parts of the region that had been a part of Germany until 1945, newcomer Poles who migrated into Upper Silesia after the war became its new political and economic elites. The native locals remained underrepresented, particularly as members and activists of the Communist Party and its social and political organizations. In an effort to gain their loyalty, the party revived the old scripts of irredentist borderland nationalism and national regionalism. Within a year, books and pamphlets on the history of local cities and folklore appeared, as did folk song and folk dance concerts. The popular nationalist radio figure Stanisław "Karlik" Ligoń—previously an outspoken anti-Communist—returned to the airwaves speaking the Polonized Silesian dialect, the so-called *gwara Śląska*, as he had before the war to further Grażyński's nationalization politics.[2] In 1955, Communist Party leaders even organized a mass rally on the Polish nationalist pilgrimage site, the Mount of St. Anne, where they unveiled a Monument to the Silesian Uprisings (officially Pomnik Czynu Powstańczego, or Monument to the Insurrectionist Deed) on the spot where the Nazis' Reich Memorial to fallen *Freikorps* fighters had stood until its destruction in 1945 (fig. 6.1).[3]

Figure 6.1. Monument to the Insurrectionist Deed, unveiled 1955. (BŚ-ZS)

The return of irredentist popular culture had mixed results. Ligoń's folkloric radio shows attracted thousands of letters and contributions of folk songs and stories by fans. In 1953 more than 6,000 locals went on state-organized trips to Warsaw, Cracow, and other parts of Poland, which marked a partial return to the "Polonization" policy of the early postwar years. Their numbers more than doubled in 1954.[4] Nonetheless, locals' alienation from the new Upper Silesia remained a reality, fed by home searches and other forms of regime terror, but also by what they saw as newcomers lording over the natives. Such attitudes found expression in tens of thousands of self-declarations of German nationality in government surveys. When in 1954 thousands of locals refused to collect their newly issued Polish identity cards, the state security agency, the UB, reported that this and similar treasonous acts had been inspired by widespread cheering for West Germany's winning team in that year's World Cup in soccer.[5]

Such explanations ignored the poverty and austerity that Stalinism imposed on the individual. While most other Poles suffered similarly—leading many to harbor dreams of emigration—Upper Silesians regularly glimpsed an alternate world in the hundreds of thousands of pieces of mail from relatives and friends in West Germany, particularly locals who had been expelled. In 1953, security agents noted that well over 9,000 Upper Silesians were engaged in such correspondence. In what these agents referred to as letters or packets from "the Reich," Upper Silesians learned how the "economic miracle" had produced a "consumer paradise."[6] As a result, thousands started to call themselves "Germans," and by the mid-1950s they demanded to be allowed to move to Germany—by which they meant West Germany.

The regime continued to dredge up the German threat to the western borderlands as a diversion from its own shortcomings. Yet the establishment of the "socialist brother state" of East Germany (German Democratic Republic, or GDR) in 1949 made problematic the once dominant myth of an eternal evil *niemczyzna* (Germandom). Indeed, in 1950, the GDR signed the Görlitz Treaty with Poland, which officially recognized the Oder-Neisse Line. Thereafter the Polish regime invoked a "Fascist" West Germany in conspiracy with its "imperialist" Western allies to revise Poland's borders. This new narrative, which could be expanded to include domestic conspirators, achieved particular prominence in the context of the regime's return to nationalist self-legitimization after 1956.[7] However, its roots lay in the Stalinist era. The UB blamed the growth of German identity among Upper Silesians on the penetration of West German "revanchist propaganda" as well as on locals who promoted "defeatism" against Poland.[8] Although the regime strategically exaggerated any actual threat to Poland's borders, the "revanchism" theme responded to the rise of West German irredentist organizations—some of them led by former Nazi officials—during the era of Chancellor Konrad Adenauer (1949–63).

The Resurgence of West German Irredentism

By 1950, over eight million expellees (*Vertriebenen*) from East-Central Europe had settled in West Germany, among them some 300,000 from Upper Silesia.[9] A nationwide umbrella organization, the League of the Expelled (Bund der Vertriebenen, or BdV), encompassed a complex network of associations that represented their interests. Expellee political activists found in Adenauer a champion of their call for border revision based on the old irredentist principles of territorial self-determination and a "right to a homeland" (*Heimatrecht*). Various homeland societies (*Landsmannschaften*), which represented the individual provinces of the "lost German east," were the lifeblood of postwar expellee political and cultural activism. The largest of these groups, the Silesian Homeland Society (Landsmannschaft Schlesien), claimed to represent both the lower and upper parts of this former German region. However, conflicts within the Silesian leadership had been an issue since the interwar era, in which the Upper Silesians asserted their regional particularity within Germany. Now the expellees fought over issues as fundamental as the nature of border revision. Upper Silesian spokesmen who refused to return to an interwar borderland "torn" between Germany and Poland renounced the mainstream German claim to the eastern border of 1937—the territorial status quo prior to Nazi expansion into Czechoslovakia—which their Lower Silesian counterparts supported. Instead, they asserted the exceedingly radical territorial claim of a return to the preplebiscite borders of 1921, thus agreeing with Hitler's demands for nullifying the Versailles territorial settlement. As a consequence, Upper Silesian irredentists found a more suitable home in their own Upper Silesian Homeland Society (Landsmannschaft der Oberschlesier, or LdO), founded in 1949 in the region of Nordrhein-Westfalen, even as they continued to work closely with the more inclusive Silesian society.[10]

This West German cohort of cultural fighters for a German Upper Silesia showed considerable continuity with borderland nationalists since the plebiscite struggles. Indeed, Otto Ulitz, the Nazi-decorated "*Volksdeutsche* hero," served as the LdO's spokesman from 1953 until his retirement in 1969. The old-timers included a number of *Heimatkundler* such as the cultural activist Karl Sczodrok and folklorist Alfons Perlick, who had promoted Hitler's *Volkstumsarbeit* (nationalization work). They were rejoined by former colleagues whom the Nazis had barred from public life because of their status as German Center Party politicians and officials. The former plebiscite campaign commissioner, Kurt Urbanek, became the LdO's founding leader, while the former German Upper Silesian *Oberpräsident*, Hans Lukaschek, rose to even greater prominence as West Germany's first federal minister for expellee affairs (1949–53). As an organization that encompassed former Nazi agents and *Ostforscher* alongside victims of Hitler's regime, the LdO was a microcosm of the larger nationwide picture of expellee elites.

As Andrew Demshuk has pointed out, the Upper Silesian expellee organization distinguished itself from other such groups in the nature of its propaganda: "[W]hile the mainstream expellee leadership fixated on the 'injustice' of expulsion in 1945 to demand the restoration of Germany's 1937 borders, Upper Silesian expellee leaders dared to insist on the 1921 borders, to repeat interwar arguments for the innate Germanness of Upper Silesians, and to glorify *Freikorps* and Wehrmacht troop maneuvers."[11] While the propaganda of all the prominent expellee societies tended to downplay or ignore Nazi atrocities—and indeed insisted that the expulsions had made Germany a victim—the leading LdO activists even glorified the Third Reich's military conquest and annexation of this borderland. They also revived the connection between irredentist politics and the religious symbolism of the German Center Party, which the Nazis had forbidden. Once again—at least in expellee propaganda—Upper Silesia officially symbolized "the land under the cross," a region and people victimized by "Polish aggression" in 1921 and now through annexation and expulsion in 1945.[12]

Invoking 1921 by viewing the plebiscite struggle and Polish uprising as "an historical landmark that anticipated the suffering of 1945," the LdO leaders, working with their all-Silesian counterparts, resurrected the kind of bombastic rallies and commemorations held at the border during the 1920s and early 1930s. Tens of thousands attended some of these events, which included Plebiscite Commemoration Day, celebrated in Freiburg in 1951, the Upper Silesian National Rally (*Bundestreffen*), staged two years later in Nuremberg, Upper Silesian Day, celebrated in Bochum four years later, and numerous similar events in later years. Like some of the Weimar-era border rallies, they featured the celebration of Holy Mass, as well as irredentist speeches by officials such as Lukaschek and Urbanek, who had spoken at the prewar events. Hitler's "recovery" of Upper Silesia in September 1939 went unmentioned at these and similar events, since the other expellee groups shared no warm feelings toward the Nazis. Nevertheless, in venerating the "heroic defense" of the region against "Polish invaders" in 1921, they borrowed a theme Hitler had used to legitimate the invasion of Poland. In addition to the attention generated from the occasional rallies, the various Silesian homeland societies also spread their irredentist messages through numerous periodicals and other publications, as well as radio and television programs.[13]

Despite impressive audiences at some irredentist rallies, most rank-and-file members of the expellee community (no matter their point of origin in Upper or Lower Silesia) preferred grassroots *Heimat* events. These more homely events were relatively apolitical compared to the gigantic rallies. Like many popular expellee publications, they promoted romantic and idealized depictions of the folkloric, architectural, and natural landscapes of the lost *Heimat*. Like the rallies, they carried on the old national regionalist theme that everything Silesian was eternally German.[14] As newcomers in West Germany, however, the borderland nationalists resisted assimilation with the surrounding German society, so as to uphold—rather than weaken—their Upper Silesian identity. Yet, despite the continuing appeal of pageants featuring Upper Silesian customs and folklore, national regionalism failed to realize its political mission, which was now to keep expellees in a permanent state of longing for a "return home" (*Heimkehr*). On the contrary, as Demshuk points out, it helped them come to terms with the loss of their old *Heimat*, assimilate into their new one, and over the years lose interest in returning. More recent Upper Silesian expellees tended to do so rather quickly, having witnessed firsthand how difficult life would be for them had they stayed in Stalinist Poland compared to a new life in a West Germany that was beginning to enjoy its "economic miracle." Any temptations of nostalgia were likely corrected by correspondence with relatives and friends still living in the lost borderland who, having avoided expulsion as officially recognized "Poles," now regretted it and wished to emigrate.[15]

Irredentism in Poland after the "Thaw"

Made official by Nikita Khrushchev's secret de-Stalinization speech, Stalinism formally ended in the Soviet Bloc in 1956, to be followed by a "thaw" in the rigidly centralized, standardized, and Soviet-controlled governments Stalin had created. In Poland, this turning point was marked by the return of deposed party leader Władysław Gomułka and the anticipated realization of his long-held promise of a "Polish road to socialism." To this end, Gomułka—formerly the chief architect of Poland's ethnic cleansing of the former German lands—reverted to his support for Germanophobic borderland nationalism, including the revival of its central promoter, the former Polish Western League (PZZ), now called the Society for the Development of the Western Territories (Towarzystwo Rozwoju Ziem Zachodnich, or TRZZ). In Upper Silesia the aging veteran insurgents were once again honored publicly as model Silesians, although they had to share this prominence with other Communist-designated "national heroes" within a regional League of Fighters for Freedom and Democracy (Związek Bojowników o Wolność i Demokracje, or ZBOWiD). Jerzy Ziętek, who remarkably had survived the Stalinist era almost unscathed as deputy regional governor, again led the veteran insurgents within the ZBOWiD as well as functioned as the honorary head of the TRZZ. In this capacity he presided over a series of official rallies celebrating the 1921 insurgencies that were held from the late 1950s into the early 1970s.[16] Academic support for irredentism also returned with a restored Silesian Institute, as were its counterparts in other western borderlands. Despite the appearance of a return to the politics of the first postwar half decade, these organizations were now under far greater control by the

Communist Party, as was signified by their new names. More significant was the reality that "recovery" of the German lands would no longer be at the center of Polish politics.[17]

Nonetheless, the rehabilitated borderland nationalists set about winning the hearts of their alienated fellow Upper Silesians. Although the "thaw" represented only a short-lived period (1956–57) of relative openness in the government and media, these formerly suppressed elites effectively used the opportunity to voice their grievances, using the press, particularly the periodical *Przemiany* (formerly *Odra*) as well as regional government assemblies to criticize earlier "re-Polonization" politics as cruel and discriminatory.[18] They even went so far as to denounce the agents of this policy for having "modeled themselves on Hitler and using his atrocities to legitimate their own [criminal] actions," thereby causing the locals' "loss of faith in Poland."[19] For the first time, they publicly criticized the regime's attempts to forcibly erase the region's "German influence" from its landscape as well as from the identity of its locals. Moreover, they exposed numerous acts of abuse and discrimination to which locals had been subjected, including expropriations and arrests based on false accusations of collaboration with the Nazis, the compulsory removal of "German" family names on identification documents and even on gravestones, and overall treatment as second-class citizens vis-à-vis the Polish newcomers.[20]

In an effort to demonstrate a new policy of tolerance, but also to allow "troublemakers" to emigrate, the Communist Party crossed an even more sensitive line and declared the existence of a German minority in the western parts of Upper Silesia. Concerned that the party had gone too far, and in doing so had threatened the basic premise of Poland's claim to the region—the myth that all Upper Silesians were Poles in their essence—the border nationalists responded with their traditional line that the party's Germans were Poles "with an uncrystallized national identity," who had begun to feel "German" only as a result of the regime's faulty policies.[21] In the words of an article in *Przemiany*, this mistaken strategy had inadvertently "Germanized Silesia in only six years, whereas the Germans could not do so in six centuries."[22]

Despite the regime's official openness to some level of "German" identity in Upper Silesia, any discussion of national indifference, that is, a nonnational regional consciousness, continued to be unacceptable. Whether critics or defenders of nationalization policy or even proponents of recognizing a "German minority in Poland," the region's newcomers and Polish-conscious Upper Silesian elites refused to allow locals to identify themselves as anything but "either/or" (German or Polish). This age-old policy of silencing nonofficial regionalism would persist until the fall of communism. Meanwhile, after the "thaw," the pro-Communist postwar version of Polish Upper Silesianism once again monopolized official representations of the region until 1989, silencing even the limited dissents raised in 1956, including the notion of a German minority.[23]

Borderland nationalism became a central pillar of the regime's self-legitimating politics during the Gomułka era (1956–70). Working with its restored nationalist elites, the regime once again staged strident irredentist rallies, particularly at major anniversaries of the "eternal struggle" for the western borderlands. Given its history of national *and* class conflict, Upper Silesia served as a useful symbol of the struggle for all the formerly German territories and even Poland itself. The regime and its borderland nationalists supported this conflict-ridden official history with servings of Germanophobia in the guise of the "West German revanchist threat." This propaganda served to legitimate the UB's continued surveillance, harassment, and even arrests of locals, although arrests declined with the end of Stalinism. The security agency's records contain many accounts of individuals suspected of "revisionism" based on reports by informers who claimed they had prayed or sung in German, publicly disparaged Poland, cared for the graves of fallen Wehrmacht soldiers, consumed Western media, received letters and parcels from West Germany, or put up swastika graffiti.[24]

Although the militant nature of some Upper Silesian expellee propaganda could have easily been exploited, Polish borderland nationalists, like their West German counterparts, focused on their domestic situation. Their primary goals were to serve the regime's new nationalist identity and to keep locals from emigrating. Nonetheless, the irredentist threat proved useful for bolstering their importance and petitioning the central government to divert more funds and attention to the region, lest they give "Mr. Lukaschek in the Federal Republic of Germany ... something to smile about."[25] In calling for the full restoration of national regionalism as a way to win the hearts and minds of locals for Poland, they continued to admire aspects of German Silesianism, pointing out, for example, the "practicality" and "popularity" of German *Heimat* almanacs (*Heimatkalender*).[26]

Exodus and Reconciliation

In the hope of gaining a fresh start by ridding itself of troublemakers, the authorities decided to allow a limited number of borderland inhabitants to leave for West/East Germany, either to join close relatives who had left Poland or in recognition of their self-identity as Germans. The resulting exodus clearly represented locals' rejection both of the regime and its policies in the formerly German territories. By 1959, some 275,000 residents had departed these regions, the largest number (114,000) from Upper Silesia.[27] Most went to West Germany, where they were officially classified as *Spätaussiedler* (late emigrants). Many more wanted to move than were allowed. "German nationality" marked the most popular reason for leaving, at least among Upper Silesians. The authorities were well aware that their treatment as potential traitors and second-class citizens as well as dreams of a better life in a prosperous and free West Germany—rather than a deeply rooted national conviction—had turned them into "Germans."

The authorities were mistaken in hoping that the removal of an alienated population would ease reintegration of those who remained. More and more residents of the formerly German territories continued to petition for departure throughout the 1960s and 1970s. When the Polish government again permitted limited emigration in the late 1970s, 250,000 individuals left the borderlands, most of them Upper Silesians. Indeed, many non-"German" citizens throughout Poland might also have chosen to emigrate had they been granted the opportunity.[28]

In 1968, reacting to rising protests against the Communist regime that followed the Prague Spring, Gomułka turned to anti-Semitism. In the official guise of an Anti-Zionist Campaign, this strategy offered a rationale for leveling charges of conspiracy against dissenters. Jews had been a target among the "unwanted" groups, most of them Germans, expelled in the late 1940s. Now they became victims of the same nationalism that both idealized an ethnically homogenous Poland and glorified struggle against "unwanted" national groups as a tool of Communist self-legitimation. This nationalism legitimated the "struggle" against West German "revanchism" and also made possible the anti-Semitic terror in 1968, which forced 25,000 individuals designated as Jews to leave Poland, including 1,500 from the eastern (Voivodeship Silesia) part of Upper Silesia.[29]

The regime's fundamentally nationalistic "Polish road to communism" assumed the permanence of conflict. At rallies on the Mount of St. Anne and at other sites of memory throughout the western borderlands, the regime celebrated Poland's long oppression at the hands of Germans and fomented conflict against West Germany by exploiting the rhetorical excesses of irredentist expellee societies. By the 1960s, the leaders of Poland's civil society were becoming aware that the end of borderland-related tensions between the two states would demolish a central ideological pillar that legitimated communism.

The initiative for German-Polish reconciliation came from the Catholic Church, which, ironically, in the early postwar years had done much to legitimate the "re-Polonization" of the borderlands. By the 1960s, however, it had ceased to cooperate with the regime, and was indeed dismayed by the continued anticlerical politics of the post-"thaw" regime, in particular the renewed use of Germanophobia as a pretext to persecute Upper Silesian priests as "German revanchist elements." The first move was made by a former bishop of the Opole Diocese, Bolesław Kominek, who earlier had himself presided over the regime's irredentist rallies in Upper Silesia (see chapter 5). As head of the Archdiocese of Wrocław (Breslau) Kominek initiated a letter to the German bishops, the main message of which was captured in the now famous phrase, "We forgive and ask for forgiveness." Bishops from throughout Poland signed the document, which went to their counterparts in West and East Germany in November 1965, only a few months before the official celebration of "The Thousand Years of the Polish State" (Tysiąclecie Państwa Polskiego), marking the millennial anniversary of what according to national historiography was the first sovereign Polish state, ruled by the medieval Piast dynasty. Anticipating that the regime would use the territorial conflict with Germany as the centerpiece of this commemoration, the church decided to stage its own competing celebration of the Millennium of Poland's Christianization, which would gesture toward reconciliation by inviting German bishops to attend via Bishop Kominek's letter.[30]

In full recognition that peace over the border issue posed a powerful threat to its nationalist identity, the regime denounced Kominek as a "pro-revisionist element." In this environment, the official 1966 celebration of the "Thousand Years of the Polish State" included some of the largest rallies postwar Poland had seen, along with the unveiling of a sizable Insurgency Monument in Katowice, one of the city's largest monuments until today. The TRZZ and veteran insurgents used these events, held on the Mount of St. Anne, in Katowice, and in other parts of the western borderlands, to explicitly denounce the bishops' reconciliation efforts and instead issue warnings of the urgent need to "defend against West German revisionists."[31]

Only four years later, the intentions expressed by the Polish bishops became the basis of West Germany's *Ostpolitik* (Eastern Policy), initiated by Chancellor Willy Brandt. As part of this policy, Brandt signed the Warsaw Treaty with the Polish government, in which he recognized the Oder-Neisse Line. This move officially ended the irredentist stance of the West German state and thereby also its official support for revisionist agitation by the expellee societies. Overall, it proved to be a decisive step toward easing tension—at least over territory—between the two nations, and was the beginning of a lasting reconciliation, which, however, did not become official until the end of the Cold War. *Ostpolitik* was symbolized by Brandt's kneeling in front of the Jewish ghetto memorial (Monument to the Ghetto Heroes) in Warsaw on 7 December 1970, a gesture that challenged one of the main myths of Polish borderland nationalism—that of Germans as "eternal aggressors."

At home, Brandt's peacemaking faced a storm of protests and scorn from expellee leaders, who defiantly vowed to continue the struggle for their inalienable "right to *Heimat*." Nevertheless, *Ostpolitik* ended these leaders' bid for territorial revision, and with time, their organizations' work was reduced largely to a struggle to keep alive the memory of territorial loss and expulsion as an element of German national identity. Indeed, these efforts have become an uphill battle for sympathy among new generations of Germans, who—having grown up conscious of Nazi crimes—favor lasting peace with Poland over expellee resentments. Indeed, in now united Germany, expellee politics have come to be associated with right-wing extremism, particularly in the new millennium.

In Poland, *Ostpolitik* immediately threatened the irredentist identities of both the regime and its borderland nationalists. Attempting to defy the new reconciliation spirit of the early détente era, they staged a series of bombastic rallies and festivities throughout the Upper Silesian industrial district to commemorate the fiftieth anniversary of the third Silesian insurgency. Other desperate efforts to keep the irredentist spirit alive included such gestures as unveiling a restoration of one of the most provocative nationalist monuments of the interwar era, the Statue of the Insurgent in Chorzów (formerly Królewska Huta/Königshütte). It used the pedestal of the earlier monument that President Ignacy Mościki had inaugurated in October 1927 (see chapter 2), which was destroyed by the Nazis.[32]

Ostpolitik formally ended German-Polish territorial antagonisms, and in Poland it finally removed one of the Communist regime's most potent self-legitimating trump cards. Nonetheless, in Poland—even more than in the reunited Germany—German expellee politics continued to raise controversy, especially after the turn of the millennium, as a result of events such as the failed bid by the Prussian Claims Society (Preußische Treuhand) to establish property restitution for expellees from Poland and the unsuccessful attempts of Erika Steinbach—the audacious leader (since 1998) of the League of the Expelled (BdV)—to set up a Center against Expulsion in Berlin. More importantly, the Polish right wing continued to use expellee politics as a pretext to fuel anti-German sentiment.[33]

Toward European Unity

It took the end of the Cold War and the fall of Communist dictatorships—notably those of Poland and the former East Germany—to truly end hostilities between Germany and its eastern neighbors. In 1990 the German government signed the German-Polish Border Treaty with the government of a democratic Poland, putting an end to any rumor that a reunited Germany might seek to "recover" its former eastern provinces. While realizing long-standing efforts that started—on the German side—with *Ostpolitik*, it also symbolized the onset of a deeper process of reconciliation between the two countries, which over time would extend far beyond government circles.

Since the new millennium, Polish and German academics have been exchanging visits to the archives of one other's countries and applying their discoveries to rewrite the histories of Upper Silesia and other contested borderlands in ways that restore their diverse identities and cultures. In the case of Poland, for example, this meant a break with a notion lasting until the end of communism: that in such regions all that really mattered were Poles and the Polish national struggle. With most of the old borderland nationalists in both countries now long retired or deceased, their libraries, institutes, and collections became research centers for reconciling antagonisms and acknowledging pluralism. In Poland the former icons of academic irredentism, such as the Silesian Institute in Opole, and in Germany the formerly *Ostforschung*-oriented Johann Herder Institute in Marburg became leading proponents of this new academic trend. Poland's entry into the European Union in 2004 opened up new possibilities for dialogue and exchange at all levels of society between the neighboring nations.

In Upper Silesia, the fall of the nationalist Communist system significantly reduced pressure on locals to identify as Poles, as well as discrimination against Germans and censorship of Upper Silesians. Moreover, locals gained a new freedom to openly declare their group identity. As a result, a picture of the region emerged that was far more complex and diverse than the simplified and homogenized one promoted by Polish and German nationalists for most of the twentieth century. Surveys in the 1990s revealed that anywhere from a quarter to half of Upper Silesia's residents identified themselves foremost as Silesians. This group in turn divided into Silesians, Polish Silesians (Silesian and Polish identity), German Silesians (Silesian and German identity), and Upper Silesians (*Oberschlesier*).[34] The results of the official 2002 census shocked the nation, as over 173,000 residents across the region declared Silesian nationality, while 224,000 declared no nationality at all. Close to 140,000 declared German nationality, while over 234,000 claimed to be of dual (German and Polish) nationality.[35] While the government officially recognized the existence of a German minority in Poland, thereby breaking with one of the Communist era's biggest taboos, it has continued the policy of refusing to recognize a Silesian one. Since the 1990s, a Silesian Autonomy Movement (Ruch Autonomii Śląska, or RAŚ) has been fighting for the official recognition of (Upper) Silesians as an ethnic/national group separate from Poles, and for regional autonomy based on this identity. The census of 2011 revealed a fourfold growth in the number of self-declared Silesians over the previous decade. Indeed, a 9 percent decline in the number of self-declared Germans makes Silesians Poland's de facto largest national/ethnic minority.[36]

Recently scholars, among them Brendan Karch and Andrzej Michałczyk, have persuasively argued that this emergent Silesian identity—or refusal to declare nationality—constituted the legacy of the (German and Polish) failure to reliably nationalize the locals after 1919.[37] In this book, I have suggested that while the borderland nationalists aimed to turn them foremost into Germans/Poles, the inherently (national) regionalist character of both nations' nationalization politics—which reinforced more than it extinguished provincial particularity—inadvertently helped locals to remain above all Upper Silesians. The transnational nature of the bilateral contest to claim the region's "national identity" allowed locals to experience both the Germanic and Slavic aspects of Upper Silesianism, especially during the interwar era, but even after the war as well, when so many local residents maintained correspondence with expellees or *Spätaussiedler* in (West or East) Germany, and thereby kept the memory of ties with this country alive at home.

The duration of the myth of Jerzy Ziętek after his death in 1985, and particularly after communism's collapse, supports this argument. Soon after the war, the Communists and their border nationalist allies invented the myth of Ziętek, the insurgent leader, to embody their self-legitimating myth of an eternally Polish Upper Silesia, which thanks to the regime had now been "recovered" by its "Polish motherland." Serving as the regime's model Upper Silesian—a Polish counterpart of sorts to what Otto Ulitz was to the Nazis during the war (see chapter 4)—Ziętek worked in the top ranks of the regional government, as vice governor, and then governor (*voivode*) for over three decades, with important functions at other levels of government. As master of ceremony during various political rallies and functions, he was the leading propagandist and proponent of Upper Silesian regional consciousness, packaged in Polish nationalist and pro-Communist guise, of which he was the central icon.[38]

In 2005, Ziętek was honored by the erection of his statue in Katowice, only yards away from the sizable Insurgency Monument he had unveiled during the official festivities commemorating "Thousand Years of the Polish State" in 1966. Why would a region so brutalized by and alienated from the postwar regime be the only one in Poland to erect a monument honoring one of its Communist governors? To locals, however, Ziętek was also a mediator between them and the "foreign" Warsaw officials, and one of the rare figures who spoke publicly in the (Polonized) Upper Silesian dialect and fought for resources to promote regional development. As a result, Upper Silesians, in particular those who had been socialized in postwar Poland and who wanted to accentuate their regional distinction from the rest of the nation, accepted him as "one of their own" particularly in memory after his death. Stripped of its Communist-serving Polish nationalism, the post-1989 myth of Ziętek depicted him as foremost a "good Silesian" who fought and worked sacrificially for the good of the region and its locals. It set aside his track record of unrelenting service to the regime, including collaboration with its crimes before and during the Stalinist era, claiming that—like other Silesians—he had been forced to conform to the borderland's ever changing foreign overlords. The myth of Upper Silesia as Poland's "recovered territory," which was supposed to turn locals above all into Poles, lost its function and following. Nonetheless, Silesians raised in postwar Poland retained and reinterpreted some of its regionalist icons, such as Ziętek, in order to accentuate their Silesian identity and support their call for Warsaw's official recognition of their regional particularity. Even though Ziętek's popularity has also been widely criticized, in 1999 *Gazeta Wyborcza*, Poland's leading liberal daily, in announcing the results of its survey, dubbed him the second "most distinguished Silesian of the twentieth century." First place went to the former Polish nationalist and insurgency leader Wojciech Korfanty, who, particularly to counter Grażyński's persecution in the late 1920s and 1930s, had reinvented himself as a leader of regional particularism.[39]

Upper Silesians appropriated not just historical figures but also some of the traditions of borderland nationalism as symbols of their "otherness" from the nation. One of the cultural legacies of the half century of German-Polish conflict over Upper Silesia is the Song and Dance Group "Silesia" (Zespół Śpiewu i Tańca "Śląsk"), which remains one of Poland's most renowned folkloric performance groups. Wearing Silesian folk costumes and specializing in simple nonpolitical songs—like the hit "Little Karolin Went to Gogolin" ("Poszła Karolinka do Gogolina")—the group serves as a symbol of regional pride and Silesian identity. Yet when created in 1953, under the auspices of Poland's Stalinist regime, the troop was intended to promote the Polish identity of Upper Silesia and to affirm Poland's claims to the region. To this end, it sang in the standardized Polish Silesian dialect, cleansed of Germanic vocabulary and expressions.[40]

Legacies of a Contested Borderland

Upper Silesia's history as a contested borderland exemplifies the long legacy of irredentism in Europe. Fueled by a persistent array of actors, institutions, discourses, and national regional traditions, the borderland nationalism examined in this book was a constant feature of Central Europe's political landscape over most of the twentieth century. It transcended national and historical boundaries, constituting a transnational political culture that shaped larger international politics from the Treaty of Versailles through the following three decades and into the Cold War years.

The politics of this era bore the marks of nationalism and World War I. Together they precipitated the downfall of multinational monarchies, thus opening the way for the rise of nation-states eager to engineer borders congruent with the location of their core ethnic groups. Heirs to their monarchical predecessors' zeal for expansion, the successor states vied with one another for territory. Thus, after Versailles, and especially in Central Europe, these "shatter zones" of the monarchical empires continued to be powder kegs awaiting a spark.[41] Borderland conflicts in the interwar era provided an impetus for a new populist irredentist politics.

Upper Silesia's identity as an iconic contested borderland was the product of geopolitical fantasies. Borderland nationalists who exploited World War I's propaganda techniques and new media technology transformed irredentism into a mass culture. Bards, artists, and academics collaborated to revive and create a local culture in the contested region that would tie it symbolically to their nation. In the cold war over Silesia, the two contenders, Germany and Poland, shaped and copied one another's irredentist discourses, dissemination strategies, and other practices. Portrayals of the contested area as a "frontier of civilization," an "endangered or bleeding borderland," and a "stolen territory that needed to be recovered" were common to both Germany and Poland, as were images of an aggressive and imperialistic "other." No matter how much linguistic diversity they tolerated in the region, neither camp of borderland nationalists saw pluralism (e.g., Silesian, German, Polish, Jewish identities) as a natural state, but rather an uneasy part of a struggle for increased homogenization along rigidly unilateral German or Polish national lines. Promoted on both sides, not just by radicals but also moderates, as well as churchmen, activists, and professionals, the border conflict fueled ethnic nationalism, mutual national hatreds, and militancy across Germany and Poland, as well as social conflicts in Upper Silesia itself.

Traditions of conflict, colonization, and nationalization made contested territories fertile fields for Nazis and Communists to pursue their utopian social engineering projects. Both regimes had inherited national—and in the latter case, also international—mandates to recover their respective contested borderlands. While guided by different motives and circumstances, both employed borderland nationalism to romanticize, popularize, and legitimate their own specific policies to build homogenous and totalitarian societies. The previous symbolic cleansing of Upper Silesia under German and Polish liberal governments, as well as the authoritarian Sanacja, facilitated the physical cleansing during the tumultuous years from 1939 to 1950. Although Nazi and Communist policies caused less displacement of populations in Upper Silesia than in other areas they controlled, they nevertheless coerced population transfers in the name of re-nationalization. In the most extreme case, the Nazis destroyed almost all of the region's Jews as part of their bid to exterminate those of all of Europe.

While Upper Silesia shared similarities with other borderlands, it differed in that both its national actors made claims not just to its landscapes but also to its people. With no clear-cut confessional and linguistic borders to objectively separate Germans from Poles, most locals were left in place to be "Polonized" or "Germanized." Indeed, their new official identity became as much the product of one-sided irredentist illusions, cleansed of any association with the culture and language of the "other," as were the borderlands themselves. Despite their best efforts, these national actors failed to shape local Upper Silesians into stable Germans and Poles. On the contrary, most efforts to renationalize annexed parts of the region failed and alienated the locals. In recognizing the locals as "recovered peoples," the Sanacja, Nazis, and Communists all subjected the Catholic majority to various degrees of discrimination, mistrust, and restrictions on their language, religious practices, and customs. Their policies deepened the locals' sense of second-class status, which the latter two regimes even formalized with strikingly similar policies of making revocable the granting of citizenship to Upper Silesians. Furthermore, all three regimes encouraged settlement by national newcomers, whose behavior was often arrogant, greedy, and—particularly after the war—violent and corrupt. The resulting clashes followed an "us versus them" dynamic that ultimately strengthened locals' indifference to the nation.

German and Polish borderland nationalists used national regionalisms: local traditions reinvented and standardized to support the approved national heritage. For both, they produced similar unintended results, as locals used these regionalisms to guard against, rather than surrender to, nationalization. In interwar Polish Upper Silesia, regionalist movements that openly resisted nationalization rallied around the defense of "Silesian autonomy," which the interwar Polish government granted as a national regionalist measure. Locals viewed folkloric entertainment like the Song and Dance Group "Silesia," use of the regional dialect in official national propaganda, and pilgrimages to the Mount of St. Anne—used by the German Center Party to promote a revisionist spirit—as symbols of overarching (nationally indifferent) regionalist pride. Upper Silesian (nationally indifferent) regionalist consciousness, which arose out of the contentious nationalist sentiments that surrounded the League of Nations plebiscite, was nurtured by subsequent border shifts and the inability of any one nation to establish a firm hold over the region. It began to emerge publicly after 1989, when locals openly called themselves Silesians and began to promote regional autonomy.

In the heyday of European nation-states, from the late nineteenth century to the end of the twentieth, borderlands served as potent symbols of divisions between peoples and cultures. States carefully monitored and shaped the production and dissemination of knowledge about these areas in order to ensure their likeness to the state laying claim to it. Any hints of incompatibility were denied or covered over, in particular those related to language, ethnicity, or culture, such as suggestions that the contested area had a right to assert its regional autonomy. Long-standing conflicts over borderlands contributed greatly to the atrocities and displacements that marked the tumultuous 1939–50 era, as did the efforts of some states to use violence to transform the symbolically cleansed identities imagined by their cultural activists into a reality. With the waning of ethnic nationalism in European politics after the collapse of communism, once divisive borderlands have become symbols of unity and integration across the continent's political borders. Thus, Upper Silesia, once a hotbed of transnational myths that long defined irreconcilable German and Polish national identities, now plays a role as a bridge between two interwoven pasts.

Notes

1. A recent study that focuses mainly on Lower Silesian expellees is Demshuk, *The Lost German East*.
2. "Analiza pracy," 1953, APK, 1793 (PZPR Wydz. Propagandy), 153, 32–51.
3. Haubold-Stolle, *Mythos Oberschlesien*, 370–74; Bjork and Gerwarth, "The Annaberg," 373–400.
4. "Analiza pracy," 1953, APK, 1793 (PZPR Wydz. Propagandy), 153, 49–51.
5. Ibid., 44–45; "Analiza zagadnienia rewizjonistycznego," May 1954, IPN Kat., 032 (Woj. Stalinogrodzkie), 59, cz. 1, 10; Madajczyk, *Niemcy Polscy*, 157, 166, 168; Czapliński et al., *Historia Śląska*, 508.
6. "Analiza zagadnienia rewizjonistycznego," May 1954, IPN Kat., 032, 59, cz. 1, 21.
7. Bernard Linek, "'Rewizjonizm niemiecki': Skala, charakter, i polityka władz bezpieczeństwa," in *Stalinizm i rok 1946 na Górnym Śląsku*, ed. Adam Dziurok, Bernard Linek, and Krzysztof Tarka (Katowice, 2007), 213–32.
8. SR, Sept. 1953, IPN Wr., 07/46 (Strzelce Opolskie), 96ff.; "Analiza zagadnienia rewizjonistycznego," May 1954, IPN Kat., 032, 59, cz. 1, 10, 21ff.
9. Haubold-Stolle, *Mythos Oberschlesien*, 377; Ahonen, *After the Expulsion*, 32.
10. Demshuk, *The Lost German East*, 63–95; Andrew Demshuk, "Wspomnienie roku 1921 po 1945 r.: Górnoślązacy wypędzenie w Zachodnich Niemczech—różne obrazy ofiary," in *Górny Śląsk i Górno-Ślązacy: Wokół problemów regionu i jego mieszkańców w XIX i XX w.*, ed. Sebastian Rosenbaum (Katowice and Gliwice, 2014), 280–313; Haubold-Stolle, *Mythos Oberschlesien*, 383–406.
11. Demshuk,"Wspomnienie," 191–2.
12. Ibid. See also Haubold-Stolle, *Mythos Oberschlesien*, 406–18.
13. Demshuk, "Wspomnienie," 280–313; Haubold-Stolle, *Mythos Oberschlesien*, 436–38, 440–41.
14. See Landsmannschaft Nieder- und Oberschlesien, *Oberschlesien: Deutsches Land, Deutsches Schicksal, 40. Jahrestag der Volksabstimmung in Oberschlesien* (Hannover, 1961).
15. See Demshuk, *The Lost German East*, esp. 250–62; Demshuk, "Wspomnienie," 280–313.
16. See Walczak, *Jerzy Ziętek*, 338–486; records on these rallies are in the files of the regional PZPR propaganda bureau in APK, 1793/1 (KW PZPR), 84, 1–162; Rada Okręgowa TRZZ, 29 Sept. 1957, APK, 310 (TRZZ Woj. Katowice), 40, 10.
17. Curp, *A Clean Sweep?*, 153–85; Strauchold, *Myśl Zachodnia*, 400–38.
18. Sytuacja Społeczno-Polityczna Wśród Ludnośći Rodzimej, n.d., APK, 1793, 182, 1–3; Posiedzienie Rady Kultury Woj. Opolskie, 1956-7, APO, 224 (PWRN), 2308, 1ff. See also Madajczyk, *Niemcy Polscy*, chap. 4.
19. "Napisałem wtedy do Gomułki," *Przemiany*, 25 Nov. 1956, 3.
20. See articles in *Przemiany*, esp. "Napisałem wtedy do Gomułki," 25 Nov. 1956; Adolf Niedworok, "Krzywdy i Nadzieje," 21 Oct. 1956, 2; Zdzisław Hierowski, "Katastrofa nie tylko Olsztyńska," 28 Oct. 1956, 5. See also Fic, *Wilhelm Szewczyk*, 137–60.
21. Zespoł *Przemian*, "Do Towarzyszy z opolskiego KW PZPR," *Przemiany*, 18 Nov. 1956, 3; Niedworok, "Krzywdy," 2.
22. "Napisałem wtedy do Gomułki," *Przemiany*, 25 Nov. 1956, 3.
23. Posiedzienie Rady Kultury Woj. Opolskie, 1956-7, APO, 224 (PWRN), 2308, 1–50, esp. 44ff. See also TRZZ Woj. Opolskie, protokoły z zebrań (1957–60), APO, 494 (TRZZ-Woj. Opolskie), 26, esp. 22 (from 15 Oct. 1959); TRZZ Woj. Katowickie, SR, 1960s, APK, 310 (TRZZ-Woj. Katowickie), 45, 1ff.
24. See the UB records in the IPN Kat., e.g., file set 032, 60 (Materiały Rewizjonizmu Niemieckiego), and IPN Wr., file set 09, 177, or 224. See file sets on *rewizjonizm* during the 1960s in

APO, 224 (PWRN Opole), 5121 to 5126, e.g., documents 1–80 in the latter (from 1965). See also Madajczyk, *Niemcy Polscy*, chap. 5; Linek, "'Rewizjonizm niemiecki,'" 213–32.

25. Posiedzienie Rady Kultury Woj. Opolskie, 1956–7, APO, 224, 2308, 45–46.

26. Ibid., 55–7.

27. Madajczyk, *Niemcy Polscy*, 258.

28. Dariusz Matelski, *Niemcy w Polsce w XX wieku* (Warsaw, 1999), 242. See also Madajczyk, *Niemcy Polscy*, 217, 294, 310.

29. T. David Curp was the first to make the connection between the expulsions and anti-Semitic campaign of 1968 in *A Clean Sweep?*, 193. See also Lech Szaraniec, "Życie Gospodarcze," in *Katowice*, vol. 1, ed. Barciak et al., 500.

30. See Thum, *Uprooted*, 386; Demshuk, *The Lost German East*, 237; Annika Frieberg, "Transnational Spaces in National Places: Early Activists in Polish-West German Relations," *Nationalities Papers* 38, no. 2 (2010): 213–26; Karolina Wigura, "Alternative Historical Narrative: 'Polish Bishops' Appeal to their German Colleagues' of 18 November 1965," *Eastern European Politics & Societies* 27 (August 2013): 400–12.

31. Obchody Tysiąclecia Państwa Polskiego, 1966, APK, 1793, 84, 59–70. See also Bartłomiej Noszczak, ed., *Milenium czy Tysiąclecie* (Warsaw, 2006).

32. On the 1971 commemoration, see files in APK, 224 (PWRN Kat.), 162. See also Hawranek et. al., *Encyklopedia Powstańcza*, 73–74, 430–32; Walczak, *Jerzy Ziętek*, 435–456ff.

33. Demshuk, *The Lost German East*, 237–40; Thum, *Uprooted*, 386–88.

34. See Czaplicki et al., *Historia Śląska*, 538–42.

35. Michałczyk, *Heimat, Kirche und Nation*, 3–4.

36. Główny Urząd Statystyczny (Warszawa), Raport z wyników, Narodowy Spis Powszechny Ludności i Mieszkań 2011, 106. Karch notes the dominant number of Silesians, based on the 2002 census, in "Nationalism on the Margins," 1.

37. These scholars base their results on the 2002 census. See Michałczyk, *Heimat, Kirche und Nation*, esp. Vorwort; Karch, "Nationalism on the Margins," esp. introduction.

38. See Walczak, *Jerzy Ziętek*.

39. See Bogusław Tracz, "Ślązak—Żołnierz—Gospodarz: Jerzy Ziętek jako przykład mitologizacji politycznej," in *Górny Śląsk i Górno-Ślązacy: Wokół problemów regionu i jego mieszkańców w XIX i XX w*, ed. Sebastian Rosenbaum (Katowice and Gliwice, 2014), 330–53.

40. Jan Myrcik, *Poł wieku Śląska: Zarys Monograficzny Zespołu Pieśni i Tańca "Śląsk"* (Koszęcin, 2004), 26–27ff.

41. See Omer Bartov and Eric Weitz, eds., *Shatterzones of Empires* (Bloomington, IN, 2013).

Appendix
Rallies at the Voivodeship Government Building (Gmach Urzędu Wojewódzkiego), Katowice/Kattowitz

Figure 7.1. May Third rally before the Voivodeship Government Building (Gmach Urzędu Wojewódzkiego), Katowice (Kattowitz), 1936. (Author unknown, APK)

Figure 7.2. Nazi Freedom Day rally, 1 September 1940. (Photo by Edgar Boidol from Heimatkalender Kattowitz, 1941, Biblioteka Śląska)

Figure 7.3. May Day rally with painting of Bolesław Bierut (right), 1946. (Author unknown, APK)

Bibliography

Archives

Archiwum Akt Nowych (AAN)
    Konsulat RP w Opolu
    Ambasada RP w Berlinie
    Ministerstwo Administracji Publicznej
    Ministerstwo Oświaty

Archiwum Biblioteki Instytutu Śląskiego (BIŚ)
    Papers of Stefani Mazurek

Archiwum Państwowe w Katowicach (APK)
    Akta Miasta Bytomia
    Akta Miasta Chorzowa
    Akta Miasta Tarnowskie Góry
    Gmina Piekary Śląskie
    Kuratorium Okręgu Szkolnego Śląskiego w Katowicach
    NSDAP Gauleitung
    NSDAP Kreisleitung Hindenburg
    NSDAP Kreisleitung Kattowitz
    NSDAP Kreisleitung Königshütte
    Oberpräsidium Kattowitz
    Polska Partia Robotnicza, Komitet Wojewódzki
    Polski Związek Zachodni, Okręg Śląski
    Polski Związek Zachodni, Bytom
    Policja Województwa Śląskiego
    Provinizialverwaltung
    Reichspropagandaamt
    Regierungsbezirk Kattowitz
    Sicherheitdienst
    Starostwo Powiatowe Bytom
    Starostwo Powiatowe Gliwice
    Starowstwo Powiatowe Katowice
    Starowstwo Powiatowe Tarnowskie Góry
    Towarzystwo Rozwoju Ziem Zachodnich
    Urząd Wojewódzki Śląski

Urząd Wojewódzki Śląsko-Dąbrowski
Wojewodzka Rada Narodowa, Prezydium
Wojewódzki Urząd Informacji i Propagandy
Związek Powstańców Śląskich
Związek Weteranów Powstańców Śląskich

Archiwum Państwowe w Katowicach—Gliwice Section (APK-Gl.)
    Akta Miasta Gliwic
    Akta Miasta Zabrze
    Zarząd Miejski Gliwice
    Zarząd Miejski Zabrze
    BDO Kreisverband Hindenburg

Archiwum Państwowe w Katowicach—Pszczyna Section
    Akta Miasta Pszczyna

Archiwum Państwowe w Opolu (APO)
    Oberpräsidium der Provinz Oberschlesien
    Prezydium Wojewódzkiej Rady Narodowej w Opolu
    Regierung Oppeln
    Starostwo Powiatowe Strzelce Opolskie

Archiwum Państwowe w Poznaniu (APP)
    Polski Związek Zachodni

Archiwum Państwowe we Wrocławiu (APWr.)
    Wydział Samorządowy Prowincji Śląskiej we Wrocławiu

Bundesarchiv Berlin-Lichterfelde (BArch)
    Deutsche Heimatbund
    N.S. (Nazi party records)
    Publikationsstelle Berlin-Dahlem
    Reichskommisar für die Festigung des Deutschen Volkstums

Bundesarchiv Filmarchiv
    Land unterm Kreuz: Ein Film von oberschlesiens schwierigsten Zeit, dir. Ulrich Kayser, 1927

Geheimstaatsarchiv Preußische Kulturbesitz (GStA PK)
    Preussische Ministerium des Innerns, "Ost-West"
    Regierung Kattowitz

Instytu Pamięci Narodowej—Katowice Section (IPN Kat.)

Instytut Pamięci Narodowej—Wrocław Section (IPN Wr.)
    PUBP, Strzelce Opolskie

Politische Archiv des Auswärtigen Amtes (PA-AA)
    Deutsche Konsulat in Kattowitz
    Deutsche Bottschaft in Warschau

Rossiskii Gosudarstvennyi Voennyi Arkhiv (RGVA)
Oberpräsident der Provinz O/S, Kattowitz

Primary Sources

Barcikowski, Wacław, et al., eds. *Odzyskane Ziemie—Odzyskani Ludzie: Z współczesnych zagadnień Ziem Odzyskanych*. Poznań, 1946.
Benisz, Adam, et al., eds. *Śląsk: Przeszłość i Teraźniejszość*. Katowice: Nakładem Okręgu Śląskiego, ZOKZ, 1931.
Bereżowski, Stanisław. *Turystyczno-Krajoznawczy Przewodnik po województwie Śląskim*. Katowice, 1937.
Bolick, J. *Beiträge zur Sprecherziehung im Grenzland*. Dortmund and Breslau: Verlag W. Crüwell, 1940.
Dienwiebel, Herbert. *Oberschlesische Schrotholzkirchen*. Breslau: Heydebrand Verlag, 1938.
Dobrolowski, Tadeusz. *Sztuka Województwa Śląskiego: L'art en Silesie Polonaise*. Katowice: Muzeum Śląski, 1933.
Echa Śląskie: Pieśni dla ludu polskiego na Śląsku Opolskim. Nakładem Związku Kół Śpiewackich na Śląsku Opolskim, 1935.
Flott, F. ed. *Heimatland O/S: Ein Heimatbuch für die oberschlesische Jugend*. Breslau, Schlesienverlag, 1937.
Förster, Wolfgang, and Friedrich Stumpe, eds. *Schönere Heimat*. Breslau: Schlesienverlag, ca. 1941.
Führer durch die Stadt Kattowitz. Fremdverkehrsverband, 1940.
Gauhauptstadt Kattowitz, O/S: Die politische, wirtschaftliche und kulturelle Mittelpunkt des neuen Gaues O/S. Unknown publisher, ca. 1941.
Grabowski, E. *Die Volkstrachten in Oberschlesien*. Breslau, 1935.
Heiß, Friedrich. *Das Schlesienbuch: Ein Zeugnis Ostdeutschen Schicksals*. Berlin: Volk und Reich Verlag, 1938.
Kauder, Victor, ed. *Das Deutschtum in Polnisch-Schlesien: Ein Handbuch über Land und Leute*. Leipzig: Verlag von S. Hirzel, 1932.
Ku lepszej przyszłości: czytanki polskie dla starszej młodzierzy szkół powszechnych i kursów dla dorosłych. Warsaw: Państwowe Zakłady Wydawnictw Szkolnych, 1945.
Łakomy, Ludwik. *Ilustrowana Monografia Województwa Śląskiego*. Katowice: E. Piecha, 1936.
Landsmannschaft Nieder- und Oberschlesien, ed. *Oberschlesien: Deutsches Land, Deutsches Schicksal, 40. Jahrestag der Volksabstimmung in Oberschlesien*. Hannover, 1961.
Landy-Brzezińska Joanna, et al. *Na Trasie: Pierwsze Czytanki dla Dorosłych*. Warsaw: Nasza Księgarnia, 1949.
Lange, Friedrich. *Ostland kehrt Heim: Memel, Danzig, Westpreussen, Wartheland und Oberschlesien*. Vol. 5. Berlin and Leipzig, 1940.
Mikulski, A., ed. *Przewodnik Po Ziemi Śląskiej*. Warsaw: Polska Agencja Telegraficzna, 1935.
Nie Rzucim Ziemi: Czytanka do Użytku na Kursach Dla Dorosłych na Ziemiach Odzyskanych. Warsaw: Państwowe Zakłady Wydawnictw Szkolnych, 1946.
Oberschlesische Volkslieder: Aus den Beständen des Oberschlesische Volksliedarchivs. Kassel: Bärenreiter, 1938.
Orłowicz, Mieczysław. *Ilustrowany Przewodnik po Województwie Śląskiem*. Warsaw and Lwów, 1924.
O/S und Seine Beitrag zum Grossdeutschen Freiheitskampf. Kattowitz and Breslau: Schlesienverlag, ca. 1941.
Perlick, Alfons, ed. *Landeskunde des oberschlesischen Industriegebietes*. Breslau: Schlesienverlag, 1943.
Die Provinz Oberschlesien: Ihre Verluste durch das Versailler Diktat, ihre Notlage, ihre Vorschläge zu deren Behebung ihr natürlicher Reichtum. Ratibor, 1931.
Ratibor: Die Stadt an zwei Grenzen—der Grenzlandturm. Publisher unknown, May 1938.
Sappok, Gerhard, Joh. Papritz, Hermann Weidhaas, et al., eds. *Oberschlesiens Großstädte: Ein Führer und Handbuch für Fremde und Einheimische*. Leipzig: Verlag S. Hirzel, 1943.

Spatz, Otto H. *Wiedergewonnenes deutsches Land.* Munich and Berlin: J. F. Lehmanns Verlag, 1941.
Szramek, Emil, et al., eds. *Pieśni Ludowe z Polskiego Śląska.* Cracow: Polska Akademja Umiejętności, 1927.
Wojciechowski, Zygmunt. *Polska-Niemcy: Dziesięć wieków zmagania.* Poznań: Instytut Zachodni, 1945.
Ziętek, Jerzy. *Powstańczy Szlak: Rozważania Powstańcze.* Katowice: Nakładem Związek Weteranów Powstańców Śląskich, 1946.

Press, Periodicals, and Almanacs

Der Angriff (1940)
Architektura i Budownictwo (1927–39)
Deutsche Monatshefte (1941)
Dziennik Zachodni (1945–53)
Głos Górnego Śląska (1926–31)
Głos Ludu (1945, 1946)
Gość Niedzielny (1945–49)
Heimatkalender des Kreises Kattowitz und der Städte Kattowitz und Königshütte (1940–42)
Katolik Codzienny (1926–39)
Kattowitzer Zeitung (1923–43)
Kulturarbeit in Oberschlesien: Ein Jahrbuch (1935–37)
Mitteilungsblatt des NSLB Gauwaltung, Schlesien & O/S (1939–43)
Nowiny Opolskie (1947–49)
Der Oberschlesier (1941–43)
Oberschlesische Kurier (1923–43)
Oberschlesische Volkstimme (1923–32)
Oberschlesische Wanderer (1931)
Odra (1945–49)
Ogniwa (1947–49)
Ostdeutsche Morgenpost (1923–45)
Polonia (1923–39)
Polska Zachodnia (1926–39, 1945)
Powstaniec (1926–39)
Przemiany (1956)
Sprawy Zachodnie (1945)
Strażnica Zachodnia (1934–39; 1945–49)
Trybuna Opolska (1961)
Trybuna Robotnicza (1945–49, 1971)
Ziemia (1928)

Secondary Sources

Ahonen, Perti. *After the Expulsion: Western Germany and Eastern Europe, 1945–90.* Oxford, 2003.
Ahonen, Perti, Gustavo Corni, Jerzy Kochanowski, Rainer Schulze, Tamás Stark, and Barbara Stelzl-Marx, eds. *People on the Move: Forced Population Movements in Europe in the Second World War and Its Aftermath.* Oxford: Berg, 2008.

Alexander, Manfred. "Oberschlesien im 20. Jahrhundert: Eine missverstandene Region." *Geschichte und Gesellschaft* 30, no. 3 (2004): 465–89.
Allen, Debra J. *The Oder-Neisse Line: The United States, Poland, and Germany in the Cold War.* Westport, CT: Praeger, 2003.
Aly, Götz, and Susanne Heim. *Architects of Annihilation: Auschwitz and the Logic of Destruction.* Princeton, NJ: Princeton University Press, 2002.
Applegate, Celia. *A Nation of Provincials: The German Idea of Heimat.* Berkeley: University of California Press, 1990.
Augusteijn, Joost, and Eric Storm, eds. *Region and State in Nineteenth-Century Europe: Nation-Building, Regional Identities, and Separatism.* Houndsmill, UK: Palgrave Macmillan, 2012.
Bahlcke, Joachim. *Schlesien und die Schlesier.* Munich: Langen Müller, 2000.
Baranowski, Shelley. *Strength Through Joy: Consumerism and Mass Tourism in the Third Reich.* Cambridge: Cambridge University Press, 2004.
Bartov, Omer, and Eric Weitz, eds. *Shatterzones of Empires.* Bloomington: Indiana University Press, 2013.
Bębnik, Grzegorz. "'Stalinizacja' jako zawłaszczenie sfery symbolicznej (na przykładzie Katowic, 1945–1956)," in *Stalinizm i rok 1956 na Górnym Śląsku,* ed. Adam Dziurok, Bernard Linek, and Krzysztof Tarka, 237–58. Katowice: IPN, 2007.
———. *Katowice we Wrześniu 1939.* Katowice: IPN, 2006.
Bergen, Doris. "Instrumentalization of Volksdeutschen in German Propaganda in 1939: Replacing and Erasing Poles, Jews, and Other Victims." *German Studies Review* 31, no. 3 (October 2008): 447–70.
———. "The 'Volksdeutschen' of Eastern Europe, World War, and the Holocaust: Constructed Identity, Real Genocide." *Yearbook of European Studies* 13 (1999): 70–93.
Biel, Urszula. "Płonące premiery: Z dziejów polsko-niemieckiego pogranicza filmowego na Górnym Śląsku." In *Kino niemieckie w dialogu pokoleń i kultur,* edited by Andrzej Gwóźdź, 321–31. Cracow: Rabid, 2004.
Bjork, James. "The National State and the Territorial Parish in Interwar Poland." In *The Germans and the East,* edited by Charles Ingrao and Franz A. J. Szabo. West Lafayette, IN: Purdue University Press, 2008.
———. *Neither German nor Pole: Catholicism and National Indifference in a Central European Borderland.* Ann Arbor: University of Michigan Press, 2008.
Bjork, James, and Robert Gerwarth. "The Annaberg as a German-Polish 'Lieu de Memoire.'" *German History* 25, no. 3 (2007): 373–400.
Blackbourne, David. "The Conquest of Nature and the Mystique of the Eastern Frontier in Nazi Germany." In *Germans, Poland and Colonial Expansion to the East: 1850 Through the Present,* ed. Robert L. Nelson, 141–62. New York: Palgrave Macmillan, 2009.
Blanke, Richard. *Orphans of Versailles: The Germans in Western Poland, 1918–1939.* Kentucky: University Press 1993.
———. *Polish-Speaking Germans? Language and National Identity Among the Masurians since 1871.* Cologne: Böhlau, 2001.
———. *Prussian Poland in the German Empire (1871–1900).* New York: Columbia University Press, 1981.
Brands, Gunnar. "From World War I Cemeteries to the Nazi 'Fortresses of the Dead': Architecture, Heroic Landscape, and the Quest for National Identity in Germany." In *Places of Commemoration: Search for Identity and Landscape Design,* edited by Joachim Wolschke-Bulmahn, 215–36. Washington DC, 2001.
Brown, Kate. *A Biography of No Place: from Ethnic Borderland to Soviet Heartland.* Cambridge, MA: Harvard University Press, 2004.

Brubaker, Rogers. *Ethnicity Without Groups*. Cambridge, MA: Harvard University Press, 2004.

———. *Nationalism Reframed: Nationhood and the National Question in the New Europe*. Cambridge: Cambridge University Press, 1996.

Bryant, Chad. "Either German or Czech: Fixing Nationality in Bohemia and Moravia, 1939–1946." *Slavic Review* 61, no. 4 (Winter 2002): 683–707.

———. *Prague in Black: Nazi Rule and Czech Nationalism*. Cambridge, 2007.

Bukowska-Floreńska, Irena. "Uwarunkowania społeczne i kulturowe folkloru śląskiego (do 1939 r.)." In *Z dziejów i dorobku folklorystyki śląskiej (do 1939 roku)*, ed. Jerzy Pośpiech and Teresa Smolińska, 13-26. Opole: Uniwersytet Opolski, 2002.

Burleigh, Michael. *Germany Turns Eastwards: A Study of Ostforschung in the Third Reich*. New York: Cambridge University Press, 1988.

Case, Holly. *Between States: The Transylvanian Question and the European Idea During World War II*. Stanford, CA: Stanford University Press, 2009.

———, ed. *Sztuka Górnego Śląska od Średniowiecza do końca XX w.* Katowice: Muzeum Śląskie, 2004.

Chu, Winson. *The German Minority in Interwar Poland*. New York: Cambridge University Press, 2012.

———. "'Volksgemeinschaften unter sich': German Minorities and Regionalism in Poland, 1918–1939." In *German History form the Margins*, edited by Neil Gregor et al. Bloomington: Indiana University Press, 2006.

Cimała, Bogdana. "Obchody Rocznic Plebiscytowych na Górnym Śląsku w latach 1924–1927." *Kronika Katowic* 6 (1996): 119–31.

———. "Uwarunkowania funkcjonowania gospodarki Górnego Śląska w organizmie Drugiej Rzeczypospolitej." In *Górny Śląsk po podziale w 1922 roku: Co Polska, a co Niemcy dały mieszkańcom tej ziemi?*, ed. Zbigniew Kapały, Wiesław Lesiuk, and Maria Wanda Wanatowicz, 64–75. Bytom: Muzeum Górnośląskie, 1997.

Confino, Alon. *The Nation as a Local Metaphor: Wüttemberg, Imperial Germany, and National Memory, 1871–1918*. Chapel Hill: University of North Carolina Press, 1997.

Connelly, John. "Nazis and Slavs: From Racial Theory to Racist Practice." *Central European History* 32, no. 1 (1999): 1–33.

Curp, T. David. *A Clean Sweep? The Politics of Ethnic Cleansing in Western Poland, 1945–1960*. Rochester, NY: University of Rochester Press, 2006.

———. "'Roman Dmowski Understood': Ethnic Cleansing as Permanent Revolution." *European History Quarterly* 3, no. 35 (2005): 405–27.

———. "The Politics of Ethnic Cleansing: The PPR, the PZZ, and Wielkopolska's Nationalist Revolution, 1944–46." *Nationalities Papers* 29, no. 4 (2001): 575–603.

Czapliński, Marek, et al., eds. *Historia Śląska*. Wrocław: Uniwersytet Wrocławski, 2002.

Dabrowski, Patricia. "Constructing a Polish Landscape: The Example of the Carpathian Frontier." *Austria History Yearbook* 39 (2008): 45–65.

Danowska-Prokop, Barbara, and Urszula Zagóra-Jonszta. *Wybrane problemy ekonomiczno-społeczne i polityczne na Górnym Śląsku w latach 1922–1939*. Katowice: Wydawnictwo Uczelniane Akademii Ekonomiczne, 1995.

Demshuk, Andrew. *The Lost German East: Forced Migration and the Politics of Memory, 1945–1970*. Cambridge University Press, 2012.

———. "Wspomnienie roku 1921 po 1945 r.: Górnoślązacy wypędzeni w Zachodnich Niemczech—różny obraz ofiary." In *Górny Śląsk i Górno-Ślązacy: Wokół problemów regionu i jego mieszkańców w XIX i XX w*, edited by Sebastian Rosenbaum, 280–313. Katowice and Gliwice: IPN, 2014.

Długajczyk, Edward. *Sanacja Śląska, 1926–1939: Zarys dziejów politycznych*. Katowice: Śląsk, 1983.

Dobrowolski, Piotr. *Ugrupowania i Kierunki Separystyczne na Górnym Śląsku i w Ceszyńskiem w latach 1918–1939*. Warsaw: Państwowe Wyd. Naukowe, 1972.

Drabina, Jan. Ed. *Historia Gliwic*. Gliwice: Muzeum w Gliwicach, 1995.
Drobek, Felicitas. "Alfons Perlick jako badacz folkloru niemieckiego w regionie Bytomskim." In *Z dziejów i dorobku folklorystyki śląskiej (do 1939 roku)*, ed. Jerzy Pośpiech and Teresa Smolińska, 91–110. Opole: Uniwersytet Opolski, 2002.
Drummond, Elizabeth A. "On the Borders of the Nation: Jews and the German-Polish National Conflict in Poznania, 1886–1914." *Nationality Papers* 29, no. 3 (2001): 459–75.
Dziurok, Adam. *Śląskie Rozrachunki: Władze Komunistyczne a byli członkowie organizacji nazistowskich*. Warsaw: IPN, 2000.
———. "Problemy narodowościowe w województwie śląskim i sposoby ich Rozwiązania." In *Województwo Śląskie, 1945–50: Zarys dziejów politycznych*, ed. Adam Dziurok and Ryszard Kaczmarek, 539–604. Katowice: Wydaw. Uniwersytetu Śląskiego, 2007.
Dziurok, Adam, Bernard Linek, and Krzysztof Tarka, eds. *Stalinizm i rok 1956 na Górnym Śląsku*. Katowice, Opole, and Cracow: Societas, 2007.
Eddie, Scott M. "The Prussian Settlement Commission and Its Activities in the Land Market, 1886–1918." In *Germans, Poland, and Colonial Expansion to the East, 1850 through the Present*, ed. Robert L. Nelson, 39–58. New York, 2009.
Ehrlich, Adam. "Between Germany and Poland: Ethnic Cleansing and the Politicization of Ethnicity in Upper Silesia under National Socialism and Communism." PhD dissertation, University of Indiana–Bloomington, 2006.
Epstein, Catherine. *Model Nazi: Arthur Greiser and the Occupation of Western Poland*. New York: Oxford University Press, 2010.
Esch, Michael. "'Ethnische Säuberungen' zwischen Deutschland und Polen 1939 bis 1950: Überlegungen zu ihrer Genese und Einordnung." In *Definitionsmacht, Utopie, Vergelung: "Ethnische Säuberungen" im östlichen Europa des 20. Jahrhunderts*, edited by Micheal G. Esch, Ulf Brunnbauer, and Holm Sundhaussen, 96–124. Berlin: Münster Lit Verlag, 2006.
———. *Gesunde Verhältnisse: Deutsche und polnische Bevölkerungspolitik in Ostmitteleuropa, 1939–1950*. Marburg: Herder-Institut, 1998.
Falęcki, Tomasz. "Nazwy miejscowe Katowic jako obraz przemian politycznych i kulturalnych." In *Katowice w 138. rocznice uzystakia praw miejskich*, edited by Antoni Barciak, 21–30. Katowice: Societas Scientiis Favendis Silesiae Superioris – Instytut Górnośląski, 2004.
———. "Regionalizm powstańców śląskich (do 1939 r.)." In *Regionalizm a separatyzm historia i współczesność, Śląsk na tle innych obszarów*, ed. Maria Wanda Wanatowicz, 46–64. Katowice: Uniwersytet Śląski 1996.
———. "Powstańcy Śląscy w ruchu kombatanckim w II Rzeczypospolitej." In *Powstania Śląskie i plebiscyt w procesie zrastania sie Górnego Śląska z Macierza: Materiały z sesji naukowej historyków powstań śląskich i plebiscytu*, ed. Anrzej Brozek, 170–76. Bytom: Muzeum Górnośląskie, 1993.
———. *Powstańcy Śląscy, 1921–1939*. Warsaw: Oficja Wydawnicza Volumen, 1990.
Fazan, Mirosław. "Wkład katowickiego środowiska naukowego i literackiego w kulturalną integrację Ziem Zachodnich." *Rocznik Katowicki* 13 (1987): 98–113.
Fic, Maciej. *Wilhelm Szewczyk: Śląski polityk i działacz społeczny (1916–1991)*. Katowice: Uniwersytet Śląski, 2007.
Fiedor, Karol. *Bund Deutscher Osten w systemie antypolskiej propagandy*. Warsaw and Wrocław: Instytut Śląski w Opolu, 1977.
Fischer, Christopher J. *Alsace to the Alsatians? Visions and Divisions of Alsatian Regionalism, 1870–1939*. New York: Berghahn Books, 2010.
Fischer, Peter. *Die Deutsche Publizistik als Faktor der deutsch-polnischen Beziehungen, 1919–1939*. Wiesbaden: Otto Harrassowitz, 1991.
Frieberg, Annika. "Transnational Spaces in National Places: Early Activists in Polish-West German Relations." *Nationalities Papers* 38, no. 2 (2010): 213–26.

Friedrickson, George M. *Racism: A Short History.* Princeton, NJ: Princeton University Press, 2002.
Fuchs, Konrad. "Zur Lage der Industrie West- und Ost-Oberschlesiens 1919–1939." In *Górny Śląsk po podziale w 1922 roku: Co Polska, a co Niemcy dały mieszkańcom tej ziemi?* Ed. Zbigniew Kapały, Wiesław Lesiuk, and Maria Wanda Wanatowicz, 39–63. Bytom: Muzeum Górnośląskie, 1997.
Głazek, Dorota. "Kolonie Robotnicze w Autonomicznym Województwie Śląskim." In *O sztuce Górnego Śląska i Zagłębia Dąbrowskiego XV–XX w. Sztuka Śląska odkrywana na nowo*, ed. Ewa Chojecka, 105–18. Katowice: Uniwersytet Śląski, 1989.
———. "Budynek Muzeum Śląskiego w Katowicach na tle architektury europejskiej lat trzydziestych XX. Wieku." *Rocznik Katowicki*, 1980, 113–21.
Glassheim, Eagle. "Ethnic Cleansing, Communism, and Environmental Devastation in Czechoslovakia's Borderlands, 1945–1989." *Journal of Modern History* 78 (March 2006): 65–92.
Godfellow, Samuel. "Fascism and Regionalism in Interwar Alsace." *National Identities* 12, no. 2 (June 2010): 133–45.
Grajewski, Andrzej. *Wygnanie: Diecezja katowicka w czasach stalinowskich.* Katowice: Księgarnia św. Jacka, 2002.
Grosch, Waldemar. *Deutsche und polnische Propaganda während der Volksabstimmung in Oberschlesien, 1919–1921.* Dortmund: Forschungsstelle Ostmitteleuropa, 2002.
———. "Deutsche und polnische Propaganda in der Zeit der Aufstände und des Plebiszits." In *Oberschlesien nach dem Ersten Weltkrieg: Studien zu einem nationalen Konflikt und seiner Errinerung*, ed. Kai Struve, 69–88. Marburg: Herder Institute, 2003.
Gross, Jan T. *Fear: Anti-Semitism in Poland after Auschwitz—an Essay in Historical Interpretation.* New York: Random House, 2006.
Gruenberg, Karol. *Nazi Front Schlesien: Niemieckie organizacje polityczne w Województwie Śląskim.* Katowice: Wydawnictwo Śląsk, 1963.
Grzyb, Mieczysław. *Narodowościowe-polityczne aspekty przemian stosunków własnościowych i kadrowych w górnośląskim przemyśle w latach 1922–1939.* Katowice: Uniwersytet Śląski, 1978.
Haar, Ingo. "German *Ostforschung* and Anti-Semitism." In *German Scholars and Ethnic Cleansing, 1920–45*, edited by Ingo Haar and Michael Fahlbusch, 1–27. New York: Berghahn Books, 2005.
Harp, Stephen L. *Learning to Be Loyal: Primary Schooling as Nation Building in Alsace and Lorraine, 1850–1940.* DeKalb: Northern Illinois University Press, 1998.
Hartwich, Mateusz J. *Das Schlesische Riesengebirge: Die Polonisierung einer Landschaft nach 1945.* Vienna: Bohlau Verlag, 2012.
Harvey, Elizabeth. *Women and the Nazi East: Agents and Witnesses of Germanization.* New Haven, CT, 2003.
Haubold-Stolle, Juliane. *Mythos Oberschlesien: Der Kampf um die Erinnerung in Deutschland und Polen, 1919–1956.* Osnabrück: Fibre, 2008.
———. "Mythos Oberschlesien in der Weimarer Republik: Die Mythisierung der oberschlesischen Freikorpskämpfe und der 'Abstimmungszeit' (1919–21) im Deutschland der Zwischenkriegszeit." In *Politische Mythen im 19. und 20. Jahrhundert in Mittel- und Osteuropa*, edited by Heidi Hein-Kirchner and Hans Henning Hahn, 279–300. Marburg: Herder-Institut, 2006.
———. "Der heilige Berg Oberschlesiens—der Sankt Annaberg als Errinerungsort." In *Schlesische Erinerungsorte: Gedächtnis: und Identität einer mitteleuropäischen Region*, edited by Marek Czapliński, Hans-Joachim Hahn, Tobias Weger, 202–20. Görlitz: Neisse-Verlag, 2005.
Hauser, Przemysław. "Von der Provinz zum Freistaat? Der oberschlesische Separatismus im Jahr 1918/1919." In *Regionale Bewegungen und Regionalismen in europäischen Zwischenräumen seit der Mitte des 19. Jahrhunderts*, ed. Philipp Ther and Holm Sundhaussen, 113–26. Marburg: Herder Institute, 2003.
Hawranek, Franciszek, et al., eds. *Encyklopedia Powstań Śląskich.* Opole: Instytut Śląski, 1982.

———. Niemiecka Socjaldemokracia w Prowincji Górnośląskiej w latach 1929–1933. Wrocław: Ossolineum, 1971.
———, ed. Dzieje Ruchu Robotniczego na Górnym Śląsku. Opole: Instytut Śląski, 1982.
Heffner, Krystian, and Wiesław Lesiuk. "Ekonomiczne i Społeczne Skutki Podziału Górnego Śląska w 1922 roku." In Podział Śląska w 1922 roku, edited by Andrzej Brożka and Teresa Kulak, 135–55. Wrocław: Uniwersytet Wrocławski, 1996.
Hein, Heidi. Der Pilsudski-Kult und seine Bedeutung für den polnischen Staat, 1926–1939. Marburg: Herder-Institut, 2002.
Heinemann, Isabel. "'Deutsches Blut': Die Raseexperten der SS und die Volksdeutschen." In Die "Volksdeutschen" in Polen, Frankreich, Ungarn und die Tschechoslowakei: Mythos und Realität, edited by Jerzy Kochanowski and Maike Sach, 163–82. Osnabrück: Fibre, 2006.
Hierowski, Zdzisław. Życie literackie na Śląsku w latach 1922–1939. Katowice: "Śląsk," 1969.
Hitze, Guido. Carl Ulitzka (1873–1953) oder Oberschlesien zwischen den Weltkriegen Düsseldorf: Droste, 2002.
———. "Oberschlesien im politischen Denken Carl Ulitzkas." In Śląsk w myśli politycznej i działalnosci Polaków i Niemcow w XX wieku. Vol. 2, ed. Danuta Isielewicz and Lech Rubisz, 171–94. Opole: Wydawnictwo Uniwersytetu Opolskiego, 2004.
Hoffmann, Stephanie. "Stadtplanung in O/S am Beispiel der Städte Beuthen, Gleiwitz, und Hindenburg." In Die Architektur der Weimarer Republik: Ein Blick auf unbeachtete Bauwerke, ed. Nikolaus Gussone, 10–28. Dülmen: Laumann-Verlag, 1992.
Hofmann, Andreas R. Die Nachkriegszeit in Schlesien: Gesellschafts- und Bevölkerungspolitik in den polnischen Siedlungsgebieten, 1945–1948. Weimar: Böhlau Verlag, 2000.
Huener, Jonathan. Auschwitz, Poland, and the Politics of Commemoration, 1945–1979. Athens: Ohio University Press, 2003.
Jaworski, Wojciech. Ludność żydowska w województwie śląskim w latach 1922–1939. Katowice: Oficja Śląsk, 1997.
———. "Jewish Religious Communities in Upper Silesia, 1945–1970." In Jews in Silesia, ed. Marcin Wodziński and Janusz Spyra, 247–66. Cracow: Księgarnia Akademicka, 2001.
———. "Kształtowanie się świadomości narodowej ludności żydowskiej w województwie Śląskim w okresie międzywojennym." In Studia Historyczno-Demograficzne, edited by Jurek Tadeusz. Wrocław: Uniwersytet Wrocławski, 1996.
Judson, Pieter M. Guardians of the Nation: Activists on the Language Frontiers of Imperial Austria. Cambridge, MA: Harvard University Press, 2006.
Kaczmarek, Ryszard. Górny Śląsk podczas II wojny światowej: Między utopią niemieckiej wspólnoty narodowej a rzeczywistością okupacji na terenach wcielonych do Trzeciej Rzeszy. Katowice: Uniwersytet Śląski, 2006.
———. Polacy w Wehrmachcie. Krakow: Wydawnictwo Literackie, 2010.
———. "W Granicach III Rzeszy." In Katowice: Środowiska, dzieje, kultura, język, społeczeństwo, edited by Antoni Barciak et al., 360–92. Vol. 1. Katowice: Muzeum Historii Katowic, 2012.
Kaczmarek, Ryszard, Maciej Kucharski, and Adrian Cybula. Alzacja/Lotaryngia a Górny Śląsk: Dwa Regiony Pogranicza, 1648–2001. Katowice: Pergamon, 2001.
Kamusella, Tomasz. Silesia and Central European Nationalisms: The Emergence of National and Ethnic Groups in Prussian Silesia and Austrian Silesia, 1848–1918. West Lafayette, IN: Purdue University Press, 2007.
———. Schlonzska mowa: Język, Górny Śląsk i nacjonalizm. Zabrze: Narodowa Oficja Śląska, 2005.
"Upper Silesia 1870–1920: Between Region, Religion, Nation and Ethnicity." East European Quarterly 37, no. 4 (January 2005): 443–62.
———. "Ethnic Cleansing in Upper Silesia, 1944–1951." In Ethnic Cleansing in Twentieth-Century Europe, edited by T. Hunt Tooley, Béla Várdy, and Agnes Huszár Várdy, 293–310. New York: Columbia University Press, 2003.

———. "The Szlonzoks and Their Language: Between Germany, Poland and Szlonzokian Nationalism." *EUI Working Papers* 1 (2003): 1–50.
———. "The Upper Silesians' Stereotypical Perceptions of the Poles and the Germans." *East European Quarterly* 33, no. 3 (Fall 1999): 395–410.
Karch, Brendan. "A Jewish 'Nature Preserve': League of Nations Minority Protections and Nazi Upper Silesia, 1933–1937." *Central European History* 46, no. 1 (March 2013): 124–60.
———. "Nationalism on the Margins: Silesians between Germany and Poland, 1848–1945." PhD dissertation, Harvard University, 2010.
Keitsch, Frank. *Das Schicksal der deutschen Volksgruppe in Ostoberschlesien in den Jahren 1922–1939.* Dülmen: Laumann-Verlag, 1982.
Kenney, Padraic. *Rebuilding Poland: Workers and Communists, 1945–1950.* Ithaca, NY: Cornell University Press, 1997.
King, Jeremy. *Budweisers into Czechs and Germans: A Local History of Bohemian Politics, 1848–1948.* Princeton, NJ: Princeton University Press, 2005.
Kłocek, Eugeniusz. *"Swoi" i "obcy" na Górnym Śląsku od 1945 roku: Środowisko miejskie.* Wrocław: Wyd. Uniwersytet Wrocławski, 1994.
Kneip, Matthais. *Die deutsche Sprache in Oberschlesien: Untersuchungen zur politischen Rolle der deutschen Sprache als Minderheitensprache in den Jahren 1921–1998.* Dortmund: Forschungsstelle Ostmitteleuropa, 1999.
Kołomejczyk, Norbert. "Polski Związek Zachodni (okręg śląski) w latach 1945–1950." *Studia i Materiały z Dziejów Śląska* 6 (1964): 305–54.
Komprobst, Markus. *Irredentism in European Politcs: Argumentation, Compromise, and Norms.* Cambridge: Cambridge University Press, 2009.
Kopec, Eugeniusz. *"My i Oni" na polskim Śląsku, 1918–1939.* Katowice: "Śląsk," 1986.
———. "Zagadnienie społeczne jendości kresów śląskich z organizmem państwowym II Rzeczypospolitej." In *Ziemie Śląskie w granicach II Rzeczypospolitej: Procesy integracyjne,* ed. Franciszek Serafin, 116–33. Katowice: Uniwersytet Śląski, 1985.
———. "Z zagadnień integracji językowej śląskich kresów Rzeczypospolitej (1918–1939)." In *Z problemów integracji i unifikacji II Reczypospolitej,* edited by Jósef Chlebowczyk, 7–48. Katowice: Uniwersytet Śląski, 1980.
Kossert, Andreas. "Masuren als 'Bollwerk': Konstruktion von Grenze und Grenzregion von der Wilhelmischen Ostmarkenpolitik zum NS-Grenzland- und Volkstumskampf, 1894–1945." In *Die Grenze als Raum, Erfahrung und Konstrukton: Deutschland, Frankreich, und Polen vom 17. bis zum 20. Jahrhundert,* edited by Etienne Françios, Jörg Seifarth, and Bernhard Struck, 211–42. Frankfurt: Campus Verlag, 2007.
Król, Eugeniusz Cezary. *Polska i Polacy w propagandzie narodowego socjalizmu w Niemczech, 1919–1945.* Warsaw: Instytut Studiów Politycznych Akademi Nauk, 2006.
Kroska, Markus. *Für ein Polen an Oder und Ostsee: Zygmunt Wojciechowski als Historiker und Publizist.* Osnabrück: Fibre, 2003.
Krzyżanowski, Lech. "Kościół katolicki a władza państwowa." In *Wieki Stare i Nowe.* Vol. 2, ed. Maria Wanda Wanatowicz and Idziego Panic, 177–85. Katowice: Uniwersytet Śląski, 2001.
Kunicki, Wojciech. *"... auf dem Weg in dieses Reich": NS-Kulturpolitik und Literatur in Schlesien 1933 bis 1945.* Leipzig: Leipziger Universitätsverlag GMBH, 2006.
Lekan, Thomas M. *Imagining the Nation in Nature: Landscape Preservation and German Identity, 1885–1945.* Cambridge, MA: Harvard University Press, 2004.
Lempart, Matthais. "Michał Grażyński: Der schlesische Woiwode, 1926–1939." In *Dzieje Śląska w XX. Wieku w świetle badań młodych historyków z Polski, Czechosłowacji i Niemiec,* edited by Krzysztof Ruchniewicz. Wrocław: Instytut Historyczny Uniwersytetu Wrocławskiego, 1998.

Lesniak, Roland. "Verkehrswesen und Bauten des Verkehrs in Oberschlesien," in Die Architektur der Weimarer Republik in Oberschlesien: Ein Blick auf unbeachtete Bauwerke, Fotodokumentation." Ed. Nikolaus Gussone, 29–48. Dülmen: Laumann-Verlag, 1992. Linek, Bernard. *Polityka antyniemiecka na Górnym Śląsku w latach 1945–1950*. Opole: Stowarzyszenie Instytutu Śląskiego, 2000.

———. *"Odniemczanie" województwa śląskiego w latach 1945–1950: W świetle materiałów wojewódzkich*. Opole: Instytut Śląski, 1997.

———. "'De-Germanization' and 'Repolonization' in Upper Silesia, 1945–50." In *Redrawing Nations: Ethnic Cleansing in East-Central Europe, 1945–1948*, ed. Philipp Ther and Ana Siljak, 121–34. Lanham, MD: Rowman & Littlefield, 2001.

———. "Mit Ziem Odzyskanych w powojennej Polsce na przykładzie Górnego Śląska (wybrane aspekty)." In *Nacjonalizm a tożsamość narodowa w Europie Środko-Wschodniej w XIX i XX w., Nationalismus und nationale Identität in Ostmitteleuropa im 19. und 20. Jhd*, edited by Bernard Linek and Kai Struve, 229–55. Opole: Instytut Śląski, 2000.

Linek, Bernard, and Juliane Haubold-Stolle, eds. *Imaginiertes Oberschlesien: Mythen, Symbole, und Helden in den nationalen Diskursen*. Opole and Marburg: Instytut Śląski and Herder-Institut, 2005.

Lis, Michał. *Ludność Rodzima na Śląsku Opolskim Po II Wojnie Światowej (1945–1993)*. Opole: Instytut Śląski w Opolu, 1993.

Liulevicius, Vejas Gabriel. *The German Myth of the East, 1800 to the Present*. New York: Oxford University Press, 2009.

———. "The Languages of Occupation: Vocabularies of German rule in Eastern Europe during the World Wars." In *Germans, Poland, and Colonial Expansion to the East*, edited by Robert L. Nelson, 121–40. New York: Palgrave Macmillan, 2009.

Loew, Peter Oliver. *Danzig und Seine Vergangenheit: Die Geschichtskultur einer Stadt zwischen Deutschland und Polen*. Osnabrück: Fibre 2003.

Loew, Peter Oliver, Christian Pletzing, and Tomas Serrier, eds. *Wiedergewonnene Geschichte: Zur Aneignung von Vergangenheit in den Zwischenräumen Mitteleuropas*. Wiesbaden: Harrassowitz Verlag, 2006.

Macala, Jarosław. *Duszpasterstwo a narodowość wiernych: Kościół Katolicki w Diecezji Katowickiej wobec mniejszości niemieckiej 1922–1939*. Wrocław: Uniwersytet Wrocławski, 1999.

Madajczyk, Piotr. *Niemcy Polscy, 1944–1989*. Warsaw: Oficja Naukowa, 2001.

———. *Pryłączenie Śląska Opolskiego do Polski, 1945–1948*. Warsaw: Instytut Studiow Politycznych Polskiej Akademii Nauk, 1996.

Marczak, Tadeusz. "Mit Słowiański jako tworzywo koncepcji politycznych w latach 1944–7." In *Polskie Mity polityczne XIX i XX w*, edited by Zofia Zmyk, 215–26. Wrocław: Wydawn. Uniwersytetu Wrocławskiego, 1994.

Maser, Peter, and Adelheid Weiser. *Juden in Oberschlesien*. Vol. 1, *Historischer Überblick: Jüdischen Gemeinden*. Berlin: Schriften der Stiftung Haus Oberschlesien, Landeskundliche Reiche, 1992.

Masurczyk, Joachim. "Wohnungsbau in Oberschlesien." In *Die Architektur der Weimarer Republik: Ein Blick auf unbeachtete Bauwerke*, ed. Nikolaus Gussone, 67–84. Dülmen: Laumann-Verlag, 1992.

Matelski, Dariusz. *Niemcy w Polsce w XX wieku*. Warsaw: PWN, 1999.

Mazower, Mark. *Hitler's Empire: How the Nazis Ruled Europe*. New York: Penguin, 2008.

Mecklenburg, Frank. "Von Hitlerjugend zum Holocaust: Die Karriere des Fritz Arlt." In *Deutsche, Juden, Völkermord: Der Holocaust als Geschichte und Gegenwart*, edited by Jürgen Matthäus and Klaus-Michael Mallmann, 87–102. Darmstadt: WBG, 2005.

Michałczyk, Andrzej. *Heimat, Kirche und Nation: Deutsche und polnische Nationalisierungsprozesse im geteilten Oberschlesien (1922–1939)*. Cologne: Böhlau, 2010.

———. "Celebrating the Nation: The Case of Upper Silesia after the Plebiscite in 1921." In *Four Empires and an Enlargement: States Societies and Individuals in Central and Eastern Europe*, edited by Claire Jarvis, Daniel Brett, and Irina Marin, 49–62. London: School of Slavonic and East European Studies, 2008.

———. "Polsko-niemiecka walka narodościowa na Górnym Śląsku: Mit historiograficzny a kwestia tożsamości górnośląskiej." In *Erinnerungsorte, Mythen, und Stereotypen in Europa*, edited by Jarosław Suchoples, Heidi Hein-Kircher, and Hans Henning Hahn, 217–36. Wrocław, 2008.

———. "Deutsche und polnische Nationalisierungspolitiken in Oberschlesien zwischen den Weltkriegen: Ein Vergleich auf Makro und Mikroebene." In *Die Destruktion des Dialogs: Zur innenpolitischen instrumentalisierung negativer Fremd- und Feindbilder Polen, Tschechien, Deutschland und die Niederlande im Vergleich, 1900–2005*, ed. Dieter Bingen, Peter Oliver Loew, and Kazimierz Wóycicki, 66–84. Wiesbaden: Harrassowitz Verlag, 2007.

Minneker, Ilka. "Schulbauten in Oberschlesien." In *Die Architektur der Weimarer Republik: Ein Blick auf unbeachtete Bauwerke*. Ed. Nikolaus Gussone, 85–102, Dülmen: Laumann-Verlag, 1992.

Miroszewski, Kazimierz. "Armia Czerwona na terenie województwa śląsko-dąbrowskiego." In *Rok 1945 w Województwie Śląsko-Dąbrowskim*, ed. Andrzej Topol, 9–31. Katowice: Uniwersytet Śląski, 2004.

Mroczko, Marian. *Związek Obrony Kresów Zachodnich 1921–1934: Powstanie i działalność*. Gdańsk: Wyd. Morskie, 1977.

Mühle, Eduard. *Für Volk und deutschen Osten: Der Historiker Hermann Aubin und die deutsche Ostforschung*. Düsseldorf: Droste Verlag, 2005.

Mühle, ed. *Germany and the European East in the Twentieth Century*. New York: Berg, 2003.

Murdock, Caitlin E. *Changing Places: Society, Culture, and Territory in the Saxon-Bohemian Borderlands, 1870–1946*. Ann Arbor: University of Michigan Press, 2010.

Musekamp, Jan. *Zwischen Stettin and Szczecin: Metamorphosen einer Stadt von 1945 bis 2005*. Wiesbaden: Harrassowitz Verlag, 2010.

Myrcik, Jan. *Pół wieku Śląska: Zarys Monograficzny Zespołu Pieśni i Tańca "Śląsk."* Koszęcin: Ośrodek Kultury i Edukacji Regionalnej, 2004.

Myszor, Jerzy. *Stosunki Kościół: Państwo Okupacyjne w Diecezji Katowickiej*. Katowice: WOK, 1992.

Naimark, Norman. *Fires of Hatred: Ethnic Cleansing in Twentieth-Century Europe*. Cambridge, MA: Harvard University Press, 2001.

———. *The Russians in Germany: A History of the Soviet Zone of Occupation, 1945–1949*. Cambridge, MA: Harvard University Press, 1995.

Nordblom, Pia. "Die Lage der Deutschen in Polnisch-Oberschlesien nach 1922." In *Oberschlesien nach dem Ersten Weltkrieg: Studien zu einem nationalen Konflikt und seiner Errinerung*, ed. Kai Struve, 111–26. Marburg: Herder Institute, 2003.

Noszczak, Bartłomiej, ed. *Milenium czy Tysiąclecie*. Warsaw: IPN, 2006.

Obersztyn, Anna, and Jerzy Jaros. "Przemysł górnośląski w organiźmie gospodarczym II Rzeczypospolitej: Ekonomiczne Aspekty Integracji." In *Ziemie Śląskie w granicach II Rzeczypospolitej: procesy integracyjne*, ed. Franciszek Serafin, 40–53. Katowice: Uniwersytet Śląski, 1985.

Odorowski, Waldemar. *Architektura Katowic w latach międzywojennych, 1922–1939*. Katowice: Muzeum Śląskie, 1994.

———. "Wieżowce Katowic i ich treści ideowe." In *O sztuje Górnego Śląska i przeległych ziem małopolskich: Materiały IV Seminarium Sztuki Górnośląskiej—Zakładu Historii Sztuki Uniwersytetu Śląskiego i Oddziału Górnośląskiego SHS—odbytego 26–7 października 1987 roku w Katowicach*, edited by Ewa Chojecka, 268–78. Katowice: Oddziału Górnośląskiego Stowarzyszenia Historyków Sztuki, 1994.

Orlowski, Hubert. *"Polnische Wirtschaft": Zum deutschen Polendiskurs der Neuzeit*. Wiesbaden: Harrassowitz, 1996.

Paczkowski, Andrzej. *Referendum z 30 Czerwca 1946 r.: Przebieg i wyniki*. Warsaw: Typografika, 1993.

———. *The Spring Will Be Ours: Poland and the Poles from Occupation to Freedom.* University Park: Pennsylvania University Press, 2005.
Peer, Shanny. *France on Display: Peasants, Provincials, and Folklore in the 1937 Paris World's Fair.* Albany: State University of New York Press, 1998.
Piotrowski, Jacek. "The Policies of the Sanacja on the Jewish Minority in Silesia, 1926–1939." *Polin: Studies in Polish Jewry* 14 (2001): 150–55.
Piskorski, Jan M., Jörg Hackmann, and Rudolf Jaworski, eds. *Deutsche Ostforschung und polnische Westforschung im Spannungsfeld von Wissenschaft und Politik.* Osnabrück: Fibre, 2002.
Polak-Springer, Peter. "'Borderless Misery': The Political Use of Refugees in German Upper Silesia during the Weimar and Nazi Eras." In *Cultural Landscapes: Transatlantische Perspektiven auf Wirkungen und Auswirkungen deutscher Kultur und Geschichte im Östlichen Europa*, edited by Andrew Demshuk and Tobias Weger. Oldenbourg: De Gruyter Verlag, 2015.
———. "Kultura ludowa, rewanżyzm i tworzenie narodowo-regionalnych kultur wysokich na polsko-niemieckim pograniczu w latach 1926–1953." In *Górny Śląsk i Górno-Ślązacy: Wokół problemów regionu i jego mieszkańców w XIX i XX w*, ed. Sebastian Rosenbaum, 116–43. Katowice and Gliwice: IPN, 2014.
———. "Jammin' with Karlik: The German-Polish 'Radio War' and the 'Gleiwitz Provocation,' 1925–1939," *European History Quarterly* 43, no. 2: 279–300.
———. "Landscapes of Revanchism: Building and the Contestation of Space in an Industrial Polish-German Borderland, 1922–1945." *Central European History* 45 (2012): 485–522.
———. "The Upper Silesian 'Dream': Re-Assimilating the Native Population, 1945–50." In *Deutschsein als Grenzerfahrung: Minderheitenpolitik in Europa zwischen 1914 und 1950*, edited by Dietrich Beyrau et al., 241–60. Essen: Klartext, 2009.
Popkiewicz, Józef, and Ranciszek Ryszka. *Przemysł ciężki Górnego Śląska w gospodarce Polski miedzywojenej, 1922–1939.* Opole: Instytut Śląski, 1995.
Porter, Brian. *When Nationalism Began to Hate: Imagining Modern Politics in Nineteenth-Century Poland.* New York: Oxford University Press, 2000.
Prażmowska, Anita. *Civil War in Poland, 1942–1948.* New York: Palgrave Macmillan, 2004.
Prusin, Alexander Victor. *The Lands Between: Conflict in the East European Borderlands, 1870–1992.* New York: Oxford University Press, 2010.
Reagin, Nancy, Krista O'Donnell, and Renate Bridenthal, eds. *The Heimat Abroad: The Boundaries of Germanness.* Ann Arbor: University of Michigan Press, 2005.
Rogowski, Stanisław. *Komisja Mieszana dla Górnego Śląska (1922–1937).* Opole: Instytut Śląski, 1977.
Roshwald, Aviel. *Ethnic Nationalism and the Fall of Empires: Central Europe, Russia and the Middle East, 1915–1923.* London and New York: Routledge, 2001.
Runzheimer, Jürgen. "Der Überfall auf den Sender Gleiwitz im Jahre 1939." *Vierteljahrshefte für Zeitgeschichte* 10, no. 4 (1962): 408–22.
Rutherford, Phillip T. *Prelude to the Final Solution: The Nazi Program for Deporting Ethnic Poles, 1939–41.* Lawrence: University Press of Kansas, 2007.
Saldern, Adelheid von. "*Volk* and *Heimat* Culture in Radio Broadcasting during the Period of Transition from Weimar to Nazi German." *The Journal of Modern History* 76 (June 2004): 312–46.
Sammartino, Annemarie H. *The Impossible Border: Germany and the East, 1914–1922.* Ithaca, NY, and London: Cornell University Press, 2010.
Schulze, Rainer. "'Der Führer Ruft!' Zur Rückholung der Volksdeutschen aus dem Osten." In *Die "Volksdeutschen" in Polen, Frankreich, Ungarn und die Tschechoslowakei: Mythos und Realität*, ed. Jerzy Kochanowski and Maike Sach, 183–204. Osnabrück: Fibre, 2006.
Serafin, Franciszek, ed. *Województwo Śląska: Zarys Monograficzny.* Katowice: Uniwersytet Śląski, 1996.

Service, Hugo. *Germans to Poles: Communism, Nationalism, and Ethnic Cleansing after the Second World War*. Cambridge: Cambridge University Press, 2013.
Siebel-Achenbach, Sebastian. *Lower Silesia from Nazi Germany to Communist Poland, 1942–49*. New York: St. Martin's Press, 1994.
Snyder, Timothy. *Bloodlands: Europe Between Hitler and Stalin*. New York: Basic Books, 2010.
———. *The Reconstruction of Nations: Poland, Ukraine, Lithuania, Belarus, 1569–1999*. New Haven, CT: Yale University Press, 2003.
Sroka, Irena, Tomasz Falęcki. "Die Deutsche Minderheit in der Wojewodschaft Schlesien." In *Wach auf mein Herz und denke! Zur Geschichte der Beziehungen zwischen Schlesien und Berlin-Brandenburg/ Przebudź się, serce moje, i pomyśl"—Przyczynek do historii stosunków między Śląskaiem a Berlinem-Brandenburgia*, ed. Klaus Bzdziach, Arno Herzig, and Wieslaw Lesiuk, 247–60. Berlin-Opole: Gesellschaft für interregionalen Kulturaustausch, 1995.
Stauter-Halsted, Keely. *A Nation in a Village: The Genesis of Peasant National Identity in Austrian Poland, 1848–1914*. Ithaca, NY: Cornell University Press, 2001.
Storm, Eric. *The Culture of Regionalism: Art, Architecture, and International Exhibitions in France, Germany, and Spain, 1890–1939*. Manchester: Manchester University Press, 2011.
Strauchold, Grzegosz. *Autochtoni Polscy, Niemieccy, czy ... Od Nacjonalizmu do Komunizmu (1945–9)*. Toruń: Adam Marszałek, 2001.
———. *Myśl Zachodnia i jej realizacja w Polsce Ludowej w latach 1945–1947*. Toruń: Adam Marzałek, 2003.
———. *Polska Ludność Rodzima Ziem Zachodnich i Północnych: Opinie nie tylko publiczne, 1944–8*. Olsztyn: Ośrodek Badań Nauk. im. Wojciecha Kętrzyńskiego, 1995.
Struve, Kai. "Geschichte und Gedächtnis in Oberschlesien: Die polnischen Aufstände nach dem Ersten Weltkrieg." In *Oberschlesien nach dem Ersten Weltkrieg: Studien zu einem nationalen Konflikt und seiner Erinnerung*, ed. Kai Struve, 1–32. Marburg: Herder-Institute, 2003.
Surowiak, Helena. "Gmach Urzędu Wojewódzkiego i Sejmu Śląskiego w Katowicach oraz jego program ideowy." *Roczniki Katowic*, 1983, 160–70.
Szaynok, Bożena. "Jews in Lower Silesia, 1945–1950." In *Jews in Silesia*, ed. Marcin Wodziński and Janusz Spyra, 213–28. Cracow: Księgarnia Akademicka, 2001.
Szczypka-Gwiazda, Barbara. *Pomiędzy praktyką a utopią: Trójmiasto Bytom-Zabrze-Gliwice jako przykład koncepcji miasta przemysłowego czasów Republiki Weimarskiej*. Katowice: Uniwersytet Śląski, 2003.
———. *Nieznane Oblicze Sztuki Polskiej: W kręgu sztuki województwa ślaskiego w dobie II Rzeczypospolitej*. Katowice: "Śląsk," 1996.
———. "Trójmiasto Bytom-Zabrze-Gliwice jako przykład nowej koncepcji urbanistycznej." In *Sztuka Górnego Śląska na przecięciu dróg europejskich i regionalnych*, ed. Ewa Chojecka, 253–81. Katowice: Muzeum Śląskie, 1999.
———. "Reprezentacyjne założenie placu forum Katowic jako próba stworzenia 'przestrzeni symbolicznej.'" In *Przestrzeń, Architektura, Malarstwo: Wybrane Zagadnienia Sztuki Górnośląska*. Ed. Ewa Chojecka, 103–16. Katowice: Centrum Dziedzictwa Kulturowego Górnego Śląska, 1995.
———. "Historia budowy katedry w Katowicach." In *O sztuce Górnego Śląska i Zagłębia Dąbrowskiego XV–XX w. Sztuka Śląska odkrywana na nowo*, ed. Ewa Chojecka, 86–104. Katowice: Uniwersytet Śląski, 1989.
Szejnmann, Claus-Christian W., and Miken Umbach, eds. *Heimat, Region, and Empire: Spatial Identities under National Socialism*. Palgrave Macmillan, 2012.
Szymon Kędryna, "Rozwój oświaty dorosłych w województwie katowickim, 1945–1963." In *Studia i Materiały z Dziejów Śląskich*, ed. Janusz Gołębiowski and Henryk Rechowicz, 414–75 Wrocław: Ossolineum, 1964.

Ther, Philipp. *Deutsche und polnische Vertriebene: Gesellschaft und Vertriebenenpolitik in der SBZ/DDR und in Polen, 1945–56*. Göttingen: Vendehoeck & Ruprecht, 1998.
———. "German History as Imperial History." In *Imperial Rule*, edited by Alexei Miller and Alfred J. Reiber. Central European University Press, 2004.
———. "The Spell of the Homogeneous Nation-State: Structural Factors and Agents of Ethnic Cleansing." In *Diasporas and Ethnic Migrants: Germany, Israel, and Post-Soviet Successor States in Comparative Perspective*, edited by Rainer Münz and Rainer Ohliger, 77–97. London: Frank Cass, 2003.
———. "Schlesisch, deutsch oder polnisch? Identitätswandel in Oberschlesien, 1921–1956." In *Die Grenzen der Nationen: Identitätwandel in Oberschlesien in der Neuzeit*, ed. Kai Struve and Philipp Ther, 169–202. Marburg: Herder Institute, 2002.
Ther, Philipp, and Holm Sundhaussen, eds. *Regionale Bewegungen und Regionalismen in europäischen Zwischenräumen seit der Mitte des 19. Jahrhunderts*. Marburg: Herder-Institut, 2003.
Thum, Gregor. *Uprooted: How Breslau Became Wrocław during the Century of Expulsion*. Translated by Tom Lapert and Allison Brown. Princeton, NJ: Princeton University Press, 2011.
———. *Die Fremde Stadt: Breslau 1945*. Berlin: Siedler, 2003.
———, ed. *Traumland Osten: Deutsche Bilder vom östlichen Europa im 20. Jahrhundert*. Göttingen: Vandenhoeck & Ruprecht GmbH, 2006.
Tilse, Mark. *Transnationalism in the Prussian East: From National Conflict to Synthesis, 1871–1914*. New York: Palgrave Macmillan, 2011.
Tooley, T. Hunt. *National Identity and Weimar Germany: Upper Silesia and the Eastern Border, 1918–22*. Lincoln: University of Nebraska Press, 1997.
Topol, Andrzej, "Przemysł ciężki w województwie śląsko—dąbrowskim." In *Rok 1945 w Województwie Śląsko-Dąbrowskim*, ed. Andrzej Topol, 165–77. Katowice: Uniwersytet Śląski, 2004.
Traba, Robert. *"Wschodniopruskość": Tożsamość regionalna i narodowa w kulturze politycznej Niemiec*. Poznań: Poznańskie Towarzystwa Przyjaciół Nauk, 2005.
Tracz, Bogusław. "Ślązak—Żołnierz—Gospodarz: Jerzy Ziętek jako przykład mitologizacji politycznej." In *Górny Śląsk i Górno-Ślązacy: Wokół problemów regionu i jego mieszkańców w XIX i XX w.*, ed. Sebastian Rosenbaum, 330–53. Katowice and Gliwice: Katowice and Gliwice: IPN, 2014.
Walczak, Jan. *Jerzy Ziętek: Biografia Ślązaka (1901–1985)*. Katowice: "Śląsk," 2002.
Wanatowicz, Maria Wanda. *Od indyferentnej ludności do śląskiej narodowości? Postawy narodowe ludności autochtonicznej Górnego Śląska w latach 1945–2003 w świadomości społecznej*. Katowice: Uniwersytet Śląski, 2004.
———. *Historia społeczno-polityczna Górnego Śląska i Śląska Cieszyńskiego w latach 1918–1945*. Katowice: Uniwersytet Śląski, 1994.
———. *Ludność napływowa na Górnym Śląsku w latach 1922–1939*. Katowice: Uniwersytet Śląski, 1982.
———. "Polski, Niemiecki i Śląski: Problemy narodowościowe Górnego Śląska w orkesie międzywojennym." In *Wrzesień 1939 na Górnym Śląsku*, ed. Grzegosz Bębnik, 17–31. Katowice: IPN, 2008.
———. "Wojciech Korfanty i Chrześcijańska Demokracja wobec mniejszości niemieckiej w województwie śląskim." In *Wieki Stare i Nowe*. Vol. 2, ed. Maria Wanda Wanatowicz and Idzieg Panic, 211–26. Katowice: Uniwersytet Śląski, 2001.
———. "Między regionalizmem a separatyzmem Śląskim." In *Regionalizm a separatyzm: Historia i współczesność, Śląsk na tle innych obszarów*, ed. Maria Wanda Wanatowicz, 11–25. Katowice: Uniwersytet Śląski, 1996.
———. "Rola ludności napływowej w procesie integracji Górnego Śląska z resztą ziemi Polskiej." In *Ziemie Śląskie w granicach II Rzeczypospolitej: procesy integracyjne*, ed. Franciszek Serafin, 72–92. Katowice: Uniwersytet Śląski, 1985.

Waszkiewicz, Ewa. *Doktryna hitlerowska wśród mniejszości niemieckiej w województwie śląskim w latach 1918–1939*. Wrocław, 2001.
Weber, Eugen. *Peasants into Frenchmen: The Modernization of Rural France, 1870–1914*. Stanford, CA: Stanford University Press, 1976.
Weitz, Eric. "Racial Politics without the Concept of Race: Reevaluating Soviet Ethnic and National Purges." *Slavic Review* 61, no. 1 (Spring 2002): 1–29.
Wiener, Amir, ed. *Landscaping the Human Garden: Twentieth-Century Population Management in a Comparative Framework*. Stanford, CA: Stanford University Press, 2003.
Wigura, Karolina. "Alternative Historical Narrative: 'Polish Bishops' Appeal to their German Colleagues' of 18 November 1965." *Eastern European Politics & Societies* 27 (August 2013): 400–12.
Wilson, Jeffrey K. "Imagining a Homeland: Constructing *Heimat* in the German East, 1871–1914." *National Identities* 9, no. 4 (December 2007): 331–49.
Wilson, Timothy. *Frontiers of Violence: Conflict and Identity in Ulster and Upper Silesia, 1918–1922*. Oxford: Oxford University Press, 2010.
Wodziński, Marcin. "Languages of the Jewish Communities in Polish Silesia (1922–1939)." *Jewish History* 16 (2002): 131–60.
Wolf, Gerhard. *Ideologie und Herrschaftsrationalität: Nationalsozialistische Germanisierungspolitik in Polen*. Hamburger Edition HIS Verlag, 2013.
Wyderka, Bogusław. "Język, dialekt czy kreol?" In *Nadciągają Ślązacy: Czy istnieje narodowość śląska?*, ed. Lech M. Nijakowski, 187–216. Warsaw: Wyd. Naukowe "Scholar," 2004.
Zagóra-Jonszta, Urszula. *Etatyzm w polskiej myśli społeczno-ekonomicznej Górnego Śląska, 1922–1939*. Wrocław: Uniwersytet Wrocławski, 1996.
Zahra, Tara. "Imagined Non-communities: National Indifference as a Category of Analysis." *Slavic Review* 69, no. 1 (2010): 93–119.
———. *Kidnapped Souls: National Indifference and the Battle for Children in the Bohemian Lands, 1900–1948*. Ithaca, NY, and London: Cornell University Press, 2008.
Ziegler, Miklós. *Ideas on Territorial Revision in Hungary, 1920–1945*. Translated by Thomas J. DeKornfeld and Helen DeKornfeld. New York: Columbia University Press, 2007.

Index

Adamski, Stanisław, ix, 45–46, 128, 150, 199–200, 209, 220
Adenauer, Konrad, 234–235
adult education/cultivation, 12, 185, 209, 223, 228n104. *See also* Volksbildung
Alsace (Alsatians, Alsace-Lorraine), 14–15, 18n31, 30, 31, 45, 143
America/American (United States of), 71, 183, 203, 206
anti-Semitism. *See* Jews
archeology, 108, 114–115
Architects Union of Silesia, 95, 100, 104
Arlt, Fritz, 152, 169
Arma, Leon Dietz d', 104, 109
Association for Germandom Abroad (VDA), 41
Aubin, Hermann, 151
Auschwitz (Oświęcim), 139, 147, 152
Austria/Austria-Hungary. *See* Habsburg Empire

Barcikowski, Wacław, 183, 191, 207
Baumgarten, Aleksander, 196
Będzin (Bendsburg), 147, 162
Berlin (German central government), 35, 40, 170; city of, 69–70, 98, 104, 106, 125, 154
Bertram, Adolf, 74
Beskidy (Beskiden) Mountains, 103
Bierut, Bolesław, 200–201, 206
Birke, Ernst, 151
Bismarck, Otto von (Bismarckian), xii, 22; and Kulturkampf, 5, 23, 25, 28, 45; Bismarck Tower, 29
"bleeding border," 2, 6, 13, 49, 59, 75, 246

Bogedain, Bernard, 28
Böhm, Dominikus, 107
Boidol, Edgar, 151, 251
Bojków (Schönwald), 121
Bolick, Joseph, 165, 170, 210
borderland nationalism/nationalists, 4–6, 13, 21, 44, 47, 78, 189, 190, 192, 205, 221, 223–224, 233, 235, 237–239, 241–242, 243, 245–246
Bożek, Arka, 194
Bracht, Fritz, 125–126, 144, 152–154, 165–166, 169
Brandt, Willy, and Ostpolitik, 241–242
Brüning, Heinrich, 72, 74, 107–108, 122
Bund Deutscher Osten, BDO. *See* League of the German East
Bureau for Upper Silesian Regional Studies, 98, 114, 151
Byrnes, Robert (and Stuttgart Speech), 206
Bytom (Beuthen), 31, 36, 49n5, 56, 59, 64, 66, 70–71, 103–106, 109, 114, 121–123, 157, 196, 215, 217–218, 225n22, 233; stadium, 72, 74, 79, 82n22, 122, 124; and Moltkeplatz, 107; Pedagogical Academy in, 119, 124, 151; Archive for Upper Silesian Folk Songs in, 119; Polish gymnasium in, 123–124; Oberschlesische Landesmuseum in, *see* museums

Calonder, Felix, and German-Polish Mixed Commission, 34–35, 44, 66, 81

Catholic (Catholicism), 28, 34–35, 39, 140; clergy in politics, 23, 25, 35, 55, 74, 128, 220, 236; and Communist regime/re-Polonization, 192, 199–200, 204, 214–215, 220, 223; Diocese of Breslau, 45, Diocese of Katowice, 39, 102, 128, 150; and regionalism, 40, 97, 99, 113; wooden churches, 115–117; and national indifference, 23; and Nazism/Nazi policy towards, 129, 161, 169, 172; "Polonization," 45, 99, 128, 169; and religiosity, 22, 46–47, 169–170–171, 172; and social/ethnic conflict, 37, 150; and German-Polish reconciliation, 240 Millennium of Poland's Christianization, 241

Catholic People's Party. *See* German Center Party

Census, Polish (2002, 2011), 25, 243; German (1939), 129, 164; fingerprint census, 145–146, 176n33

Center Party. *See* German Center Party

Central Institute for Upper Silesian Regional Research (ZIOF), 152, 169

Christian Democratic Party (ChD). *See* Korfanty, Wojciech

Churchill, Winston (and Iron Curtain Speech), 205–206

Cieszyn (Teschen, in Poland after 1922), 34, 36, 100, 120, 128

Cold War, 131, 184, 206, 222, 242, 245

cold war (over Upper Silesia), 9, 21, 43, 47, 57–58, 65, 90, 93, 98–99, 106, 130–131, 140, 184, 221, 223, 245

Communists (of Poland/Polish Communists/regime), 10–11, 33, 79, 82, 190, 193–194 201, 242–244; interwar Polish Communist Party (KPP), 24, 39–40, 198; postwar Polish communist regime (Polish Worker's Party, PPR), 186, 190–192, 195–198, 203, 212, 215–217, 219–220; and propaganda bureau, 196, 199, 204–207, 209; Communist Polish United Worker's Party (PZPR), 221, 223–224, 233, 238, 241, 244, 246; Communist Union of Polish Youth, 220

Cracow/Cracovian, 67, 97, 100; Małopolska 116, 139, 204, 234

Curzon Line, 187

Czechoslovakia/Czechs, 29–30, 45, 67, 75, 110, 125, 143, 184, 162, 235; and Sudetenland, 113, 120, 139; and Hultschin, 30, 143

Częstochowa, 67, 220

Dąbrowa Basin, 37, 139, 143, 171, 186; ghettoes in, 147, 148, 162, 214

Danzig, 7, 9, 31, 70, 142

Deutsche Volksliste. *See* ethnic categorization

Dmowski, Roman; and National Democracy (Endecja), 5, 8, 27, 29, 41–43, 197, 223; and nationalism, 184, 205–206; and postwar era, 190–191

Dobrowolski, Tadeusz, 98, 114–115

Dudek, Andreas, 126

Eichendorff, Joseph Freiherr von, 60

Endecja. *See* Dmowski, Roman

ethnic categorization, German Ethnic List (Deutsche Volksliste, DVL), 12, 140, 148–149, 167, 173–174, 177n48, 188–189, 194, 220; verification/rehabilitation (verified), 12, 189, 194, 209, 213

ethnic cleansing (cultural cleansing, expulsion, genocide, homogenization, nationalization, forced assimilation), 6, 8, 33, 45, 47–48, 90, 110, 131, 140, 142–143, 147–148, 150–151, 153–154, 156–157, 160–161, 164, 166–167, 184–185, 188, 192, 193, 195, 197, 199, 203–205, 207–208, 211–213, 216–220, 222–223, 232, 237, 246

Falcon Society (Sokol), 27, 76

film, 3, 5, 12–13, 16, 69–70, 91–92, 114, 122, 153

Fojc, Jan, 195
folklore/folk culture/ethnography (*see also* Sczodrok, Karl *and* regionalism), 75, 90, 92, 99, 113, 120, 124, 130–131, 140, 153, 237, 245; folk costumes, 121–123, 126, 146, 167, 203, 233, 245; folk music/songs, 119–120, 169; folksong books, 119–120, 123–124, 128, 233–234, 245; folk song and dance groups/choral societies/concerts, 123–126, 129, 167, 203, 233, 247;Heimatkundler/ Heimatkunde (regionalist/folklorist), 90–91, 98, 107, 113, 132n4, 140, 151–153, 161–162, 165, 169–170, 174, 177–178n57, 185, 208, 235; Heimatforscher/Heimatforschung (*see also* Ostforschung), 91, 115, 185; and wooden architecture/churches, 115–117, 159
France/French, 13–14, 29, 31, 34, 40, 45, 59–60, 66, 70, 139, 143, 155

Galicia, 30, 36, 41, 120, 148
Gau Oberschlesien, 147; architecture/ symbolic landscape, 156–159; acculturation/cultural politics in, 152–159, 165, 170, 174; conflict between locals and newcomers in, 150, 164, 187, 247; cultural cleansing, 151–153, 165; Gau Office for Local Administration (local administrators), 155, 159–160; language policy in, 165–167, 169, 213, 216–219 (*see also* language); Operation More Beautiful Silesia, 159–161, 216–217; tourism in, 159, 162; treatment of Jews in, *see* Jews; treatment of Poles in, 158–160
Gau Schlesien, 125, 143, 152; border rallies in, 144. *See also* Katowice
Gawlik, Zygmunt, 103
General Plan for the East, 143
Generalgouvernement (GG), 148, 150, 164, 167, 169, 171–172
Geneva Convention (1922, Geneva), 35, 36, 41, 43, 46–47, 57, 92, 110

Gerlach, Henry, 106
German Army, Reichswehr, 79; Wehrmacht, 138–139, 150, 164, 173, 236, 239
German Block, 38–40, 43, 46
German Center Party (Catholic People's Party/centrists), 23, 25, 28–29, 34, 40–41, 43, 46, 48, 56, 62, 68, 70, 72–74, 77–79, 81–82, 91–92, 113, 126, 129, 141, 150, 162, 169, 235–236; Catholic youth, 73
German Communist Party (KPD, German communists), 39–40, 79–80, 129
German consulate in Katowice, 59
"German east," 2, 8, 13, 70, 91–95, 114, 125, 142–143, 165
German Eastern Marches Society, 26–27
German Foreign Office (Auswärtiges Amtes), 59
German Foundation (Deutsche Stiftung), 41
German Homeland Patriots (VVHO), 43, 53n93, 53n95, 57–59, 63–65, 69, 74, 81, 84n22
German minority, 1, 7, 35, 41, 43, 46–47, 48, 66, 79, 110, 117, 125–126, 139, 142, 146 157, 238. *See also* Volksbund
German National People's Party (DNVP), 41, 84n22, 108
German paramilitary groups, (Freikorps, Selbstschutz, Landeschutz), 32, 58, 69, 74, 78, 84n22, 110, 139, 141, 194, 201, 233, 237
German-Polish Non-Aggression Pact, 81
German Social Democratic Party (SPD), 74, 79–80, 93
Germanization (re-Germanization), xii, 8, 24, 26–27, 29, 47, 90, 128, 143–144, 145, 153–154, 157, 159–161, 163, 165, 169–173, 208, 210, 216, 220
Germany/Germans,
East Germany (GDR), 206, 232, 234, 242
German Federal Republic, and German-Polish Border Treaty, 242
Imperial Germany (Hohenzollern empire), 21, 27, 29, 34, 37, 48, 90, 191

Germany/Germans (*cont.*)
  Nazi Germany (Third Reich, Nazi era), 1–2, 56, 81, 98, 100, 104, 114, 116, 122, 126, 128, 130, 138, 141, 148, 151, 153, 190, 215, 236; Annexed Territories, 138, 140, 142–144, 147–148, 154, 157; invasion of Poland, 138, 142, 174, 202, 205; Reich Tourist Association, 159. *See also* Nazis
  Postwar Germany, 183, 239, 241
  Weimar Republic (Weimar Germany/ German republic/Weimar era), 2, 5–7, 8–10, 13, 16, 30, 32, 35, 43, 57, 60, 62, 75, 122, 126, 143, 146, 169; government of 70, 78, 82, 113, 115; and hyperinflation, 38, 92; Eastern Aid (Osthilfe), 38; Reichstag elections, 39–40, 46; and revisionism/ revanchism, *see* irredentism)
  West Germany (FRG), 206, 222, 232, 234–235, 237, 240
Gestapo, 47, 124, 140
Gliwice (Gleiwitz), 1–2, 31, 36, 43, 49n5, 59, 64–65, 67, 69, 105–107, 110, 121, 194, 207, 213–215, 217–219, 233, concentration camp in, 216, 219; radio station in, 71, 110; attack on radio station (Gleiwitz incident), 1–2, 82, 110, 142, Nazi opponents in, 1, 130, 137n139, 141–142, 175n10
Goebbels, Joseph, 126, 156, 172
Gomułka, Władysław, 191, 199–200, 204–206, 221, 237, 239; and Anti-Zionist Campaign, 240
Gottschalk, Walter, 138
Grażyński, Michał, 34, 42, 70, 79, 128, 141, 145, 150, 194–196, 211, 221–223, 233, 245; cultural politics/events, 71, 81, 94, 97–98, 102–105, 110, 113, 117, 120, 147, 152–156, 159, 191, 211; and personality cult, 42, 68, 98; and Korfanty, 41–42, 45, 77; and "Polonization" of industry, etc., 36, 43–45, 110; and Sanacja, 39, 42, 45–46, 79, 196; and Silesian insurgency, 41; *see also* Polonization, German minority, national indifference, *and* Jews
Great Britain (England/United Kingdom), 8, 37, 39, 70, 183, 203; and London, 124
Great Depression, 37–39, 43, 92
Gross Strehlitz (Wielkie Strzelce/Strzelce Opolskie), 67, 215, 217–218, 220
Gutberlet, Heinrich, 157

Habsburg (Habsburg/Austrian Empire, Austria-Hungary), 6, 22, 29, 34, 100, 139, 143, 191; Austria, 70
Harvest festival, 121–123, in postwar era, 200–203, 206, 227n63
Hasiński, Maks, 210
Haus Oberschlesien, 106
Hayduk, Alfons, 73
Heimat, xiii, 7, 13, 18n23, 130, 132n4, 139–140, 152–153, 160, 163, 174, 232, 235–237, 241
Hierowski, Zdzisław, 195–196
Himmler, Heinrich, 148–149, 151–152
Hindenburg (Zabrze), 31, 36, 49n5, 64, 74, 105–107, 129, 233
Hindenburg, Paul von, 40, 56, 93
Hitler, Adolf, 2, 6–8, 81, 125, 141–144, 146, 184, 192, 205, 212–213, 235, 238; Adolf Hitler Canal, 110
Hitler Youth (HJ), 108, 153, 165, 215
Hlond, August, 61
Hoefer, Karl, 74, 78
Holocaust. *See* Jews/Jewish
Hungary/Hungarian, 184; and Romania
Hultschin. *See* Czechoslovakia

industrial district. *See* Upper Silesia
Insurgent League (ZPŚl, veteran insurgents) (*see* Grażyński, Michał), 1–2, 42–44, 58–61, 67–68, 82, 141, 193, 195–197, 204, 216, 237, 241, 243; and refugees, 65–66, 77; Veterans League of Silesian Insurgents, 193–194
Inter-Allied Commission. *See* Le Rond, Henri

irredentism, irredentist politics, xii, 1–8, 10–14, 16n6, 16n7, 21, 26, 40, 41–43, 45, 48–49, 57, 62–63, 66, 69, 73, 77–80, 81–82, 91–92, 100, 103, 105, 107, 131, 232, 233–234, 245; German irredentism/revanchism, 40, 42, 68, 79–80, 125–126, 141, 143–144, 146, 239–241; Polish irredentism/revanchism, 66, 192, 195, 203, 205, 232, 246
Izdebski, Zygmunt, 208

Jews/Jewish (and anti-Semitism), xiii, 25, 27, 42, 46–48, 157; and propaganda on landscape/architecture, 155–156; and expulsion to Poland, 47; Nazi policy towards/the Holocaust, 140, 143, 147–148, 151–152, 160, 162–163, 174, 193, 246; and National Democracy, 27; treatment in postwar Upper Silesia/Poland, 187–188, 218–219, 222–223, 225n22, 240–241; Reich Pogrom Night (Kristallnacht), 47; Lublin Nisko Reservation, 147

Kalide, Theodor, 117
Kate, Georg, 152–153
Katowice (Kattowitz), 31, 33, 67–68, 71, 77, 82, 122–123, 145, 148, 152, 173, 201, 225n22; architecture/buildings/symbolic landscape in, 58–59, 76, 95, 128, 154, 160; Forum Katowice, 96–97, 100–103, 106, 198, 222; South Park, 117; synagogue in, 156; Administration Office Building, 100, 157; Cathedral of, 102–104; House of Education, 100, 104, 152; Silesian Library in, 146, 152; Silesian Technical Science Institutes, 100, 104; skyscraper, 101–102, 104, 156, 179n82; Freedom Day rally in, 144, 146–147, 156, 169, 172; migration of German newcomers to, 150; Kattowitz District, 165; postwar Jews in, 188; and Stalinogród, 221–222; and Voivodeship Silesia-Dąbrowa, 186–191, 197

Kauder, Viktor, 146, 151, 162–163
Kayser, Ulrich, 69, 91–93, 122. *See also* film
Khrushchev, Nikita, 237
Kielce, 139; and pogrom, 188
Kluge, Ing, 107
Kończyce (Kunzendorf), 107
Königsberg (Kaliningrad), 70
Königshütte (Chorzów), 31, 33, 55, 102, 117, 120, 159
Konopicka, Maria (and *Rota*), 71, 76
Korfanty, Wojciech, 24; and Polish Circle, 28; Polish Plebiscite Commission, 31; and Christian Democratic Party (ChD), 38–39, 42, 45, 48, 58, 61, 68, 69, 72, 75, 77–78, 82, 99, 113, 120, 194, 245; and conflict with Grażyński, 45, 77–78, 128; and regionalism, 45, 80, 94
Kornke, Rudolf, 58
Kościuszko, Tadeusz, 60
Krause, Walter, 98
Kresy (Poland's eastern territories), 30, 196
Kustos, Jan, 38, 45, 72, 80, 128
Kłębowski, Witold, 102
Kominek, Bolesław, 199–200, 204, 240–241
Kultur (German culture), 7, 70, 95, 109, 114, 115, 122, 131, 132n5, 162; and Arbeit, 26, 90, 105, 146; and Volkstumsarbeit, 151, 165; and Aufbauarbeit, 93–94; and Kulturaufbau, 151, 177n56; and Kulturarbeit (cultural work), 90, 110, 124, 126, 147, 151, 157; and Kulturträger, 90–91, 142; and Zivilization, 155
Kultura (Polish culture), 90–91, 103–105, 107, 109–110

language, and bilingualism/multilingualism, 40, 45–46, 56, 80, 113, 129, 163, 170, 219, and German (High German), 22, 39, 47, 119, 140, 145, 156, 164, 166, 169, 171, 210, 216; and

language (*cont.*)
    language courses, 165, 166–167, 170; enforcement of, 165–167; prohibition of, 209, 211, 213, 215, 217; and minority schools, 35; And Nazi cleansing of, 160–161; And Polish (High/literary Polish), 22, 26, 28, 37, 120, 123, 129, 145, 164, 210; and re-Polonization courses/language lessons, 209–213, 219; and schools, 153; And Silesian dialect (Wasserpolnisch, Oberschlesisch, gwara śląska), 22, 28, 34, 47, 120 163, 169–170, 172, 208, 218–219; gwara śląska, 120, 123, 233, 244, 247; Wasserpolnisch/Oberschlesisch, 128–129, 164, 166, 210–211; and folk songs, 119–120. *See also* folklore
League of the Expelled (BdV), 235, 242
League of the German East (BDO), 10, 26, 47, 81, 104, 116, 120, 124, 128–130, 141–142, 145, 151, 152, 165, 167, 192–193, 226n41
League of Nations, 21, 35, 43, 64, 66, 247
League of Upper Silesians (BdO), 32, 34, 50n38
Le Rond, Henri, and Interallied Commission, 31
Ligęza, Joseph, 208
Ligoń, Juliusz, 55
Ligoń, Stanisław, 120, 123, 195, 233–234
Lisiecki, Arkadiusz, 45, 97
Lithuania, *and* Polish war against, 29–30
locals (ordinary/native Upper Silesians/Volksdeutsche), 1, 3–4, 9–15, 22, 63, 65, 75, 77–79, 128–130, 140, 144, 159–160, 162–163, 164, 166–167, 171–173, 186, 195, 207, 210, 235, 237; Zwischenschicht, 146, 149; threes, 167, 169, 173–174, 189, 204, 214, 216–219, 222–223, 225n30; Polish autochthons/recovered people, 186, 194–195, 200–201, 204, 207–208, 212–215, 220, 233, 246–247; conflicts with newcomers, 187, 189, 215, 218–219, 221–222, 233, 247; contacts with West Germany, 234, emigration from Upper Silesia, 239–340; and Silesian Autonomy Movement (RAŚ), 243, and postwar Silesian identity, 243–245. *See also* Voivodeship
Locarno Agreements (1925), 40–41
Lompa, Józef, 28, 120
Lower Silesia, 22–23, 28, 102, 113, 116, 125, 143, 152, 184, 189, 232, 235–236
Lukaschek, Hans, 74–75, 78, 108, 235–236, 239
Lutman, Roman, 191, 195, 208

Mączyński, Franciszek, 103
Magistrale, 99
Marxist-Leninism (communism/"democracy"), 8, 196–197, 203–204, 208, 212, 214, 218, 223
Masuria, 27, 30, 43, 232
Mazurek, Stefani, 210
Męclewski, Edmund, 183, 193, 206–208
Miarka, Karol, 28
Mikołajczyk, Stanisław (and Polish Peasant's Party, PSL), 198, 204, 215
Ministry of Recovered Territories (MZO), 191, 193
modern/modernist architecture, 89, 96, 102, 109; Art Deco, 107; monumentalism, 11, 76, 96, 100, 103; Jugendstil, 107; Neue Bauen, 105–106; Cubism, 156; avant-garde, 157; "social realism," 222
Molotov-Ribbentrop Pact, 139
Morcinek, Gustav, 120, 195, 221
Mościcki, Ignacy, 55, 70, 75, 98, 242
Mount of St. Anne, xii, 33, 48, 74, 78–80, 122, 141, 198, 200–205, 233, 241, 247; and Reich Memorial, 110, 129, 200, 233; and Monument to the Insurrectionist Deed, 233
Munich, 75; Munich Conference (1938), 7–8

museums, 3–4, 11–13, 90, 131;
  Oberschlesische Landesmuseum,
  108–109, 114–115, 151, 157, 196;
  Silesian Museum 98, 99, 108–109,
  114, 157, 196, 222

National Democracy (Endecja). See
  Dmowski, Roman
national indifference. See regionalism
Nazis (Nazism, National Socialism,
  NSDAP, Nazi regime), 1–4, 7–8,
  10–12, 16, 33, 41, 46–47, 77, 81–82,
  90, 96, 104, 108, 110, 120, 122, 123;
  124–125, 129–131, 138, 142–144,
  145–147, 150, 151, 153–155, 156,
  160–161, 163–164, 166–167, 173,
  185, 187, 189, 190, 194, 202, 208,
  211–212, 215, 218–219, 222,
  234–235, 241–243, 246; Labor
  Union (DAF), 153, 165; population
  politics, 148, 193; Strength Through
  Joy (KdF), 153, 165; SA (Nazi
  Sturmabteilung), 48, 79, 110, 167;
  SS (Nazi Schutzstaffel), 48, 148, 151;
  and Union of German Girls (BDM),
  165; Women's League (NSF), 153,
  165. See also Germany
Neisse (Nysa), 60
Niemczyzna (Germandom), 120, 204–205,
  210, 216–219, 223, 227n79, 234
North and East German Research Society/
  NOFG. See Ostforschung
Northern and Western Territories (of
  Poland). See Western borderlands
Nuremberg, Nuremberg Laws, 47; city, 236

Oberschlesische Stiftung, 153
Oder-Neisse Line/border (western border),
  8, 183–184, 195, 206, 212, 222, 234;
  and Warsaw Treaty (1970), 241;
  Oder-Neisse Territories, see Western
  Territories
Oder River, 59, 82, 116, 203
Odorkiewicz, Edmund, 196
Oppeln (Opole), 15, 56, 66–67, 105, 114,
  122, 194, 198, 200, 206, 215, 227n63
Optants, 35

Organization for Upper Silesian Regional
  Studies, 73, 104, 113–114, 151
Ostflucht, 25, 105, 115–116, 120
Ostforschung (North and East German
  Research Society/NOFG), 10, 12, 43,
  98, 104, 114–115, 128, 143, 151, 185,
  235, and Johann Herder Institute,
  243
Ostoberschlesien/Ostoberschlesier, xii, 78,
  92, 138, 143, 146, 151, 170, 174, 193.
  See also Voivodeship Silesia

Pan-German League, 5, 26–27
Papen, Franz von, 108
Paukszta, Eugeniusz, 197
Pawlukiewicz, Konstanty, 70
People's Referendum (and Sejm elections),
  198, 204, 215–216
Perlick, Alfons, 120–122, 123, 151, 163,
  165, 170, 208, 235
Pfünzenreiter, Franz, 151, 161
Piast, and myth, 27, 29, 190, 197; and
  dynasty, 27, 185
Piekary Śląskie (Deutsche Piekar),
  121–123, 162, 172, 220
Pilichowski, Czesław, 196
Piłsudski, Józef (and Sanacja), 29, 41–42,
  45, 68, 122, 196, 246; cult of, 69
plebiscite, 9, 15, 29–30, 31, 63–64, 92,
  199, 235–236, 247; and the émigrés,
  31; and prior campaigning/activists,
  34–35, 42, 48, 69, 194, 216; and
  Plebiscite Day/commemoration/
  rally, 41, 57, 59, 62–65, 68–69, 72,
  74–75, 91–93, 98, 107, 122, 126, 128,
  143; postwar rallies, 236; and Polish
  counter-rally, 64–65, 67–68, 80–82,
  103
Poland (Polish), 21, 75, 125; Polish-
  Lithuanian Commonwealth, 25,
  34; Prussian Poland, 25–29; Russian
  Poland, 28; Interwar Poland, 48, 82,
  103, 110, 113, 192; occupied Poland,
  138–144, 147; Generalgouvernement
  (GG), 139; Communist Poland
  (People's Poland), 183–187, 191–192,
  195, 213, 222, 242; and fate of Jews

in, 188; Ministry of Education, 209–210, 212, 214, state security agency (UB), 216, 234; Postcommunist Poland, 242; The Thaw, 237–239
Polenlager, 148
Polish consul(ate), 64, 67–68, 70, 94, 120, 122, 125–126
Polish Corridor, 30, 77, 98–99, 142, 201
Polish exile government in London, 190, and Delegatura, 190, 193,
Polish minority, 66, 122, 124, 130, 142, 194. See also Union of Poles in Germany
Polish scouts (ZHP), 67, 76, 98, 214–215, 229n126
Polish underground and civil war (against communism), 216, 225n30
Polish Western League (PZZ). See Western Territories Defense League
"Polnische Wirtschaft," 29, 91, 104, 146, 155, 205
Polonization (re-Polonization/nationalization) (see also Grażyński, Michał; Western Territories Defense League and Polish Western League), 2, 15, 24, 27, 34, 38, 42–45, 95, 97–98, 102, 113, 117, 128, 156, 173, 191, 199–200, 204, 207–209, 215–216, 223–224, 233–234, 238, 240; re-Polonization courses, 209–215, 219, 221, 229n122; and de-Germanization, 199, 207, 212–213, 216–218, 220
Pomerania, 27, 184, 232
Popiołek, Franciszek, 195
Potsdam Conference, 183, 216
Poznań (Posen, Poznania), 22, 25–27, 36–37, 43, 67, 70, 77, 81; Warthegau, 148; Wielkopolska Uprising, 30; Polish General Exhibition, 70, 86n68; Western Institute, 191
press/printed propaganda, 13, 73–74, 78–80, 84n22, 88n101, 94, 98–99, 102, 104, 108–109, 121–122, 128, 142, 145, 153, 156, 160, 162–163, 167–168, 192–193, 199, 208, 217, 236, 238, 244, novels; 120; schoolbooks/educational materials, 120, 212
Proske, Alfons, 43, 56, 62–64, 74
Province Upper Silesia (Provinz Oberschlesien/Provinz, Western Upper Silesia), xii, 33–35, 43, 56, 77, 94, 186, 194; rallies, see plebiscite; cultural politics in, 62–64, 69, 70, 91–95, 97, 108, 113, 116, 122; built and symbolic landscape in, 105–106; industry/economy in, 37–38; paramilitary groups in, 82
Prussia/Prussian (Prussian era), 8, 10–11, 22–23, 67, 78, 90, 95, 97, 113, 117, 128, 143, 145, 147, 149, 154, 156, 162, 184, 204–205; Prussian east (Prussian Empire), 25–28, 91, 105, 139, 143; East Prussia (Prussian eastern provinces), 36, 184, 232; Prussian State, 34, 56; Prussian State Bank (Preußische Seehandlung), 38; Prussian Claims Society, 242; Prussian Settlement Commission, 25–27
Pszczyna (Pleß), 121, 172

radio, 114, 153, 160; German radio, 71, 236 (see also Gliwice); Polish Radio Katowice, 71, 76, 98, 120, 152, 196
Ratibor (Racibórz), 93, 141, 194; Borderland Tower in, 110
"Recovered Territories" Myth (Myth of the "Recovered Territories"), 4, 8, 12; for Poland, 103, 192, 202, 208, 212, 221; western territories myth, 195, 223, 237, 242, 244, 246; for Germany, 138–140, 148, 143–144, 165, 167, 169, 174, 192, 236
"Recovered Territories" of Poland. See Western borderlands
Red Army. See Soviet Union
Reden, Friedrich Wilhelm von, and Reden/Liberation Hill, 117, 159; Reden Festival, 167–169

refugees (*see also* Voivodeship), Verdrängte, 65, 76; in Polish Silesia (uchódcy, Silesian Refugees League), 65–66, 76
regionalism, 13–15, 40, 78; and national regionalism, 48, 90, 113, 129, 131, 141, 167, 169, 200, 210, 243, 245, 247; and propaganda, 92, 94; and German Silesian regionalism, 73, 78; Pan-Silesia(nism), 113–116, 125, 130, 140, 143, 151–153, 174, 177–178n57, 236; and minorities, 48; national indifference (non-national regionalist sentiment), 15, 23–24, 29, 34, 36, 39–40, 45–46, 64, 79, 80, 83, 113, 128, 143, 163, 167, 170, 172–173, 195, 203, 208, 218, 223, 238, 247; and Polish Silesian regionalism, 28, 94–95, 97–100, 109–110, 115, 117, 120, 122–123, 128, 152–154, 191, 195–196, 203, 211, 221, 233, 237, 244–245; and separatism, 48, 80, 113, 128
Ręgorowicz, Ludwik, 103
Reich Commissioner for the Strengthening of Germandom (RKF), 151–152, 160
revanchism/revisionism. *See* irredentism
Richthofen, Bolko von, 108, 115
Roger, Juliusz, 120
Rola-Żymierski, Michał, 206
Romania/Romanian, 139, 184; Bukovina, 171
Romer, Jan, 82
Rosenberg, Alfred, 153
Rozbark (Roßberg), 121–123
Ruhr, and French occupation of, 59; and bombing of, 139
Russia (Russians, Imperial Russia/ Romanov empire), 29, 191. *See also* Soviet Union
Rybnik, 65, 215
Rydz-Śmigły, Edward, 98

Sanacja, 39, 40, 42, 44, 45–46, 68–69, 72, 75, 77–79, 82, 90, 98, 102, 131, 189–190, 194. *See also under* Piłsudski, Józef *and* Grażyński, Michał

Schabik, Karl, 106–107
Schayer, Karol, 109
schools/pupils/teachers/curriculum planners, 73, 76, 83, 98, 107, 123–124, 153, 164–166, 169–170, 210, 212–213, 217, 220–221, 229n122; Silesian Education Department, 120; Nazi Teacher's Union (NSLB), 153, 165; Silesian school district, 210, 214; school books, *see* press
Schramm, Erwin W., 155, 160
Schultis, Antoni, 59
Sczodrok, Karl, 104, 107, 114, 123, 128, 151, 177–178n57, 235
Severing, Carl, 74, 93–94, 97, 126
Silesia. *See* Upper Silesia, Lower Silesia, Province Upper Silesia, *and* Voivodeship Silesia
Silesian dialect. *See* language
Silesian Homeland Society, 23
Silesian Institute, 98, 152, 191, 196, 208–209, 210–211, 237, 243
Silesian insurgencies (uprisings), 30–33, 60, 63, 68, 98, 120, 141, 194–195, 202, 204; and German fighters, 79 (*see also* German paramilitary groups); insurgents, 70, 78, 110, 138, 145, 162–163, 201, 204 (*see also* Insurgent League); and commemorations of (May Third/3 May/Third of May rallies) 60–65, 67–68, 70, 72, 75–76, 78–80, 82, 98, 103, 121, 198, 201, 207, 227n75, 241–242. *See also* Mount of St. Anne
Silesian Propaganda Month, 110, 115
Silesian Union for Heimat Defense, 151
Silesianism. *See* regionalism
Skowron, Eryk, 196
Śląsk Opolski, 76, 186, 193. *See also* Province Upper Silesia
Slavic (Slav, Slavdom), 22, 26, 108, 113–115, 157, 165; Pan-Slavism, 206, 213, 243
Sosnowiec/Sosnowitz, 162

Soviet Union (USSR), 8, 30, 183, 186, 191, 194, 203–204, 206, 218; policies in Upper Silesia, 186–187, 215; Polish-Soviet War, 29–31; Red Army (Soviet troops), 30, 139, 183, 186, 203, 212; Soviet Bloc, 206, 237; Soviet communism, 184
Speer, Albert, 139
Springorum, Walter, 165
Stabik, Antoni, 28
Stahlhelm, 69, 84n22
Stalin, Joseph (Stalinism/Stalinist), 183, 185, 190–191, 216, 220, 232, 234, 206, 237, 239, 244–245
statues/monuments, 24, 55, 56, 72, 117–118, 141, 145, 156, 161, 167–168, 241–242, 244
Steinbach, Erika, 242
Stresemann, Gustav, 40
Stütz, Albert, 106, 108
Szaffranek, Jozef, 28
Szczepański, Edward, 64, 94, 122
Szewczyk, Wilhelm, 195–196
Szramek, Emil, 120

tariff war (Polish-German tariff war), 37, 62, 92, 105
Tarnowitz (Tarnowskie Góry), 65, 117, 164, 170–171
Teschen (Tešin/Zaolzia), 7, 30; and Karviná, 120, 139, 143. *See also* Czechoslovakia
Treaty of Versailles (Versailles), 2, 7, 10, 30, 75; Versailles Powers, 141–142, 245
Treviranus, Gottfried, 40
Tyc, Teodor, 43

Ukraine, 148, 183–184, 192; Polish war against, 29–30
Ulitz, Otto, 34, 41, 95, 146, 156, 235, 244. *See also* Volksbund
Ulitzka, Carl, 24, 43, 78, 91
Union of Poles in Germany (ZPwN), 35, 47
Union of Soviet Socialist Republics (USSR). *See* Soviet Union

Upper Silesia (*see also* Province Upper Silesia *and* Voivodeship Silesia)
as annexed territory in the Third Reich, 138; and cultural politics, 139, 236; and population politics, 147–148. *See also* Gau Schlesien
and anthem ("Upper Silesian Oath"), 73–74
and border/borderland, 1–15, 33, 75, 77, 79, 89, 92, 102, 114
and conflict/war/struggle over/events of 1921, 10, 29, 31–33, 43, 80, 81, 93, 149, 169, 196, 199, 201, 204, 236. *See also* plebiscite *and* Silesian insurgencies
and economic relations, 9, 100
and emigration of locals from, 239–240
and industrial district, 23, 30–31, 33, 49n5, 92, 114, 120, 145, 154, 159, 163, 168–170–171, 173, 187, 204, 222, 242; tricity (*see also* Beuthen, Hindenburg, *and* Gleiwitz), 36, 64, 71, 79–80, 105, 124; Tricity Project, 106–107
and labor camps in, 187, 209
and Polish national movement, 23, 25, 28, 48. *See also* Dmowski, Roman and Korfanty, Wojciech
and postwar Poland, 183–186, 193, 205
and society, 23–24, 36
and Stalinist era, 185, 200, 220, 232–234
Upper Silesian Defense League (ZOG), 38, 45, 80, 88n110, 128, 150, 162
Upper Silesian Homeland Patriots. *See* German Homeland Patriots
Upper Silesian Homeland Society (LdO), 235–236
Upper Silesian Person (Oberschlesische Mensch/Volk/Lud Śląski), 78, 99, 140, 161–163, 170, 172, 186, 216; new Pole/new man, 192, 194–195, 207–209, 211–213, 216, 221, 244
Upper Silesian Regional Homeland League (OHB), 152–155, 159–160, 162, 165–167, 169, 206; and Deutsche Heimatbund, 153, 156–159
Urbanek, Kurt, 31, 70, 92, 235–236

Vereinigte Verbände Heimattreue Oberschlesier. *See* German Homeland Patriots

Vertriebenen (expellees), 235; Upper Silesian expellees, 236–237, 244; Spätaussiedler, 239, 244

Voivodeship Government Building (VGB), 76, 96–100, 103, 106, 109, 144, 145; Gau House, 156–157, 179n82. *See also* Katowice

Voivodeship Silesia (Województwo Śląskie, Polish Silesia, Eastern Upper Silesia), 33–34, 40, 51n46, 65, 68, 71, 75, 77, 82, 122, 138, 186
  as annexed territory of the Third Reich, 138–144, 145, 151, 153, 162, 165, 169. *See also* Gau Schlesien *and* Gau Oberschlesien
  and autonomy/semi-autonomy, 34, 38, 80, 113, 197, 247
  and built and symbolic landscape, 55–56, 95–103, 107, 117, 154–155, 159. *See also under* Kattowitz (Katowice) *and* folklore
  and Bureau for Architecture and Construction, 95
  and Bureau for Building and Planning, 103, 105
  and conflict between locals and newcomers, 37–39, 48, 77–78, 80, 128, 156, 162, 187
  and elections, 39, 41, 43
  and German minority, 39, 92, 110. *See also* German minority *and* Volksbund
  and industry/economy, 34, 37–39, 41, 94
  and Jews (*see* Jews)
  and migration/forced migration, 36–37, 43, 45, 65, 92, 100, 150, 247
  and rallies (*see* Third of May *and* plebiscite)
  and Silesian Sejm, 34, 96 (*see also* and elections)

Voivodeship Silesia-Dąbrowa (Stalinogród) (*see also* Upper Silesia) autonomy, 197

concentration camps (labor/work camps) in, 187, 216, 219
conflicts between newcomers and locals, 187, 189, 193, 215, 218–219, 221–222, 234
expulsions from, 187, 219, 232
Görlitz Treaty, 234
migration in/newcomers, 186–187, 195, 207, 213, 217, 218, 220, 222, 233, 238, 247
"Struggle against the Resurgence of Germandom," 216–220, 229n131, 229n134
struggle against illiteracy, 221, 230n156, 230n158
Western Upper Silesia (Śląsk Opolski/Opolian Silesia), 213–215, 222–223

Volhynia, 30

Volksbildung (Volk cultivation), 141, 144, 151, 164, 167, 169; Volks Cultivation Agency (VBW), 165, 175n7, 209, 211, 228n104

Volksbund, 34–35, 38, 47, 78, 80, 95, 145–146, 194; and Kulturbund, 146, 151. *See also* Ulitz, Otto

Volksdeutsche. *See* German minority

Volksdeutsche Resettlers (Umsiedler), 148, 160, 169, 171; "Home to the Reich" myth, 143

Volksgemeinschaft, 125–126, 163

Wagner, Joseph, 138, 143–144, 146–147, 170

Warsaw (and Central Government of Poland), 30, 35, 38, 40, 64, 67–68, 125; city of, 70, 94, 234, 241, 244; Voivodeship Warsaw City, 34, 81, 102, 122; Choral Congress in, 124–125

Wasserpolnisch. *See* language

Weimar Republic. *See* Germany

Western borderlands (of Poland/western territories/recovered territories/Piast lands), 4, 8, 184–186, 190–191, 193, 196, 206–208, 212, 215, 220–221, 239

Western Borderland Thought (of Poland, Polska myśl zachodnia), 10, 12, 42–43, 71, 115, 120, 184, 191, 207
Western Territories Defense League/Polish Western League (ZOKZ/PZZ), 10, 42–44, 47, 53n91, 57–58, 67, 71, 81, 103, 110, 115, 123, 183–184, 191–192, 194–197, 199, 205–210, 212–216, 218, 220–221, 226n41, 226n45; and Society for the Development of the Western Territories (TRZZ), 237, 241
Wieszowa (Randsdorf), 124
Wilson, Woodrow/Wilsonianism, 4, 6, 17n11
Wojciechowski, Zygmunt, 191

Wolny, Konstanty, 98
World War I (Great War), 28–29, 34, 48, 75, 90, 139, 195; and Allied Powers/Allies, 30–31, 92
World War II, 24, 92, 131, 183, 223, 245; and Allies (western Allies), 144, 206, 216
World War III, 222, 247
Wrocław (Breslau), 70, 102, 105–106, 114, 116, 125, 126, 128, 143, 152, 240

Zawadowski, Henryk, 97
Zawadzki, Aleksander, 186, 194, 216
Ziegler, Gerhard, 154–155
Ziętek, Jerzy, 24, 194, 204, 220, 237, 244
Żywiec (Saybusch), 148

www.ingramcontent.com/pod-product-compliance
Lightning Source LLC
Chambersburg PA
CBHW072146100526
44589CB00015B/2108